A Birder's Guide
to
Southern California

A BIRDER'S GUIDE
TO
SOUTHERN CALIFORNIA

completely revised by
Brad Schram
1998

revisions to the original version by
Harold R. Holt

original version by
James A. Lane
1968

American Birding Association, Inc.

Copyright © 1998 by American Birding Association, Inc.
All rights reserved. No part of this publication may be reproduced, stored in a retrieval system, transmitted in any form or by any means, electronic, photocopying, or otherwise, without prior written permission of the publisher.

Library of Congress Catalog Number: 98-72346
ISBN Number: 1-878788-17-5
Fourth Edition
  1   2   3   4   5   6   7   8
Printed in the United States of America

Publisher
  American Birding Association, Inc.
  George G. Daniels, Chair, Publications Committee
Editor
  Cindy Lippincott
Associate Editor
  Bob Berman
Layout and Typography
  Cindy Lippincott; using CorelVENTURA, Windows version 5.0
Maps
  Cindy Lippincott; using CorelDRAW version 5.0
Cover Photography
  front cover: *Yellow-billed Magpie;* Herbert Clarke
  back cover: *California Condor;* Herbert Clarke
Illustrations
  Shawneen E. Finnegan
Distributed by
  American Birding Association Sales
  PO Box 6599
  Colorado Springs, Colorado 80934-6599 USA
  phone: (800) 634-7736 or (719) 578-0607
  fax: (800) 590-2473 or (719) 578-9705
  e-mail: abasales@abasales.com
European and UK Distribution
  Subbuteo Natural History Books, Ltd.
  Pistyll Farm, Nercwys, Nr Mold, Flintshire, CH7 4EW UK
  phone: 1352-756551; fax: 1352-756004;
  email: sales@subbooks.demon.co.uk

Dedicated to
Dianne, Kate, and Kirk,
and for Norma May Swift

with love

TABLE OF CONTENTS

ACKNOWLEDGEMENTS

This is the fourth edition of *A Birder's Guide to Southern California*. The reader can readily appreciate, therefore, that the information contained in this volume owes a tremendous debt to those whose contributions produced the three earlier versions of this book. Starting with Jim Lane and then Harold Holt—both of whom received the help and cooperation of dozens of Southern California birders—through the current edition, this has been a project of continuous teamwork. We build on the foundation laid by others.

Many of Southern California's excellent birders gave generously of their time to update and revise birding routes from the previous edition. Experts on the status and distribution of Southern California birds reviewed and upgraded the graphs and Specialties. Others wrote new contributions to the described birding sites. Volunteers drove routes double-checking for accuracy or reviewing written material, making suggestions and upgrades, while others responded to simple factual queries. This guide would not be possible without them. Contributors participating in this project include: Keith Axelson, David Blue, Bill Bouton, Martin Byhower, Peter Cantle, Wanda Dameron, Stella Denison, Bill Deppe, Tom Edell, Richard A. Erickson, Sylvia Ranney Gallagher, Kimball Garrett, Karen Gilbert, Bill Grossi, Robert A. Hamilton, Roger Higson, Charles Hood, Joan Easton Lentz, Chet McGaugh, Robert Mesta, Stephen J. Myers, Michael A. Patten, Stacy J. Peterson, James Pike, Phil Pryde, Mike San Miguel, Kirk Schram, Kevin Seymour, Arnold Small, Greg Smith, Steve Tucker, Phil Unitt, Ken Weaver, Richard E. Webster, Walter Wehtje, and Thomas E. Wurster. Others, unnamed, provided site- or bird-specific data of a factual nature in response to a single inquiry. We thank them all.

In a project of this scope there are inevitably certain individuals whose commitment of time, breadth of knowledge, and creativity deserve special mention. Keith Axelson upgraded his text in the Eastern Kern County route, providing updated information and insight into that extremely interesting, varied route. Martin Byhower volunteered to write a new Palos Verdes Peninsula route, an area undergoing rapid change; the result is an insider's approach to a rich area on the edge of the state's largest megalopolis. Sylvia Ranney Gallagher upgraded her Coastal Orange County chapter and wrote portions of the Santa Ana Mountains chapter as well as the boxed section on Santa Ana River shorebirding spots. Robb Hamilton likewise wrote portions of the Santa Ana Mountains chapter; his expertise in the canyons and byways of the Santa Ana Mountains was critical to the chapter's depth of information. Charles Hood not only wrote the Antelope Valley chapter, but also upgraded the Joshua Tree National Park chapter and reviewed the Introduction, making helpful suggestions. Chet McGaugh rewrote the Western Riverside County chapter, adding much expert contemporary information about this surprisingly rich birding area. Tom Wurster wrote a new chapter for the San Gabriel Mountains, a fascinating birding route offering the possibility of solitude in the mountains above the Los Angeles Basin—his joy in the experience there flows through his descriptions. Arnold Small field-checked the Santa Monica Mountains Loop, rewrote portions of the chapter, and responded kindly to numerous questions about the area and its birds. Steve Tucker contributed directions to the Oxnard Plain Tamarisks in the Santa Monica Mountains Loop chapter.

Richard Webster reviewed the San Diego County chapters, making many relevant, helpful suggestions regarding both birding and presentation of the area to birders. Phil Unitt also reviewed the San Diego County chapters, adding much substantive information, and responded to numerous questions of fact regarding San Diego County birds. Joan Lentz field-tested and revised the Santa Barbara County route, and also reviewed the new Suggested Itineraries chapter, making many helpful suggestions. Martin Byhower, Karen Gilbert, Jim Pike, and Mike San Miguel all wrote descriptions of important birding areas appearing in the Other Good Birding Spots chapter. Walter Wehtje wrote an excellent description of how to bird yet another good birding spot—but his site had to be withdrawn on request of the location's on-site manager. Such are the fortunes of birding in Southern California. Roger Higson contributed his intimate knowledge of Imperial Valley, and wrote the boxed segment in the Salton Sea Loop. Robert Mesta, Condor Program Coordinator for the U. S. Fish and Wildlife Service, kindly answered each of many requests for relevant data in comprehensive detail. Wanda Dameron generously supplied her list of the butterflies of Southern California for publication herein. I don't even want to think about the hours Stacy Peterson put in. He field-checked, totally revised, and largely re-wrote the Salton Sea Loop; he also field-checked, provided up-dated text, and served as consultant on both the San Bernardino and San Jacinto Mountains routes.

All birders using this guide owe a debt of gratitude to this talented group of generous volunteers.

A birdfinding guide without accurate information on the status and distribution of the birds to be found would be an absurdity. Dick Erickson and Michael Patten reviewed the graphs of the birds of Southern California, making many upgrades and changes. This was an exacting task, requiring attention to detail by persons of unusually comprehensive knowledge—exactly the people who generously volunteered their time in this instance. Michael Patten and Kimball Garrett (co-author with Jon Dunn of *Birds of California: Status and Distribution*) reviewed and upgraded the Southern California Specialties chapter. Their acute understanding of Southern California's birds produced a much enhanced edition of this guide.

viii

When Paul J. Baicich in the ABA office asked me to undertake this revision I knew that success would depend on the work of others. Cindy Lippincott took over as Editor shortly after I agreed to proceed with the new edition. Her substantive suggestions, critical eye, generosity, patience, and sense of humor have been critical to the success of the enterprise. Cindy's maps are, of course, wonderful—giving order to a chaos of urban streets and vague rural birding sites. Bob Berman's skill in manipulating and presenting the graphs and related text are a mighty contribution to the guide's usability.

In the process of gathering and massaging all this information, I used my own discretion regarding the inclusion and presentation of the material. It must be assumed, therefore, that any errors are mine.

Shawneen Finnegan's outstanding drawings of some of Southern California's bird specialties enhance the guide in a manner impossible to convey in words. A well-rendered bird is a wonderful thing. We thank Herbert Clarke for his marvelous photos on the covers.

Two more individuals deserve my thanks as well. Paul Lehman suggested to ABA staff that I be contacted to oversee the revision of *A Birder's Guide to Southern California*. I have enjoyed my involvement with the talented team responsible for this guide, birding friends all, and I thank Paul for the suggestion. Finally I thank my wife, Dianne, the poster child for patience and support.

This book will need updates and revisions in the future. I hope that the American Birding Association will carry on with readers' help. Please send corrections and update notes to ABA's office in Colorado Springs.

Brad Schram
Arroyo Grande, California
May 26, 1998

ix

INTRODUCTION

California's motto, suggests a wag, should be: "As seen on TV." Only New York City can rival California for the clarity of mankind's preconceptions on the nature of life, landscape, atmosphere, and essence of the place. This is *especially* true of Southern California. There is, one confesses, a reason for the stereotype—and yet, like all stereotypes, it is superficial and ignores a much deeper, broader reality. Ask a native of Katmandu or Nairobi, Sydney or Vladivostok about California and you usually will get a reasoned response based in celluloid: automobiles, urban sprawl, freeway-chases ending in fireballs, Rodeo Drive shops, and movie stars. In short, the popular conception of Southern California is little more than a lyric from the theme song of "The Beverly Hillbillies." Birders, however, know better.

Southern California is a magnet for birders. Few regions in North America offer such biological and topographic diversity. Favored location and climate have made it rich in endemic birds. Where else would one go to look for Xantus's Murrelet, Allen's Hummingbird, Nuttall's Woodpecker, Island Scrub-Jay, Yellow-billed Magpie, California Gnatcatcher, Wrentit, California Thrasher, or California Towhee? Add to this the seasonal migrations of pelagic, shorebird, waterfowl, raptorial, and passerine species coupled with the phenomenon of vagrancy from the east, the world's oceans, Siberia, and Mexico. The result is an exciting, challenging avifauna. Southern California, quite simply, is one of the supreme destinations for North American birders.

The purpose of this guide is to help birders find birds in Southern California.

We define Southern California as an area from San Luis Obispo and Kern Counties, a few hours north of Los Angeles, south to the Mexican border. One may well ask "why, then, have you included Death Valley in the guide?" To which we answer: Death Valley is contiguous with Southern California and is most easily reached from Southern California—besides, it offers great birding!

Southern California is about the size of Florida (Death Valley not included) with an elevational relief giving it more surface area, a factor to ponder when planning a birding trip. Southern California's lowest point is the Salton Sea, at 226 feet below sea level; its highest point is the summit of San Gorgonio Mountain at 11,502 feet elevation. These elevational extremes, added to California's geographic position—the Pacific Ocean to the west, Sonoran desert to the east, Mexico to the south, and the Bering Sea (well) to the

1

north—mean that it is situated in a location guaranteed to produce a varied bird list. The list, exceeding 555 bird species recorded in Southern California (introduced birds not meeting ABA listing criteria excluded), qualifies handsomely as a varied list.

This richness, and the size of Southern California's counties (San Bernardino County is larger than New Hampshire and Vermont combined), have caused local birders to keep careful county lists. There are active birders in most coastal counties with personal lists exceeding 400 species in their home county. The obsessive quest for birds and birding spots by local birders has produced most of the information presented in this guide.

WHERE TO BIRD?

A big subject—the whole point of this guide, as you know. A few words in shorthand before you read further, however.

Birding can be as simple as watching out your window with binoculars nearby, or as arduous as compiling a *want list*, researching habitat requirements and chronological patterns of occurrence, consulting maps, graphs, experienced birders, and textual resources, then mounting an expedition. This guide strives to make the latter approach less arduous, although practitioners of the former can use it to help them expand their experience.

You will find, on reading further, that much reference is made to *migrant traps*. Migrant traps are local segments of habitat along migration routes, restricted in size and circumscribed biologically in some way, that attract migrating birds. Butterbredt Spring in the Eastern Kern County chapter is a classic migrant trap. It is a patch of green offering food, shelter, and water to passing migrants in the midst of hundreds of square miles of desert. Riparian corridors bisecting chaparral habitat, a coastal lagoon set amidst suburbia, a grove of trees on a coastal promontory (e.g., Point Loma), and desert golf courses are further examples. The migrant traps referred to in this guide are locations that have been birded regularly for many years. Migrant traps are not the only place to find birds, of course—indeed some birds could never be seen if you limited yourself to birding only migrant traps! They are, however, among the best places to find a variety of species during the most exciting times of the year—the semi-annual migrations.

SOUTHERN CALIFORNIA'S BIRDING YEAR

Although the visitor from out-of-state may be most interested in our endemic species, he or she is wise to account for the birding seasons.

One of the hoariest preconceptions of Southern California is that it lacks seasons. Granted, seasonal change in the lowlands is subtle. For the birder, however, seasonal change is marked by significant migrational movement.

California birders, like their counterparts elsewhere, pay close attention to the calendar. The problem lies in how to define a particular season.

Does spring, for instance, start in mid-January with the arrival of the first male Allen's Hummingbirds? Not really, although their arrival and subsequent displays on the occasional warm January or February day conveys a strong spring-like atmosphere to their surroundings. Does fall begin in late June with the arrival from the far north of the first shorebirds—passing impossibly late shorebirds still going north? You see the nature of the problem.

Generally speaking, all seasons in Southern California provide the birder with excitement. The *least* exciting time of year is probably March, when many wintering birds have left and spring migration is not yet in full swing. Otherwise, there always is interesting birding somewhere in Southern California.

In order to get the clearest picture of our birding year it may be best to turn to the graphs in the back of this guide. Look at the pelagic species graphs, the shorebird graphs, then look at the warbler graphs. You can see the birding seasons change by studying the likelihood of seeing a particular shorebird, pelagic bird, or migrant passerine at a specific time. The presence or absence of migratory birds, and their relative abundance through time, define the seasons for California birders. Those seasons, although conforming to the usual names, may look strange to the visitor.

• SPRING •

Ignoring the sturdy Allen's Hummingbird, the most obvious sign of spring's imminent return is the swallow flights, predominantly Tree and Violet-green, moving through under storm clouds in February and beyond. By late May passerine migration is slowing down—by now Pacific-slope Flycatchers may be feeding nestlings in the same lowland riparian habitat through which the last north-bound migrants filter—but this is optimum time for spring passerine vagrants in the desert migrant traps. Spring in the lowlands is over in June with the passage of the last stragglers moving toward the boreal forests. In the high mountains spring—defined by wildflowers, new growth, and nesting birds, not by the calendar or northward movement—can continue into August.

Let's, for the sake of clarity, *define* spring traditionally—mid-March through mid-June. Pelagic, lowland (especially riparian), shorebird, coastal promontory, and desert birding (especially migrant traps) are all productive in spring. Spring passerine migration is more noticeable in the desert oases than it is along the coast, and spring vagrants are more frequent in the desert at this season. Most spring vagrants appear later in the season. Birders are well-advised to include migrant traps in the eastern desert and the Salton Sea in their birding itinerary at this time of year. Although we typically do not get the waves of migrants seen in the East or along the Gulf coast (they tend to filter through continuously across a broad front, although there *are* unpredictable spurts of abundance), after a good flight-night the birding can be very good indeed.

• SUMMER •

Mid-June to mid-September comprises the summer months. They are characterized by the migration of shorebirds commencing in late June, the start of the fall passerine migration in August, breeding activity, and post-breeding dispersal. Summer is the time when frigatebirds and boobies, if any, move into the Salton Sea (more rarely, to the coast), and vagrant herons from Mexico may wander northward in post-breeding dispersal. If you have a strong constitution you will want to bird the Salton Sea shore for vagrant shorebirds and southern surprises. Summer is also a fine time to bird the high mountains. By September Southern California birders bird desert and coastal migrant traps assiduously, looking for eastern vagrant species among their western cousins.

• FALL •

It should be clear by now that "fall" (mid-September to the second week in December) is a relative term for Southern California birders. It is axiomatic among them that mid-September through mid-October are typically the best days of fall migration here, but fall birding is good generally. There is often a late fall spurt in early December when a new group of eastern vagrants arrive.

No other season produces the same feelings of panic among the initiated when finding themselves far from a telephone. The introduction of cellular telephones and pagers into the birding scene will not find a more thankful group than that of active Southern California birders in fall, for we know that being out of touch after Labor Day can result in serious birding dysfunction. Better you should be birding Tierra del Fuego and unable to do anything about it than to learn, on returning home from a day in the field, that the first state record of Great Knot was seen that day at Ventura's Santa Clara River estuary—and you have to work the next day. The possible combination of eastern, pelagic, Siberian, and Mexican vagrancy means that any fall day can produce an experience told and retold among birders for years to come. Fall migration edges out spring as the most exciting, frenetic time of year for local birders.

While birding Southern California in the fall you will do best to take a pelagic trip or two, concentrate on the coastal and desert migrant traps, the shorebird-rich estuaries and mudflats, and the Salton Sea (this leaves few other choices!). Unlike spring, when most of the rarities are found in the desert, fall produces vagrant species in the coastal migrant traps with regularity. All following chapters including coastal routes will give directions to the best-known migrant traps in their areas.

• WINTER •

Mid-December to mid-March officially comprise our winter months, mild though they are by standards common to most of the ABA Area. The annual Audubon Christmas Bird Counts often produce stake-out rarities among the normal wintering species. It is the "stake-out" nature of winter rarities here that characterizes much that is exciting about winter birding in Southern California. Every winter seems to bring a vagrant Siberian shorebird or duck, eastern warblers, a sparrow, or a flycatcher from the southwest—usually multiple examples of each of these categories—and others. Winter birding for the native is always rewarding, and one can usually plan the time and itinerary of a "chase" because wintering rarities tend to stay put for the season. This is much appreciated following fall's recurrent panics.

Visiting birders will have much to do in winter, whether or not they are concerned with rarities. Chaparral-adapted species and our native raptors, gulls, woodpeckers, and desert residents are all available and the weather is—usually—very good (the standard El Niño disclaimers apply). Add to these the complement of wintering pelagics, waterfowl, raptors, shorebirds, gulls, and passerines and you have an interesting avifauna to explore. All habitat types save for the high mountains provide good birding in the Southern California winter.

TOPOGRAPHY, GEOLOGY, AND MAN

The history of Southern California is dominated politically and economically by its search for and acquisition of water. Consider the fact that a region of its size has no large river within its boundaries—indeed, hardly any permanent rivers at all. It has no natural large freshwater lakes. Add to this geographic curiosity over 15 million people, all thirsty and needing baths. The quest for water has therefore been a determining factor in its human history. This is no less true of its natural history.

Generally speaking, the Southern California lowlands and foothills west of the mountain ranges lie in a dry, moderate Mediterranean climate while those east of the mountains—in their rain shadow—are true deserts characterized by little water of any kind and a xeric flora. The Pacific Ocean is the source of the prevailing weather pattern, the westerly onshore movement of cool ocean air. The rainy season, such as it is, starts in November and ends in April. This is, in some ways, the most beautiful time of year in Southern California. The days between the infrequent rains tend to be clearer and cooler than at other seasons, wildflowers abound in spring, and rolling grasslands in inland valleys and on the coastal slope challenge the green of the Irish countryside.

If its human and natural history is essentially a story involving water, Southern California's topographic history is a story dominated by geological faulting. Scores of faults exist, with new ones being found continuously—many near or under population centers. Most of these faults run a northwest-to-southeast course, thus determining the direction of valleys and mountain ranges. Southern California has lots of faults.

Two notable exceptions to this north-south trend should be noted: the east-west trending Tehachapi Range forming the northern edge of the Mojave

Desert along the Garlock Fault (and normally considered to form the northern boundary of what constitutes "Southern California"), and the Transverse Ranges within and around which is a complex series of west-east trending faults. The Transverse Ranges terminate in the west at Point Arguello, and in the east in the mountains of Joshua Tree National Park—a distance of roughly 325 miles. They include the northern channel islands of Anacapa, Santa Cruz, Santa Rosa, and San Miguel. The importance of the Transverse Ranges faunistically is shown in this guide's inclusion of routes in the Santa Barbara, California Condor, Santa Monica Mountains, San Gabriel Mountains, San Bernardino Mountains, and Joshua Tree National Park chapters—all within the Transverse Ranges.

The west-east Transverse Ranges are comprised of uplifted marine sediments in the Santa Ynez Mountains, becoming igneous in the footings of the Santa Monica Mountains with marine sediments above. The San Gabriels are largely igneous, with schists, gneisses, and granites predominating, while the San Bernardinos immediately to the east are largely granitic with marine sediments forming the northern and eastern flank. By the time one reaches Joshua Tree National Park the spectacular jumbles of weathered rock are granitic.

The so-called Peninsular Ranges trend northwest to southeast and include the Santa Ana, San Jacinto, Santa Rosa, Cuyamaca, and Laguna Mountains, all including numerous birding routes within them. This extensive system of mountain ranges extends to the tip of Baja California some 775 miles south of San Diego, thus the name.

The Peninsular Ranges are largely igneous in nature, primarily granites, although the Santa Ana Mountains contain significant segments of volcanic and sedimentary components. The dramatic weathered forests of granite boulders in eastern San Diego County are elegant curiosities on the eastern edge of this geological province.

Southern California's urban centers lie south of the Transverse Ranges and west of the Peninsular Ranges. Outside of this megalopolis the birder has the chance to encounter bits of Old California. This is, after all, where natural habitats survive.

SOUTHERN CALIFORNIA HABITAT TYPES

Many references are made in the text following to particular habitat types in Southern California. The explanations below describe the essential features of these habitats.

Suburban Gardens—Ornamental plantings characterize Southern California neighborhoods. The moderate climate ensures blooming flowers of one variety or another throughout the year, a fact noted with approval by numerous species of birds. The flowers, the insects drawn to them, and the seeds and berries available all ensure an interesting, if limited, list of birds in suburban gardens. Anna's Hummingbird is one of the most characteristic and most appreciated birds common to suburban gardens throughout the region. The introduced Blue-gum Eucalyptus common in Southern California blooms in winter at which time its giant boles ring with the chips of Yellow-rumped Warblers and the zip of Anna's hummers. The Yellow-rumps eat insects attracted to the flowers and drink their nectar, as well. Southern California birders know that it is important to bird these flowering trees in winter because they may hold a wintering *Selasphorus* hummingbird or out-of-season warbler, tanager, or oriole—and occasionally a wintering vagrant bird reported far and wide. Many a Christmas Count has benefited thereby.

Chaparral—Chaparral is not a species, it is a habitat type characterized by tough—often impenetrable—hard-stemmed brush adapted to periodic fires; the fire burns it to the ground and it grows anew from the roots. Anyone who watches CNN has seen thousands of acres of Southern California burn annually—almost invariably chaparral. This remarkable habitat is composed of a rich flora with chamise, various sages, Toyon, Lemonadeberry, scrub oak, manzanita, and numerous species of *Ceanothus* predominating. Many species of wild flowers also inhabit the chaparral; some, like Bush Poppy, are very showy indeed. The chaparral is home to an interesting list of resident, wintering, and migratory bird species, including many endemics. Characteristic birds of the chaparral include: California Quail, Anna's Hummingbird, Bewick's Wren, Wrentit, California Thrasher, Spotted and California Towhees, and Lesser Goldfinch. Wintering birds common in chaparral include Ruby-crowned Kinglet, Hermit Thrush, and Fox ("Sooty") and Golden-crowned Sparrows.

Coastal Sage Scrub—Coastal sage scrub is often referred to as "soft chaparral". It is lower growing (usually around waist height or a little taller) and not as dense as chaparral, which is frequently head high or taller. You can typically walk through coastal sage scrub, but you cannot easily walk through chaparral. Plants characteristic of coastal sage scrub include various sages, California Buckwheat, California Sunflower, and Coastal Prickly-Pear. Like chaparral, many more species can be included within this habitat. Chaparral requires more water than coastal sage scrub, and typically occurs at higher altitudes (this is a rough generalization—coastal sage scrub can be found on exposed slopes up to 5,000 feet and chaparral down to the coast). The most famous avian resident of coastal sage scrub is the endangered California Gnatcatcher, whose range is restricted to this habitat—to the chagrin of developers in Orange and San Diego Counties who constantly search for new areas to "improve."

Riparian Corridors—Riparian corridors in Southern California occur throughout the region, except above treeline on the highest peaks. The species of trees and shrubs vary with altitude, but all are characterized by mature trees and/or shrubs growing alongside a river or streamcourse. These corridors provide cover, foraging, and breeding habitat for a diverse list of birds. Characteristic breeding birds of these corridors in the coastal lowlands include Red-shouldered and Red-tailed Hawks, Acorn (where oaks are nearby), Nuttall's, and Downy Woodpeckers, Pacific-slope Flycatcher, Black Phoebe, Western Kingbird, Tree Swallow, Bewick's Wren, Western Bluebird, Swainson's Thrush (northern coast), Warbling Vireo, Yellow Warbler, Common Yellowthroat, Black-headed Grosbeak, Spotted Towhee, Song Sparrow, and Bullock's Oriole. Because these corridors are not so much a unique habitat type as an acknowledgement of trees along watercourses, the list varies with altitude and location east or west of the mountains. Riparian corridors are particularly significant to the birder, however, due to their talent for drawing migrants in spring and fall.

Fresh Water—Southern California, west of the Colorado, does not have any large permanent bodies of flowing water—known in the rest of the world as "rivers." Yes, we have watercourses carrying the name of river; these serve as a source of amusement to most visitors. Their channels may be roaring torrents during winter storms, but in summer they are usually shallow trickles at best. Shallow trickles, however, are attractive to birds in a dry land. Generally, wherever there is standing fresh water in California, there will be birds whatever the season.

Mountain, coastal, and desert lakes, ponds, and sewage plants play host to numerous waterfowl species in winter. Many species of waders, shorebirds, rails, and raptors are to be found around the edges. Ospreys and Bald Eagles visit larger inland lakes in the winter. The chapters that follow discuss the most important of these bodies of water for the birder.

Oak Woodlands and Savannas—Dense live-oak woodlands are widespread in Southern California, found in canyons and on damp hillsides west of the deserts and below the coniferous zone. Characterized by Coast Live Oak as the dominant species, the crowns touching and shading the ground beneath, these magical places support an interesting avifauna. Bird specialties of these forests (density and occurrence varying somewhat north to south) include Band-tailed Pigeon, Western Screech-Owl, Acorn and Nuttall's Woodpeckers, Pacific-slope Flycatcher (summer), Western Scrub-Jay, Oak Titmouse, Bushtit, Hutton's Vireo, Orange-crowned Warbler, and Spotted and California Towhees.

Southern California's oak savannas were formerly more extensive, many having fallen under subdivisions. The remaining broad interior valleys with majestic Valley Oaks punctuating the grasslands, usually fringed by Blue Oaks, are one of our most visually attractive habitats. Extensive oak savannas remain in Southern California in Santa Barbara and San Luis Obispo Counties: the Santa Ynez, Los Alamos, western Cuyama, Huasna, and southern Salinas Valleys are all exemplary of this habitat type. Characteristic birds of the oak savannas include Red-tailed Hawk, American Kestrel, Barn Owl, Acorn Woodpecker, Nuttall's Woodpecker, Western Scrub-Jay, Yellow-billed Magpie, Oak Titmouse, White-breasted Nuthatch, Western Bluebird, European Starling (sadly), Lark Sparrow, and Bullock's Oriole.

Deserts—East of the Transverse and Peninsular Ranges the insignificant annual rainfall produces California's extensive deserts. These are loosely divided into the Colorado and Mojave Deserts, the Mojave being "high" desert (roughly 1,000 to 4,500 feet), the Colorado being "low" desert (below sea level to 1,000 feet). This rule of thumb is not particularly useful; much of the Anza-Borrego Desert—a segment of the Colorado Desert—is above 1,000 feet elevation. A geographic definition is somewhat more useful: the Mojave Desert starts roughly in Joshua Tree National Park, extending northward through San Bernardino County, and west through northern Los Angeles and eastern Kern Counties. Death Valley in eastern Inyo County is a transitional area between the Mojave and Great Basin Deserts—typical of neither—although its flora more closely fits that of the Mojave, *sans* Joshua Trees. The Colorado Desert's flora is dominated by creosote bush in its lowest reaches, and by Ocotillo, cholla, agave, and barrel cactus at higher altitudes. It often has Ironwood and Smoke Trees along the washes, and spring-fed fan palms in hidden canyons. The Mojave is characterized by Joshua Tree woodlands interspersed with creosote bush; some segments of the Mojave (e.g., the Lanfair Valley east of Mojave National Preserve) become grassland in the spring during years of abnormally high rainfall. Winter frosts are to be expected in the higher elevations of the Mojave Desert. All desert types tend to have Frémont Cottonwoods growing at fresh water oases, along with willows and mesquite and sometimes introduced Tamarisks. These oases attract migrant birds like dollar bills attract congressmen.

Suffice it to say, it is difficult to characterize Southern California's deserts. It is just as difficult to construct a *characteristic* bird list due to the deserts' variability and many species' restricted ranges (see Specialties chapter). Birds resident in our deserts not appearing (apart from vagrancy) elsewhere in Southern California include: Gambel's Quail, White-winged and Inca Doves, Gila and Ladder-backed Woodpeckers, Gilded Flicker, Verdin, Black-tailed Gnatcatcher, Bendire's and Crissal Thrashers, Lucy's Warbler, and Abert's Towhee. Northern Cardinal and Elf Owl (the latter so local that no locations are accessible) have extremely local populations on the Colorado River, and Bronzed Cowbird is likewise a fairly local non-resident breeder. Vermilion and Brown-crested Flycatchers, Le Conte's Thrasher, Summer Tanager, Black-throated Sparrow, and Scott's Oriole are primarily desert species, having few restricted breeding populations west of the deserts.

Mountains—Southern California's mountains, like its deserts, defy description in a simple paragraph. Their geology was roughly outlined above. C. Hart Merriam's studies in Arizona almost 100 years ago noted that for every 1,000 feet gained in elevation, the flora changed equivalent to that 300 miles farther north—the well-known "life zone" concept was the result. The principle is valid, although in Southern California the vagaries of precipitation and direct or oblique exposure to the sun often hinder its direct application. The dominant flora of a particular mountain slope, added to its altitude, precipitation, and relative location east to west, north to south, determines its bird list. The chapters that follow include routes in every mountain province in Southern California; consult them for information on the special birds of each.

Generally speaking, Southern California's complex mountains fall into three broad categories: 1) lower mountains and mountain slopes like the Santa Ynez and Santa Monicas and the lower slopes of the San Gabriels, San Bernardinos, and the Peninsular Ranges, where chaparral is the dominant vegetation type, and typical birds include those noted for chaparral above; 2) higher mountain regions characterized by yellow pine (i.e., Jeffrey and Ponderosa Pines) forests interspersed with Incense Cedar, White Fir, and Black Oak—characteristic birds include Great Horned Owl, Red-breasted Sapsucker, Hairy and White-headed Woodpeckers, Olive-sided Flycatcher, Western Wood-Pewee, Violet-green Swallow, Steller's Jay, Clark's Nutcracker, Mountain Chickadee, Pygmy Nuthatch, Western Bluebird, Townsend's Solitaire, Green-tailed Towhee, and Dark-eyed Junco; and 3) dry slopes, (e.g., the desert side of the San Gabriels and San Bernardinos, desert mountains like the Providences and New Yorks, the lower elevations of Mount Pinos, Tehachapis, and the like) usually above 3,000 feet elevation, characterized by Pinyon Pines, junipers, and scrub oaks. Interesting breeding bird complexes are found in these areas, which are more variable than those of the yellow pine forests. Birds characteristic of the higher pinyon/juniper/scrub oak slopes (varying by location) include such species as Common Poorwill, Acorn Woodpecker, Gray Flycatcher, Western Scrub-Jay, Pinyon Jay, Juniper Titmouse (eastern desert mountains), California Thrasher, Gray Vireo, Black-throated Gray Warbler, Spotted Towhee, and Chipping and Black-chinned Sparrows.

Beaches—From "Gidget" to "Baywatch," from the 1969 Santa Barbara Channel oil spill to El Niño of 1998, Southern California's beaches have been the subject of national attention. They are not ignored by birds, either.

Although the media spends most of its time on the sandy bathing beaches, Southern California also has many wonderful rocky beaches and dramatic coastal cliffs. The rough, rocky shore is most common north of Point Conception, but rugged segments are found in every coastal county; read the text describing birding locations in these areas—rocky shorebird habitat is always noted. Rock breakwaters at the many marinas along the coast supply artificial habitat meeting the minimal requirements of migrating shorebirds and should not be ignored. Shorebirds to watch for along the rocky shores during spring and fall migration include Wandering Tattler, Ruddy and Black Turnstones, and Surfbird; Double-crested, Brandt's, and Pelagic Cormorants should be watched for in this niche as well; any inshore species can show up. Black Oystercatcher is a common resident of rocky shores north of Point Conception; it is increasingly uncommon as one moves south.

Sandy beaches are, or are not, productive largely in inverse proportion to the amount of human disturbance they endure. Remote beaches, or those at or near the mouths of protected estuaries, are most attractive to birds favoring this habitat. Sandspits at the end of harbor breakwaters (e.g., Santa Barbara Harbor) are also examples of habitat favored by sandy-shore-adapted species of shorebirds, gulls, and terns. Almost without exception, the sandy beaches at the mouths of the estuaries noted below are productive sandy shores; they are noted in the appropriate chapters.

Estuaries—The sad fact forces itself into the Southern California birder's consciousness: only about five percent of our original estuarine habitat remains. Its importance to the health and diversity of the ocean has been demonstrated in many biological case studies. The present depaupered state of this habitat is therefore of great concern. There is good news, however, in that governmental agencies and a significant part of the population now recognize the importance and endangered status of the remaining estuaries. This makes one cautiously optimistic that these beautiful, productive habitats will endure—with our vigilance. This is absolutely critical for many species of breeding, migrant, and wintering birds.

Starting with the Tijuana River Estuary in the southern extreme of this guide's range, and ending with Morro Bay in the north, the Southern California estuaries are both beautiful and bountiful—although some of those remaining are sadly impacted and reduced from their former glory (e.g., northern San Diego County's Buena Vista Lagoon, Santa Barbara County's Goleta Slough). Estuaries such as Tijuana River, San Elijo, and Batiquitos in San Diego County, Upper Newport Bay and Bolsa Chica in Orange County, the mouth of the Santa Ynez in Santa Barbara County, and Morro Bay in San Luis Obispo County are all important bird habitats that are accessible to birders. The Santa Clara River mouth in Ventura and the Santa Maria River mouth in Santa Barbara County are less viable as estuarine breeding habitat, but are outstanding birding sites.

The estuaries, characterized by *Salicornia* flats and drainage channel borders, usually include stands of cattails and tules at the upper edges above the high tide line. They are home to a fascinating resident avifauna as well as to numerous species of migrant and wintering birds. Each species' subtly differing requirements produces some anomalies in distribution; one cannot assume that because, for instance, Clapper Rail is found in the Tijuana and Upper Newport Bay Estuaries that it must therefore be found in similar (and less impacted) habitat in Morro Bay—it isn't. Likewise, Black Rails stalk parts of the Morro Bay estuary but are nowhere to be found in similar habitat at the mouth of the Santa Ynez River not far to the south—indeed they are very rare coastally south of Morro Bay (consult a reference such as Garrett and Dunn, 1981, for a full appreciation of such distributional questions). You get the picture. The coastal chapters to follow will explain more about the estuaries and their distinctive species. While visiting the estuaries be sure to take note of the dark, heavily streaked "Belding's" subspecies of Savannah Sparrow endemic to Southern California's estuaries from Morro Bay south.

Ocean—Southern California's oceanic environment can be divided roughly into inshore and pelagic regions.

Inshore habitat varies in its distance from shore, depending on ocean depth and temperature, among other factors. An imprecise rule of thumb may be as follows: inshore habitat is that part of the ocean readily birded from land with the help of a telescope. This part of the ocean is characterized (allow for seasonal variability) by such species as Red-throated and Common Loons, Western Grebe, Brown Pelican, the cormorants, scoters, and various species of gulls and terns. Genuinely pelagic species are seen occasionally in inshore waters. These are usually fly-bys seen from coastal promontories, usually in the spring (the annual flocks of Sooty Shearwaters north of Point Conception following bait fish inshore in summer are a regular exception). Generally speaking, however, inshore waters produce the same species you can see in any harbor along the coast.

Pelagic habitat, by definition, is open ocean far from land. Southern California has plenty of that (note, however, that ABA listing rules prevent one from adding to our lists species found more than 200 miles offshore).

Pelagic habitat is surprisingly, if subtly, diverse. Currents, depth, upwellings, surface temperature, seasonal winds, and variable salinity all combine to make one segment of the otherwise identical ocean surface more or less attractive to a particular species. Add seasonal variability and migration and you have a complex, but decipherable, situation. Pelagic trips are usually clustered around the spring and fall passage of pelagic birds off our coast. The most consistently productive trips, those with the highest numbers and species lists, tend to be long-range trips out to sea beyond the northern Channel Islands and trips north of Point Conception. This is not to say that trips to the south do not have high potential, but simply that one predicts more individuals of more species in the deep, colder waters to the north. See the Pelagic and Island Birding chapter for information on trip scheduling.

Islands—Southern California's Channel Islands are remote and otherworldly when compared with the mainland coast and its dense human population, but some islands allow surprisingly easy access. Regularly scheduled trips travel to Santa Catalina, Santa Cruz, and Anacapa Islands (see Pelagic and Island Birding chapter). Although much of the birding focus is on Santa Cruz Island due to the endemic Island Scrub-Jay, other offshore islands offer fine birding during spring and fall migrations, as well. Many eastern vagrant species have been recorded from the Channel Islands during these seasons. The rugged, rocky shorelines are a haven for shorebirds, while Leach's, Ashy, and Black Storm-Petrels, Pigeon Guillemots, Xantus's Murrelets, and Cassin's and Rhinoceros Auklets breed on one or more of the islands. The westernmost beach on San Miguel Island has the most impressive pinniped rookery south of Alaska. In summary, if you can get aboard a boat visiting one of the islands during spring or fall migration, do it. You will be doubly rewarded by pelagic birding during the passage and the chance of migrants on shore.

TRAVEL RESOURCES

• MAPS •

The Automobile Club of Southern California (AAA) publishes excellent maps for each of Southern California's counties, and a separate map of Death Valley. California birders include these maps as an essential part of their tool kit. AAA maps of specific cities and the entire state are also excellent. Maps of the National Forests are available at Forest Service offices. Bookstores sell maps of the region locally, the Rand McNally state map includes an index, a state park chart, metropolitan area maps, and a mileage log for inter-city distances (also see inside front cover of this guide). A number of atlases are on the market, of which DeLorme's treatment is a well-known example.

Although each chapter includes maps of the area(s) covered, visitors to Southern California will need regional maps such as those mentioned above in order to gain a wider context for their travels.

• TRAFFIC STATUS •

Traffic—how to survive in it, avoid it, and plan for it—is one of the unpleasant facts of life in Los Angeles, Orange, and western Riverside, San Bernardino, and San Diego Counties. Every day Monday through Friday and, to a lesser degree, on weekends, the extensive freeway systems in these areas become hundreds of miles of eight-lane parking lots during the morning (5–9 AM) and afternoon (3–7 PM) rush hours. Friday evenings and Sunday afternoons are nightmarish; the rush to the deserts and resorts on Friday and the return Sunday should be avoided. If you must travel during the rushes, plan it so that you are going *against* the flow if possible. You will run into slow spots, but it is far superior to going with the flow. The whole scene is reminiscent of the wildebeest migration across the Serengeti, the roadside breakdowns serving in place of lion kills and gawking motorists as the curious, albeit undeterred, herd. Although popular media would have you believe that flak vests and high-caliber weaponry are required equipment, this is not so. Birders, however, will do well to factor potential traffic snarls into their plans.

Radio station KNX, 1070 AM, has traffic and weather updates for the greater metropolitan area of the Los Angeles basin every six minutes. Monitoring this station will apprise you of trouble on the freeway system, allowing you to plan an alternate route if possible. In the San Diego area, station 760 AM gives a traffic report on the hour with bulletins if necessary.

If—after planning and precaution fail—you find yourself stuck hopelessly in traffic, it is best to adopt a Zen attitude and listen to taped bird songs, music, or books-on-tape. Like Brer Rabbit and the Tarbaby, the more you struggle, the greater the despair.

SOUTHERN CALIFORNIA RARE BIRD ALERTS

The Rare Bird Alerts (RBAs) below typically offer Audubon chapter and field trip information as well as rare bird news. You will also be able to leave a message about a rare bird sighting on these tapes.

Los Angeles   213/874-1318
Covers Los Angeles County as well as highlighting rarities around Southern California.

Morro Bay   805/528-7182
San Luis Obispo County and the Santa Maria River mouth.

Orange County   714/487-6869
Orange County, often with updates from around the region.

Southeastern   909/793-5599
Imperial, Riverside, and San Bernardino Counties, often with updates on special rarities from throughout Southern California.

San Diego   619/479-3400
San Diego County and rarities news from Imperial County.

Santa Barbara   805/964-8240
Santa Barbara and Ventura Counties.

"Birdbox" Southern California   818/952-5502
Covers rarities throughout the region. This is a voice mail system; you will hear recent messages in the original voice, as it was relayed to the mail box. In order to enter you will be prompted to insert the number of loon species recorded in Southern California: hint—all of them.

WEB SITES

The proliferation of sites on the World Wide Web has resulted in an amazing amount of information just a modem and mouse-click away. The sites outlined below are current as of spring 1998. More are appearing with regularity (and some sites may change servers, but they usually leave a link to the new site behind). Use a search engine like Yahoo or Alta Vista to find information on a birding location by typing the location name in the query box—you may be surprised to find valuable information instantly available.

Experiment, run a trial: type the *Yahoo!* Internet address in the Location box (http://yahoo.com) of your web browser, followed by Enter. When the Yahoo home page comes up, type Cibola National Wildlife Refuge in the Search box, then press Enter. You will see links to this rather obscure refuge appear on your screen. By clicking on the refuge link you find directions to the refuge, nearby services listed, birds to be expected, and other relevant information. Be creative, follow this practice for any birding site you care to visit; you may find information available that will surprise you.

Some of the sites below have links to numerous other birding-related sites; since these links are often up-dated, the ready information available is growing rapidly—and will continue to do so.

• CALIFORNIA RBA SITES •

California RBA Sites
http://www.birdware.com/lists/rba/_us/ca/caindex.htm
Contains links to California on-line Rare Bird Alerts, updated as events warrant.

• SOUTHERN CALIFORNIA AUDUBON SOCIETIES •

Audubon in Southern California: http://www.audubon.org/chapter/ca/socal/
An excellent source about field trips in southern California. Just click on the day of the month on the interactive calendar under "field trips" and see where you can join Audubon Society chapters or other groups on field trips that day. You can also access the homepages of other nearby Audubon chapters. Have you wanted to know how to subscribe to birding e-mail lists? This web page will tell you.

Buena Vista Audubon Society, Oceanside, San Diego County:
http://www.audubon.org/chapter/ca/buenavista/

Kerncrest Audubon Society, Eastern Kern County:
http://www1.ridgecrest.ca.us/~hallowel/kerncrest/

Los Angeles Audubon Society, Los Angeles:
http://pw1.netcom.com/~laas/index.html

Morro Coast Audubon Society, Morro Bay, San Luis Obispo County:
http://www.morrobay.com/Audubon/

Palomar Audubon Society, interior San Diego County:
http://www.audubon.org/chapter/ca/palomar/

San Fernando Valley Audubon Society, Los Angeles County:
http://www.audubon.org/chapter/ca/sfvas/index.html

Santa Monica Audubon Society, coastal Los Angeles County:
http://www.audubon.org/chapter/santamonicabay/homepage.htm

Sea and Sage Audubon Society, Orange County:
http://users.deltanet.com/users/ader/seasage/

• WESTERN FIELD ORNITHOLOGISTS •

Western Field Ornithologists
http://www.wfo-cbrc.org
Information about Western Field Ornithologists, their activities and publications, and the California Bird Records Committee (CBRC). Contains the Official California State List as well as rarities photos and a rarities report form.

• NATIONAL BIRDING RESOURCES •

American Birding Association:
http://www.americanbirding.org/
Wide range of on-line information about ABA and American birding generally.

Birdlinks:
http://www-stat.wharton.upenn.edu/~siler/birdlinks.html
This site provides links relevant to California and just about anything else a birder wants—an outstanding resource that almost single-handedly can get a birder anywhere in the birding web-world he or she can dream of going.

Cornell Laboratory of Ornithology:
http//www.ornith.cornell.edu/
Spend a day (or more) here. Accesses selected articles from current issue of Living Bird, contemporary research, pictures, volunteer contributions to bird knowledge, and more.

ID Frontiers Archive:
http://207.201.150.188/AT-nbhccoID_FRONTIERSquery.html
Provides access to discussions of field identification of challenging birds.

National Audubon Society:
http://www.audubon.org/

Virtual Birder:
http://www.virtualbirder.com/vbirder/
A popular and useful internet birding magazine filled with fun articles, prizes, virtual tours of popular birding spots, and tons of other information. From the "Real Birds" link you can access any transcribed Rare Bird Alert across the nation.

• Miscellaneous California Birding-related Sites •

Banded birds:
http://www.pwrc.nbs.gov
This is the site of the Patuxent Wildlife Research Center. It includes a wealth of bird-related information, including how to report banded birds on-line.

Big Morongo Canyon Preserve List:
http://www.cyberg8t.com/cvag/242.html
Provides bird list for this fine migrant trap/desert riparian site. Includes abundance, seasonal codes.

Birder:
http://www.birder.com/birding/index.html
Contains much birder-related information national in scope, plus checklists for all states.

California Condor recovery program:
http://www.peregrinefund.org/CACondor.html
Provides information on the status of the California Condor recovery efforts and related issues.

Eaton Canyon Nature Center (Pasadena):
http://www.znet.com/~schester/angeles_mtns/guides/
Unusual web site gives information on Eaton Canyon Nature Center via a link, and Angeles National Forest hikes with in-depth info. Also includes northern San Diego County hikes. Get out of your car (and away from your computer) and explore.

Field Trip announcements:
http://www.audubon.org/chapter/ca/socal/
See description in "Audubon in Southern California," above.

Gull Photo Archive:
http://www.agecon.ucdavis.edu/homepages/hampton/gulls.htm
You want photos of gulls? This site has photos of gulls: cryptic gulls, rare gulls, gulls to die for (or at least to travel to a sewage plant for), California gulls—and others.

Gjon Hazard's Web Site:
http://www.humboldt.edu/~gch3/index.html
Includes birding links, California bird list, and links to many California natural history museums.

Imperial Valley:
http://www.imperial.cc.ca.us/birds/iv-birds.htm
Numerous photographs of birds in the Imperial Valley plus other information on that region.

Inland Counties Birding Atlas:
http://www.gg.klever.net/~birds/
A fine web page covering San Bernardino, Riverside, and Imperial Counties should be of great interest to birders in California's southeastern counties. Rare Bird Alerts and other birding information in this region are provided.

Joe Morlan's Web Site:
http://fog.ccsf.cc.ca.us/~jmorlan/
Contains photographs of California rarities, updated regularly, and links to other birding sites in California—and elsewhere. A California-bound, web-surfing birder would be well advised to check into this page and hang ten over the keyboard.

• MUSEUMS •

Natural History Museum of Los Angeles County:
http://www.lam.mus.ca.us/webmuseums/
Natural history information from California and around the globe.

San Bernardino County Museum:
http://www.cyberspacemuseum.com/n5_11.html
Contains basic information on the San Bernardino County Museum.

San Diego Natural History Museum:
http://www.sdnhm.org/
An outstanding web site for introductory (and beyond) information about San Diego County and Southern California. Includes a bird list for San Diego County, Q and A on birds (and more) in the county. Also has lists for mammals, reptiles, plants, etc. Click the "field guide" link and spend a few hours.

Santa Barbara Museum of Natural History:
http://sbnature.org/
Introduces the museum and much local natural history information.

Smithsonian Institution:
http://www.si.edu/organiza/startold.htm
All right, so it's not California. It does, however, give you access to information in and about the national natural history museum.

• BUGS •

Butterflies of California:
http://www.npwrc.org/resource/distr/lepid/bflyusa/ca/toc.htm
A listing of all the butterflies of California with a hot link to each species; one click and you have a photo of the beast, life history information, and its range on the California map.

Butterfly Web Resources:
http://www.chebucto.ns.ca:80/Environment/NHR/lepidoptera.html
"Electronic Resources on Lepidoptera" bills itself as "the most complete and comprehensive website on Lepidoptera on the internet" which it may well be.

Digital Dragonflies:
http://www.dragonflies.org/Welcome.html
Information on the dragons and link to the Digital Dragonfly Museum, featuring photos of dragonfly species—among the most beautiful images on the web.

Dragonflies and Damselflies:
http://gnv.ifas.ufl.edu/~entweb/draghome.htm
Information, and hot links to other resources, on the Class Odonata.

• MISCELLANEOUS USEFUL SITES •

MAPQUEST:
http://www.mapquest.com/
This site will give you detailed directions with mileage to or from almost anywhere in the United States.

Weather:
http://www.weather.com/weather/us/states/California.html
This is the California-specific site from The Weather Channel, giving you information on a city-by-city basis. Forecasts, radar maps, and a vast array of weather-related information.

PERILS

The **California Highway Patrol** now has radar. Not only that, they use it on freeways. This may seem strange, given prevailing speeds which range from a dead-stop to averaging ten miles per hour over the posted speed limit. It is most useful to them in rural areas where high speed often is safer—and individual cars are easier to pick out.

When birding in Southern California one should always be aware that the state boasts of numerous poisonous **snakes** (no, we don't mean those in wingtip shoes). An impressive list of rattlesnake species is to be found here; most habitat niches—including high altitude—have their own type. Many native birders have never even seen a rattlesnake in the field after many years of birding—but many others have. Use common sense; watch where you put your feet and hands when in the field. If you see a snake, don't try to kill it—simply move quietly away.

There are no documented records of Lyme Disease originating in California. We do, however, have our share of noxious **bugs**. Mosquitoes are the most obvious and pernicious of pests, but biting flies are common in the mountains late spring through summer, and we have our fair share of ticks. Use of insect repellent is an effective way of lessening the minor threat posed by these various pests.

Some of the following chapters include birding sites in **urban** areas. An attempt has been made in the body of the text to identify those likely to pose a higher risk. Just because a given site does not include a warning, however, should not cause a birder to be oblivious to possible perils. Always lock your vehicle, whether in an urban or rural area, and do not allow valuables to be visible from outside. If you are renting a car, ask if the rental agency will provide a steering wheel locking device (The Club); a visual sign of vigilance is helpful. Be aware of others around; if you see or otherwise sense something in the surroundings that is not quite right—go somewhere else. It is always best to bird with others in urban and suburban settings.

Use good sense in protecting yourself from the **sun**. It is a rare birder indeed who does not know of the dangers of too much sun, but some do not know of its power to penetrate our chronic summer coastal low clouds. You can get a vivid burn on the gloomiest of summer days, so do not let down your guard.

The sacred CNN triumvirate of **floods, fire,** and **earthquake** do occur in Southern California on occasion (though, one suspects, not often enough for the media). These are about as likely to affect your birding as a case of mumps: possible, but the percentages mean that it's not worth losing an opportunity due to fear of them. The exception, of course, is flash floods. You can avoid trouble by staying out of dry washes and streambeds when it is raining higher up in the drainage. Use caution when crossing dips on roads during and after rainstorms.

Your Papers Are in Order? FOREST ADVENTURE PASS

Visitors to all National Forests in Southern California (Angeles, Cleveland, Los Padres, and San Bernardino) have the opportunity to pay for an annual **Forest Adventure Pass** in order to enjoy them. The annual Forest Adventure Pass costs $30.00 (1998), and a second-car pass (two vehicles traveling together) is $5.00; another alternative, a daily pass, is $4.00 per day per car. Although not required for those merely driving through, if you intend to stop the car and get out, you **must** have a pass. The penalty for not having a pass is steep (currently $100), and people are being ticketed. The pass is not license plate specific; you may use it in whichever car you happen to be driving. Keep it in your car at all times while in a National Forest, hanging it from your rear-view mirror while you are outside the vehicle.

In order to procure the *required* passport to adventure, stop at any US Forest Service business office and buy one there. Many sporting goods stores, private campgrounds, and convenience stores near National Forests also carry the pass. On holidays and weekends, passes may also be available at roadside Forest Service information facilities, but don't expect them to be open early enough to accommodate a birder's early start.

ROADKILL

Much can be learned, if morbidly, from an area's roadkill. Characteristic reptiles and mammals—and occasionally birds—of a region inevitably end up on or beside the highway in a pathetic heap. It is instructive, along a rural, little-used road, to stop to examine roadkill in order to learn what is running, creeping, crawling, or slithering about the area. Where possible and practical, it is a good idea to remove roadkill from the road so that local scavengers

(Coyotes, vultures, Golden Eagles, magpies, ravens) don't become statistics as well. One should *not* handle rodents, however, due to the slight possibility of picking up an illness from their viruses or parasites. Roadkill analysis is not for everyone, but it does provide information that may not be otherwise attainable under normal field conditions.

HOW TO USE THIS BOOK

This guide is constructed with primary and secondary goals. The primary goal is straightforward and no surprise to the reader: helping birders find birds in Southern California. The secondary goal, we hope, may be discernible as well: we wish to help make *your* birding more interesting by providing a broader perspective on the region, its birds, and other natural features.

What is a bird's context? How does it make its living? When does it arrive or leave? What habitat is it adapted to exploit? Although not attempting to discuss behavior or biology, we hope to have provoked questions in the reader's mind which will lead to further study and involvement with the world of birds. Take the Gray Vireo as an example. The San Bernardino and Laguna Mountains chapters point out two of the most reliable places to find this low-density species in Southern California. This begs a question: Southern California positively bulges with fine Gray Vireo habitat—why are there so few? We do not have an answer. It is an interesting question. There are many more implied throughout the book. You will find questions of your own, some of which may be answered within.

After perusing the book's overall plan and the birding routes it presents, turn to the graphs. These are intended to illustrate the likelihood of seeing a given species in appropriate habitat at a specific time of year. Next, if you are looking for a specific target bird, read about it in the Southern California Specialties section, then turn to the index to find places in the text where the bird is mentioned. This will guide you to likely locations to find your bird. You may choose to follow an entire route, or simply to focus on a certain location—it's up to you. Do remember that the routes are constructed by birders with considerable field experience in those locations; the sites noted have proven trustworthy through time, as described.

Notice that genuine rarities are not graphed, but rather are listed following the graphs. These species are not predictable—indeed, some are so out-of-range in Southern California that future appearances are virtually incredible. You may have heard of a specific event involving one or more of these species in our area; do not expect to see it on a given day or season. If you do encounter one of these species, document it in writing (if it is a review species of the California Bird Records Committee, send them your documentation: c/o Michael M. Rogers, Secretary, P.O. Box 340, Moffett Field, CA 94035), call the local Rare Bird Alert (RBA)—the numbers are on page 14—that same day, and treat yourself to a celebratory dinner that evening!

Use this guide in conjunction with a good **map** of the area you are birding. You will inevitably note other spur roads in rural areas that are not included in the text you are following. Explore, find new things, do not allow your birding to be restricted to the tried and true routes within these pages; then write to the ABA office with suggestions for additions or corrections to this guide.

Note that each chapter, whether loop or linear route, includes **bold-faced** place names. These locations are the most interesting and productive along the route. Decisions regarding which stops to make or which to save for another day will depend on many factors, of which time of year is among the most important (again, consult the bar-graphs). Note that most locations give you an idea of their specialties and the most productive seasons—make your decisions accordingly.

Mileages between points in the chapters are typically included in parentheses (1.6). *Mileage presented in this format is invariably the distance from the last point so mentioned.* You may choose to reset your trip-odometer at each measured site to make the next point easier to find, or not, depending on your own approach to following directions. In any case, if you find a serious discrepancy in the mileage or in directions to a particular site, please let the ABA office know so that it may be corrected in a future printing.

WEATHER

Everyone knows that it never rains in Southern California. The phantom rainy season extends from November through April and it is best not to tempt fate if you are here during that time; bring light rain gear. Winter, spring, summer, and fall are typically mild along the coast. Summer temperatures in inland valleys and in the deserts range from warm to intensely hot. Winter in the mountains can be bitterly cold (as can the bow of the boat on a pelagic trip any day of the year). Californians typically dress in layers. Expect cool mornings and evenings most places, and pleasant mid-days and afternoons.

ACCOMMODATIONS

Unless your home address is the Tibetan Plateau, you know that coastal Southern California offers a tremendous variety of accommodations. The rural towns noted in the chapters that follow are, however, another matter. Note that comments regarding local accommodations along the route are included at the end of each chapter. If you are a visitor intent on camping, such facilities are also pointed out at each chapter's conclusion, as appropriate. You should also consult one of the published camping guides to California for more detailed information.

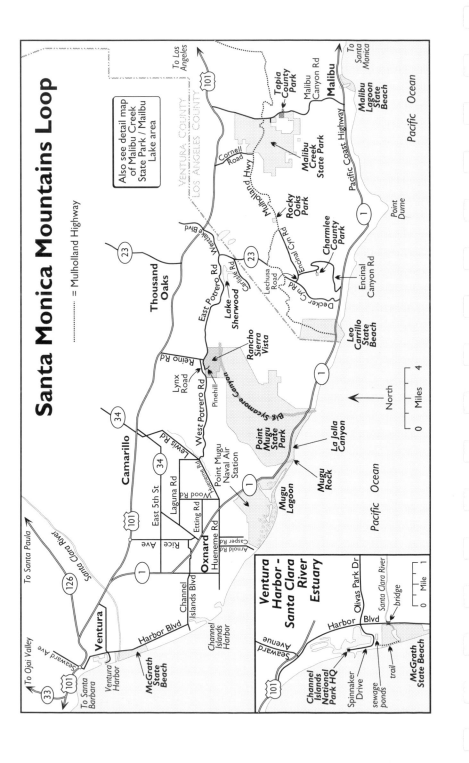

Santa Monica Mountains Loop

······· = Mulholland Highway

Also see detail map of Malibu Creek State Park / Malibu Lake area

Ventura Harbor – Santa Clara River Estuary

SANTA MONICA MOUNTAINS LOOP

Compared with other California mountains, the Santa Monica Mountains are more like hills. Part of California's Transverse (that is, trending west-east instead of north-south) Ranges, their highest point is Sandstone Peak with an elevation of only 3,111 feet. However, what they lack in height is offset by their rugged canyons and coastline. The only forests are occasional stands of live oaks and sycamores along the streams. Most of the vegetation is lush chaparral. This loop will take you through these habitats as well as to some interesting coastal sites.

This is not one of the best birding areas in Southern California, but it *is* close to Los Angeles. The best time to visit is during April and May, when the birds are singing and the flowers are in bloom, although fall migration is the best time to bird the Oxnard Plain to the west; overall, the birding can be fairly good at any season. Most of the birds of Southern California's chaparral and oak-woodland habitats can be found on this loop.

The starting point is the intersection of the Pacific Coast Highway (Highway 1) and Webb Way in Malibu, about 13 miles west of Santa Monica. Before starting up Malibu Canyon, drive east on Highway 1 for one-quarter mile to **Malibu Lagoon**. On the right (south), just before the bridge over Malibu Creek, you will see the entrance to Malibu Lagoon State Beach (fee). The parking lot is open 9 AM–sunset, and the fee is steep, but there is on-street parking on the south side of Pacific Coast Highway or near the shopping mall across the highway. *You should not leave valuables in the car when parking in these locations.*

The lagoon and beach can be very rewarding at any time of year, with a varying assortment of gulls, terns, small shorebirds, large waders, ducks, and marsh birds. In late summer and fall check for Elegant Terns. In fall and winter you should scope the offshore waters for loons, grebes, cormorants, sea ducks, and Black-vented Shearwaters. A sudden mass flight of birds may mean only a playful dog in the water, but it could also mean a raptor overhead. Walk under the bridge and upstream to look for a variety of streamside songbirds and, in winter, waterfowl.

A walk across the bridge over the creek (take a moment to scan the lagoon from here) takes you to Adamson House and Museum, where a fine growth of exotic trees and shrubs surrounds an attractive Spanish-style mansion. On your left, as you enter the grounds, a brick wall covered with luxuriant Cape

23

Honeysuckle is excellent in spring for Allen's and occasionally Rufous Hummingbirds. The property also offers alternate access to the east side of the lagoon, which may not be accessible from the west side when the intermittent sandbar serving as a path is not there. A viewing platform on the bank above the lagoon often produces such secretive species as Sora and Virginia Rail. Return to Webb Way and turn right. Go one block and turn left onto Civic Center Way, then turn right onto Malibu Canyon Road (0.7).

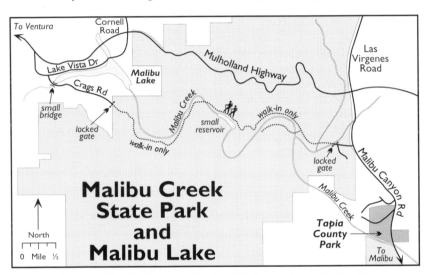

Turn left into **Tapia County Park** (4.5) (fee), where Malibu Creek, lined with dense willows, can offer good birding. Nearby are areas of large cottonwoods, sycamores, and Coast Live Oaks. Common resident chaparral birds which you can expect are Acorn, Nuttall's, and Downy Woodpeckers, Western Scrub-Jay, Oak Titmouse, Spotted and California Towhees, and Lesser Goldfinch. California Quail, Bewick's Wren, Wrentit, and California Thrasher can be heard calling from the chaparral on the surrounding hills. Along the stream Green Heron, Belted Kingfisher, and Common Yellowthroat are found, and Red-shouldered Hawks often perch in the sycamores. Among the oaks, you may find Band-tailed Pigeon and Hutton's Vireo. Spring brings Lazuli Buntings and an assortment of transient flycatchers, vireos, and warblers. In winter Golden-crowned Kinglet and mixed flocks of White-crowned and Golden-crowned Sparrows may be seen. In fall eastern vagrants show up regularly. At any time of year, an early morning birder may come upon a Bobcat.

Continue up Malibu Canyon Road and turn left into **Malibu Creek State Park** (1.3) (fee). This oasis of natural beauty is rapidly becoming encircled by development. Set in rugged, chaparral-covered mountains, the park contains creeks, grassy flats, thick groves of oaks, and a man-made lake. Birding here is good for the same species listed for Tapia Park. Phainopepla is fairly common, especially in spring and summer, and Lazuli Bunting can be seen in spring. Canyon Wrens are found regularly where the creek flows close to the steep cliffs. An occasional White-tailed Kite may be encountered in grassy areas. Be on the lookout for Golden Eagles and other raptors sailing over the rugged peaks.

Turn left as you leave the park, then left again at the signal light onto Mulholland Highway (0.2). For the next 30 miles or so, you will be in a good area for Golden Eagles, but most of the large soaring birds will be Red-tailed Hawks and Turkey Vultures.

At the stop-sign at Cornell Road (3.2) turn left onto Lake Vista Drive, which skirts Malibu Lake. The lake and the land on both sides of the road are private, but you might try to get permission at the office of the Malibu Lake Mountain Club (0.4) to bird the road on the east side of the lake, the property around the office, and up the hill behind. The lake abounds with ducks and other waterbirds, particularly in winter. Crags Road (1.1) branches to the left for 0.7 mile and ends at the western entrance (walk-in only) to Malibu Creek State Park, but there is no parking here. Shortly after turning onto Crags Road, you will reach a small bridge. This is a good vantage point for scoping the lake on the left and a reedy area to the right, which can sometimes be productive. Turn left onto Lake Vista Drive as you leave Crags Road and almost immediately rejoin Mulholland Highway, where you turn left. During the next 20 miles you will pass many side roads which may be explored, but the habitat is all about the same.

Stay on Mulholland Highway to Rocky Oaks Park, Santa Monica Mountains National Recreational Area (4.7), where you'll find a nice mix of easily birdable oaks and chaparral. Continue on Mulholland Highway, bearing left at the fork (0.8). Go left down Encinal Canyon Road (past the junction with Lechusa Road) to Charmlee County Park on the right (4.7). Across the road from the nature center is a small water-drip and pool where most of the typical chaparral birds are easily seen.

From Charmlee County Park return to the Lechusa Road junction (1.2), continuing straight ahead to a right turn onto Decker Canyon Road (Highway 23), eventually becoming Westlake Boulevard, to Carlisle Road (5.0). The last two miles are narrow and winding, so drive slowly.

Turn left onto Carlisle Road to drive through a beautiful oak-lined canyon. Just beyond the turn, look up at the cliffs to the right where White-throated Swifts and Cliff Swallows nest. Both sides of the road are private property, but birding from the road is fine. This dead-end road is only about two miles long, but it can be alive with birds, particularly after the first mile. Return to Westlake Boulevard, turn left, continue to Potrero Road (1.5), and turn left again. To access **Lake Sherwood**, turn left at the second Lake Sherwood Drive (1.7) and stop at the fire station to scan the lake.

Those who have known this area in the past will be shocked at the changes. The road around the lake no longer exists, nor do the tules which held

Red-winged and Tricolored Blackbirds. Most of the houses, trees, and other vegetation which formerly ringed the lake have been removed in order to make way for a development of about 600 million-dollar homes. But the ducks and other waterbirds don't seem to mind, and a flock of American White Pelicans has been present here in some winters. Return to Potrero Road and continue west through Hidden Valley, an area of beautiful farms and huge Valley Oaks (also known as California White Oaks). The fields hold Western Meadowlark, Horned Lark, Lark Sparrow, and, in winter, American Pipit. Check the oaks for Oak Titmouse and Acorn Woodpecker. The utility poles in this area are often riddled with holes drilled by these colorful woodpeckers, who use them for acorn storage.

Continue west past Lake Sherwood, turning left at the intersection with Reino Road (5.5) onto West Potrero Road. At Pinehill Avenue (0.5) turn left into the Santa Monica Mountains National Recreation Area/Rancho Sierra Vista. The nature center is about a one-half-mile walk from the parking lot (0.4). The area has several short trails which may be productive, and an 8-mile trail through Point Mugu State Park which ends at the ocean at Big Sycamore Canyon. The grasslands here have singing Grasshopper Sparrows in early spring, Western Kingbirds in summers, and Say's Phoebes in winter. On the hillsides you will see unusual, stalked plants: Giant Coreopsis or Sea Dahlia, which grow only on the Channel Islands and the adjacent mainland as far north as San Luis Obispo County. Here they are small, but on the islands they may grow to ten feet tall. Return to Reino Road and turn left on Lynx Road continuing west to the Oxnard Plain.

Near the satellite campus for Cal State University, Northridge (8.0) the road is bordered by rocky hills with a heavy growth of cactus. Look here for Cactus Wren (at the westernmost limit of its range) and Rufous-crowned Sparrow. In winter you might find a Prairie Falcon here. Bear left across the bridge at Lewis Road (1.2) onto Hueneme Road (y-KNEE-me). The newly-plowed fields in this vicinity are good in winter for Horned Lark, Mountain Bluebird, and American Pipit. Red-throated Pipit occurs in October rarely.

The **sod farms** just off Hueneme Road, north of Mugu Lagoon on the Oxnard Plain, should be birded in fall. Pacific Golden-Plover, other wet-field-loving shorebirds, Horned Lark, American and Red-throated (very rare) Pipits, and longspurs (rare) should be looked for at this season. To get to the sod farms, continue on Hueneme Road, going under the Highway 1 bridge (2.3), to Casper Road (1.8). Turn left and scan the sod fields to the west of the GTE building, and left along Casper Road to the gate at the end. Additional sod farms are found along Arnold Road (left at 0.5 mile along Hueneme Road farther west). *Do not in any circumstances walk on the sod or enter the roads into any of the sod farms; they must be scanned from public roads.*

If you are here from late August to the end of October, birding nearby **Tamarisk rows** is highly recommended. Good numbers of western migrants and the occasional eastern vagrant (mid-September through mid-October best) are attracted to the "Tams." Common Ground-Doves are fairly common nearby year round. The three rows of Tams noted below produced twenty species of warblers and four species of vireos (including two Yellow-greens) in September and October 1997.

To reach the Tams after birding the sod farms, retrace your route on Hueneme Road, traveling east. Cross under Highway 1, parking on the right (0.3) opposite a beige two-story house next to a long row of Tamarisks running perpendicular to the road. Walk along the row on the dirt road that parallels it. This is the longest row on the Oxnard Plain, with the tallest trees. Thicker than other rows of Tams, it normally produces the best records each fall. *Do not venture into the surrounding fields and orchards—they are all private property.* It is a privilege to bird this row, as it is to bird other locations on the Oxnard Plain.

Proceed to Wood Road (0.5), turning left. Continue on Wood Road to Etting Road; turn left and bird the large Tams (1.6) across from the intersection with Hailes Road. Return to Wood Road, turning left. Pull over at concrete Revlon Flood Control Channel crossing under the road (0.6). You can bird from the bridge or walk downstream. This is a good place for Solitary Sandpipers in fall when the water level is right, and occasionally for other shorebirds. The riparian section downstream may produce a rare bunting or sparrow.

Continue north to the intersection of Wood and Laguna Streets (0.4), turning left on Laguna. Stop at a row of Tams on the left (1.1), the thinnest of the three rows discussed, making it easy to bird—it is right along the road.

Black-vented Shearwaters
Shawneen E. Finnegan

Return to Highway 1 and Hueneme Road. Travel south to Mugu Lagoon (3.8), which is located within the boundaries of off-limits Point Mugu Naval Air Station. It usually abounds with birds, but unfortunately it can be birded only with difficulty through the chain-link fence along the Pacific Coast Highway. Since the birds are usually at a considerable distance, a good telescope is necessary. Still, it is worth a try. With luck you may be able to identify some of the larger waders, such as Long-billed Curlew, Marbled Godwit, Willet, and the like. There are usually some Brant present in winter.

*If you are particularly frustrated here and wish to visit a good, accessible coastal site on this loop, see the Boxed Text on the next page for directions to the **Santa Clara River Estuary**. Otherwise, read on for directions for birding Point Mugu State Park and the remainder of the loop route.*

From Mugu Lagoon continue east to **Mugu Rock** (0.8). Parking is available on both sides of the rock, so both can be checked for loons, grebes, sea ducks, and Black-vented and occasionally other shearwaters in fall and winter. Flights of Sooty Shearwaters, loons (predominantly Pacific in spring), Brant, and Surf Scoters may be seen here in spring and fall. Black-vented Shearwaters may be seen in fall and winter, and jaegers are also spotted sometimes. An impressive array of pelagic rarities has been seen from this location. A pair of Rock Wrens is usually visible on the rock itself, and White-throated Swifts often course overhead.

From Mugu Rock, continue on Pacific Coast Highway to La Jolla Canyon (fee) in **Point Mugu State Park** (2.6). You'll find a nice section of riparian growth along a small streambed here, as well as lush chaparral. It is worth a brief stop in spring and fall to check the riparian growth for migrants. **Big Sycamore Canyon** (1.6) is always worth checking—especially the usually wet creekbed upstream from the bridge. In some years masses of Monarch Butterflies assemble here in the fall. You can park outside the entrance (on the ocean-side) to avoid the fee.

As you continue east, stop occasionally at turn-outs to look for flocks of sea ducks and grebes and to scan the beach for Snowy Plovers and other shorebirds. Check the trees on the ocean-side of the highway for migrants. The wooded area at Leo Carrillo State Beach (5.4) can be very good for warblers in migration. Continue on Highway 101 toward Malibu. At Encinal Canyon Road (3.1) you can turn left for 3.8 miles to reach Charmlee County Park, if you have not already visited it.

Campgrounds are located at Point Mugu State Park (Sycamore Canyon), Leo Carrillo State Park, McGrath State Beach, and Malibu Creek State Park. Motels are clustered along Highway 1.

BIRDING THE SANTA CLARA RIVER ESTUARY

To reach the estuary from Mugu Lagoon, go west and north on Highway 1 to US-101 (9.9; refer to map and inset map at the beginning of this chapter). *(To bypass downtown Oxnard you may want to go north on Highway 1 to the Channel Islands Boulevard off-ramp a few miles north, turning right at the off-ramp to Rice Avenue, then left on Rice all the way to US-101. Travel west on US-101—the sign will say "Highway 101 North"—to the Seaward Avenue exit.)* Take US-101 west to the Seaward Avenue exit in Ventura (5.3). Go one-half block south, and turn left onto Harbor Boulevard, which parallels the highway. Turn right onto Spinnaker Drive (1.6), which borders the south edge of **Ventura Harbor**. At the end of Spinnaker Drive is the headquarters for Channel Islands National Park and the dock where you can make arrangements to go to Santa Cruz Island for Island Scrub-Jay (see Pelagic and Island Birding and the Specialties chapters). In winter you will find loons, grebes, and scoters in the harbor and, on the beach, gulls, terns, and shorebirds.

To reach the estuary, go back to the chain-link fence at the south end of the harbor and park in the lot on the opposite side of Spinnaker Drive. To get to the **Santa Clara River mouth**, walk south along the beach from this point. In spring you will pass a protected breeding colony of the endangered California subspecies of Least Tern. The river-mouth area is very good for waterfowl, gulls, and terns. Elegant Terns are numerous in summer and fall. A few Thayer's Gulls are present each winter in the large gull flock. Shorebirding is generally excellent here, but it s all highly dependent on the season and the water level (a low water level is best). The sewage ponds inside the fence are excellent for ducks in both summer and winter. The entrance to the facility is a little farther along Spinnaker Drive. Birders are welcome to walk or drive around the ponds, *but first must sign in at the office.*

For alternative approaches to this estuary, return to Harbor Boulevard and turn right. Park just before reaching the bridge to check for swallows and terns. The estuary can be approached from here if you climb down the bank at the west corner of the bridge. (You may have difficulty making your way through the dense vegetation, but a path can usually be found.) Birds will be encountered along the river all the way to the ocean. The south side of the estuary can also be checked from **McGrath State Beach** (camping; fee) (0.5). The brushy areas of the park are excellent for warblers and small landbirds during migration. White-tailed Kites are usually seen hovering over the fields along Harbor Boulevard beyond the park.

You can continue the Santa Monica Mountains Loop by returning to Mugu Lagoon. Alternately, you can get a jump on the Santa Barbara County chapter by heading north on US-101.

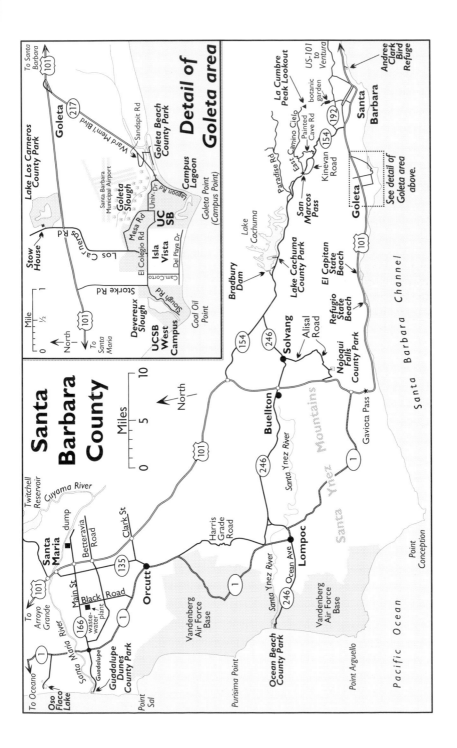

Detail of Goleta area

Santa Barbara County

SANTA BARBARA COUNTY

When the Spaniards were picking sites for missions, they surely must have selected Santa Barbara for its ideal climate and beautiful setting. The mission rises on a slope among gnarled live oaks and sycamores at the base of the Santa Ynez Mountains; looking southeast from its steps one looks over the city and across the Santa Barbara Channel to Anacapa Island. The contemporary city of Santa Barbara values both its heritage and exquisite setting, making this a most attractive destination. Add to this the over 460 species of birds recorded here and little more reason is needed to provoke a visit. It is doubtful that you will find anything approaching that many species, unless you decide to retire and stay. After seeing this attractive town, you will probably think that this is not a bad idea.

The route below comprises two to three days of birding, and can easily be divided into north and south Santa Barbara County segments.

Before beginning this route, visitors to the Santa Barbara area ought to be aware that the coast here runs east-west, not north-south. The ocean is therefore to the south (not west) and the mountains—at the western end of California's east-west Transverse Ranges—are to the north (not east), unlike most of coastal California. Adding to the visitor's navigational unease, the downtown and waterfront areas boast streets named Cabrillo, Castillo, and Carrillo in close proximity. It is best to suspend disbelief and merely follow the directions.

The starting point is the intersection of US-101 and Hot Springs Road east of downtown Santa Barbara. **Andree Clark Bird Refuge** is just southwest of this intersection and serves as a good entry point and introduction to Santa Barbara's rich avifauna. To reach this refuge exit US-101 at Hot Springs Road, turn south onto Cabrillo Boulevard, and take the first right turn, Los Patos Way. The lake and parking lot are located immediately to the left. There are always ducks of some type on this freshwater pond. From late fall though winter there may be a fairly good selection, occasionally including Wood Duck among the more expected species. Check the *Myoporum* bushes on the islands for roosting Double-crested Cormorants, Great Blue and Green Herons, and Black-crowned Night-Herons. All three phalarope species occur here in migration, although Red is most unusual.

This is an excellent area to study gulls. They are accustomed to being fed and are very tame. Western, California, and Ring-billed Gulls are present all year. Glaucous-winged, Herring, Thayer's (rare), Heermann's, Mew, and Bonaparte's Gulls arrive for the winter.

31

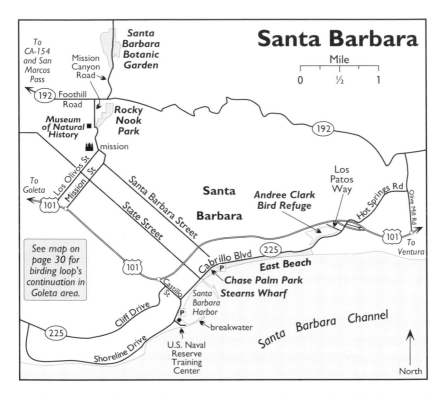

To continue the waterfront area tour, turn right onto Cabrillo Boulevard and follow it to **Chase Palm Park**, best accessed by a parking lot at the base of Santa Barbara Street (1.9) (fee in summer and on weekends). From here you can see **Stearns Wharf**. A walk on the wharf may be productive, especially in winter, for close looks at loons, grebes, and scoters. From late August through April, however, you will probably see more birds by looking around the beach in front of the parking lot.

First, follow the bike-path to your left (east) where an outfall channel creates a large pool in the sand. All sorts of gulls and terns gather here to roost, especially in late fall and winter; this is probably the best waterfront location for finding Thayer's Gull. A large flock of Black Skimmers winters on the beach here. From time to time rarities such as Black-headed Gull and Glaucous Gull show up. The more common shorebirds forage near the edges of the pool.

As noted earlier, a walk on the wharf can be worthwhile, but it is probably better to spend your time on the breakwater which protects **Santa Barbara Harbor**. To reach the harbor area, turn left (west) from the parking lot at Chase Palm Park and follow Cabrillo Boulevard for another mile. One-half mile past the traffic light at Castillo Street turn left into the harbor parking lot (fee). Follow the sidewalk past the US Naval Reserve Training Center and the seafood restaurants to the breakwater. At the end of the breakwater you will see a sandspit where Snowy Plovers and other shorebirds rest (early fall through early spring); Wandering Tattler is seen frequently on the rocks in spring and fall. Gulls and terns are usually common. In late summer and fall this is a good spot to pick out Heermann's Gull and Elegant Tern. Mew Gulls and Royal Terns come in late fall and winter.

Return to Castillo Street and turn left (north). After three blocks you can access US-101 for the trip to Goleta. Turn up-coast on US-101 (the signs will say "Highway 101 North" although you will actually be traveling west at this time) to Ward Memorial Boulevard (Highway 217) (7.0) which you will take toward UCSB and Goleta Beach. Turn right onto Sandspit Road (1.9), and then left at the stop-sign toward **Goleta Beach County Park** on your right. From the inland side of the main parking lot check the channel to the mouth of the slough for herons, egrets, ducks, shorebirds, gulls, and terns. Elegant Terns occur from July to October; Royal Terns are present from October to March. Walk out on the fishing pier to look for loons, grebes, and scoters. In winter and spring a handful of Tricolored Blackbirds is sometimes in the parking area near the base of the pier.

Leave the park, turn left, go under the highway (0.2), and turn right onto Ward Memorial Boulevard to the gate of the **University of California at Santa Barbara** (fee for parking, Monday–Friday—ask for a campus map). Go left on Lagoon Road and park, only where your permit allows, near the end of the road (ask the guard at the entrance kiosk). Bird Campus Lagoon beyond the Marine Science building. The lagoon is fairly good from fall through spring for grebes, cormorants, waterfowl, and terns.

To reach **Goleta Point** (also called Campus Point), walk west from the Marine Science building down to the beach and then up onto the bluffs, bearing to your left at the top. The Point is marked by an old piece of concrete foundation; you can see rocky outcroppings directly below in the surf. These rocks can be good fall through spring for Ruddy and Black Turnstones at low tide, but the bluff-top is the best vantage point for scanning the Santa Barbara Channel. A telescope is very helpful. This is the favored spot for observing the spring coastal seabird migration from mid-March through late May (with April being best). Many thousands of loons (mostly Pacific), Brant, scoters (mostly Surf), phalaropes, gulls, and terns may be seen moving up-coast (west). All sorts of surprises are possible. Late afternoon and early morning are the best times of day to see a large number of birds here.

To reach the west side of campus, return to Lagoon Road and go straight ahead to University Drive. Follow University Drive to its intersection with Mesa Road. Turn right onto Mesa Road and follow it around to Los Carneros Road, 0.9 mile from the entrance kiosk. Turn left (south) onto Los Carneros Road, then right onto El Colegio Road. At the University West Campus sign (0.5), turn left (south) onto the entrance road to Devereux Slough.

Birding **Devereux Slough** (part of the Coal Oil Point Natural Reserve) can be great, depending on water levels. In recent years, however, it has become a challenge due to strictly enforced parking regulations. Unless you wish to stay with your car and scan from the several pull-outs, you must obtain a permit (fee) to park at any time in the designated West Campus areas. Permits are available from the Marine Science Institute, University Reserve System, UCSB, Santa Barbara, CA 93106; phone 805/893-4127, weekdays 9 AM–5 PM; and from Parking Services, UCSB, Santa Barbara, CA 93106; phone 805/893-2346, weekdays 7:30 AM–4 PM.

If you cannot get a permit beforehand, try parking on surface streets in nearby Isla Vista and walking west toward the slough. Camino Corto, which turns south off El Colegio Road, is a possibility, or you may drive all the way to the end of Camino Corto, turn right onto Del Playa Drive, and drive to its end, where you can park on the street.

When it has water (usually dry by late summer) from late fall to mid-summer, the slough has good numbers of ducks, gulls, and terns. If water levels are low (late summer and early fall), it is very good for shorebirds. Over the years such rarities as Sharp-tailed Sandpiper, Ruff, Little Gull, Eurasian Wigeon—and an immature White/Black-backed Wagtail—have been found. The vegetation bordering the slough can be good for migrating and wintering landbirds. One or two pairs of Cassin's Kingbirds are resident in the area. Allen's Hummingbirds breed from March to July. One or two Tropical Kingbirds are sometimes present in fall or winter.

At **Coal Oil Point** (named in reference to the permanent natural petroleum seep from the channel floor just offshore) at the end of the road, a low tide exposes rocks. Look for Ruddy and Black Turnstones during fall and winter. Large numbers of Brandt's Cormorants are usually found offshore at this time. The point is fairly good for scanning the ocean at any season. A sizable wintering flock of Snowy Plovers frequents the beach several hundred yards up-coast, present late August to April.

Retrace your route to the intersection of El Colegio Road and Los Carneros Road. Turn left onto Los Carneros Road and follow it over the freeway to Stow House and **Lake Los Carneros County Park** (1.9 miles from the intersection of El Colegio and Los Carneros Roads). Park in the lot behind the fire station and walk to the house, birding the ornamental plantings there. Then follow the driveway to Lake Los Carneros County Park, a good spot for ducks, herons, and migrating passerines. Most of the 1,043-acre park, including the lake, is in a semi-wild state. The trees around the house itself may be particularly good during migrations and winter. The footbridge over the channel at the north end of the lake is a good place from which to watch for Virginia Rail, Sora, Common Moorhen (rare here), and American and Least Bitterns. The Least Bitterns breed, but are difficult to see. Lake Los Carneros County Park is best August through April.

To continue the loop, return to US-101 and go south (east) to Mission Street in Santa Barbara (7.8). Exit US-101 at Mission Street and go left four blocks to State Street. Turn left at State Street, go two blocks to Los Olivos Street, and turn right. Continue on Los Olivos Street past historic Santa Barbara Mission and bear left at the fork onto Mission Canyon Road.

Your first stop should be **Rocky Nook County Park.** Turn right off Mission Canyon Road just after it crosses a small bridge about one-quarter mile past the Mission. The Coast Live Oaks and California Sycamores which grow along Mission Creek create a beautiful oak woodland frequented by Acorn and Nuttall's Woodpeckers, Western Scrub-Jay, Oak Titmouse, Bewick's Wren, Hutton's Vireo, and Spotted and California Towhees. In fall and winter the flocks of Bushtits may contain migrant and wintering warblers, including Black-throated Gray (rare in winter) among the more abundant species. Pacific-slope Flycatchers breed here, and Black-headed Grosbeaks and Western Tanagers are showy among the other spring transients. The park can be crowded with picnickers on weekends.

The adjacent **Santa Barbara Museum of Natural History** (open daily; fee) west of Rocky Nook County Park can be reached by footpath or by following the signs along Mission Canyon Road. It has excellent exhibits of native birds and mammals. The interesting Museum store stocks bird checklists and a nice selection of natural history books. The Museum grounds boast an assortment of oak-woodland birds similar to those found at Rocky Nook, especially in the winter months. American Robin, Cedar Waxwing, Townsend's Warbler, and Wrentit are usually present at this season. Spring migration can bring migrants to the Museum grounds—vireos, warblers, tanagers, Black-headed Grosbeak, and orioles can be abundant at this time. To walk through the Museum grounds, look for the trailhead at the west end of the main parking lot.

Return to Mission Canyon Road and turn left. At Foothill Road (Highway 192) (0.3), jog right 2 blocks and then left, continuing on Mission Canyon Road to the **Santa Barbara Botanic Garden** (fee) (1.0). If you can tear yourself away from the fine display of native plants, you will find many chaparral and oak-woodland birds.

The trail following the creek at the bottom of the canyon is productive for woodland species, and the drier upper garden and along the road above are particularly good for chaparral species. Permanent residents here include California Quail, Anna's Hummingbird, Nuttall's Woodpecker, Oak Titmouse, Wrentit, California Thrasher, and Spotted and California Towhees. Summer is the time to look for Pacific-slope Flycatcher, Hutton's Vireo, Black-headed Grosbeak, and Hooded Oriole. Winter Wren (uncommon), Townsend's Warbler, and Golden-crowned Sparrow are present in winter.

For a longer trip west of Santa Barbara, return to Foothill Road (Highway 192) and turn right. At San Marcos Pass Road (Highway 154) (3.0) turn right for the climb up the pass. The hills here are covered with fine stands of chaparral. You are now entering Los Padres National Forest and a Forest Adventure Pass is required for all but through traffic. See information on the regulations and how to obtain one of these passes (fee) in the Introduction. A stop anywhere along this road could produce resident California Quail, California Thrasher, and Wrentit, but the traffic and noise make the side roads noted below more advisable—and enjoyable—places to search for these species.

At the crest of the highway (San Marcos Pass) turn right to drive out **East Camino Cielo** (6.9). At the fork with Painted Cave Road (2.0) keep left and bird your way out East Camino Cielo seven miles to the La Cumbre Peak fire lookout. All along this road in spring and early summer look for California and Mountain Quail, Greater Roadrunner, White-throated Swift, Costa's and Anna's Hummingbirds, Ash-throated Flycatcher, California Thrasher, Wrentit, Canyon Wren, Lazuli Bunting, and Rufous-crowned, Black-chinned, and "Bell's" Sage (*A. b. belli*, uncommon here) Sparrows. The dropped-ping-pong-ball song of the Wrentit is heard more often than the bird is seen, but if you squeak, it may come out to investigate. Townsend's Solitaires sometimes winter in the pines in the La Cumbre Peak area, and Golden-crowned and "Sooty" Fox Sparrows are common in winter.

Retrace your route to Highway 154. From East Camino Cielo cross Highway 154 to reach **Kinevan Road**. *(Kinevan Road can be reached from Santa Barbara by turning left off Highway 154, below the summit of San Marcos Pass, onto West Camino Cielo/Kinevan Road, 6.2 miles from the Highway 192 junction.)* Turn left immediately onto the frontage road and then right onto Kinevan Road. This shaded canyon along a stream is an especially good place to see Cassin's Vireo, Black-chinned Hummingbird, and Swainson's Thrush from mid-April through the summer. In winter look for Winter Wren and Varied Thrush. *The land on both sides of the road is private property; be careful not to trespass.* The southern end of Kinevan Road soon rejoins Highway 154.

Turn left (north) onto Highway 154 and travel to **Lake Cachuma,** best in winter when the ducks, grebes, Bald Eagles, and Ospreys are about. There are only two reasonable locations to bird the lake. The first is **Lake Cachuma County Park** (fee) (10.4), and the second is the overlook at **Bradbury Dam** (1.2). From the County Park there are naturalist-led cruises on the lake twice a week in winter. Your best option is to pay the entrance fee at the County Park and explore the margins of the lake or arrange in advance to take one of the naturalist-led cruises. For reservations on the Eagle Cruises (Wednesday–Sunday, two hours, November through March), call at 805/686-5050 weekdays 9 AM–4 PM.

By far the most productive time to visit is November through March when numbers of wintering ducks—including Greater (rare) and Lesser Scaups, Ring-necked Duck, Hooded and Common Mergansers, and Common Goldeneye—attract Bald Eagles. Other birds of prey such as Osprey, Northern Harrier, Red-shouldered and Red-tailed Hawks, and Golden Eagle may be around also. Both Western and Clark's Grebes breed at the lake, as do Tree Swallows and Wood Ducks. To bird from the shore, try the campsites marked "Overflow Area," reached by turning right (east) shortly after passing the entrance kiosk. To rent a boat or to rendezvous for the naturalist cruises, go straight ahead and follow the signs to the boat dock.

The oak woodland by the lake shelters such birds as Acorn Woodpecker, Oak Titmouse, and Western Bluebird. In winter look for Lewis's Woodpecker (rare). At the dam, look for California Quail, Oak Titmouse, Wrentit, California Thrasher, and California Towhee in the oaks and chaparral by the overlook. An impressive number of waterbirds is visible from this vantage

SANTA YNEZ VALLEY AND FIGUEROA MOUNTAIN SIDE TRIP

After leaving Bradbury Dam you may want to explore in the Santa Ynez Valley a bit more before turning west toward Solvang and Lompoc. Leaving the dam and driving west on Highway 154, turn right onto Armour Ranch Road (3.3) immediately after crossing a bridge over the Santa Ynez River. Turn right onto Happy Canyon Road after one mile, and then right again following **Happy Canyon Road**, a little over two miles from Highway 154. Grassland birds abound in the pastures, Acorn and Nuttall's Woodpeckers in the oaks, and California Quail just about anywhere. Springtime's Western Kingbirds and Bullock's Orioles are replaced in winter by Say's Phoebe and White-crowned Sparrows. This is also a good area for raptors. Yellow-billed Magpies are common residents of the ranches in the oak savannah. This is a beautiful drive and the birding can be very good.

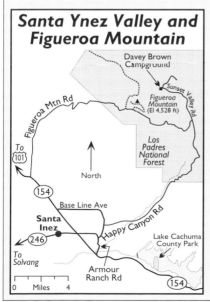

Santa Ynez Valley and Figueroa Mountain

Continuing farther on this road takes you to Figueroa Mountain (Forest Adventure Pass required) in the backcountry. If you want to explore along the dirt Forest Service roads, procure a AAA map of Santa Barbara County or a Los Padres National Forest map as a guide. Figueroa Mountain (El. 4,526 ft) is crowned with Jeffrey Pines and pockets of Bigcone Douglas-fir in the damp creases on the northern slope. Owls of these forests and the live oak groves of the lower slopes and canyons include Western Screech-, Great Horned, Northern Pygmy-, Spotted, and Northern Saw-whet (rare). Among the Jeffrey Pine forest's spring and summer guests are Olive-sided Flycatcher, Western Wood-Pewee, and Violet-green Swallow. Mountain Quail, Acorn and Hairy Woodpeckers, Steller's Jay, Mountain Chickadee, and Pygmy Nuthatch are resident.

point in winter, with Golden-crowned Sparrows fairly common in the chaparral at this season.

Return to Highway 154 and drive north. *[See Boxed Text above for an optional side trip.]* At Highway 246 (5.2) turn left toward Solvang (5.0). This replica of a Danish village is famous for its pastry and artwork. It's a pleasant little tourist trap that includes a bookstore or two which stock books on local natural history subjects.

Just past Santa Ines Mission east of the town center, turn left onto Alisal Road for a drive down beautiful **Alisal Canyon**. Look over the golf course for Western Bluebirds and Yellow-billed Magpies. The latter, along with Island Scrub-Jay, is the only California bird never verified outside the state. After you reach Alisal Creek, stop anywhere to check the lush vegetation. Acorn Woodpeckers abound, and in summer you may see Hooded and Bullock's Orioles, Black-headed Grosbeak, Hutton's and Warbling Vireos, Lazuli Bunting, and Chipping Sparrow. Look for Hermit and Varied (rare) Thrushes and numerous sparrows in winter. Stop at **Nojoqui Falls County Park** (*NAH-ho-wee*) (5.0) for the tame Acorn Woodpeckers and the Purple Martins (a rare and local bird in Southern California) which breed in the sycamore trees around the ranger's house (April–August), and to hike the trail to the falls.

The short hike up to the falls is best in spring, taking you through typical California Central Coast moist-woodland-canyon habitat. Here you will find many resident birds, usually including Band-tailed Pigeon, Anna's Hummingbird, Acorn, Nuttall's, Downy, and Hairy Woodpeckers, Oak Titmouse, California Thrasher, and Hutton's Vireo. Summer brings Black-chinned and Allen's Hummingbirds, Pacific-slope and Ash-throated Flycatchers, Violet-green Swallow, Warbling Vireo, Yellow Warbler, Black-headed Grosbeak, and Bullock's Oriole. In winter look for Winter Wren, Ruby-crowned Kinglet, numerous Hermit Thrushes, and Townsend's Warblers among the Yellow-rumps. It is best to bird this area early before the crowds arrive.

Leaving Nojoqui, turn left on Alisal Road to its T-intersection with Old Coast Highway, turning right to reach US-101 (1.7).

You now have a choice. You may turn north toward Lompoc, Santa Maria, San Luis Obispo, and Morro Bay (instructions for San Luis Obispo and Morro Bay are in the following chapter), or you may wish to return to Santa Barbara. If you want to go east to camp on the beaches, or head back to Santa Barbara, read on.

To complete the loop back to Santa Barbara, turn south onto US-101. After going through Gaviota Pass you will quickly reach the ocean. There are several state parks along the route back to Santa Barbara that are worth checking in migration and in winter, but are far too crowded in summer. El Capitan State Beach (19.2) has the best habitat and many of the same oak- and riparian-woodland birds as above except for Yellow-billed Magpie and Purple Martin.

Resume driving east (freeway signs will say "South") on US-101 approximately 24 miles through Goleta to Santa Barbara.

If, however, on leaving Nojoqui you wish to continue your tour farther west and north, drive north on US-101 to its junction with Highway 246 (4.9). Exit, turning left toward Lompoc, where Highway 246 crosses Highway 1 (17.5). Rather than turning north in downtown Lompoc to follow Highway 1, continue west on Ocean Avenue (Highway 246) until you reach the turn-off to Ocean Beach County Park (8.3) (no fee, no camping) and the **mouth of the Santa Ynez River**. From the parking lot follow the trail under the railroad trestle to the beach. From May through August you should scan the ocean for Sooty Shearwaters, and in fall (September to late November or December) you have a chance of seeing Black-vented Shearwaters. In winter the ocean off the river mouth supports large numbers of Surf Scoters, a few White-winged Scoters, and lesser numbers of Red-throated, Pacific, and Common Loons. From July to October good numbers of Elegant Terns appear along with smaller numbers of Royal Terns (the Royals remain through the winter).

The amount of water in the Santa Ynez River varies greatly, depending on the amount of rainfall in its drainage system. During high water levels, the river mouth is good for herons, ducks, gulls, and terns. On the other hand, shorebirds are numerous during periods of low water. Least Terns breed locally. The willow-riparian vegetation along the river to the east is the southern edge of the Chestnut-backed Chickadee's range.

Return to Lompoc and turn left onto Highway 1 (H Street). At Orcutt (19.0) follow Highway 135 to the right and continue north on it to Betteravia Road (5.4); then turn left (west) to Black Road (3.0). Formerly, this area's lush pastures offered very good birding, but the best fields have been converted from pasture to strawberries and other row crops. Just to the northeast of this intersection are shortgrass fields and gently rolling hills (some grazed by cattle and sheep) which somewhat regularly support small numbers of Mountain Plover from early November through mid-February. The green fields southeast of the intersection occasionally have Pacific Golden-Plovers in fall and winter. These birds prefer dry shortgrass habitat and are not present every winter. You may find wintering Ferruginous Hawks here. *This is all private property, so please bird from the public road.*

Continue west on Betteravia Road, watching the agricultural fields on both sides for concentrations of birds in wet or newly plowed fields. At Main Street (Highway 166) (5.4) turn left, continuing across Highway 1 to Main Street's end at the entrance kiosk for Guadalupe Dunes County Park (3.8) (no fee, no camping). The park is open from 8 AM–6 PM (or dusk depending on the season) seven days a week. The **Santa Maria River mouth** at the end of the road ahead is a very good birding spot—especially during spring and fall shorebird migrations. A riparian area of thick willows meanders between the kiosk and the dunes; bird from the road *(it's private property beyond the fence)*. Swainson's Thrush, Hutton's and Warbling Vireos, and Yellow and Wilson's

Warblers breed. Migrants are attracted to the willow-riparian thickets in spring and fall; bird the willows early when mixed flocks of Chestnut-backed Chickadees and migrants tend to come to the east side for morning sun. In fall, these flocks have produced many eastern vagrants. Continue toward the parking lot at the beach. On cresting the dunes past the Gordon Sand plant you are presented with a panoramic view (unless it is foggy) that is worth stopping to admire. The wild dunes and coast to the west are not only beautiful, but also are home to rare plants and animals.

Shorebirds abound on the mudflats at the river mouth in spring and fall—if the tide has not dammed it, creating a small temporary lake. Numerous rarities have been recorded over the years, including several fall records of Ruff and Sharp-tailed Sandpiper. The area also can be fairly good for waterfowl in winter and fall. Snowy Plovers breed here, as do Least Terns. In summer and fall you should find lots of Elegant Terns and Heermann's Gulls; it is a fine place to study gulls on a winter afternoon. You will be well-served by a pair of calf-high rubber boots while birding the river mouth. If boots are unavailable to you, expect to get your feet wet and muddy.

The beach near the parking lot is an excellent platform from which to scope the ocean for Sooty Shearwaters in summer and Black-vented Shearwaters and the occasional jaeger (both Pomarine and Parasitic) in fall. Three species of loon, with Common and Pacific predominating, are seen in winter along with a large raft of scoters, mostly Surfs.

On completing your birding at the river mouth you have a choice. You may return east on Main Street to Highway 1 and travel north to Oso Flaco Lake (occasionally productive), or continue east through Santa Maria to the local refuse dump for gulls. If you want to look for waterfowl or migrant passerines, turn left onto Highway 1, driving through Guadalupe (excellent Mexican restaurants!) north to Oso Flaco Lake Road (4.8). Turn left to its dead-end, 3.2 miles later, where thick willows and sand dunes surround natural **Oso Flaco Lake** (fee). In spring and fall, migrant passerines may be found here (best in September and October). Resident willow birds include Anna's Hummingbird, Nuttall's and Downy Woodpeckers, Black Phoebe, Chestnut-backed Chickadee, and Wrentit, with California Thrasher around the margins. Winter produces an assortment of ducks, including an occasional surprise. American Bitterns are seen frequently, Common Moorhens are uncommon, while Virginia Rails and Soras are common in the cattails and tules at lakeside. Caspian, Forster's, and Least Terns are common in spring and summer.

The picturesque dunes behind the lake and along the coast have been preserved by The Nature Conservancy, which also built a boardwalk across the lake. Walking across the lake in spring brings you close to flocks of migrant swallows, usually at least five species, coursing about overhead; in winter the boardwalk affords a closer view of the numerous ducks. Continue along the trail on the other side of the lake, birding the willows (usually not as productive as those before the boardwalk) on your way through the dunes to the ocean. Oso Flaco Creek enters the Pacific just south of trail's end;

shorebirds usually work the shallows here. On completing Oso Flaco, retrace your route south through Guadalupe to Main Street (Highway 166), turn left, and follow the directions below to the wastewater treatment facility and the Santa Maria dump.

After birding the river mouth, and desirous of birding gull flocks at the dump, return east on Main Street to the intersection with Highway 1. Continue east on Main Street to Black Road (4.8), where you should turn right to visit the **Santa Maria Wastewater Treatment Plant** (0.4). Open 8 AM–4:30 PM on *weekdays only*, the plant has a variety of dirt-embankment settling ponds which can host many hundreds of shorebirds during migration—if the water level is right. Stop at the administration building and sign the guest book, telling whoever is on duty that you are a birder and that you want to drive the dikes around the ponds to the west. You may drive these dikes (words of caution being superfluous), looking for good shorebird conditions among the settling basins. Although the quality of birding varies widely depending jointly on the vagaries of migration and current water levels, you may hit it right and have very good birding indeed. This location has, over the years, produced a variety of rare shorebirds, some of which cause birders to undertake long-distance drives (or flights) when found anywhere in North America. In winter, Mew and Bonaparte's Gulls hover over the treatment tanks.

On becoming convinced that you have birded the plant thoroughly, return to Main Street. Turn right and stay on Main Street through Santa Maria to the **Santa Maria Municipal Landfill** (5.9). This has been one of the best localities in Southern California for finding Thayer's Gull, although numbers have been lower in recent years than during the 1980s (one January day in 1985 produced 50). Constant reconfiguration of the dump can make it difficult to see the birds from the road. Entering the dump is not permitted unless you have a truckload of trash—a prop not included in most birders' kits. You can, however, bird from the road with a telescope by parking outside the fence beyond the entrance adjacent to where active dumping is taking place. From November through March multiple Thayer's per day may be seen, almost all in first-winter plumage. Other gulls present are Mew, Ring-billed, California, Herring, and Glaucous-winged. Western Gulls are rare inland from the immediate coast and typically, therefore, are not found here.

Upon becoming satiated with dump gulls through the fence, return west to US-101. From here you may drive north to the start of the San Luis Obispo–Morro Bay trip at the junction of US-101 and Grand Avenue in Arroyo Grande (15.1), start the California Condor Trip, or turn south toward Santa Barbara.

There are campgrounds in the Santa Ynez Valley and at the state beaches west of Santa Barbara. Motels are plentiful in Santa Barbara, Lompoc, and Santa Maria.

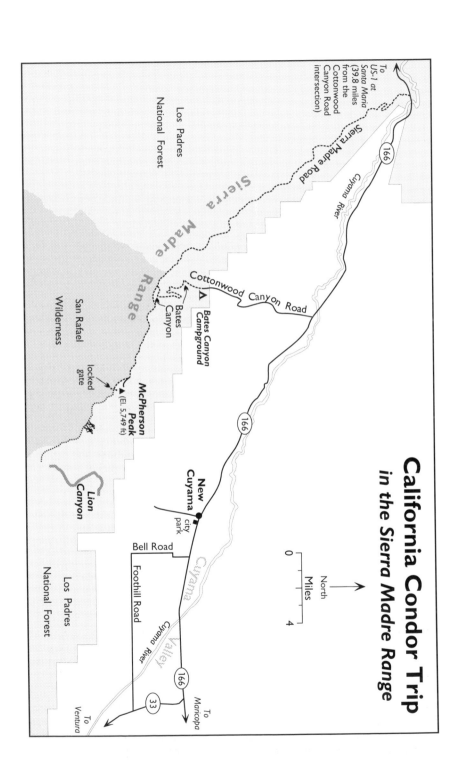

California Condor Trip
in the Sierra Madre Range

CALIFORNIA CONDOR TRIP

In his monumental (if quaint by contemporary standards) 1923 four-volume *Birds of California*, William Leon Dawson wrote "...for me the heart of California lies in the Condor country." The following route takes you through Condor country in Santa Barbara County's interior. This is genuine Old California. The region has changed little since Dawson's time or, indeed, since the Chumash painted their complex geometric designs on cave ceilings throughout the region. If you follow the instructions below, you will immerse yourself deep within chaparral-clad mountains, damp canyons, Coast Live Oak and Blue Oak forests and savannahs, and dry-prairie cattle country, ending on a peak from which you can see both the Pacific Ocean and the Sierra Nevada on clear days. With luck, you will also see a California Condor.

We hasten to note a few practical matters about this trip before selling it further. After leaving Bates Canyon Campground, there are no restroom facilities of any kind, and the road degrades from poor to bad in places—during wet weather some spots may be best described as "pre-Columbian." Although Volvo sedans have been seen making the drive up Bates Canyon, one assumes that they were rental cars. Bates Canyon requires a fairly high clearance, although four-wheel drive is not necessary except during and immediately after a storm. The canyon can be driven in a pick-up truck or a van with a little care. Those making the effort to take this route will be amply rewarded by the splendid scenery and populations of chaparral-adapted species. You are entering Mountain Lion and Black Bear country here, although they are rarely seen; Mule Deer and Bobcats are common.

Following the instructions below will get you to within a few miles of the top of Lion Canyon in Santa Barbara County's Sierra Madre Range. Captive-bred California Condors were released from hacking stations in Lion Canyon in 1993, 1995, 1996, and December 1997, with more releases planned for future years. Although totally unrestrained, these immense birds show a degree of fidelity to Lion Canyon—partly because the Condor Recovery Team still maintains feeding stations nearby. Placing yourself atop the Sierra Madre ridge (known by locals, with reason, as Hurricane Deck) gives you the most predictable chance of seeing free-flying California Condors in California's wild backcountry.

This foray into Condor country starts at the intersection of US-101 and Highway 166 in San Luis Obispo County, immediately north of Santa Maria. Proceed east on Highway 166 through the Coast Range, following a canyon cut by the Cuyama River. As you drive you will occasionally cross the river; as you do you will be crossing from San Luis Obispo County to the north into

43

Santa Barbara County to the south, and vice-versa. This is important information for county listers! The high quality, lonely, two-lane highway is driven at high speed. There are multiple turn-outs along the way, although you are encouraged to keep moving toward the goal because species seen next to the highway are found easily once you leave it in the Cuyama Valley. While driving, however, watch for Golden Eagles, which are commonly seen along this road, as are Ferruginous Hawks in winter in the Cuyama Valley.

Approximately 28 miles east of US-101 the mountains start to recede to the north and south as you enter the western edge of the Cuyama Valley. Yellow-billed Magpies are commonly seen at roadside among the Blue Oaks in the cattle country here, but it is difficult to stop along this stretch. There will be magpies in Cottonwood Canyon, so be patient.

Turn right off Highway 166 at Cottonwood Canyon Road (39.8). The trip from Highway 166 up Bates Canyon to McPherson Peak takes approximately 1½ hours in good weather. Newcomers probably will drive more slowly, stopping more often.

Cottonwood Canyon Road sneaks up on a driver unexpectedly when traveling at traffic speed on Highway 166, so watch your odometer. Follow the road south through rangeland *(both sides are private until reaching National Forest lands; do not trespass)*, home to resident Turkey Vulture, Red-tailed Hawk, Golden Eagle, American Kestrel, and Prairie Falcon. Northern Harrier and Ferruginous Hawk are consistently seen here in winter, while Rough-legged Hawk and Merlin are rarely encountered. The road dips into Cottonwood Canyon (2.5) and crosses the wash. A colony of Yellow-billed Magpies nests in trees here and along the road ahead. They will always be in the immediate area in spring and early summer and can be seen with patience on the valley floor here year round. Oak Titmouse, White-breasted Nuthatch, Western Bluebird, and Phainopepla nest in nearby oaks, while Say's Phoebe and Mountain Bluebird are winter visitors. Lark and White-crowned Sparrows are abundant in winter, with Fox (predominantly "Sooty") and Golden-crowned Sparrows more common in the chaparral ahead.

Not long after a sign reading "No Hunting: Trespassers will shot. The remains will be prosecuted," the road bears 90 degrees right. You soon come to a fork in the road (approximately 5 miles from Highway 166) at which a sign points toward White Oak Campground to the left. Take the left fork to National Forest land (Forest Adventure Pass required) and ultimately up Bates Canyon.

Cottonwood Campground is usually closed, so proceed to Bates Canyon Campground (4.4) (El. 2,500 ft) where you may wish to stop to stretch your legs, use the facilities—such as they are—and watch and listen for the multitude of oak grove and chaparral birds in the area. Resume your drive into the mountains.

The road starts a steep ascent up **Bates Canyon** in a damp fold at the base of the Sierra Madre among California Bay trees (1.4). Varied Thrush has occasionally been seen here in winter in moist areas. As you drive up the mountainside, stop from time to time to listen—Northern Pygmy-Owl is sometimes heard on this slope. At any time of year, save at mid-day, you will hear the voice of the chaparral—the bouncing-ping-pong-ball song of the Wrentit. You should also hear California and Mountain Quail in spring and early summer (the latter has a hollow call reminiscent of Phainopepla's call note when heard at a distance), Western Scrub-Jay, California Thrasher, and Spotted and California Towhees. The chorus varies with the season, of course, but these are dependable residents. Patient squeaking and pishing will produce most of them. California Quail should be seen at roadside near the campgrounds below. Mountain Quail, heard frequently morning and afternoon in spring and summer, may be flushed from roadside on the mountain—although they are always unpredictable and difficult to see.

On reaching the ridgetop at approximately 4,500 feet elevation (4.5) turn left onto the broad dirt road running along the ridge, traveling east toward McPherson Peak. A turn to the right would ultimately take you back to a junction with Highway 166 far to the west. The thick chaparral (unless you arrive following one of the cyclical fires) on both sides of the ridge is home to the species list noted immediately above as well as Rufous-crowned Sparrow, Black-chinned Sparrow, and "Bell's" Sage Sparrow, April–August.

Although it has been theoretically possible—if extremely unlikely—to see a California Condor since entering the mountains east of Santa Maria, on reaching the ridge you should be especially alert. From here your vision is limited only by the curvature of the earth and the moisture content of the air brought in off the Pacific.

Since their first release in Lion Canyon a few miles to the east in 1993, condors have used the winds and thermals coming off this ridge as a highway, expediting their travel east and west as they forage. They are no different from their ancestors in this regard; condors have used this and other ridges stretching beyond sight in this manner since large furry elephants foraged the Cuyama Valley below. Man had not yet entered the western hemisphere.

The released birds have explored in all directions, going as far up the coast as Monterey County and as far northeast as Bishop, east of the Sierra Nevada. They are, in brief, behaving like condors, not like pets. Their genetic curiosity occasionally gets them in trouble, however, and if you are lucky enough to see one up close, show it the respect it is due. You could conceivably come round a corner and see one standing at the roadside overlooking the expanse downslope. If it does not fly, do not approach it. These birds should be taught to avoid humans, not to learn how friendly some of us are. Learning the wrong things could (and has) prove fatal to a bird.

Continue east along the ridge, stopping and birding at will, until you come to a left-hand fork (7.2) which goes up **McPherson Peak**. The right fork takes you to a locked gate 1.5 miles farther along. Take the left fork and either drive to the top (0.8) with its US Air Force microwave tower, or park along the road here where you might like the vantage point. Looking east along the ridge with binoculars you will see an area of massive rounded sandstone formations about five miles distant—the top of **Lion Canyon**. If you have a telescope you will find it most useful.

Golden Eagles are commonly seen soaring along the ridge here, as are Red-tailed Hawks, so be cautious. When peering into the far distance it is possible to mistake one of these large soaring birds for a condor if care is not taken. The condor, when seen well, is unmistakable. Even though all birds currently out (1998) are immatures, and the strong black-white underwing features are not yet remarkable at a distance, their steady flat-winged glide is unique. Their proportions are also quite different from those of eagles and hawks. The depth of wing, from leading edge to trailing edge, seems substantially broader in proportion to wing length than that of Golden Eagle, and the massive body hanging beneath the nine-foot wingspan is proportionately very different from that of eagles or buteos. In the far distance their movements may best be described as "stately," and their steady, level glide has caused them to be mistaken for small planes. When circling, their turns are wider and slower—again, more stately—than those of eagles or buteos.

With luck, condors may be seen soaring in the distance over the ridge or might suddenly appear nearby, without warning. Condors have a remarkable ability to materialize overhead shortly after one has done a complete 360-degree scan of the skyline, seeing nothing. There is no predicting them, but if you are lucky enough to see one, you will not soon forget it.

Following your trek up to McPherson Peak, retrace the route to Highway 166. *From here you may return to the west and US-101. At that junction you will be between the Santa Barbara and San Luis Obispo chapters in this guide and may travel either north or south as you please. If you turn east on Highway 166, you are traveling toward the Carrizo Plain/Mount Pinos junction at Cerro Noroeste Road approximately 20 miles distant.*

If you would like to bird the **Cuyama Valley** further, turn east on Highway 166 toward the community of New Cuyama. There is a town park with restroom facilities here, 13 miles east of Cottonwood Canyon Road.

Traveling two miles east beyond the park on Highway 166 brings you to Bell Road. Turn right and 2.5 miles farther you can stop to scope distant Lion Canyon, approximately 45 degrees to your right in the Sierra Madre, from below. Although the view is of far distant silhouettes at best, condors are sometimes seen soaring above the canyon from this vantage point. Bell Road takes a 90-degree turn to the left a little farther along, becoming Foothill Road. Winter routinely produces multiple Ferruginous Hawks in the Bell Road/Foothill Road area, as well as all the other raptors listed above; Common Ravens are abundant. Condors do, of course, forage in the Cuyama Valley, but their rarity, coupled with their extensive range, makes a valley encounter with them unlikely.

Although the number of species is limited, the Cuyama Valley is a birdy place in winter. Mountain Bluebirds may be found at this season along with abundant Horned Larks and American Pipits. Occasionally a Vesper Sparrow is seen among the common wintering sparrows. Lawrence's Goldfinch, legendary for its unpredictability, is possible in the Cuyama at any season—although most normally March–July. Watch for them with flocks of Lesser Goldfinches and House Finches in weedy fencerows or near farmhouses where trees and water are available.

A dairy a few miles east on Foothill Road often produces Tricolored Blackbirds among the Red-wings, Brewer's, and ravens. Tricolors are usually found in the Cuyama Valley in winter as well as in spring. Drive the back roads and watch for blackbird flocks. Losing one's way would take significant talent in this mountain-circumscribed, almost treeless valley with few roads.

There is a store, a restaurant, a gas station, and a small motel (the Buckhorn) in New Cuyama; motels and other services are abundant in Santa Maria to the west, just south of the Highway 166/US-101 junction. Camping is always available in Bates Canyon Campground.

Mountain Quail
Shawneen E. Finnegan

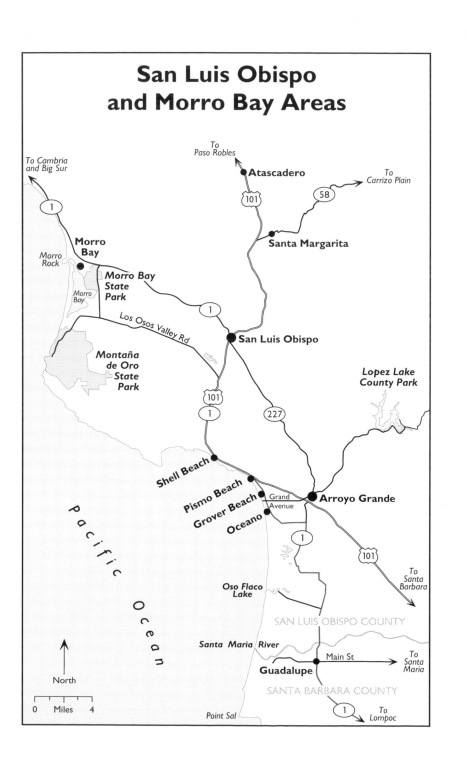

San Luis Obispo and Morro Bay Areas

SAN LUIS OBISPO AND MORRO BAY AREAS

This route will take the birder through the hillside and coastal habitats in the San Luis Obispo and Morro Bay areas. Two main north-south highways—famous California Highway 1 on the coast and US-101 through the interior—provide parallel tracks from which all birding trips mentioned below depart. Visitors from the East may find many western and California specialties here with ease, given the right season and habitat. Conversely, westerners may be treated during migration (especially fall) to eastern vagrants in many of these locations.

US-101's Grand Avenue off-ramp in Arroyo Grande is the starting point for both the Lopez Lake and Oceano trips. It is located 12.3 miles north of the Santa Maria River, which marks the boundary between Santa Barbara and San Luis Obispo Counties.

Lopez Lake (see map on next page) is a large reservoir amid oak-covered rocky hillsides and cattle-grazing land. In winter its waters (especially at the east end from within the county park) are good for diving ducks, Ospreys, and the occasional Bald Eagle. The oak-clad slopes are year-round host to numerous species, including Red-shouldered Hawk, Band-tailed Pigeon, Western Screech-Owl, Acorn and Nuttall's Woodpeckers, Oak Titmouse, and Western Bluebird, while White-throated Swifts may be seen hawking overhead. Yellow-billed Magpies are resident in the hillside oak savannah, but are not plentiful. Chestnut-backed Chickadee is a permanent resident in the willow-riparian area along nearby Hi Mountain Road. The latter area is best visited in spring and early summer when breeding Western Wood-Pewees, Pacific-slope Flycatchers, Warbling Vireos, MacGillivray's Warblers, Yellow-breasted Chats, Black-headed Grosbeaks, Lazuli Buntings, and Bullock's Orioles are present. As with all streamside habitat in San Luis Obispo County (SLOCo to the locals), Black Phoebes are year-round residents, while California Thrashers and California Towhees populate the edges.

To reach **Lopez Lake**, turn east off US-101 at the Grand Avenue exit. Drive through the old village of Arroyo Grande, following the highway signs pointing east toward the lake. Be sure to bear right (following the sign) at the junction with Highway 227 (0.8). As you drive through the decreasingly populated countryside, stay alert for roadside birds (the first 1.3 miles off US-101 are good for Hooded Oriole between April and August when they nest in ornamental fan palms). In spring and summer you may see Western

49

Kingbirds perched on the fences in open country, while Say's Phoebes take over this territory in winter. Raptors might include White-tailed Kite (uncommon). After reaching the west end of Lopez Lake (no access), continue driving until you find a small, gated, dirt track off to the right behind a "no parking" sign (9.9). Park on the dirt drive and check the inlet waters, which extend under the highway and up a small oak-lined canyon. Birds often seen here (November–March) include Gadwall, Hooded Merganser (rare), and Common Merganser.

After crossing a bridge, you will see paved Hi Mountain Road leading off to the right (0.1). Before investigating it, winter visitors will first want to continue on the main road into Lopez Lake County Park (fee); the entrance is straight ahead (0.3). Wild Turkey, introduced into the county many years ago, is commonly seen in the campground east of the lake; winter mornings are best for this bird. The park's oak-covered hillsides contain species typical of this habitat, noted earlier, while the lake-shore has its own specialties. From the entrance kiosk proceed straight uphill on Lopez Drive to a large parking lot on the left (0.7). Between November and March there is usually a large mixed flock of Ring-necked Ducks,

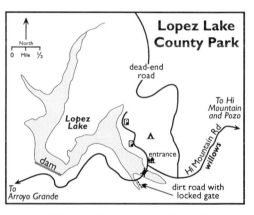

Lesser Scaups, and Buffleheads on the lake at this location. Both Western and Clark's Grebes are regular in winter. Tufted Duck (very rare) has been seen here. Drive to the end of the road (0.8), park, and walk a few hundred yards farther to a vantage point on narrow Wittenberg Arm of the lake. During high water levels this arm can be filled with diving ducks, possibly including all of those noted above. The enclosing oaks may be productive also. From mid-April through summer the lake will be unproductive, but the riparian and oak habitats will then be at their best.

Return to Hi Mountain Road and follow it 1.2 miles to an area of thick willows on a curve where roadside parking is easy. All land on both sides of the road here is private, so bird the edges of the oaks and willows from the lightly-traveled road. If you continue farther up 13-mile-long Hi Mountain Road, it becomes a four-wheel-drive dirt track transecting some wonderful oak, grassland, sycamore-riparian, and chaparral habitat—but this is only for the hardy, and local advice should be sought before attempting the drive. Those whose constitution and vehicle are up to the challenge will be rewarded with fine chaparral birding. Rufous-crowned Sparrows nest on brushy, sunny slopes, and Northern Pygmy-Owls reside in Coast Live Oak groves.

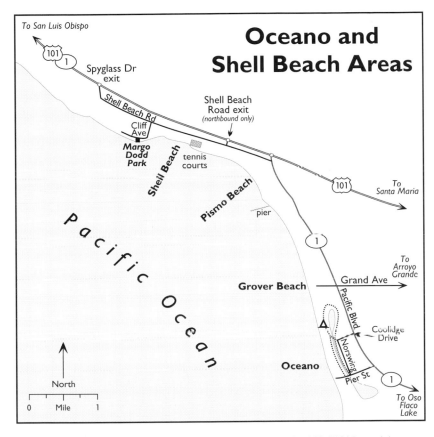

Oceano and Shell Beach Areas

Oceano Campground is easily reached from the US-101/Grand Avenue junction. Drive west (toward the ocean) on Grand Avenue through Arroyo Grande and Grover Beach to the intersection with Highway 1 (2.7). Turn left onto Highway 1 and continue to the first street on the right, Coolidge Drive (0.9). Turn right onto Coolidge Drive and park at its end, one block away at the intersection with Norswing Drive. From the corner of Coolidge and Norswing you will see a path entering the willows behind wooden barrier posts. Turn right and follow this approximately one-mile-long path as it circles the pond. Bird the willows around the pond, the pines behind the tile-roofed homes across from the north end of the pond, the willows and cattails along the channel extending north from the pond's end, and the pines in the campground and along the dunes. These areas are good for western migrants. In fall, vagrant warblers, the primary target, may occur in impressive numbers, but many other vagrant passerines also have been found here. After a good migration flight-night this search should take no less than two hours, often more.

Oceano should be birded before 10 AM to avoid the regular afternoon winds. This is a classic coastal California vagrant trap during fall migration, centering on a small pond surrounded by willows with nearby pines, just a few hundred yards of sand-dunes inland from the ocean. The best time is in September and October, especially the latter month, although eastern vagrants have been found here through December. There are only a few records from spring. The resident willow birds are Anna's Hummingbird, Nuttall's and Downy Woodpeckers, Chestnut-backed Chickadee, Wrentit (easily seen here), and Hutton's Vireo. In winter you will find a full complement of visiting warblers and sparrows such as you might see anywhere on the California coast. Black Phoebe is a permanent resident, as is Marsh Wren in the cattails and tules, while patches of dry scrub provide cover for California Thrashers. California Quail may be found in many locations; California Towhees outnumber their Spotted cousins.

An extension of the park, across Pier Street from the entrance, has a pond surrounded by grass and willows. This area holds the predictable assortment of domestic waterfowl and panhandling gulls, but an occasional wintering Snow (rare) or Ross's (uncommon) Goose may be found, and wintering Thayer's Gulls (uncommon) are sometimes seen after mid-October. Look among the Western Grebes on the pond for the occasional Clark's Grebe. The nineties have brought a very nineties phenomenon to the pond—much strutting about, raucous display, and general noise in the form of a growing colony of Great-tailed Grackles, San Luis Obispo County's first.

The cliffs at **Shell Beach**, just up-coast from Arroyo Grande, are a fine place for birding at any time of year. Wintering birds easily seen just offshore include three species of loons, both Western (abundant) and Clark's (uncommon) Grebes, and rafts of scoters (Surf is abundant, White-winged very uncommon, and Black is rare). Resident Brandt's and Pelagic Cormorants are common on rocks just offshore, as is Black Oystercatcher. Winter shorebirds include Willet, Wandering Tattler (uncommon), Whimbrel, Marbled Godwit, Ruddy (uncommon) and Black (common) Turnstones, Surfbird (uncommon), and Sanderling, while the resident Western Gulls' numbers are augmented by the influx of wintering gulls from the north. From October to mid-March small flocks of Black-vented Shearwaters (uncommon) may be seen offshore with the aid of a spotting scope.

Birding from the cliffs can be especially rewarding during spring through summer when migration is underway, cliff-nesting birds are breeding, and the summer influx of Brown Pelicans, cormorants, and gulls (especially Heermann's) make impressive numbers here. Pigeon Guillemots arrive on the cliffs during April, and by May dozens may be seen from numerous vantage points. From June to August scores of thousands of Sooty Shearwaters are commonly spotted from the cliffs. From August through the fall, Royal Tern is often seen, and Elegant Tern is common from mid-July through early October, when its numbers decrease until this species disappears locally by mid-November.

From the Grand Avenue overpass take northbound US-101, drive through Pismo Beach, and exit at Shell Beach Road (4.7). Turn left under the freeway to Shell Beach Road, which parallels the cliffs. Turn right onto it and drive to the tennis courts on the left side of the road (0.3); park in the lot, taking care to be as unobtrusive as possible—*this is private property.* Birders, and others, park here with regularity and it seems not to be a problem; however, it is best to park in the westernmost lot, away from the players' entrance to the courts, keeping a low profile. *If coming from the north, exit at Spyglass Road, 5.9 miles south of Los Osos Valley Road, turn right at the stop-sign, and then left onto Shell Beach Road. Drive 1.8 miles to the tennis courts.* Peregrine Falcon is sometimes seen here in spring and summer, as is Osprey during migration.

Drive north from the tennis courts, turn left onto Cliff Avenue (0.6), and stop at very small, bluff-top Margo Dodd Park (0.3). The birds are similar to those at the tennis courts, but a bonus is close-range views of Pigeon Guillemots at the entrances to their nest burrows from mid-April to July. Several active Black Oystercatcher breeding territories are visible from this point. From here you have a panorama of the entire coast from Point Sal in Santa Barbara County to the Port San Luis Lighthouse up-coast to the right; this is an exquisite spot! Look closely at the low, flat rock just offshore for

Heermann's Gull
Shawneen E. Finnegan

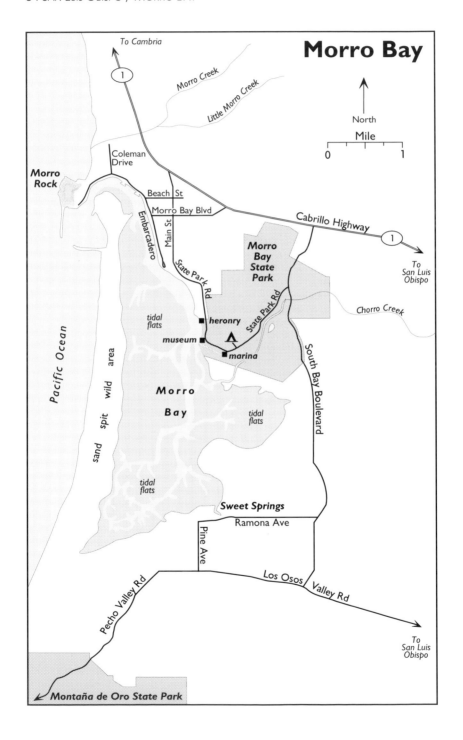

Morro Bay

shorebirds and the numerous Harbor Seals normally hauled out there. Sea Otters are often seen from this point, as are Gray Whales during migration and Common Dolphins in late spring and summer.

Montaña de Oro State Park, located just south of Morro Bay, is another productive birding area. MDO, as locals call it, and Oceano have produced more vagrants than all other SLOCo locations. The park's western border is a series of lovely cliffs, small beaches, and the finest tide-pools in the county. The cliffs and coastal waters, at the appropriate time of year, harbor the same species noted for Shell Beach. Winter scoping from the cliffs often produces sightings of Northern Fulmar (irregular), Parasitic and Pomarine Jaegers, Common Murre, Marbled Murrelet (rare), and Rhinoceros Auklet. Scoping here can produce hundreds of Pacific Loons, Brant, and scoters per hour in spring (especially April and May).

Local birders pay closest attention to MDO from late August through November, when it becomes another classic California coastal migrant/vagrant trap. The cypresses at park headquarters, and especially the pines in the campgrounds and the adjacent willow-lined creek, host migrating warblers and other passerines in fall. The list of eastern and Mexican/southwestern vagrants historically found here is impressive. All species typical of California coastal chaparral can be located on the hillsides. Rufous-crowned Sparrow (uncommon) is resident on the south-facing chaparral hillsides. MDO has the virtue of being birdable at any time of the day.

To reach Montaña de Oro from US-101 take the Los Osos Valley Road off-ramp in San Luis Obispo (5.9 miles north of Spyglass Drive) and drive west toward the ocean. Pass through the community of Los Osos (10.0), following the signs to MDO as the road sweeps to the south and uphill, affording spectacular views of Morro Bay and the coastal dunes. Park at the white headquarters building (5.1). To hike the bluffs, walk uphill from the parking lot to the obvious trail which skirts the cliffs south of jewel-like Spooner's Cove, and continue walking down-coast for about three miles. The beauty of this walk is such that it almost makes any birds found an unnecessary bonus.

Anna's and Allen's (except in winter) Hummingbirds, Nuttall's Woodpecker, Chestnut-backed Chickadee, Wrentit, California Thrasher, and Hutton's Vireo are all common, and Pacific-slope Flycatcher is a common breeder, but it is the migration seasons which make this park most interesting. Aside from the cliff-top pelagic birding possibilities, the willows along the creek behind and below park headquarters can be very productive (especially fall) for western and, occasionally, vagrant eastern migrants. The most predictably active birding locations, however, are the pine groves in the campgrounds. After birding the cypresses near park headquarters, walk inland from your car about one-quarter mile to the campground pines, birding the fringe of willows on one side and chaparral on the other along the way. Sort through the western species for the occasional eastern vagrant. Bird numbers vary depending on month (September, October, and to a lesser extent May are best) and flight conditions, but on some days the numerous mandible-snaps of feeding warblers quicken the heartbeat.

The campground is also a very good location for visitors from other states to bird some typical California chaparral. Simply watch the edges along the road above the campground (pishing helps), or walk through the campground to its easternmost point where a trail continues east through chaparral with the willows below eye-level to your left.

If visiting in winter, a side-trip to Sweet Springs on an inlet of Morro Bay is called for when leaving MDO. Retrace the route taken into the park (the only entrance/egress) from headquarters 4.2 miles, then turn left next to a church onto Pine Avenue. Turn right at the bottom of the gentle hill onto Ramona Avenue and park in front of a mobile-home park, 0.7 mile from where you turned off Los Osos Valley Road. Walk through the cypress and eucalyptus to the *Salicornia*-edged bay where hundreds of ducks and Brant feed daily. Occasionally, Greater Scaup (rare) are among the Lessers and other diving and puddle ducks, but the major attraction is the opportunity to see Eurasian Wigeon. For at least twenty years, one or more male Eurasian Wigeons have wintered here amidst a flock of several hundred American Wigeons. Other birds (depending on the tide) at this time of year typically include Willet, Long-billed Curlew, Marbled Godwit, Sanderling, Western and Least Sandpipers, and Long-billed and Short-billed Dowitchers. Peregrine Falcon and Merlin are occasionally seen making air strikes.

After birding Sweet Springs, return to Los Osos Valley Road. To continue on to Morro Bay, turn left and drive to South Bay Boulevard (1.1), turn left, and then left again onto State Park Road (3.3), which skirts the estuary and takes you toward Morro Bay Campground. You can continue through the state park along State Park Road to the town of Morro Bay, where the road becomes Main Street.

The environs of the picturesque town of **Morro Bay** provide worthwhile birding year round, although winter offers the most variety. Morro Bay's primary industry is tourism (fishing is second). Famous Morro Rock (El. 581 ft), a Miocene era volcanic plug, guards the bay while housing nesting colonies of Brandt's and Pelagic Cormorants, Western Gulls, and Pigeon Guillemots in spring. But it is the Rock's status as a Peregrine Falcon nesting site that brings it its most publicized avian distinction. Although Peregrines are resident here, the best time to see them is typically in May and June, when they are feeding and fledging young. The spectacle of Peregrines winging about to the accompaniment of crashing Pacific rollers, mingled with the cries of gulls, songs of the enigmatic resident Canyon Wrens, and the dash of White-throated Swifts, makes the Morro Rock experience dramatic indeed.

Winter brings loons (Common and Red-throated are common, Pacific uncommon), grebes, cormorants, Brown and American White Pelicans, flocks of shorebirds, Brant, and ducks to the bay. Caspian Terns may be seen year round, although they are decidedly uncommon in winter. Royal Terns are present from September through March, while Elegant Terns, most abundant from July through early October, are not found here in winter. A mixed flock of wintering gulls, terns, and shorebirds on a sandy beach across the bay inlet from Coleman Drive is best scrutinized with the aid of a spotting scope. The extensive *Salicornia* marsh in the upper bay supports thousands of wintering and migrant shorebirds, and Morro Bay State Park campground, under the pines on the bay's margin, is regularly birded in fall for the vagrants sometimes found among mixed flocks of Chestnut-backed Chickadees and western migrants.

To reach Morro Bay from US-101, turn west at the Highway 1 Morro Bay exit (Santa Rosa Street in San Luis Obispo). Turn right (west) onto Highway 1 and proceed to the South Bay Boulevard exit (11.2). Turn left onto South Bay Boulevard, continue to the sign for Morro Bay State Park (0.7), turn right onto State Park Road, and proceed to the campground entrance (0.9).

Park next to the campground and bird the pines. In fall the canopy contains migrant flocks mingling with the resident birds. This area is most easily birded in the morning when the sun strikes the pines lining the road. Walk across the street opposite the campground to look for shorebirds in the *Salicornia*. About 200 yards past the campground entrance, on the opposite side of the street, you will see a parking lot behind eucalyptus trees with a small marina beyond. Take the path past the marina across a *Baccharis*-and-willow-covered peninsula; then follow the peninsula's shoreline, scoping the shorebird concentrations. The hour before and after high tide is best, but any time can be good.

Elegant Terns
Shawneen E. Finnegan

A few "Large-billed" (*rostratus*) Savannah Sparrows and Nelson's Sharp-tailed Sparrows have been found wintering on this peninsula over the years. They favor emergent shrubs at the edge of the marsh within 100 yards to the left when facing the marsh after having walked straight across the peninsula from the parking lot. They are only possible during winter tides high enough to cover the *Salicornia*, forcing them out of the marsh.

Continue driving on beyond the campground entrance to visit the Morro Bay Museum of Natural History (fee) (0.3), where the displays, information, and bay overlook are all worth the traveler's attention. (You can buy a SLOCo checklist here.) When you leave the museum, continue toward the town of Morro Bay. An active heron rookery (0.3) is an interesting stop in spring and early summer. Double-crested Cormorants, Great Blue Herons, Great Egrets, and Black-crowned Night-Herons nest here, with the attendant clamor, sights, and smells associated with these elegant birds. Red-shouldered Hawks, common in the southern and western part of SLOCo, are frequently seen and heard here as well.

Continue north on Main Street to Beach Street (1.5), turning left to reach Embarcadero and the waterfront (0.2). Turn right onto Embarcadero toward the Rock, keeping your eyes open for Coleman Drive (0.4), a dirt road on the right. If you are here in fall, follow Coleman Drive about one-tenth of a mile to a dead-end on Morro Creek. Walk the creek (frequently dry in fall; if not—rubber boots required), looking for mixed chickadee/warbler flocks. Return to Embarcadero and turn right toward Morro Rock, where you can park on either side of the road. Look through the gull flock in the parking lot and watch for Peregrines here as well as resident White-throated Swifts, Black Phoebes, Bewick's and Canyon Wrens, and "Nuttall's" White-crowned Sparrows; watch the bay for waterbirds.

Retrace your way to Morro Bay Boulevard, either to return to Highway 1 and then US-101, or to continue up-coast on Highway 1 beyond the scope of this book to the beautiful Big Sur Coast in Monterey County via the equally beautiful San Luis Obispo County coast. Turn-outs along the coast north of Cambria and in the San Simeon area are good overlooks for shorebirds, while those north of San Simeon also produce Northern Elephant Seals.

To hook up with the Carrizo Plain–Maricopa–Mount Pinos trip, see the instructions at the beginning of the next chapter for starting this route from Highway 1 and US-101. If traveling south, both the Santa Maria area and California Condor routes begin in southern San Luis Obispo County.

There are plenty of campgrounds in the areas covered in this chapter (e.g., Lopez Lake, Oceano, Pismo Beach, Montaña de Oro, and Morro Bay State Park). Motel accommodations in most price ranges abound in such areas as Arroyo Grande, Pismo Beach, Shell Beach, San Luis Obispo, and Morro Bay.

SAN SIMEON COAST

When in Morro Bay you are at the south end of Highway 1's famous stretch that travels north through Big Sur to Monterey. San Luis Obispo County's rocky north coast is likewise beautiful—and plays host to all the rock-loving shorebirds to be expected in Southern California. Peregrine Falcon nests at various points along this coast. A side trip here is worth your time, or you may choose to continue traveling north to Monterey—unless it is winter, in which case the traditional mudslide(s) will have closed the road somewhere south of Big Sur.

If you have time to travel north of Morro Bay, your first stop should be at the Cayucos Pier 6 miles up-coast in Cayucos. The pier attracts birds at almost any time of year, but winter may be best, with its assortment of scoters, gulls, and the occasional alcid. Summer often brings large flocks of Sooty Shearwaters inshore as they chase bait fish.

Cambria, 15 miles north, is set amidst a Monterey Pine forest inhabited by Acorn and Hairy Woodpeckers, Steller's Jay, and Pygmy Nuthatch. The willows along Santa Rosa Creek paralleling Highway 1 at Cambria's north end (turn left at the signal on Windsor Boulevard and park by the wastewater treatment plant—alas, sealed) have hosted many eastern vagrants in fall; walk the creek (in the creekbed) toward the ocean. Bird the willows along Windsor Boulevard, too.

San Simeon State Park campground is on San Simeon Creek 1.5 miles north of Cambria. The creek mouth itself is a good place to look for Snowy Plovers, gulls, and terns along with occasional wintering ducks. Walk the streambed upstream from the bridge. During migration, shorebirds frequent the shallows, while passerines are to be found in the willows at streamside.

The grassland alongside the road north of Cambria provides habitat for resident Turkey Vulture, Red-tailed Hawk, and American Kestrel, while winter often brings Ferruginous—and rarely Rough-legged—Hawks to add to the mix. Long-billed Curlew routinely winters in this pastureland.

As you travel north to San Simeon and beyond to the Monterey County line you will want to stop at the numerous pull-outs along the bluff overlooking the rocky shore. Black Oystercatcher (resident), Black Turnstone, Surfbird, and Wandering Tattler are found all along this coast. Wintering loons and scoters can be seen at any point along the coast in winter. In lovely San Simeon Bay below Hearst Castle you will occasionally see interesting in-shore birds around the pier or on shore at the mouth of a small creek. It is, in any case, a beautiful place to visit.

A parking lot just south of the lighthouse (no entry) at Point Piedras Blancas, about 21 miles north of Morro Bay, affords access to a trail along the bluffs northward to a point overlooking a beach favored by a Northern Elephant Seal colony. An information display in the parking lot, and docents seven days a week in the winter, provide valuable information about the beasts. The spectacle here is particularly impressive in winter, with some animals lingering into April—individual animals are often found here or nearby throughout the year. Use of a telescope from the bluffs in April and May (morning best) routinely produces large northbound flights of loons (overwhelmingly Pacific—over 45,000 one fine April day), Brant, and Surf Scoters—and occasionally a major surprise.

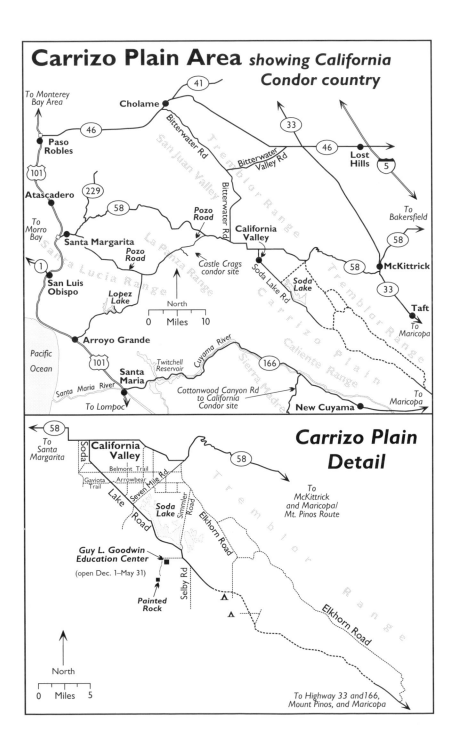

Carrizo Plain Area *showing California Condor country*

To Monterey Bay Area

Cholame — 41

Paso Robles — 46

101

Atascadero — 229

58

Santa Margarita

Pozo Road

To Morro Bay

1

San Luis Obispo

Lopez Lake

Bitterwater Rd

San Juan Valley

Bitterwater Rd

Bitterwater Valley Rd

46 — Lost Hills — 5

33

Pozo Road

California Valley

Castle Crags condor site

Soda Lake Rd

Soda Lake

58 — McKittrick

To Bakersfield

58

33

Taft

To Maricopa

Tremblor Range

La Panza Range

Santa Lucia Range

Carrizo Plain

Caliente Range

North

0 Miles 10

Arroyo Grande

101

Santa Maria

Twitchell Reservoir

Cuyama River

166

Sierra Madre

Pacific Ocean

Santa Maria River

To Lompoc

Cottonwood Canyon Rd to California Condor site

New Cuyama

To Maricopa

Carrizo Plain Detail

58

To Santa Margarita

California Valley

Belmont Trail

Gaviota Trail

Arrowbear

Soda Lake Road

Seven Mile Rd.

Soda Lake

Simmler Road

Elkhorn Road

58

To McKittrick and Maricopa/ Mt. Pinos Route

Tremblor Range

Guy L. Goodwin Education Center

(open Dec. 1–May 31)

Painted Rock

Selby Rd

Elkhorn Road

North

0 Miles 5

To Highway 33 and166, Mount Pinos, and Maricopa

CARRIZO PLAIN, MARICOPA, AND MOUNT PINOS AREA

If you are traveling Interstate 5 north of Los Angeles County, are looking for condors in Santa Barbara County, or are birding San Luis Obispo County, you need to know about several productive birding areas between the coast and Interstate 5. Time of year will be a factor influencing your chosen route. Although winter offers the best birding in the Carrizo Plain, Soda Lake Road can become impassable (infrequently) after a big winter storm—ask locally—and Mount Pinos will be a focus for snow fun. As you can see, although these areas are within easy driving distance of one another, the best birding is in opposite seasons, and you need to plan accordingly.

To reach the Carrizo Plain from coastal San Luis Obispo County, drive north on US-101 from its intersection with Highway 1 in San Luis Obispo. At the El Camino Real exit (8.8), leave the freeway and head east toward the town of Santa Margarita. Drive through this small community to a right turn across the railroad tracks onto Highway 58 (1.6). For the next 35 miles you will traverse oak savannah and chaparral with an avifauna especially interesting to out-of-state visitors. Acorn (abundant) and Nuttall's (common) Woodpeckers, Oak Titmouse, and Western Bluebird are among the most characteristic birds here year round. Yellow-billed Magpies are very conspicuous along the route. "Bell's" Sage Sparrow (*Amphispiza belli belli*) breeds locally in the chaparral along Highway 229 just north of its junction with Highway 58, but its numbers seem to be decreasing here as the habitat matures.

When you reach Pozo Road (35.1), turn right and park opposite the first oak tree in the pasture on the right. A small resident population of Lewis's Woodpeckers used to be predictable here, but in recent years has become less so. Look for them flying from tree to tree here and also along Highway 58 to the west. This is a good area for close-up looks at Yellow-billed Magpies. Check the stock tanks for Lawrence's Goldfinch, and watch for Prairie Falcon, often seen here. *This is also the junction for a side-trip to a California Condor release site; see the Boxed Text on the following pages for directions.* Return to Highway 58 and travel eastward over some low hills to Soda Lake Road (10.5) on the Carrizo Plain.

You can also reach the Carrizo from the east via westbound Highway 58 out of Bakersfield, or, if you are coming from Yosemite or the northern Central Valley, via Bitterwater Road off Highway 46. To reach the Carrizo from Highway 46, turn south on Bitterwater Road 2.2 miles west of the

61

CASTLE CRAGS CONDOR RELEASE SITE

While traveling Highway 58, you are in the ancestral California Condor heartland. Look around in all directions. To the north rolling rangeland, extending to the Salinas Valley in Monterey County, is a tapestry of grassland, chaparral, and pine-oak woodland supporting a varied biota. During a good wildflower spring the profusion of blooms from a dozen species bewilder the eye—where to look next? This was—and is becoming again—prime condor foraging country. To the south lies the north slope of the Santa Lucia Mountains, chaparral-clad with hidden spring-fed oak canyons, isolated patches of pine woodland, and rugged geological structures. In 1911, hiking with a pack horse along roughly this same route, William Leon Dawson and Kelly Truesdale—Kelly an amateur ornithologist and professional egg-collector from nearby Shandon—came in search of a nesting condor. Dawson relates the adventure in *The Birds of California*, a story from a bygone time.

The location of the nest they were looking for? The site is in a massive outcropping of conglomerate, known today as **Castle Crags**, on the edge of the Machesna Mountain Wilderness. Although your own condor search along the detour to Castle Crags will not be as arduous as Dawson and Truesdale's, there will come a point at which you likewise will need to resort to footwork if you are not in a high-clearance vehicle. There may be moments, as you jolt over ruts and rocks, when you would *prefer* to be on foot. In any case, and no matter how far your vehicle can take you into Los Padres National Forest (Forest Adventure Pass required), the country is representative of California before its "improvement."

Turn right onto Pozo Road at its intersection with Highway 58. This will take you through rangeland (watch for Yellow-billed Magpies, Western Bluebirds, Lark Sparrows, and in spring and summer Western Kingbirds) for a few miles before starting to climb upward; the blacktop becomes a good dirt road shortly after beginning the climb. Six miles from Highway 58, just before the saddle, a narrower dirt road goes to the left—the Queen Bee Mine Road—turn onto it. The old mine itself is 1.5 miles farther, but it is the steep dirt road on the right 2.3 miles from the Pozo Road that you are looking for. Up to this point a normal passenger car, with a little driver dexterity and courage, will make it in normal weather conditions. The road up to the crags 2.3 miles east of Pozo Road should be attempted only in a high-clearance vehicle; turn right onto this road.

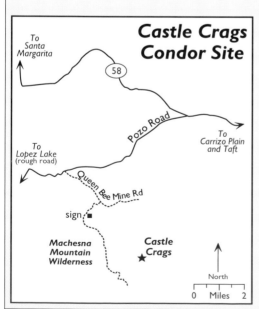

At 0.7 mile from the Queen Bee Mine Road you should see a small sign on the left telling you that you have arrived at the condor lookout. There is a short trail to a picnic bench on the hill to the left. You can stop here, watching the sky above the ridge and, especially, the gigantic rocky outcropping, for condors. If you have a four-wheel-drive vehicle, you might want to continue to the 3,000-feet-elevation ridge-top 0.9 mile farther, from which you may get a closer look at any birds that happen to sail by.

Four fledgling California Condors were released here in 1996 as part of the condor recovery effort. They were fed here, but wandered the rangeland to the north and east and west along the ridges, as well. They quickly became acquainted with the flock released in Lion Canyon in Santa Barbara County. Members of the Lion Canyon flock were often found with the Castle Crags birds—Lion Canyon birds have red, numbered patagial tags and the Castle Crags birds have yellow tags. Eleven condors were seen together here one evening.

A devastating forest fire during the summer of 1996 toasted the area, denuding it of much of its cover. Before the fire, spring mornings would ring with the sounds of the chaparral as Mountain Quail, Western Scrub-Jay, Wrentit, California Thrasher, and Spotted and California Towhees sang their boasts. Until the chaparral regenerates these birds will be largely missing here, but the burned Knobcone Pines still host Nuttall's and Hairy Woodpeckers and Northern Flickers. Raptors of many species ride the thermals and occasionally use the crags as sites for their aeries.

The fire also destroyed the Condor Recovery Team's equipment near the crags, and the birds are no longer fed there. They do, however, still sail the ridge and appear over the crags on occasion. It is worth checking if you are in the area and have the time, a sturdy vehicle, and a tolerance for rough roads.

junction of Highways 46 and 41, just west of Cholame (Sha-LAM—gasoline, restaurant, post office, James Dean Memorial). This is cattle range, and wintering raptors are sometimes seen along this road in substantial numbers. At 9.3 miles south of the turn, take the right fork in the road, following the "To Highway 58" sign for another 22.8 miles to its end at Highway 58. Turn left at the intersection with Highway 58 for the remaining 6.3 miles to Soda Lake Road.

Turn south from Highway 58 onto Soda Lake Road toward the little settlement of California Valley. The California Valley Motel and Restaurant (phone 805/475-2363) is open seven days a week, year round, and reservations are recommended. They have been very accommodating to birding groups in the past, opening the restaurant for groups of six or more (there is a fixed meal charge based on group size—inquire). Although the motel plans to reopen the local gas station in the future, the Carrizo Plain is over fifty miles from the nearest service station, and you should plan accordingly. If it has rained recently, the dirt roads splitting off Soda Lake Road are not recommended. Although winter daytime temperatures in the Carrizo will typically be in the 60s, nighttime temperatures can drop to the teens, and early mornings are best described as "crisp."

November through March is the best time for birders to visit the Carrizo, fortuitously among the most comfortable months climatically. Summer on the Carrizo is hot, very dry, and relatively birdless. This remote, desolate, inland desert-like valley is separated from the San Joaquin Valley to the east by the Temblor Range running along the infamous San Andreas Fault. Historically home to extensive grain, cattle, and sheep ranches, the Carrizo is now also home to the Carrizo Plain Natural Area, designed to preserve this largest-remaining undeveloped slice of the southern San Joaquin Valley topography, flora, and fauna. California birders regularly visit the Carrizo in winter to enjoy the solitude and to look for Sandhill Cranes, Mountain Plovers, wintering raptors, and grassland specialties.

Raptors are among winter's most characteristic birds here, and you will usually see White-tailed Kite and Golden Eagle; Prairie Falcon is seldom missed. Like the rarer Rough-legged Hawk, Merlin numbers vary from winter to winter between uncommon and rare status. Burrowing Owls (uncommon) can best be seen along Soda Lake Road south of Soda Lake. Common winter birds of the Carrizo include Northern Harrier, Red-tailed and Ferruginous Hawks, American Kestrel, Say's Phoebe, Horned Lark, Common Raven, Savannah Sparrow, House Finch, and Western Meadowlark. Mountain Plover (uncommon and local), Mountain Bluebird, and Vesper Sparrow are regular wintering species.

Soda Lake Road is paved until well south of Soda Lake, and is thus driveable whatever the weather conditions. As you drive you will pass dirt roads going off to both sides and gigantic high-tension-line towers transecting the valley west to east. Sometimes the sagebrush along Seven Mile Road north of the towers is productive in winter for Sage Thrasher (uncommon to rare here) and Short-eared Owl among the White-crowned and (less common) Sage Sparrows (*A. b. canescens* here). A winter drive on the dirt roads to plowed fields west of Soda Lake Road sometimes produces Mountain Plovers and Mountain Bluebirds. Belmont Trail, intersecting Soda Lake Road from the west between "town" and the high-tension lines is especially good for Mountain Plovers. Drive west on Belmont Trail and look in the dry fields to the north of the road.

Continuing south on Soda Lake Road you will cross under the high-tension lines, eventually coming to a sign proclaiming "Carrizo Plain Natural Area" (8.0). Across the road from this sign a large pasture stretches east to the edge of **Soda Lake**, approximately one-half mile distant. Sandhill Cranes arrive here in October and are gone by the end of March, feeding wherever the year's grain crops take them. Park anywhere along the road to watch for Sandhill Cranes flying in to the lake in the afternoon. The one predictable place to see the Sandhills, providing that there is water in the lake, is in and around Soda Lake in mid-to-late afternoon. The lake is their roosting site through the night. The sight and sound of hundreds—or thousands—of cranes flying in toward the lake for a night's roost is one of nature's great sensory experiences.

Soda Lake is a shallow, mineral-encrusted pan several thousand acres in extent in the middle of the Plain. The most heavily-vegetated area of the Carrizo surrounds the lake; Sage Sparrow is resident here. All of the birds mentioned above can be found within a few miles of Soda Lake, while the reintroduced Tule Elks and Pronghorns range anywhere within hundreds of square miles.

If you continue farther south on Soda Lake Road, you will reach Simmler Road (6.4), a dirt track running east. It will take you through Sage Sparrow habitat south of Soda Lake to Elkhorn Road, a north-south dirt track traversing much of the Plain's east side. You may wander this and similar dirt tracks, when they are dry, with a chance of seeing any bird mentioned for the Carrizo, although the birds' locations will vary from year to year and sometimes from day to day. Le Conte's Thrasher has nested in open juniper, sage, *Ephedra* habitat at the base of the Temblor Range along Elkhorn Road—but is wildly unpredictable.

As you drive south on Soda Lake Road, watch weed-stalks and fence-lines for Mountain Bluebirds in winter. Burrowing Owls are best seen along this road and Elkhorn Road to the east, usually around California Ground Squirrel colonies. The huge Horned Lark flocks have, on rare occasions, harbored longspurs. Wintering Vesper Sparrows (uncommon) are usually found by checking birds perched on the barbed-wire fences and foraging on the ground near the fence-line.

Past Simmler Road 1.2 miles on the right is a dirt road taking you to the **Guy L. Goodwin Education Center** (805/475-2131), a small natural history museum and information center open from December 1 through May 31. The exhibits are well presented, giving close-up views of mounted mammals characteristic of the area, while labeled native plants outside may answer some of your questions about local botany. A free map is available here that details the Carrizo Plain and provides relevant information. If you continue on the dirt road behind the museum you will come to a parking area from which you can walk to Painted Rock. This unique sandstone formation emerging from the plain near the base of the Caliente Range contains a natural gallery in its sandstone interior. Area Chumash painted their complex geometric patterns on it long ago; it is now a monument to a lost culture as well as home to nesting Barn Owls, Cliff Swallows, Common Ravens, and Rock Wrens.

A few miles south of Selby Road, Soda Lake Road changes from all-weather paved to a good quality dirt road for about 20 of the approximately 32 miles to its intersection with Highway 33/166 just west of Maricopa. (At this intersection, you will be 65.4 miles east of US-101 at Santa Maria via Highway 166.)

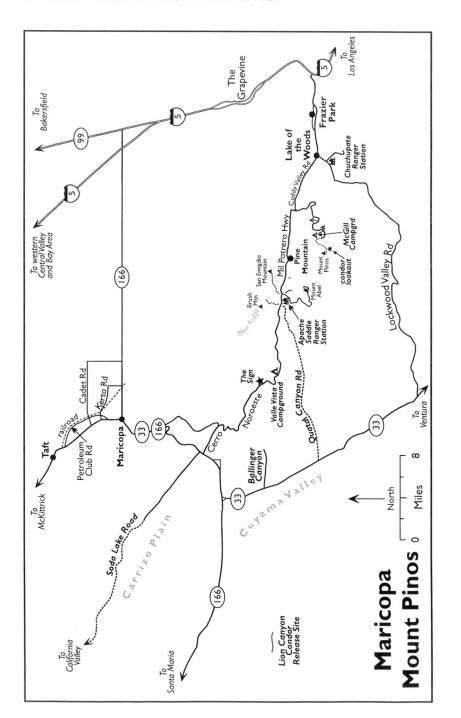

Maricopa Mount Pinos

MARICOPA AREA

After you visit Soda Lake, if the weather does not favor dirt-road driving, retrace your way through California Valley to the junction of Soda Lake Road and Highway 58. If you want to return to the coast, you will turn left. A desire to search for Le Conte's Thrasher will cause you to turn right and follow the directions to **Maricopa** to the east. This highway traverses the Temblor Range, joining Highway 33 just south of the town of McKittrick (27.2). Turn right to Taft (15.1) and stay on Highway 33 a little farther to Petroleum Club Road (0.2). Turn left and take Petroleum Club Road south toward Cadet Road (3.7) in Maricopa.

It is more likely, however, that you will be able to continue south through the Carrizo Plain on Soda Lake Road to Highway 33/166. The entire length of Soda Lake Road is good for wintering raptors and the open-range birds noted above. You may come across a herd of Pronghorns, as well; this antelope-like native to the Carrizo was reintroduced in the 1980s. The small, striped ground squirrel you occasionally see with its tail curved over its back is the San Joaquin Ground Squirrel; it is much outnumbered by the larger brown California Ground Squirrel. Other mammals on the plain include Kit Fox, Coyote, Badger, and a variety of kangaroo rats, including the endangered Giant Kangaroo Rat. All of the latter species, except Coyote, are more readily spotted after dark.

Arriving at Highway 33/166, turn left toward Maricopa 9 miles to the east. On reaching the stop-sign in Maricopa, Highway 33 turns north toward Taft, while Highway 166 continues east to Interstate 5. Turn left onto Highway 33 to Petroleum Club Road (1.3). Turn right, cross Kerto Road (0.6), and continue to a wide dirt pull-out at the top of the slope (0.4). Park off the road. You are now in the middle of an area good in recent years for Le Conte's Thrasher. The birds can be anywhere along the road between Kerto and Cadet, on either side. This section of road has many virtues for one seeking this elusive bird: it is lightly traveled, the vegetation is ideal for Le Conte's, there are no active oil wells on either side of the road, there are no "no trespassing" signs, and finally—there is more than one Le Conte's territory in this stretch. If you arrive in the early morning, it is unlikely that you will need to leave the road to find the bird. Although much has been made of their fondness for washes over the years, this is not necessarily true here. Patience, they say, is a virtue—this is especially true when searching for Le Conte's Thrashers.

These skulkers prefer the light-colored terrain of desert flats and washes and are usually seen on the ground running between the low and widely-scattered bushes. Although they are found in nearly all of the low deserts of Southern California, nowhere are they more common than here at the south end of the San Joaquin Valley. Even in this favorable habitat, Le Conte's is a shy, unapproachable bird, usually found only with difficulty. Listen for their song, but be aware that Northern Mockingbird is also resident and singing here.

Le Conte's Thrashers are most active mornings and evenings, when they often sing while perched on top of the higher vegetation and, uncommonly, even telephone poles. A good strategy for seeing one is to walk slowly along the road, scanning across the distant bushes. Your best chance is to look for them during the breeding season (February–April). Arrive early before it warms up, making the birds less active.

Other species here include Red-tailed Hawk, American Kestrel, Mourning Dove, Greater Roadrunner, Say's Phoebe, Western Kingbird (spring/summer), Horned Lark, Rock Wren, Northern Mockingbird, Loggerhead Shrike, Sage (*canescens*) and White-crowned (winter) Sparrows, and House Finch. Coyote, Black-tailed Jackrabbit, Cottontail, and California and San Joaquin Ground Squirrels are also frequently seen.

If you do not find Le Conte's Thrasher between Kerto and Cadet Roads, return south on Petroleum Club Road to Kerto Road. Park and check the flat northeast of this intersection, walking north to the wash, and in the wash east to the railroad tracks.

After your thrasher encounter, return south to Maricopa. *If you are headed for Los Angeles and wish to bypass the Mount Pinos section of the route, turn left on eastbound Highway 166 and drive 22.6 miles to its intersection with Interstate 5.*

Sage Thrasher
Shawneen E. Finnegan

MOUNT PINOS AREA

The following route is best done mid-April through October, although any time of year can be interesting; winter weather in the mountains is the limiting factor.

At the stop sign in Maricopa bear right and follow combined Highway 33/166 south to Cerro Noroeste Road (9.3), turning left onto it. This good, if winding, road takes you through Bitter Creek National Wildlife Refuge toward Mount Pinos 31 miles to the east. Bitter Creek is in the midst of a vast open section of Southern California; it was purchased in the 1980s and set aside as California Condor foraging range. Much of the drive is atop a ridge exceeding 4,000 feet in elevation and trending southeast, from which you have a wonderful view of the southern Central Valley and the Tehachapi Range to your left as well as the Ventura and Santa Barbara County backcountry on your right. The Sierra Madre ridge, the current heartland for the re-introduced California Condor population, is in sight to the west. This is a wonderful wildflower drive in March and April.

Birds commonly seen in the open grassland on Cerro Noroeste Road include Northern Harrier, Red-tailed Hawk, Golden Eagle, American Kestrel, Mourning Dove, Great Horned Owl (nocturnal), Northern Flicker, Western Kingbird (spring–summer), Horned Lark, Western Scrub-Jay, Common Raven, Western Bluebird, Loggerhead Shrike, Lark Sparrow, and Western Meadowlark. When driving the road in fall, almost anything can whiz overhead as birds from the Central Valley and points north are moving south. Cerro Noroeste has not proven to be a classic hawk-watch site, but raptors do move through the area along with passerines, Northern Flickers, and the occasional flight of waterbirds (there is no water nearby); do not be shocked if a flock of Double-crested Cormorants appears overhead, moving south around the flanks of Mounts Abel and Pinos ahead.

Stop at the **Los Padres National Forest sign** (9.7) (Forest Adventure Pass required). Before the last California Condor was captured for the captive breeding program on April 19, 1987, "The Sign" was the most predictable spot from which to see these far-ranging birds. The view here is spectacular, most of the birds noted for Cerro Noroeste Road can be seen from this spot, given time, and the pinyon-chaparral slope below produces Wrentit, California Thrasher, and Spotted and California Towhees.

Leave The Sign and continue along the ridge toward Valle Vista Campground. The long high ridge on your left is Blue Ridge, topped by Brush Mountain and its higher neighbor to the east, San Emigdio. The canyon between San Emigdio and Mounts Abel and Pinos served as a condor flyway from mountain roosts to open-country foraging areas, and may become so yet again. Drop into the Valle Vista Campground (2.4) immediately downslope on the left. It is shaded by Pinyon Pines, and offers modest restroom facilities. The view of the valley to the north is, again, spectacular. The campground is good in summer for Black-headed Grosbeak, Lazuli

QUATAL AND BALLINGER CANYONS SIDE TRIP

If you are traveling in a high-clearance vehicle, you may wish to take the side trip to Quatal and Ballinger Canyons. You may do this, depending on time of day, on your way to Mount Pinos, or for a day-trip from mountain camping. Either way, spring birding is rewarding in Quatal and Ballinger Canyons, best done in morning or evening.

A dirt road extends downslope to the right (south) from Cerro Noroeste Road 1.1 miles west of Apache Saddle. *Alternately, you may start at the bottom from Highway 33 and ascend Quatal Canyon to Cerro Noroeste Road.* This dirt road descends through pinyon/juniper forests to **Quatal Canyon**, becoming chaparral and ending in the grassland of the valley floor almost 3,000 feet below. The 14.7-mile dirt road is usually in good condition, especially as it broadens in its lower reaches. It terminates on Highway 33 in the southeastern arm of the Cuyama Valley about 5 miles south of the four-county corner where San Luis Obispo, Santa Barbara, Ventura, and Kern Counties come together. This area is a county-lister's paradise.

Quatal Canyon Road is marked with mileposts. The unfenced land in the upper part of the canyon belongs to the US Forest Service (don't forget your Forest Adventure Pass) and is open to the public. Sage Sparrows (*canescens*, just at the edge of the *canescens/belli* subspecies [species?] ranges) prefer the low, brushy areas with a few scattered bushes between miles 3 and 8. Brewer's Sparrows are generally limited to the pure sage areas, particularly around mile 3.8. Scott's Orioles (declining in the four-county-corners region for reasons unknown) and Black-chinned Sparrows (common) range throughout most of the canyon from mile 3 to mile 12.

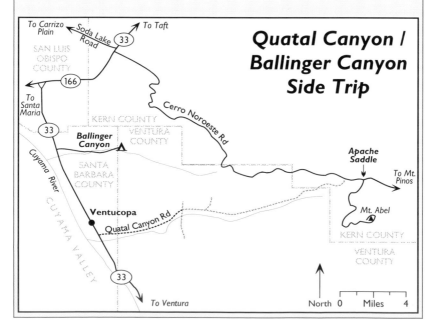

Quatal Canyon (like Ballinger Canyon just to the north in Santa Barbara County) is most productive from mid-April to early June, when nesting birds are in full song and migrants contribute to the diversity. Summer residents you might expect to find, in addition to those species mentioned for Ballinger Canyon below, are Common Poorwill, Ash-throated Flycatcher, Common Raven, Oak Titmouse, Phainopepla, Black-chinned and Lark Sparrows, and Lesser Goldfinch. At the higher elevations look for Cooper's Hawk, Olive-sided Flycatcher, Western Wood-Pewee, Violet-green Swallow, Black-throated Gray Warbler, Black-headed Grosbeak, and Chipping Sparrow. Many other species common in Southern California are also present. Gray Flycatcher has nested in the canyon between mileposts 9 and 11, so watch for them along this segment of road.

On leaving Quatal Canyon in the valley, turn right onto Highway 33 to **Ballinger Canyon Road**, 5.3 miles north. Turn right onto it, stopping for roadside birding and short walks from the road. The road ends at a campground (3.3) favored by dirt-bikers, who have designated areas for their land-shredding. The hillsides in the canyon are the northwestern limit of the ranges for a number of desert species. It is best to walk the canyon to the east, away from the dirt-bikers' activity. Some of the breeding birds you may find from mid-April to mid-July include Mountain Quail, Greater Roadrunner, Lesser Nighthawk, Costa's Hummingbird, Rock Wren, California Thrasher (the only thrasher here or in Quatal Canyon), Brewer's, Black-throated, and Sage Sparrows, Scott's Oriole, and Lawrence's Goldfinch.

Bunting, and Chipping, Brewer's, Black-chinned, and Lark Sparrows. In winter, look for Fox, Lincoln's, Golden-crowned, and White-crowned Sparrows. Resident birds include Western Scrub-Jay, Wrentit, California Thrasher, and Spotted and California Towhees.

Continuing on toward Mount Pinos, you will reach Apache Saddle (9.7). The forest at this higher elevation is now predominantly Jeffrey Pine, although Pinyon Pines are still in evidence, predominating on the hot, dry southwest slopes. You may choose to take the right turn to explore 8,286-foot-high Mount Abel after the Forest Service reopens the road following clearing of the winter debris in early May. Mount Abel has essentially the same bird list as Mount Pinos immediately to the east, but it is not as large an area; no water is available in the lone campground on its summit. Mount Pinos is open all year (although its highest slopes may be closed in winter) and has water in McGill and Mount Pinos Campgrounds (fee).

Continue downslope (Cerro Noroeste Road has now become Mil Potrero Road) through the forest, through the little community of Pine Mountain (motel, gasoline, restaurant, grocery store), and up the steep winding road beyond to the intersection with Cuddy Valley Road at the base of Mount Pinos (8.6). Turn right to ascend **Mount Pinos**.

As you travel upward through the wooded areas, watch for Mountain Quail, Clark's Nutcracker, Cassin's and Purple Finches, Green-tailed Towhee, and "Thick-billed" Fox Sparrow. **McGill Campground** (5.3) (El. 7,500 ft) has good facilities and enticing birding possibilities. One of the best areas is below the group campsite on the back side of the campground. Look for Band-tailed Pigeon, White-headed Woodpecker, Williamson's Sapsucker (rare), Steller's Jay, Clark's Nutcracker, Pygmy Nuthatch, Red Crossbill, and Yellow-rumped Warbler. At night, you may find Northern Pygmy-Owl, Flammulated Owl, and Northern Saw-whet Owl. Driving Mount Pinos' lower slopes at night will sometimes produce Common Poorwill on the road—watch for the eyeshine.

You will see several old logging roads as you continue up the road; all are dirt, dead-end, and about a mile long. Their names are more impressive than the roads themselves, but they do allow you to get off the main road. Iris Point Road (1.6) on the left leads to the warm south side of Mount Pinos, where Violet-green Swallows and Western Bluebirds abound. Fir Ridge Road (0.2) on the right ends on the shaded north side of the mountain in a stand of White Fir, an indicator of the Canadian Life Zone.

A large parking lot ends the paved Mount Pinos Road (1.7). The little swale (named **Iris Meadow**) just beyond is usually good for Mountain Quail, Calliope Hummingbird (breeds mid-May to late June), Dusky Flycatcher, Green-tailed Towhee, and "Thick-billed" (*stephensi*) Fox Sparrow.

"Thick-billed" (stephensi) Fox Sparrow
Shawneen E. Finnegan

Just as you enter the parking area, a small dirt road begins through the forest on the left. Formerly open to vehicle traffic, it is no longer maintained and is routinely closed. It makes a wonderful walk with all of the mountain's birds listed above possible along its 1.2-mile length to the west and Mount Pinos' summit (El. 8,832 ft). The rich, old-growth **Jeffrey Pine forest** is most impressive on foot; the aroma alone is worth the walk. The forest begins to open up into scrubby-edged iris meadows as you continue west. On reaching the westernmost point you come to a magnificent overlook of the saddle stretching between Mount Pinos and Sawmill Mountain, with Mount Abel beyond. This is the old "Condor Lookout" from the 1960s and 1970s. It is still a fine spot to watch for raptors in September and October (although not a classic "hawk-watch site"), with a 270-degree view from the Sierra Nevada to the Sespe.

The most common mammals on Mount Pinos are Gray Squirrel and California Ground Squirrel, although you may find others, particularly at night. Look for Mule Deer, Black Bear, Long-tailed Weasel, Gray Fox, Coyote, Bobcat, Lodgepole Chipmunk (in forested areas), and Merriam's Chipmunk (in brush).

Return to the base of the mountain, stopping where the Mount Pinos road intersects with Mil Potrero Road on the left and Cuddy Valley Road straight ahead (8.8). Check the patches of wild rose in spring and summer for nesting Brewer's and Black-chinned Sparrows and Lazuli Bunting.

At Lake of the Woods (5.2) the road forks. The right fork (Lockwood Valley Road) takes you to the Chuchupate (*Chu-chu-PAH-tay*) Ranger Station (phone 805/245-3731). Beyond Chuchupate lie 27 twisty miles on Lockwood Valley Road through remote backcountry, finally connecting with Highway 33. The habitat, and thus the bird list, is similar to that in Quatal Canyon minus Black-throated Sparrow and Scott's Oriole. The left fork at Lake of the Woods is Frazier Mountain Park Road, leading to the Golden State Freeway (Interstate 5) (7.0).

If you wish to bird the Eastern Kern County Loop, southbound Interstate 5 connects with eastbound Highway 138, which will take you to northbound Highway 14 and Mojave, the loop's starting point. This routing will also take you through parts of Antelope Valley, right by the Lancaster Sewage Ponds (see Antelope Valley chapter). Consult your map of California: a return to Highway 166 gives you a route to Mojave via connections with Highways 99, 223, and 58. Conversely, turning south on Interstate 5 and continuing for approximately 50 miles delivers you to Los Angeles.

There are motels in California Valley (see text), New Cuyama, Maricopa, Taft, Bakersfield, and Gorman. Campgrounds can be found on Soda Lake Road (primitive), Cerro Noroeste Road (Valle Vista), Mount Pinos, Mount Abel, and in Lockwood Valley. The best camping area for birding is McGill Campground on Mount Pinos.

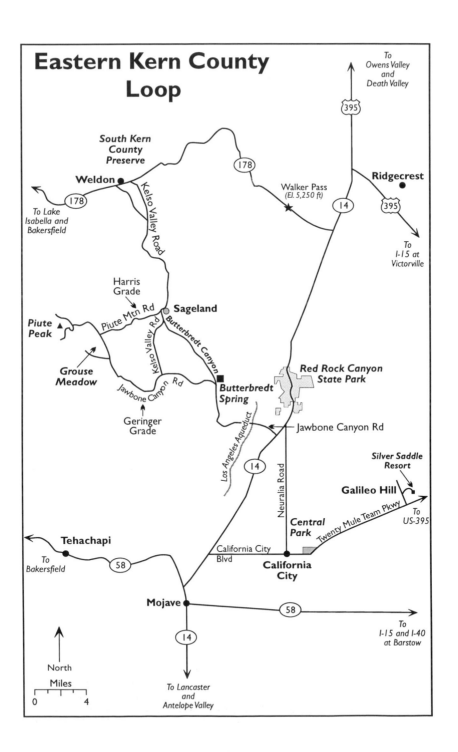

Eastern Kern County Loop

To Owens Valley and Death Valley

395

South Kern County Preserve

178

Walker Pass (El. 5,250 ft)

Ridgecrest

Weldon

178

14   395

To Lake Isabella and Bakersfield

Kelso Valley Road

To I-15 at Victorville

Harris Grade

Piute Mtn Rd   Sageland

Piute Peak

Kelso Valley Rd   Butterbredt Canyon

Red Rock Canyon State Park

Grouse Meadow

Jawbone Canyon Rd   Butterbredt Spring

Geringer Grade

Los Angeles Aqueduct

Jawbone Canyon Rd

14

Silver Saddle Resort

Neuralia Road

Galileo Hill

Central Park

Twenty Mule Team Pkwy

To US-395

Tehachapi

To Bakersfield

58

California City Blvd

California City

Mojave

58

To I-15 and I-40 at Barstow

14

North

Miles

0   4

To Lancaster and Antelope Valley

EASTERN KERN COUNTY LOOP

by Keith Axelson

Over 270 species of birds have been observed within this loop, and a visit during spring migration in particular promises a good variety. Start your trip quite early in the morning for best results.

To begin this adventure, drive north from Mojave along Highway 14 to the intersection of Jawbone Canyon Road (19.9). Turn left (west) and drive past the white aqueduct pipe until you reach the *black* Los Angeles Aqueduct pipe which passes under the road (2.9). Stop to check the trees around the nearby house *from the road* (good migrant trap). Chukars are occasionally seen on the steep slopes on both sides of the canyon from the house.

The pavement ends at about 3.9 miles. You are now in the middle of a BLM-designated Off-road Vehicle Open Area. Bear right (north) up and out of Hottman Canyon. *The condition of this road is normally adequate for the passage of a standard sedan, but conditions change with the weather and maintenance schedule.* The turn-off on your right into Butterbredt Canyon (11.1 from Highway 14) is easy to find. At the intersection a white range sign still stands, but shooting has obliterated its former message. Across the cattle-guard on the right, however, is a **Butterbredt Spring Wildlife Sanctuary** sign. Butterbredt Spring (0.9) is down the rough, sandy road to the right. At the lower end of the road you will see the spring directly ahead. (Low-clearance vehicles may wish to avoid this last stretch of road, although it is rarely necessary; one can park at the turn-off and walk down the road in 10 minutes—take water.)

There are no facilities of any kind at the sanctuary and the area is considered primitive, so please pack out your trash. Observe all desert precautions such as having sufficient water, gasoline, and proper clothing. The area is checkerboarded with private and public land, and camping is *not* permitted at or near the spring. The spring remains private land, but through an agreement with the Onyx Ranch, Keith Axelson, Santa Monica Bay Audubon Society, and the Bureau of Land Management, the Butterbredt Spring Wildlife Sanctuary was created and fenced. *Birders should never open any gates here.* Cattle now water from a trough outside the fence. Butterbredt Canyon is included within the largest Area of Critical Environmental Concern (ACEC) administered by the BLM. All vehicle travel within Butterbredt Canyon is restricted to Butterbredt Canyon Road and Gold Peak Road.

75

Le Conte's Thrasher in Jaw-bone Canyon. Jawbone Canyon, managed by the BLM, is a classic example of the damage caused by unrestricted off-road vehicle use. Even though most of the hillsides look like a battle zone (and in fact some have been battle zones, as scenes from *Starship Troopers* were filmed near here), the sandy wash in the first mile of canyon is home to several pairs of Le Conte's Thrashers. To look for them, park by the first of two large aqueduct pipes which cross the paved entrance road half a mile west of Highway 14. Walk the wash between the two pipes, looking especially in the low brush at the edges of the main channel. (See Le Conte's Thrasher in the Specialties section for ID comments.)

If you have no luck here, occasionally Le Conte's Thrashers can be seen in the Joshua Tree woodland on the way to Butterbredt Spring. After the road forks and begins to climb out of Jawbone Canyon heading north, look for them anywhere between that point and the turn-off to Butterbredt Spring. (Do be aware that California Thrashers can occur at the spring.)

A note of caution is in order. Except in winter, rattlesnakes are active in this habitat. During heavy winter rainstorms or late summer thunderstorms—both rare but annual—the wash can be very dangerous. If it is raining in the mountains, do **not** hike in the wash bed. Flash floods can be fatal. Floods in September 1997 washed out not only the Jawbone Canyon Road, but also sections of Highway 14.

There are no designated motorcycle trails through this fragile environment. A letter from you to the BLM, Ridgecrest Resource Area, 300 South Richmond Road, Ridgecrest, CA 93555, in favor of continued motorcycle closure will help to keep it this way.

Butterbredt Spring Wildlife Sanctuary and the immediate vicinity offer a diverse variety of habitat. Marsh vegetation has filled the pond, and typical desert plants such as Joshua Tree, cholla cactus, sage, and Rabbitbrush dot the hillsides. Cottonwoods and willows follow the water east as it resurfaces down the wash.

Most birders spend their time in the oasis formed by the main spring. After wet winters, water trickles through the area, attracting numerous birds. The El Niño winter of 1998 was a little too wet. Flash flooding through the canyon knocked down a few trees, ripped out much of the willow stand, and generally scoured the canyon below the oasis. The remaining willows and, especially, the cottonwoods will hold many migrants—but it will be a few years before regrowth of the understory restores extensive skulker habitat.

At all times the large cottonwoods play host to birds, as well as giving a much-needed windbreak and relief from the sun to birders watching them. A lookout on the southeast side of these trees offers you a great vantage point. This spot allows a clear view of the canyon as it trends southeastward, letting you see what is flying upcanyon toward you. Because most of the birds will fly past close to the spring, you will be able to test your ability to identify passerines on the wing.

Butterbredt Spring is among the Mojave's best birding localities in spring. Western migrants are best from mid-April to mid-May, although the vagrants are what draw many birders at this season. To date, over 30 species of warblers have been seen in this oasis. While vagrants may show up at any time, late April to early June is best. Fall, while less spectacular, also has its share of migrants and vagrants.

In some years Calliope Hummingbirds have been common (early May). Scott's Orioles nest in the area, as do the ever-so-popular Chukars. Other birds to look for are Ladder-backed Woodpecker, Cactus Wren, Le Conte's Thrasher (Be careful: California Thrashers breed at and near the spring and are sometimes paler in hue.), and Brewer's, Sage, and Black-throated Sparrows.

After you have birded the spring, a leisurely walk/drive up Butterbredt Canyon can reward you with excellent high-desert scenery—and add to your bird list. The canyon opens into a broad, bowl-like valley filled with Joshua Trees. Scott's Orioles nest throughout the area, as do Blue-gray Gnatcatchers. Golden Eagle and Le Conte's Thrasher are seen regularly. A few Bendire's Thrashers have also been reported from this area. You might hear their distinctive song if you drive along slowly with your windows rolled down. (Nesting Bendire's were reported one time near the summit of this road.)

If road conditions allow (and they usually do), continue on through Butterbredt Canyon to the summit (El. 5,220 ft) (5.0), where you will be able to see the Piute Mountains in front of you, due west. Pressing on, about one mile past the summit, stop to listen for Pinyon Jays, which are often found foraging through the Joshua Trees. Down the hill you will come to paved Kelso Valley Road (2.6). Turn right toward the site of Sageland (1.3). Only a concrete historical marker still stands at this intersection.

At this point, you may choose one of two routes to reach the summit of Piute Vista (El. 8,326 ft). Piute Mountain Road, climbing up the Harris Grade, departs from Sageland. Jawbone Canyon Road (Geringer Grade) departs 7.7 miles south of Sageland where Kelso Valley Road intersects with Jawbone Canyon Road. This latter route is described several paragraphs hence.

If you have chosen to follow Piute Mountain Road, turn left (west) onto it for a 16-mile trip to the summit of Piute Peak. **Piute Mountain Road** can be productive for montane species such as White-headed Woodpecker, Williamson's Sapsucker (very rare), Clark's Nutcracker, and Rufous Hummingbird. Take time to investigate some of the side roads you pass as long as they lead uphill. Once you have traveled 9.7 miles from the Sageland intersection, you will come to Jawbone Canyon Road leading left. Turn left onto it to reach Grouse Meadow (3.1). Blue Grouse formerly occurred here, but are now apparently extirpated locally. The area has been heavily logged.

Return to Piute Mountain Road and continue on to the Piute Vista turn-off on the right (5.1). It is now clearly signed: Piute Vista, 2 miles, 28S17. (A USFS Sequoia National Forest map is helpful.) The last 400-yard stretch requires a four-wheel-drive vehicle, but if you don't have one, park and walk—the lichen-covered rocks and the view are worth it.

To reach Piute Peak, if you have not driven all the way through Butterbredt Canyon, return to Jawbone Canyon Road (where you entered the canyon) and turn right (west). At the intersection with Kelso Valley Road (6.9), you could continue straight ahead on Jawbone Canyon Road, taking the Geringer Grade route to the summit of Piute Peak. However, the Geringer Grade is a difficult road with many switchbacks, and is not recommended for passenger cars. Even with four-wheel drive it should not be attempted during or immediately after bad weather. Snow and mud often block the road in winter. Another option from this intersection is to drive the Geringer Grade route only until you reach a Blue Oak woodland on your right (north) and an open grassland on your left (2.8). Lewis's Woodpeckers can be seen here in spring or fall and appear in this area intermittently throughout the year.

To reach the smoother route (Harris Grade/Piute Mountain Road) to Piute Peak and the good birding previously described, turn right (north) on Kelso Valley Road. As you approach a house (1.5) among some willows and cottonwoods, watch on the left about 100 yards below the road for three ponds where, in season, you may find shorebirds, ducks, and many passerines. *Please observe from the road and do not trespass or agitate the cattle—this is private land.* Farther up the valley watch for nesting Brewer's Sparrows. As you near the pass, stop to listen for Black-chinned Sparrows which nest on both sides of the pass.

There is a fine view from the summit of the pass (El. 4,850 ft) (4.0). To the west you will see the Piute Mountains and a portion of the southern Sierra Nevada to the north. To the south you can see the northern part of the Tehachapi Mountains. Continue driving north and you will pass, on your right, the north end of the Butterbredt Canyon Road (1.2). At the Sageland site (1.3), described earlier, a left turn will send you up the Harris Grade and Piute Mountain Road. Proceeding straight (north) will take you to a massive cottonwood/willow riparian area along Kelso Creek (2.0). Park and walk into the trees and along the creek to look for owls, woodpeckers, flycatchers, vireos, and warblers. You are now in different habitat, as evidenced by the nesting birds, which include Western Scrub-Jay, Western Bluebird, and Spotted Towhee. Nuttall's Woodpecker, found throughout the riparian area, is known to hybridize with Ladder-backed Woodpecker in nearby areas.

Continue north on Kelso Valley Road to the town of Weldon (15.2), site of Audubon California's **Kern River Preserve**. Turn left onto Highway 178 and look for the sign (75 yards) marking the headquarters on the right side of the road. Stop in and pick up a map of the Preserve's trail systems. Some of the trails are partly under water. Birding on the Preserve is best in June; it is generally hot there during the summer. You can contact the Preserve in advance to arrange a tour or use the self-guided nature trail (PO Box 1662, Weldon, CA 93283; phone 760/378-2531).

Species you might expect to find include "California" Yellow-billed Cuckoo (on the state endangered list), Willow Flycatcher (federal endangered list), Bell's Vireo (rare), Summer Tanager, Blue Grosbeak, Lazuli and Indigo

Buntings, and other riparian species such as kingbirds and orioles. The cuckoos, the last migrants to arrive, come in late June.

When you are ready to continue the loop, drive east on Highway 178 to its junction with Highway 14 (33.0), where you turn right. After passing through Red Rock Canyon State Park (check for Verdin and, with lots of luck, Le Conte's Thrasher by the campground), bear left onto Neuralia Road (21.2). At California City Boulevard (12.2), turn left (east) to **California City**. This town exists primarily as a bedroom community for people from Edwards Air Force Base. North of the main road at the east side of town is large Central Park, which has a pleasant small lake surrounded by ornamental trees and bushes, and a golf course. Park in the main parking lot and walk south to the hill with a waterfall—usually flowing—which is attractive to a large number of birds. Walk around the lake as far as possible (avoid the private property). The islands of vegetation on the north side of the park serve as the most reliable spots for migrants and vagrants (spring is best). Large numbers of flycatchers, thrushes, and warblers are found. Lawrence's Goldfinch occurs here in spring and fall, as well as at the resort at Galileo Hill (below). The best months for both are April and May, and late August to the end of October.

Twenty Mule Team Parkway borders the northeast side of the park. Follow it east about ten miles, turning left and then right, following the signs to **Silver Saddle Resort** at the foot of Galileo Hill. This is a private resort and birder access to this fine migrant trap is due to the generosity of resort management. Their generosity, alas, has not always been repaid by good birding manners. While birding here one must adhere to a few resort requests—and basic common sense: 1) always park only in the large main parking lot fronting the resort restaurant, 2) do not bird near the private residential units, 3) do not walk through ornamental plantings, and 4) always respect the privacy of guests and resort employees while exercising common courtesy toward all. This man-made oasis has a most impressive list of vagrants in its immediate past and is thus one of the premier desert birding spots in both spring and fall. One can easily spend a half-day birding here. Continued access depends on birders behaving like guests in another's home.

Retrace your route to Central Park in California City and back out to Highway 14; turn left toward Mojave to complete the loop.

If you decide to spend more than one day on this loop, you will find motels at the Silver Saddle Resort, in California City (by the park), and in Mojave, Tehachapi, and Lake Isabella (13 miles west of Weldon on Highway 178). One would be well advised to budget a minimum of two days in order to bird the entire loop. When birding here during peak migrant season, visitors may well want to confine their mornings to the oases noted above.

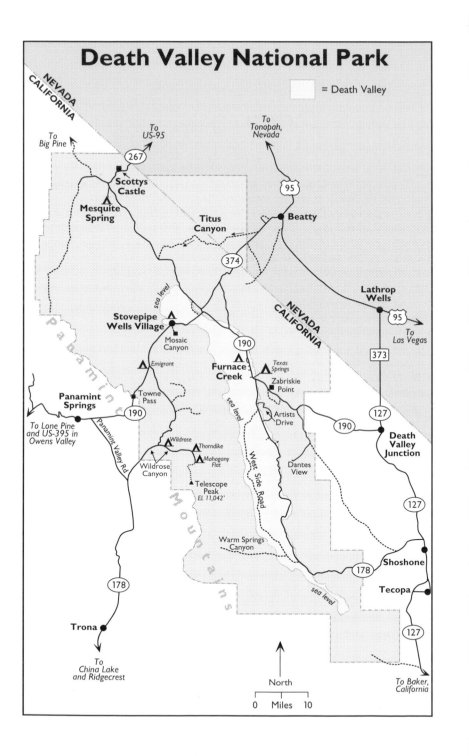

Death Valley National Park

☐ = Death Valley

DEATH VALLEY

Death Valley—which other of North America's famous birding sites is blessed with such an extraordinary name? To be sure, certain place-names evoke the spectacle of migration, exceptional natural beauty, and a memory of wonder: Cave Creek Canyon, Point Pelee, Cape May, High Island, the Kougarok Road north of Nome. The Dry Tortugas may stand alone in competition with Death Valley for the birding destination whose very name is to be reckoned with—a name requiring a mental pause so one may simply savor the words, the concept, the mythology of the place.

Wholly enclosed within Death Valley National Park, Death Valley is not dead. It is, however, a *valley*, and a fairly long one at that; it runs some 130 miles from Last Chance Spring in the north to Saratoga Springs in the south. Tucked in eastern Inyo County amid mountain ranges named Cottonwood, Grapevine, Panamint, Black, and—more picturesquely—Funeral, Last Chance, and Owlshead, the valley is a deep faulted slash into Paleozoic rock punctuated with volcanism, latter-day stream-washed sediments, and the caustic mineral pans left by prehistoric lakes. It is an extreme place; therefore it is fitting that one can stand at the lowest spot in the United States near Badwater, 282 feet below sea level, and look west to Telescope Peak in the Panamints, at 11,042 feet elevation. The total distance is approximately thirteen miles. Gazing upward from the chemical stew in the company of Common Ravens at Badwater, you are looking toward nearby habitat whose breeding birds include Clark's Nutcracker, Mountain Chickadee, and Mountain Bluebird. It is also much cooler up there.

Lurid tales of lost pioneers aside, Death Valley *can* be a pretty grim place. The birder, however, knows that it is rife with opportunity. The possibilities depend on two factors: water and migration. One does not bird Death Valley because it has rare or endemic residents not found elsewhere. There is no one stand-out species drawing birders the many long, dry miles to this remarkable place. *Birders bird Death Valley for its migrants and the rarities that show up during migration.*

Do not bother birding Death Valley in the summer (further elaboration should be unnecessary). Winter on the valley floor is delightful with cold nights, crisp mornings, and moderate daytime temperatures under clear skies; annual precipitation averages less than two inches. Winter also brings an interesting assemblage of ducks and wintering passerines to the verdant oases. Fall and spring migrations at the oases can produce wonderful days among western migrants leavened with vagrant surprises. Birding Death Valley is essentially a progress from oasis to oasis, thus the plan of this chapter.

You can reach Death Valley National Park (fee) easily (after a long drive) through entrances in the west, east, and south. Try to procure the AAA map to Death Valley before starting your trip. Many Southern Californians prefer the route through Trona and the Panamint Valley on Highway 178, continuing to Highway 190, turning there east toward Towne Pass and Death Valley beyond. However you approach the valley, be sure to arrive with as full a fuel tank as possible (gasoline is readily available in the park, but prices are steep); carry extra water, and bring plenty of snacks. A broad-brimmed hat, lightweight clothes, and sun block are required equipment; in winter, bring a warm shirt or sweater and a windbreaker as well. If you intend to do any hiking, appropriate rugged footwear is necessary. People still occasionally go for a hike up a side canyon and disappear; take warnings about water and accurate navigation seriously.

Disclaimers notwithstanding, Death Valley is a wonderful place for explor- ing—best done from November through April when the temperatures are more reasonable. The birding, although good, is not as exciting at this time. The mornings can be given to birding while mid-day and afternoons can be spent exploring this fascinating place. A fairly extensive network of four- wheel-drive tracks provides access to hidden canyons and geological curiosi- ties. The one-way drive through Titus Canyon in the Grapevine Mountains (accessed via Highway 374 just west of Beatty, Nevada) is justly famous. As with all desert travel, one should stay away from canyons during infrequent storms in the mountains (especially in summer); carrying extra water *inside* the vehicle is only one of the traveler's concerns at such times.

Our birding route starts at **Furnace Creek Ranch** in mid-valley, and will be completed in one day. Depending on your time available, you may wish to explore the Panamint Mountains *(see Boxed Text at end of this chapter)*, or other byways, on your second day here, re-doing the valley on the third. This gives more migrants time to arrive (or leave), providing new possibilities. Furnace Creek Ranch can also serve as your overnight lodging destination with motel rooms (760/786-2345), swimming pool, store, restaurants, and a campground available. This man-made oasis includes surface streams, small ponds, date palm groves, a golf course, tennis and basketball courts, historic museum, post office, and a gas station. You should stop at the Park Headquarters and Visitors Center on the northern edge of the Furnace Creek complex, pay your entry fee, and peruse the fine selection of books relevant to Death Valley, California desert history, natural history, and deserts generally. A Greater Roadrunner may be stalking nearby in front of the building, as White-winged Doves call hollowly from the Tamarisks. The improved campground (fee) is behind the visitors center.

Although much of interest and natural beauty lies south of Furnace Creek, this oasis forms the southern terminus of the birding route. The valley south of "The Furnace" is not very productive from a birding perspective; a morning sight-seeing trip to Zabriskie Point four miles southeast on Highway 190 is, however, highly recommended after birding the oasis itself.

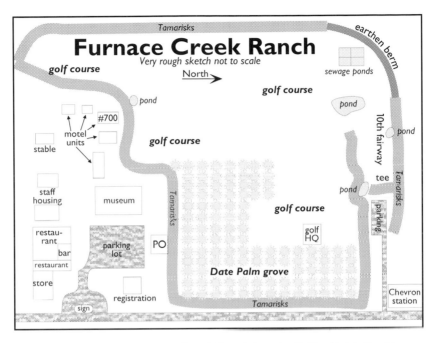

The golf course at Furnace Creek Ranch lives in California birding history as the source of many accidental vagrant records including: Mississippi Kite, Garganey, Purple Gallinule, Upland Sandpiper, Le Conte's Sparrow, Smith's Longspur, Streak-backed Oriole, and a host of others. It has also provided some very entertaining birder stories; maybe someone will write them down one day.

A word about Furnace Creek Ranch and the golf course. It is *private property* and birders are not welcome on the fairways or greens while others commit golf. You may, however, bird from the fringes and among the date palm groves which intrude into the course plan from the eastern edge like peninsulas bordering a lake. This is a large area to bird but you will be amply rewarded following a good flight night (conversely, after a night when few migrants are moving through, birding can be quite dull). Put yourself in a nocturnal migrant's place: you have been flying all night and as the stars begin to fade the ground some few thousand feet below starts to become clear. And that is precisely what comes clear—ground. Hundreds of square miles of inhospitable, desiccated, rocky, sandy, mineral-encrusted, treeless, hot wasteland. To the west are the 9-11,000 foot Panamints, to the east the lower, but still formidable Blacks and Funerals. Yet there before you, illogically, are a few hundred acres of trees, green grass, and running water. Where would you choose to alight?

Western Kingbird, Warbling Vireo, Orange-crowned, Yellow, and Wilson's Warblers, Western Tanager, Black-headed Grosbeak, and Bullock's

Oriole will be among the most common migrants found here and throughout the Death Valley oases. Wintering species dominating the scene include Ruby-crowned Kinglet, American Pipit (on the lawns and fairways), Yellow-rumped Warbler, White-crowned Sparrow, and Brewer's Blackbird; there is usually an *Accipiter* or two lurking somewhere nearby. Although migrants and the occasional vagrant can be anywhere (California's first known Common Grackle was found on the small lawn by the sign at the entrance to the tourist complex), there are a few areas that have proven especially good through the years.

Bird the **Tamarisk** trees (or Salt Cedars as they are sometimes called) lining the fairways from the fringe, the ponds, the date palm groves, and the Tamarisks around the public areas. You are likely to come across a Greater Roadrunner hunting the golf course and fringing areas (they have been seen snatching exhausted migrants from the lower branches), and the cacophony of Great-tailed Grackles will be one of the dominant sounds. Bird the date palm groves and public areas last.

Start your morning at dawn—or as soon as you have birdable light *before* dawn in the heat of late spring or early fall. Drive a tenth of a mile north of the tourist center (store, restaurants) to the Chevron gas station, turning left onto the road along its south side. Drive to the end and park in the golfers' parking lot. Bird the surrounding Tamarisks and the small pond at the parking lot's edge. Walk northwest through the shrubs to the paved road running west from the campground along the **northern edge** of the course. An often-damp fringing ditch parallels the 10th fairway. Walk along the ditch on the paved road, birding the Tamarisks and shrubs. The ditch can be accessed through the tangled greenery at many points. Bird the shrubs and scan the fairway and patches of fringing weeds; many vagrant birds have turned up here, including more than one Le Conte's Sparrow. There is a small pond with cattails that attracts birds about half way down the fairway adjacent to the ditch. Continue west to where you can see the fairly large pond inside the northwest corner of the course. In winter this pond consistently holds wintering ducks and geese; it is a good place for Snow and Ross's Geese if any are around (and have not been grabbed by one of the aggressive local Coyotes). When you reach the northwest corner of the golf course you will find that a large earthen berm has been pushed up. Walk along the top of this berm as it curves south to the new Furnace Creek Ranch **sewage ponds**. The ponds attract migrant and wintering shorebirds, as well as insects and insectivorous birds. Eastern vagrants—most commonly Rose-breasted Grosbeak, Indigo Bunting, and Bobolink—are sometimes close by here and elsewhere on the course in late spring and in fall. Lucy's Warblers breed in the Catclaw just outside the oasis.

Continue birding the fringing line of Tamarisks and accessible ponds nearby. Yellow-headed Blackbirds are often found among the cattails. The pond behind motel unit 700 and the Tamarisks in the vicinity consistently turn up unusual birds, while the stables at the southern edge of the complex regularly has a mixed flock of blackbirds. Strange things happen during migration—a Cape May Warbler was once found among cattails in a golf course pond in late May. In late May and early June evenings you should watch for migrant Common Nighthawks (rare) among the Lessers overhead. Bird the Tamarisk line along the date grove—and the date grove itself—back toward the parking lot from the motel units, watching for birds on the lawns and wherever there are plantings. Even the ornamental Oleanders sometimes attract migrants.

Bird the **date palm groves** thoroughly (and save these for last, after golfing is in full swing), especially those being irrigated at the moment. These groves are irrigated by running water over the flat orchard soil, where it stands among weeds in low spots. These wet weedy patches and nearby vegetation usually produce birds, as do the date palms themselves. If the dates are ripe, watch for birds in the fronds, hunting insects attracted to the dates. The palm groves are especially good for wintering birds, and in migration regularly produce many species of migrant flycatchers, warblers, buntings, and icterids. Be careful where you step among the date palm fronds; Sidewinders can show up here and elsewhere around the golf course. Barn and Great Horned Owls are occasionally found roosting among the date palm crowns. Do not neglect the Tamarisk row separating the date grove's eastern edge from the highway.

When you have completed your birding at Furnace Creek, probably by mid-to-late morning, drive north up the valley to your next birding destination, **Stovepipe Wells**. Turn west on Highway 190 at its right-angle turn 18 miles north of Furnace Creek, and continue to the village of Stovepipe Wells (7 miles farther) where there is a motel, store, and gas station. Watch the House Sparrows in the parking lot fly up under your vehicle's grill so they can pick insects off the radiator. Although not a good birding spot normally, ignore it at your peril during migration. Many species of eastern vagrants have been found here, and waterbird surprises occasionally occur. Birders once found a Least Bittern wandering the broken center-line on Highway 190 here—you just never know. Bird the Tamarisks and shrubs around the motel for migrants. There is a settling pond about 300 yards northeast of the gas station. There is a multi-strand wire fence atop the berm surrounding it. When the ponds (there are two) were improved recently, excess dirt was piled along the berm on the western edge. Climb to the top of the dirt pile and scan the ponds; they are small enough that this can be done quickly. Ducks, gulls, and shorebirds are usually seen here, as the seasons dictate. If there are only a few birds around you will be able to bird Stovepipe Wells in ten minutes, although you may want to linger in the shade with a cold drink before the 45-minute drive north to the next stop.

Leaving Stovepipe Wells, retrace your steps east to the road turning north (7.1), following the signs up the valley toward Scottys Castle. Turn left here and settle in for the drive north (32.9 miles) to the Mesquite Spring turn-off. By now it will be quite warm, a good time to be out of the sun in an air-conditioned car. During the 1970s when a hard core of California birders ran this route every Memorial Day weekend (usually without air-conditioning), they played a game: "how many species will we see on the drive from Stovepipe to Scottys?" Two species formed the base number, Common Raven and Horned Lark. Beyond that, it was sparse. Very low numbers (the term "on the fingers of one hand" comes to mind) often won. Make your own prediction before starting out.

Take the turn-off to **Mesquite Spring** campground on the left (32.9); drive down the gentle slope to the small natural oasis adequately described by its name. Park in the shade and bird around the mesquites. The draw here is the same as elsewhere in the valley—the possibility of migrants at an oasis in the midst of desolation. One never knows, on driving in, what will be there. California's first record of Varied Bunting was found here in November 1977.

Leave Mesquite Spring; return to the main road and turn left (north). Follow this road as it turns east into the lower reaches of Grapevine Canyon (0.5), and continue to **Scottys Castle** (2.9). You are now at 3,000 feet elevation, having climbed gradually since leaving Stovepipe Wells; but it is still warm—or worse. Relax on the lawn under the cottonwoods, a good place for a mid-day siesta. If you're curious enough to pay the entry fee, now would be a good time to tour the castle; it's cooler inside and birding will improve in mid-afternoon. There is a small restaurant, gift shop, and gas station here, but no lodging is available.

Bird the willows along the small stream just below the castle grounds, the lawn and cottonwoods by the parking lot, and the tangle of mesquite, Catclaw, and other growth along the stream above the parking lot. Chukars are sometimes seen nearby in morning or evening as they come down the rocky slopes to the stream. Watch for rattlers; birders have encountered the unusually aggressive, highly venomous Mojave Rattlesnake here. This particular species of rattlesnake has no sense of humor.

Park administration occasionally succumbs to an impulse to tidy the rank desert plantlife upstream from the castle, cleaning out the undergrowth. This is unfortunate for migrants and breeding species alike, who depend on the cover and its abundant insect life. During winter 1997–1998 the Park Service yielded to this temptation, thus despoiling nesting habitat for the endangered "Least" Bell's Vireo. Once the habitat restores itself, looking hopelessly untidy, the upstream tangle will be a fine place for birds and birding again.

If you find the castle area has lots of birds, you may profit by driving farther up the canyon and parking where you can to bird the small mesquite thicket that winds upcanyon a short distance. Passerine migrants are occasionally abundant here. Even farther upcanyon, in the narrows, Chuckwallas (large, flattish, prehistoric-looking lizards) are often seen sunning themselves on flat rocks.

On finishing your birding of Scottys Castle you can retrace your route, possibly to lodgings at Furnace Creek one hour south, or you may want to continue north through Nevada, west to the Owens Valley and eastern Sierra Nevada, or return to Southern California.

In any case, you may choose to leave the park through Towne Pass (El. 4,956 ft) on Highway 190 west of Stovepipe Wells. If so, stop briefly to bird the sparse Tamarisks at Emigrant Campground before continuing on. Stop at Panamint Springs, a tiny settlement in the north end of Panamint Valley just west of the junction of Highway 190 and Panamint Valley Road to bird the ornamental plantings for migrants (a good practice in any desert oasis during migration).

If you choose to leave through the eastern entrance to Death Valley Junction, and drive from there south to Baker and the Mojave National Preserve route, be sure to stop at the Tecopa marshes described on page 93 en route.

Furnace Creek Ranch is approximately 113 miles north of Baker, 176 miles north of Barstow, 40 miles southwest of Beatty, Nevada, and 106 miles east of Lone Pine. It is a 3½-hour drive from Mojave in the Eastern Kern County Loop. There are facilities at these locations as well as in Death Valley. Campgrounds in Death Valley National Park include those at Furnace Creek, Mesquite Spring, and Emigrant, and in the Panamint Mountains at Wildrose, Thorndike, and Mahogany Flat.

The Southeastern California RBA and the web site (see pages 14-15 in the Introduction) regularly reports rarities known to be in Death Valley and the surrounding region.

The **Panamint Mountains** are starkly beautiful. Although they exceed 11,000 feet at Telescope Peak, their position east of the Sierra Nevada places the Panamints in the rain shadow. The Panamints leach as much water as they can out of the remnant clouds reaching them, but still receive little precipitation. They therefore boast only xeric forests on their heights—composed primarily of Pinyon Pines with Bristlecone Pines, as well, on the higher slopes. Characteristic resident birds here include Northern Flicker, Hairy Woodpecker, Common Raven, Western Scrub-Jay, Pinyon Jay, Clark's Nutcracker, Mountain Chickadee, Mountain Bluebird, and Dark-eyed Junco.

Although not a birding hotspot, the Panamints make a pleasant side trip. The view of Death Valley from Mahogany Flat Campground and the trail to Telescope Peak is spectacular. Travel here at any season but winter, when it can be bitterly cold. A lone road gets you into the Panamints. It can be reached at its junction with the Panamint Valley Road, 14.4 miles south of its junction with Highway 190, or from Emigrant Canyon's intersection with Highway 190 near the Emigrant Campground. This is a slow road in many places, with hairpin turns and steep grades, not recommended for trailers. Watch for feral burros on the road. It will take most of a full day to explore this route—longer if you hike the 14-mile round-trip trail to Telescope Peak.

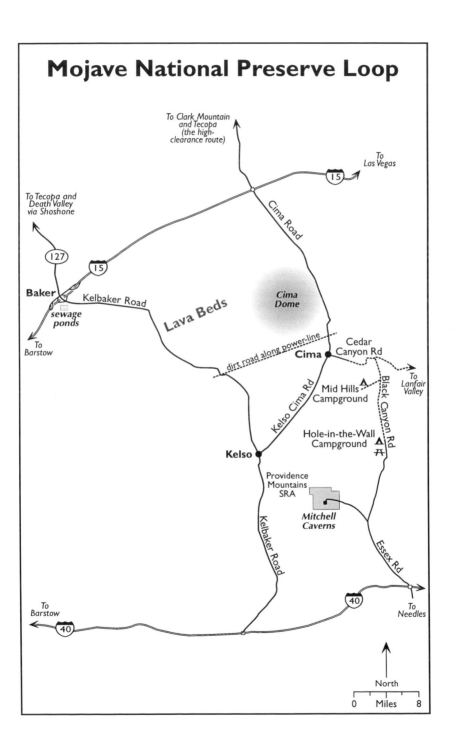

Mojave National Preserve Loop

To Clark Mountain and Tecopa (the high-clearance route)

To Las Vegas

15

Cima Road

To Tecopa and Death Valley via Shoshone

127

15

Baker

Kelbaker Road

Lava Beds

Cima Dome

sewage ponds

To Barstow

dirt road along power-line

Cima

Cedar Canyon Rd

To Lanfair Valley

Kelso Cima Rd

Mid Hills Campground

Black Canyon Rd

Hole-in-the-Wall Campground

Kelso

Providence Mountains SRA

Mitchell Caverns

Kelbaker Road

Essex Rd

To Barstow

40

40

To Needles

North

0   Miles   8

MOJAVE NATIONAL PRESERVE LOOP

This route, with the exception of the town of Baker ("Radiator Hose Capital of California"), is contained within the Mojave National Preserve. The preserve was established in 1994 by act of Congress, encompassing an area of some 1.4 million acres. Within this area are desert mountain ranges, enough geological forms to astonish even the seasoned traveler, and a few birds with unusually local populations in Southern California. Species of special interest along this loop include Ladder-backed Woodpecker, Gilded Flicker, Juniper Titmouse, Bendire's and Le Conte's Thrashers, Black-throated Sparrow, and Scott's Oriole. The Baker sewage ponds add an aquatic note to the day that appears somewhat incongruous when attached to the list above.

The Joshua Tree forest in the vicinity of Cima, eastern San Bernardino County, is the largest in the world. It is also one of the most beautiful segments of desert in California. This birding route is a classic loop, starting and ending in Baker after approximately 140 miles of desert travel. The tour starts at 1,000 feet elevation in Baker among creosote bush and reaches its highest point at 5,500 feet in Mid Hills Campground amidst a pinyon/juniper forest. The route traverses Cima Dome, an unusually symmetrical granite feature of approximately 75 square miles. It then enters the campgrounds in the Mid Hills between the Providence and New York mountain ranges before turning southwest to Kelso. The return to Baker along the western edge of a field of more than thirty young (only 1,000 years old) volcanic cinder cones tours a remarkable geological landscape.

The geology along this route is varied, rugged, and beautiful to behold. Much of it is volcanic in origin, although Cima Dome is a batholith (formed and cooled deep within the earth's crust), and the Providence Mountains forming the backdrop east of Kelso are made of limestone. The loop is a scenic tour as well as being rewarding to the birder. Mid-April through May is the best time to bird this area; the breeding birds are all singing and active, migrants are coming through, and wildflowers are blooming. There are many nearby sites that are interesting as well, and these will be noted below.

Observe the normal desert precautions—temperatures can exceed 100 degrees in late spring and summer. You will need to consume at least a gallon of water a day while birding in this weather. Carry more water in the car than you think you can reasonably need, and start with a full gasoline tank;

89

there are no services anywhere on the loop after leaving Interstate 15. Stop at the Mojave Desert Information Center (760/733-4040) under "The World's Tallest Thermometer" (it may be best not to look) on the Baker strip. The Park Service employee behind the counter will have up-to-date information about the area, as well as campground information and a free map. There is also an informative selection of books available.

Although the tour can be driven in a day, we suggest that you arrange your timing in such a way as to be in the Joshua Tree forest in the morning to get the full benefit of birding this wonderful habitat. From here you can proceed higher into Mid Hills Campground to bird the pinyon/juniper woodland in later morning, if you have not camped there overnight. However you approach it, morning in the Joshua Trees is a must. For the sake of organization and description we will start in Baker.

Start on the south side of the overpass of Interstate 15 in Baker where Highway 127 and Kelbaker Road connect. Looking toward the southwest corner of Kelbaker Road and Interstate 15, you will see impoundments surrounded by a chain-link fence. These are the **Baker sewage ponds**. They must be birded from outside the fence, but this is possible. Walk the east edge, scanning the near, lower pond as you go. There are four, higher ponds in the southern part of the complex. Bird these from the south edge where the elevated ground gives you a view. Various common ducks will be seen here in winter, and spring and fall migrations can bring a real surprise among the regular migrant Western and Least Sandpipers—birds like Whimbrel or Sanderling deserve a call to the RBA due to their out-of-range location. Eared Grebe, Killdeer, Black-necked Stilt, Yellow-headed Blackbird, and Great-tailed Grackle are likely to be seen.

Drive east on Interstate 15 to Cima Road (26.8), exiting and turning south. You will quickly start a gradual ascent of the eastern segment of Cima Dome which crests at 5,000 feet before descending toward Cima. As you drive across the dome watch for Bendire's Thrasher teed up among the Joshua Trees and creosote bushes. Le Conte's Thrasher also occurs here, and either thrasher can be anywhere along this road, as can Ladder-backed Woodpecker, Gilded Flicker, Black-throated Sparrow, and Scott's Oriole. Common birds likely at roadside include Red-tailed Hawk, American Kestrel, Mourning Dove, Loggerhead Shrike, and House Finch. You need to keep in mind the fact that Northern Flicker is present here also, so look carefully at any flicker you see; the wing-linings on a flying bird are, of course, a dead give-away.

You will notice as you drive that there are numerous private in-holdings in Mojave National Preserve. Cattle grazing, mining, and hunting are permitted in the Preserve. Heed all "no trespassing" signs.

About a mile north of Cima, giant high-tension power-lines cross the road from east to west. A dirt road (16.7) leads off to the right on the south side of these lines, extending for many miles to the west beside them. The road is driveable by a vehicle with a decent ground clearance; it traverses classic

Joshua Tree forest away from the main road (which may be unimportant; the "main road" has little traffic). All the birds noted for Cima Dome may be found along this road, best in the first 7 to 8 miles. You will have to go through two wire gates soon after leaving the highway. *Be sure to close all gates you open after passing through—this is cattle country.*

If you take this side road, on your return turn right to Cima (essentially a little ghost town with post office and small store of uncertain hours), and turn right again at the "intersection" (1.2) onto the Kelso Cima Road. You are still in thrasher country, so watch carefully as you parallel the railroad track toward Kelso.

Take the Cedar Canyon Road on the left (4.7), gaining altitude as you drive east to the Mid Hills. The road becomes dirt after the first few miles. The habitat is the same as on Cima Dome, with the same bird possibilities. The road is rough, but wide, and of generally good quality. Although it would be possible to pull a trailer here, it would severely try its ability to store crockery without damage—a better example of washboard will be found nowhere in this guide.

Continue on the Cedar Canyon Road until you come to the Black Canyon Road on the right (6.2). Turn right onto Black Canyon Road. You will climb in open juniper country to the right turn (2.9) toward the **Mid Hills Campground** turn-off. Drive the two miles to the campground and park. The campground is carved into a pinyon/juniper forest at 5,500 feet elevation and is much cooler than the lowlands. Although you may see Pinyon Jay and Black-throated Gray Warbler here, the primary bird of interest is Juniper Titmouse, recently split from the Plain Titmouse complex. If you are camping in the area from May through September, this is the place to camp. Its altitude and shade make this much the coolest place along the route, although the availability of water in the campground is sporadic.

Leaving Mid Hills Campground, return to Black Canyon Road, turning right toward Hole-in-the-Wall Campground (5.4), where the road returns to pavement. Hole-in-the-Wall is at 4,500 feet elevation, exposed to sunlight until late afternoon. It makes a good winter and early spring campsite, but will be too hot during the remainder of the year. Continue past Hole-in-the-Wall on Black Canyon Road for a short distance to the Hole-in-the-Wall picnic area, visible from the road. The "hole-in-the-wall'" is a picturesque defile cut through the volcanic ridge behind the picnic area parking lot; it is worth a look and, for the adventurous, a climb-through to Banshee Canyon, using the steel rings set in the rock. White-throated Swift, Ash-throated Flycatcher, Rock Wren, Bushtit, Black-throated Sparrow, and Scott's Oriole are included among its list of breeding birds, while Crissal Thrasher also is reputed to be in the area.

You can continue south along the paved road to the desert floor west of the Providence Mountains if you wish. Le Conte's Thrashers nest among the cholla cactus in the area. Mitchell Caverns, approximately 13 road miles southwest in the

Providence Mountains are a picturesque series of limestone caves, administered by the California Park Service. Continuing farther south you will come to Interstate 40 about 17 miles south of Hole-in-the-Wall.

Return north on Black Canyon Road to Cedar Canyon, turning left (west) to rejoin the Kelso Cima Road. Turn left toward Kelso. The next 14.5 miles to Kelso can produce Bendire's and Le Conte's Thrashers teed up in the morning. Kelso itself used to have a leaking water tower near the old Union Pacific railroad station, attracting migrants in spring and fall—including eastern vagrants. The tower, alas, is no longer and the generally dry nature of this small community (no services) is not very attractive to migrants these days. Maybe the long-rumored remodeling of the railroad station will one day occur along with ornamental plantings and a watered lawn. When (and if) that day comes, "Kelso" will reappear attached to rarities records for the California Bird Records Committee.

If you turn south at the three-way junction in Kelso, in 21 miles you will reach Interstate 40.

Turn north on the Kelbaker Road for the 35-mile drive back to Baker at Interstate 15. As you gradually ascend the land north of Kelso you will have a magnificent view of the rugged western face of the Providence Mountains to the east. If you look to the north you will see the graceful arc of Cima Dome's highest point beyond a small range to the left. On reaching the crest of Kelbaker Road, the road begins a long, gradual downslope toward Baker. As you drive you will skirt the edge of a few of the 65 lava flows in the large lava field, a land of Prairie Falcon and Common Raven.

Baker is about 50 miles south of the Tecopa marshes (see following page) and 113 miles south of Furnace Creek Ranch, Death Valley National Park. It has all the services a traveler needs.

TECOPA – INYO COUNTY

If your birding route includes Highway 127 between Baker and Death Valley Junction, the eastern gateway to Death Valley National Park, you should take a quick side-trip to the Tecopa Marshes. (See location map on page 80.) The tiny town of Tecopa, formed around mineral hot springs, offers little in the way of services—it is essentially a desert get-away for a hardy few—but an impressive marsh forms west of town. There is virtually no passerine habitat in the vicinity.

The marshes can be sampled from the northern access road approaching town from Highway 127, 63 miles south of Furnace Creek Ranch. Drive into town (notice the large wooden cut-outs of Red-headed Woodpeckers in some of the yards—if you see the real thing, shoot up a flare!), turning into the small private campground on the right. Drive to the back and you will see the Tecopa "sewage lagoon" behind a chain-link fence. Bird this small pond, which produces wintering and migrant ducks and, occasionally, a selection of migrant shorebirds. You may work your way out to the marshes from here.

The Tecopa area has produced vagrants on occasion; on surveying this remote location one suspects that more rarities would be reported given better coverage. It is truly an oasis.

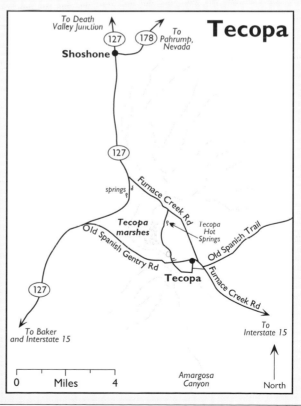

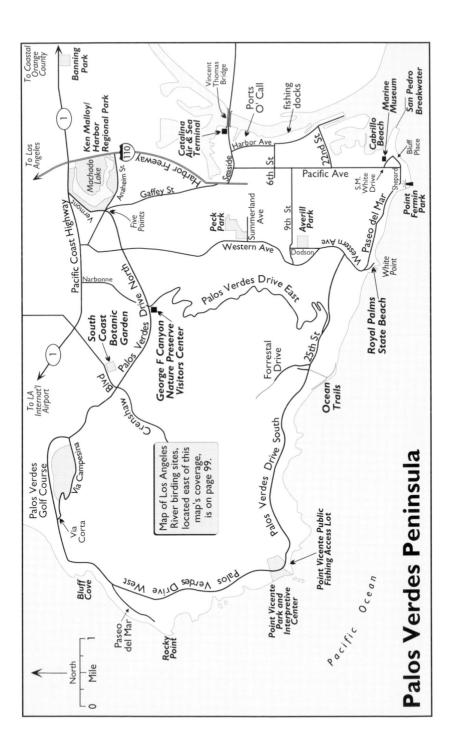

Palos Verdes Peninsula

Map of Los Angeles River birding sites, located east of this map's coverage, is on page 99.

PALOS VERDES PENINSULA

by Martin Byhower

The Palos Verdes Peninsula is famous for its scenic coastline and beautiful homes and, as birders discover it, it becomes famous for its birds as well. Much of the original native habitat has been lost to past grazing practices and suburban development, but several ongoing and successful restoration efforts are bringing back representative, albeit small, samples of the coastal sage scrub, coastal bluff, vernal marsh, and willow-riparian communities. It also appears that some of the native birds are beginning to recover. Meanwhile, extensive planting of exotic shrubs and trees has greatly increased the number and variety of small land birds, and the geography of the peninsula contributes to the great diversity of avian life found here, particularly during fall migration and winter. Local birders know that "The Hill" and the surrounding coastal lowlands are species-rich and vastly under birded secrets in Los Angeles County where, at one time or another, virtually anything can and eventually does show up.

Much of the Palos Verdes area was once one of Southern California's offshore channel islands and, biologically, it maintains a closer affinity with them than with other nearby mountain ranges. The peninsula is now separated from the Santa Monica and San Gabriel Mountains, not by water but by the highly urbanized Los Angeles basin. The island of Palos Verdes first emerged between 1 and 2 million years ago. It joined the mainland relatively recently, at the end of the last ice age, between 10 and 20 thousand years ago, as the Los Angeles basin filled with debris from the erosion of the nearby Transverse Ranges. Afterwards, defying gravity, it underwent further uplift even as sea level rose following the ice age.

Whether or not portions were ever previously connected to the mainland, organisms that were stranded on the island and/or colonized it later were isolated from the mainland long enough for new species and subspecies to diverge. Some species that might be expected in this habitat, such as Wrentit, Oak Titmouse, and California Thrasher, seem unwilling to cross the Los Angeles basin in order to inhabit the area (can you blame them?).

Isolation has its benefits, as well. Perhaps the non-migratory *sedentarius* race of Allen's Hummingbird evolved on the island of Palos Verdes; it continues its dispersal to surrounding areas even today. In any case, the Palos Verdes Peninsula may be the only area where the Allen's is as common a

95

resident as Anna's Hummingbird. In winter, check the abundant flowering eucalyptus planted throughout the area. Year round, Allen's can be found easily in the local canyons and parks and in residential neighborhoods at any nectar-rich flowers or sugar-water feeders.

The Palos Verdes area hosts the resident, rather dull (but endearing) channel island *sordida* subspecies of Orange-crowned Warbler. Based upon subtle variations in plumage and call or song, some meticulous observers believe that we probably also have our "own" versions of Pacific-slope Flycatcher, Spotted Towhee, and possibly others, as well. But it is the excellent assortment of fall migrants and vagrants that really draws the binocular-toting crowds.

The Palos Verdes Peninsula also hosts an eclectic group of stable breeding populations of exotics. Spotted Doves, Peafowl, and Mitred Parakeets are locally abundant. Yellow-chevroned Parakeets seem to be replacing the closely-related White-winged Parakeet. Only the doves are countable by ABA standards.

An excellent starting point for observing a representative sample of Southern California species as well as some regionally scarce specialties is **Ken Malloy/Harbor Regional Park**. Through the years over 300 species have been documented here—a very large number for such a small area! Much of the habitat has been and continues to be degraded, but ongoing preservation and restoration efforts are helping somewhat. Start at the intersection of Pacific Coast Highway (Highway 1) and the Harbor Freeway (Interstate 110). Go northwest on Pacific Coast Highway, turning left (south) at the traffic light onto Vermont Avenue (0.5). Pull into the first lot on the left (quickly pass the harmless but eager undocumented day-laborers at the semi-official pickup work station at the lot entrance). Park where the lot curves around to the right, paralleling Pacific Coast Highway.

A walk eastward along the (remaining) riparian forest (the "north-end willows" as locals call them) can turn up excellent vagrants during late fall migration into the winter, and sometimes in late spring, as well. Earlier in the morning is best here. Try to locate the warbler/Bushtit flock(s) and then seek out the unusual members. Residents in the willows here include a few Allen's Hummingbirds, Downy Woodpecker, the Palos Verdes race of Orange-crowned Warbler, California Towhee, and other species. Many years a Plumbeous Vireo winters in the area. Yellow Warblers, Bullock's Orioles, and maybe a few Swainson's Thrushes still nest here in season.

To continue, walk or drive parallel to **Machado Lake** southward along Vermont Avenue. (You can choose to walk the length of the lake or leapfrog to the succeeding parking lots along the west shore.) There are always a few grebes, ducks, gulls, and shorebirds visible from this area southward to the dam/spillway, and the numbers increase significantly in winter. This can be a good area to pick up Mew, Glaucous-winged, and (usually juvenile) Thayer's Gulls, especially after mid-November, as well as the more common gull species. Watch out for the Western x Glaucous-winged hybrids which show up frequently. Be sure to scan the groups of feral geese and ducks for surprisingly easy-to-miss individuals like Brant, Ross's Goose, Wood Duck, and the like. In late May, check this area at dusk for Black Swift and other unusual migrants.

Search the tules on your side as well as on the opposite shore for Sora, Common Moorhen, Marsh Wren, Song Sparrow, Red-winged and Tricolored Blackbirds, and other marsh birds. Tricoloreds often segregate by sex and/or age, but there are usually at least a few around. The very-dark-bellied females are sometimes less difficult to separate from the Red-winged Blackbirds than the juveniles or males. Unfortunately, Great-tailed Grackles have been taking the area by storm lately, threatening the regionally endangered nesting wetland species.

In late spring and summer the south end of Machado Lake is one of the best locations in Los Angeles County to look for Least Bitterns. Look for them in the tules along the east shore or flying across the lake. Better yet, park in the lot closest to Anaheim Street and Vermont Avenue and walk out along the spillway. (The author currently leads regular birding and nature walks for the Palos Verdes/South Bay Audubon Society from this location at 8 AM on the second Sunday of each month.) Standing along the dam in the morning or at dusk in June and July affords an excellent opportunity to spot Least Bittern, as well as Least Terns teaching their young to fish for the Mosquitofish stocked in the lake. During winter and migration this is also an excellent place to spot a variety of herons, egrets, ducks, and other waterbirds on the lake; sparrows and warblers frequent the weedy bushes below the dam.

Continuing across the dam, follow the trail next to the lake around to the left. *Do not walk up onto the adjacent golf course.* You will be harassed and threatened by the management, taking some of the fun out of dodging errant golf balls or coming up with witty replies to golfers' off-the-wall comments.

A less stressful option is to go back the way you came and head south from the west side of the spillway, then east around the bend, entering an area of dirt trails bordering the seasonally-inundated lower wetlands. Trails then loop through Camp Machado, an occasionally productive area composed mostly of non-native trees and shrubs.

Note: Past editions of this guide have warned about the possibility of encountering gangs and unsavory individuals here. This is an unlikely scenario. There is some reason for caution both here and at Banning Park, but birding in the morning or afternoon, especially when accompanied by a partner, is probably a safe bet here or nearly anywhere else in Southern California. The best advice is to be wary but friendly at these locations. You may opt to skip this part if you feel at all vulnerable.

In fall bird **Banning Park** for migrants. This park ranks among the best fall vagrant havens in California. Better yet, since wind, park patrons, and mariachis kick up by mid-morning, go here before you visit Harbor Park. Many Southern California birders have seen their life eastern vireos, warblers, tanagers, and more here. It is also a good place to hone your skills in identifying an assortment of *Empidonax* flycatchers.

To reach Banning Park, drive east on Pacific Coast Highway from the corner of Vermont Avenue to Eubank Street (2.0), turn right, then right again on Robidoux, and execute a quick right into the park. Bird the entire park (less than 0.25 square mile), which can be dead one day and hopping with birds the next. The best bet is to check out the tree where you find the omnipresent local birders. The flowering eucalyptus, ash, and Siberian Elm trees along the channel on the west perimeter are often good, as are the carob trees on the east perimeter. Fruiting ficus on the Pacific Coast Highway-side by the rose garden are often loaded with Western Tanagers and Black-headed Grosbeaks during migration; in this general area, a Yellow-green Vireo shows up almost annually. If you arrive early on a warm day, after the sprinklers have shut off, the ponds and puddles along the pathways throughout the park will be hopping with bathing birds. If you have a chance, check out this park on several successive days because the lineup of avian players can change daily.

If you're visiting during shorebird migration (which begins in earnest in mid-to-late July) and wish to catch an excellent peep show, head from Banning Park over to the nearby **Los Angeles River** (yes, we still call it a river, despite conflicting efforts to further entomb it in concrete versus restore it to something beautiful and useful once again). Continue east another 2 miles on Pacific Coast Highway to the Long Beach (710) Freeway and drive north about 4 miles to Del Amo Street. Take the East exit across the river to the first right (Oregon Avenue) and park in the residential area across from the religious school (read the parking signs to avoid street-sweeper-day viola-tions). Walk back (west) along the chain-link fence, down the hill, and then up to the pathway along the east edge of the levee. The birding is best from here southward for about one-half mile to where Compton Creek enters into the channel. Morning is best from this side, since you will be looking toward the west.

Among the hundreds to thousands of Western and Least Sandpipers that begin to arrive in July, try to pick out the much rarer Semipalmated, Baird's, and Pectoral Sandpipers, all of which regularly occur here (late August and September) in small numbers. Semipalmated Plovers, Greater and Lesser Yellowlegs, Long-billed and Short-billed Dowitchers (the former dominate in August, the latter in September), and other waders are regular here. Peri-odically an Osprey may fly over or a marauding Peregrine Falcon may swoop down to snack on a peep (or to merely harass the flocks to show who's boss).

Uncommon species like Franklin's or Glaucous Gulls (see seasonal status in the bar-graphs) can also show up along this and nearby stretches of the Los Angeles River, particularly at another good spot south of here: the **Willow Street crossing**. Willow Street should be checked year round,

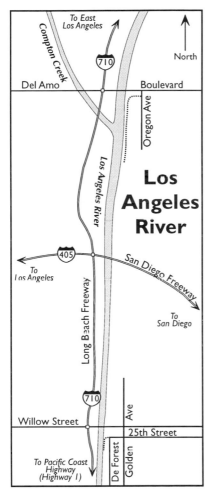

because something interesting is nearly always present if you look hard enough. Retrace your drive back about 3 miles south to the first exit north of Pacific Coast Highway, and take the Willow Street East off-ramp. Cross the river, turning right onto the first street, Golden Avenue. Immediately turn right onto 25th Street, parking a block away at its intersection with DeForest. Walk up the embankment and bird along the river for about 100 yards southward. Depending on the season, and whether or not the county crews have scraped the channel bottom recently, you can see a good-sized flock of Blue-winged Teal and other ducks, American Avocets and Black-necked Stilts (both of which may nest here in June and July), a good assortment of egrets, herons, gulls, terns, plovers, and many of the species seen at the previous site. Watch the weedy areas along the banks here and at Del Amo for Blue Grosbeak, Lazuli Bunting, and maybe even a Bobolink in fall.

Harbor Park is central to many of the other good birding spots in the area. If, instead of chasing vagrants, you choose to look for species of the coastal sage scrub and riparian canyon communities, George F Canyon is a great place to visit. You will see many of the same birds that occur at the South Coast Botanic Garden, but more of them, in a more natural habitat, without paying a fee.

The **South Coast Botanic Garden** (fee) is a good place to pick up some migrants in fall and spring and a few odd vagrants in late fall and winter. There are regularly-scheduled bird walks on the first Sunday and third Wednesday of the month at 8 AM. However, the plants and habitat are limited due in part to problems related to the botanic garden's location on a shifting, out-gassing landfill. If the gift shop is open, you can pick up the checklist of the large number of birds that have visited in the past, but don't expect to see more than 10 to 20 percent of the species on the list at any one time. To get to the South Coast Botanic Garden from the 5-way intersection (Five Points) at the southwest corner of Harbor Park, where Anaheim Street, Gaffey, Vermont, and Palos Verdes Drive North all come together, head west (uphill) on Palos Verdes Drive North to Crenshaw Boulevard (3.5), then go right to the South Coast Botanic Garden entrance on the right (0.3).

George F Canyon is closer to Harbor Park. From the Five Points Intersection (see above) take Palos Verdes Drive North west to its intersection with Palos Verdes Drive East (1.8). Go left (south) on Palos Verdes Drive East and immediately park on the right (on the southwestern corner of the intersection) at the delightful George F Canyon Nature Preserve Visitors Center (restrooms, bookstore; open weekends only) or drive to the main trailhead of Lower George F Canyon (0.1). Pick up a trail guide at the kiosk on the trailhead and head up this lovely riparian canyon, home of the only significant perennial stream on the peninsula.

Because of the water and the fact that the canyon faces northward, the local habitat is uncharacteristically green and lush for this dry region. Hike the entire trail (0.75 mile) for an excellent introduction to the local botany and geology as well as the birds. During migration, this is a good area for Pacific-slope and Ash-throated Flycatchers, Warbling Vireo, most of the western warblers, and Black-headed Grosbeak. Phainopepla, Swainson's Thrush, and some of the previously-mentioned migrants breed in this canyon and the upstream watershed. In winter look for Red-shouldered Hawk, Anna's and Allen's Hummingbirds, Downy Woodpecker, Northern Flicker, Western Scrub-Jay, Bewick's Wren, Ruby-crowned Kinglet, Blue-gray Gnatcatcher, Hermit Thrush, Orange-crowned, Yellow-rumped, and Townsend's Warblers, Common Yellowthroat, Spotted and California Towhees, "Sooty" Fox Sparrow, and Song, Golden-crowned, and White-crowned Sparrows. At the top of the trail watch for White-throated Swift and swallows as well as for soaring hawks.

From the Lower George F trailhead, take Palos Verdes Drive East south to Palos Verdes Drive South (6.2); this road parallels the cliffs on the south part of the peninsula, giving you access to the coast at various places. You can choose to go right to Forrestal Canyon and the Ocean Trails area, or to go left (east) to visit Royal Palms State Beach/White Point, and then either head north up Western Avenue to Averill and Peck Parks or continue east to Point Fermin Park, Cabrillo Beach, and Vista Vizcaino.

To bird **Forrestal Canyon**, turn right onto Palos Verdes Drive South, drive 0.7 mile to Forrestal Drive, and turn right, parking at the gate at the end of the road.

This area has been mined and was slated for development, but due to the extraordinary efforts of the Palos Verdes Peninsula Land Conservancy and some wise decision-making by the city of Rancho Palos Verdes, this unique gem seems safe from development for now (alas, however, not the area on the coastal side of Palos Verdes Drive South). The best time to visit here is in spring, in the early morning.

About 50 feet past the gate walk up a dirt road to the right. In spring, this is a great place to encounter the relatively docile Pacific Rattlesnake, so long pants, boots, and caution are advised. A year-round natural spring is about one-quarter mile up the road. You can listen for it but you won't actually see water since it descends back underground nearly as quickly as it emerges. The spring is located at the end of a crater-like depression, which locals call the Quarry Bowl. The cliffs, bottom of the bowl, and the spring are all good areas for California and Blue-gray Gnatcatchers (see discussion following), and for Allen's Hummingbird, Pacific-slope Flycatcher, Cactus (declining), Rock, and Bewick's Wrens, Rufous-crowned, Golden-crowned, and White-crowned Sparrows, and Spotted and California Towhees. The last covey(s) of California Quail on the peninsula (which, granted, may consist entirely of re-introduced birds at this point) come down to drink at the spring in the early morning and at dusk.

Walk back to the road and continue uphill, away from the gate. Watch along the cliffs for roosting Great Horned Owl, and also for White-throated Swift, Loggerhead Shrike, Costa's Hummingbird, and Lazuli Bunting in spring and summer. Where the road turns left, go straight onto a dirt path. This area and the top of a hill to your left are also good spots for birding and observing wildflowers, Miocene fossils, and some interesting metamorphic rocks and crystals.

By now you may have encountered a California Gnatcatcher. (If you haven't, read on to the next section.) Your first clue that the gnatcatcher you are watching isn't a Blue-gray is that the latter is absent from early March until late September. The best field mark is actually the call: the California's is a rising, then dropping, kitten-like mew, clearly different and less assertive than the speeeee call of the Blue-gray Gnatcatcher. The breeding male's black cap is a good mark. The brownish tinge occasionally visible on the wings and back on the California is absent on the Blue-gray. If you get a look at the undertail, that should be the clincher; the California's is almost entirely black, while the Blue-gray's is largely white. The Blue-gray's outer tail feathers show a good deal of white from the top, unlike the narrow or nearly absent white on the California. (For details on the tails of our gnatcatchers, see the illustrations above.) Of course, most of the Californias you find in this area have been tagged, so unless you have a new recruit, check for colored ankle ornaments.

The Palos Verdes Peninsula represents virtually the northwestern-most limit of the California Gnatcatcher's range (a few were discovered recently in Ventura County). The California Gnatcatcher inhabits arid late-successional and climax sage scrub in gullies, canyons, lower slopes, and washes. This habitat is being nearly eliminated locally even as these words are being written.

Granted, developers have been required to preserve and restore narrow strips or small blocks of habitat, but whether these will be extensive enough to provide buffering against nest predation and allow this isolated population

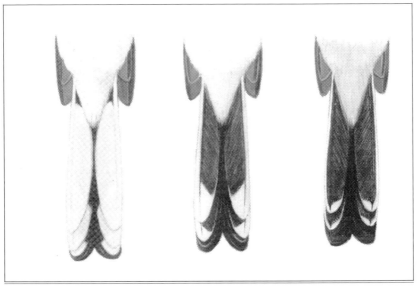

GNATCATCHER TAIL PATTERNS, FROM BELOW

left: Blue-gray Gnatcatcher, *Polioptila caerulea*

center: Black-tailed Gnatcatcher, *P. melanura lucida*

right: California Gnatcatcher, *P. californica*

Dunn, Jon L., and Kimball L. Garrett. 1987. The Identification of North America Gnatcatchers. *Birding:* Vol. XIX, No. 1, pages 17-29. Reproduced with the kind permission of the artist, Jonathan Alderfer.

a large enough gene pool to maintain adequate diversity is the subject of controversy. The number of breeding pairs of California Gnatcatchers seems to fluctuate significantly from year to year; ongoing studies have yet to determine the net impacts of habitat restoration versus overall habitat loss, but some fear that by the time we can say anything conclusive, it may be too late.

If restoration efforts compensate for habitat loss, the easiest place to find California Gnatcatchers, Cactus Wrens, and other coastal scrub specialties may continue to be along the coastal walking trails at the new **Ocean Trails** Development, which in 1998 was still under construction. Access is available now, and presumably will be in the future, from a gate at a dirt lot 0.1 mile west of Forrestal Drive on Palos Verdes Drive South, on the south side of the highway, opposite Conqueror Lane. Walk toward the coast and follow the trail in either direction. Check the remnant and restored stands of Lemonadeberry, Coast Sagebrush, Bush Sunflower, and both cactus species for the birds noted above as well as for Say's Phoebe, Western Scrub-Jay,

Loggerhead Shrike, Common Yellowthroat, both towhees, Song and Rufous-crowned Sparrows, and an occasional Blue Grosbeak (the latter have been breeding here in small numbers, but the development will probably exclude them). Of course, look above the cliffs for swifts and swallows and out over the water for Western and Clark's Grebes, Brown Pelican, California's three cormorants, and gulls, terns, and the occasional pelagic bird.

If you like, you can continue on to Point Vicente Park and Interpretive Center (4.0), where you can again look over the ocean for pelagic species, best in spring. This park was built in 1985 and serves mainly as a whale-watching area. (Gray Whales may be seen offshore between December and April.) The hours are 10 AM–5 PM, closed holidays. At dawn or dusk you can usually see or call in a Great Horned Owl at the adjacent lighthouse.

A better place to spot pelagic species, however, is the **Point Vicente Public Fishing Access Lot**, which overlooks the water just southeast of Point Vicente Park. This lot is always open, offers a public restroom, and you can scope offshore or at the cliffs behind you to your heart's content. Coming from the east/south along Palos Verdes Drive South, make a U-turn at Point Vicente Park (at this point, Palos Verdes Drive South changes name to Palos Verdes Drive West) and drive back 0.3 mile to the lot, which is on the seaward side of the highway. Hooded Orioles nest in the California Fan Palms at the east end of the park, and you might hear (and even see, if you use a scope) Cactus Wrens, California Gnatcatchers, and Rufous-crowned Sparrows behind you on the cliffs. During spring migration this is a great place to spot Western Kingbirds and other migrants.

You probably came here, however, for the excellent show of coastal and pelagic species offshore; if you arrive at the right time (especially in early morning) and season you will see remarkable numbers and diversity. The loon show alone is worth the trip: in addition to wintering birds look for large numbers of Red-throateds (late March to early April) Pacifics (mid-April through May), and Commons (early April to early May). In late summer through early spring, check for Black-vented Shearwaters just offshore (in winter it is possible to see up to 10,000 go by in a few hours). Also watch for Northern Fulmar (winter), Sooty and Pink-footed Shearwaters (late spring through early fall), Royal, Forster's (winter), Caspian, and Elegant Terns (spring and summer), Pomarine and Parasitic Jaegers, and phalaropes (spring migration). If you arrive early and look carefully, Xantus's Murrelets (mainly spring), Cassin's Auklet (year round), and Rhinoceros Auklet (winter) are all possibilities. Of course, check the flocks of Surf Scoters for White-wings and Blacks, and watch for marine mammals while you're at it. For hikers, there is a steep trail to the rocky beach below, which may in winter yield rocky-shore birds, but Royal Palms (see below) is a more accessible and reliable spot for all of these.

Return to the intersection of Forrestal Drive and Palos Verdes Drive South, then continue on until Palos Verdes Drive turns into 25th Street and intersects Western Avenue (2.3). Go right on Western Avenue toward the ocean. When Western Avenue ends (0.5), bear left onto Paseo del Mar. Go one block and make a sharp right turn down the hill to the **Royal Palms State Beach** on White Point (fee). Better yet, if you want to save some time and money, park on the cliff at the entrance, or, to avoid the fee, on either end of the entrance, and scope from the cliffs. At a bluff about 100 yards west of the entrance you can get an excellent view of all of the Southern California rocky-shore birds out on the rocks past the lifeguard tower or on the exposed rocks to the east. If you arrive at high tide you might find Black-bellied Plover, Black Oystercatcher, Surfbird, Wandering Tattler, Whimbrel, and both turnstones, not to mention all three cormorants, a variety of gulls, and more. For any of these that you miss, continue on Paseo del Mar, stopping along the way to scope the rocks.

About 1.6 miles past Royal Palms you arrive at Point Fermin Park in San Pedro. The over-trimmed trees are starting to grow back, and occasionally they can draw some interesting migrants. Anna's and Allen's Hummingbirds are common all year. Don't be surprised if you see some Mitred and Yellow-chevroned Parakeets flying around. On the cliffs below the lighthouse, you may find Double-crested, Brandt's, and Pelagic (winter) Cormorants. Black Oystercatchers are occasionally seen here.

From the park, turn right onto Shepard Street to Pacific Avenue and jog right to Bluff Place, which leads down the hill to Cabrillo Beach (0.6) (fee for parking, although you can park above the entrance and walk in for free). The free museum has fine marine exhibits. The main attraction here is the **San Pedro Breakwater**.

By walking the breakwater and the beach in early morning, you can find nearly all of the birds which frequent the inshore ocean and bays. This can be a great place to compare tern species on the buoys just offshore.

Pacific Golden-Plover and Black-bellied Plovers
Shawneen E. Finnegan

Heermann's, Ring-billed, California, and Western Gulls are abundant on the beach, and others often show up. Later in the morning the crowds and jet-skis inevitably disperse the birds. At dawn there is a good chance of seeing a few pelagic birds. They often come close to shore at night, but move out to sea as the boats leave the harbor. If you pay to drive in, or are up for a hefty walk, go past the disappointingly unproductive "restored estuary" just north of the museum, past the youth camp on the right, along Vista Vizcaino/Shoshonean Drive. In recent years, a fine assortment of migrating vagrants has stopped to rest and feed on the bluffs and in the little parkway on the west side of the road.

Another spot to check both for residents and migrants is **Peck Park**, also in San Pedro. From Averill Park, take Dodson north to 9th Street (0.2), then go west back to Western (0.4). Turn north onto Western Avenue to just past Summerland (0.8) to reach the park entrance on the right, and park either in the first lot on the right, or drive all the way to the east end of the entrance road, turn right, and park in the lot there. Either spot gives you good access to some very birdy habitat. There are trails on both sides of the canyon running through the center of the park, and these are worth walking for the usual assortment of resident species. The extensive plantings of trees, particularly the groves on the southwest and northwest ends, are excellent spots to turn up migrants and vagrants.

A generous local birder, David Moody, has compiled and will send you, free of charge, a checklist that includes many of the above areas, with the request that you send word of any additions back to him. Send a self-addressed stamped, legal-sized or larger envelope with US55 cents postage and your request to him at 315-B North Gertruda, Redondo Beach, CA 90277.

Good maps of the area include the Los Angeles/Orange County Thomas Guide and the AAA Metropolitan Los Angeles Southern Area map. There are no campgrounds along the Palos Verdes Peninsula route, but motels are abundant in the communities surrounding the peninsula.

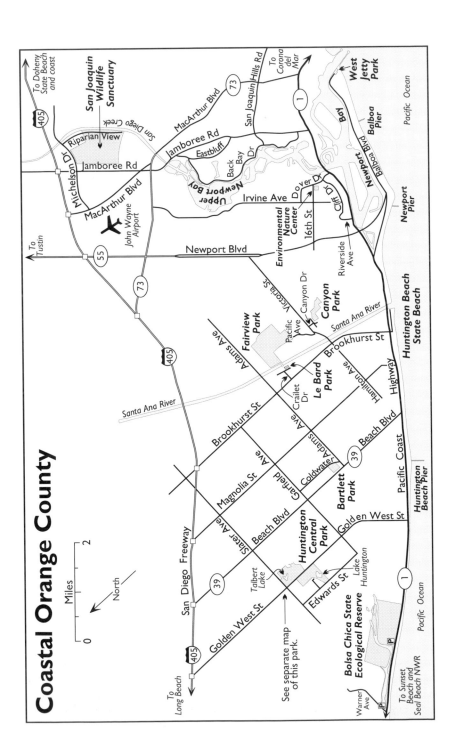

Coastal Orange County

COASTAL ORANGE COUNTY

by Sylvia Ranney Gallagher

Surprisingly, some excellent birding spots in Southern California are found right in the middle of the urban sprawl of coastal Orange County. Two coastal saltmarshes—Upper Newport Bay and Bolsa Chica State Ecological Reserves—are choice places to visit. San Joaquin (*wah-KEEN*) Wildlife Sanctuary has recently been recontoured and opened to the public. Since the birding world discovered its potential, Huntington Central Park has proven to be the best place in the county for rare-to-accidental passerines. Crystal Cove State Park is an excellent place for rocky coastline birds and also for birds more common in the foothills. If you're a gull fancier, as well as a rarity chaser, Doheny Beach State Park is also a must. Between these major stops are a number of smaller areas, which are worth a visit if you have time. If you are in the area on a business trip and have a few hours for some birding, the many locations below are spread among Orange County's business centers, providing opportunities for convenient birding adventures.

The starting place for this tour is the junction of Interstate 405 and Highway 55, located where the cities of Irvine, Santa Ana, and Costa Mesa come together, just north of the John Wayne Airport.

Drive southbound on I-405 to the Jamboree Road exit (1.5). Turn right at the end of the off-ramp; then, at the first signal (0.3), go left to Michelson Drive. Turn right at Riparian View (0.7) and stay on the creekside road to **San Joaquin Wildlife Sanctuary** (0.7), where Sea and Sage Audubon Society has its headquarters and bookstore (8 AM–4 PM daily except holidays). Valuable resources available for sale here include both an *Orange County Breeding Bird Atlas* (1996) and an Orange County status and distribution book (1996). A list of recent sightings at the sanctuary is posted on the porch, as well as the latest Orange County rarities.

In 1997 sanctuary ponds were recontoured and new trails established. As a result, the area currently (1998) looks rather barren, but has great potential as a wildlife area. Ponds hold a wide variety of shorebirds and waterfowl. White-faced Ibises are present all year, and this is a favorite wintering haunt of Black-necked Stilts and Long-billed Dowitchers. In late summer and early fall Pectoral, Baird's, and Semipalmated Sandpipers turn up with regularity, while Solitary and Stilt Sandpipers are less dependable. There are few spring migrant records of these species here.

Wintering waterfowl include Canada and Greater White-fronted Geese, Gadwall, Redhead, and Ring-necked Duck along with the more common Orange County wintering waterfowl. The sanctuary also has an extensive area of willows that should be especially productive during migrations.

To continue the route, retrace your way to northbound Interstate 405. Follow this to the Brookhurst Street exit (6.2). At the end of the off-ramp, turn right, then immediately left onto Slater Avenue. Follow this street west 2.9 miles. About 100 yards short of the traffic light at Golden West Street, turn left into the parking lot for **Huntington Central Park**.

This large city park is one of the few public parks in urban Orange County which has not been trimmed to within an inch of its life. It has lots of shrubs, willow clumps, weedy patches, and other places where birds can find cover. That is not to say that the City of Huntington Beach hasn't tried to tidy up the place, but public pressure keeps them from going too far in this endeavor.

Huntington Central Park is good just about any time of year, except perhaps in the heart of the summer. Spring and fall migrations bring all sorts of unusual species for a few days of rest and recuperation. Each winter a number of choice rarities stay several months. The official park bird list contains well over 200 species, including 16 flycatchers, 10 vireos, 36 warblers, and counting! A recent addition to the local avifauna, the introduced Nutmeg Mannikin, is sometimes encountered in grassy areas. These and other attractive little exotics are not countable.

As you walk south into the park, you will come to a large area choked with willows. In wet years, you will walk on the outskirts peering in. In dry years, when the water-table is low, you can enter the area and wander around. Sparrows, finches, and other seed-eaters are especially likely here. Continue south to an expanse of lawn with a small restaurant on the west side. Alder trees here have been good for warblers and other passerines. Still farther south is Talbert Lake, although it may look more like Talbert Green in dry years. If there is lots of water in the lake, wintering ducks and possibly even a loon may occur here. If the water level is low, expect shorebirds.

If you are birding here in a wet year, you will have to walk the trail around the south end of the lake, but if it is dry, you can cut across to the trees on the other side. Look them over for passerines, then continue on to the east.

The city library will be on your right. The trees in the large southeast section of the park have yielded many of the choicest birds over the years.

Be sure to check the bits of marsh in this area wherever they exist. Pied-billed Grebe and Common Moorhen nest here in wet years, and you might spot a Virginia Rail or Sora. The northeast corner of the park consists mainly of trails and Myoporum bushes which have been less productive than other areas. The trail through here finally brings you back to the parking lot.

To take in the rest of the park, return to your car and exit the parking lot, turning left. Drive west on Slater Avenue to Edwards Street (0.6) and turn left. Watch on your right for the small green Huntington Central Park sign, and turn left (0.4). Park in the lot at the end of the street (0.3).

At the north end of the parking lot is a well-marked trail leading to Shipley Nature Center (usually opens at 9 AM). This is worth a visit, especially if you're looking for Tricolored Blackbirds. The eucalyptus trees in the parking lot are home to resident Allen's Hummingbirds. This area has also proven good for warblers and other insectivores. Birders haunt this area during migration.

The pine grove well east of the parking lot is productive. Red-breasted Nuthatches are often found in winter, when Mountain Chickadees, Golden-crowned Kinglets, or Varied Thrushes are occasional visitors.

Lake Huntington, at the south end of the parking lot, usually has water even when Talbert Lake is dry. Check it for ducks; Wood Ducks are occasionally found. The cattails around the edge might harbor Yellow-headed or Tricolored Blackbirds.

The next important place to visit is **Bolsa Chica State Ecological Reserve**. Retrace your route almost back to your first parking lot at Huntington Central Park, but turn right onto Golden West Street. At Pacific Coast Highway (Highway 1) (3.0) turn right and drive up the coast to the second signal (2.5). Just beyond turn right into the little parking lot. (A second parking lot is 1.5 miles farther north just around the corner to the right on Warner Avenue. The first lot usually produces the best birding.)

Bolsa Chica is an estuary with saltmarsh, mudflats, and open water (and an upland mesa favored by hawks—slated for development). It is excellent at any time of year, but what has really put the place on the map is the colonization, starting in 1985, by hundreds of terns and Black Skimmers. Before that year only a few California Least Terns (endangered) nested there. Then, over a period of just four years, it became the breeding ground for Elegant, Forster's, Caspian, and Royal (few) Terns, as well as Black Skimmers. A Sandwich Tern arrived in the summer of 1995 and was also present 1996–1997—it mated with an Elegant Tern. So far the influx of the other species has not hurt the Least Terns, which continue to thrive.

Bolsa Chica is also home to a large number of "Belding's" Savannah Sparrows (*P. s. beldingi*). This endangered subspecies (California list only) is a permanent resident of the pickleweed (*Salicornia sp.*) of the saltmarsh.

The best way to tour Bolsa Chica is to take the 1.5-mile loop trail which starts in the parking lot. Most of the typical birds of a coastal estuary can be found. Many are the same species that may be seen more readily at Upper Newport Bay, but a few that are more easily seen here should be mentioned. During winter it is usually possible to find Clark's and Horned Grebes among the more common Western and Eared. Red-throated and Pacific Loons are sometimes present, although most loons will be Commons. Rarely, a Greater Scaup is found in the large raft of Lessers. Other somewhat regular waterfowl, good for Orange County, include Brant, White-winged Scoter (Surf is common), Common Goldeneye (Barrow's is accidental), and Common Merganser (Red-breasted is common). A wide variety of shorebirds is also present. Bolsa Chica may be somewhat better than Upper Newport Bay for Wilson's and Red-necked Phalaropes in July and August and for Red Knot and Lesser Yellowlegs (both rare) in winter when they are missing elsewhere.

Beyond the Bolsa Chica parking lot on Warner Avenue (1.5) are Sunset Beach and Seal Beach National Wildlife Refuge (2.0). There are lots of birds here, but access is currently restricted and it's hard to find a place from which to observe the birds. At present your best bet is to bird from Pacific Coast Highway. A few Pacific Golden-Plovers can usually be seen September–April.

Turn around and drive southeast on Pacific Coast Highway. The **Huntington Beach Pier** will be on your right 3.5 miles south of the Bolsa Chica parking lot with the loop trail. As with other piers, winter is best and you can look for loons, Western and Clark's Grebes, or scoters (usually only Surf) and other seabirds here. Northern Fulmar, Black-vented Shearwater, Oldsquaw, and Black-legged Kittiwake turn up once in a while—although the presence of a King Eider one winter shows the location's potential.

Turn left on Beach Boulevard 1.0 mile past the pier. Drive north to Adams Avenue (1.6) and turn right. At the first signal (0.1), turn left onto Coldwater Lane. Bartlett Park will be on your left. Park on the street near one of the inconspicuous gates in the fence, walking in to explore the mainly willow-riparian habitat for a variety of passerines. A Streak-backed Oriole was a sensation here the winter of 1996–1997.

Return to Adams Avenue and turn left, continuing to Brookhurst Street (1.9). Turn right onto Brookhurst, then left on Crailet Drive (0.4), then right onto Craimer Lane at the end of Crailet. You will quickly come to Le Bard Park. This tiny city park occasionally has rare land birds in the trees, but it is mainly recommended as an access point to the **Santa Ana River**. A bicycle bridge crosses the river here, allowing you to bird both sides easily. Look out for the bikes! They can be more dangerous than cars, because you can't hear them coming. It is possible to bike along the river 2.5 miles south to the ocean or 31 miles north to the Riverside County line.

The riverbed usually has some shallow pools of water which attract a variety of shorebirds and herons. **Fairview Park** across the river can be reached by crossing the river on the bike bridge. Walk north on the east side of the river about 100 yards past the apparently inaccessible footbridge over the flood-control channel, then double back to it on a parallel trail.

Most of Fairview Park is being kept natural, and new native plants have recently been put in. Look for California Gnatcatchers and Cactus Wrens (*C. b. sandiegensis*) on the cliff face, where coastal sage scrub is found. *Please note that playing taped calls to attract California Gnatcatcher is always inappropriate*—this species is endangered in California. When the sea breeze strikes the cliff face in the afternoon, hawks hang motionless in the updraft and can be observed at close range.

Another access point to the Santa Ana River can be reached by returning to Brookhurst Street and turning left. Go to Hamilton Avenue (1.1), turn left, then make an immediate right into the parking area behind the gas station. Walk up onto the bridge approach, then right onto the public bike trail. Here you can expect some of the same birds you saw near Le Bard Park. Among the flock of Bonaparte's Gulls which often rests here during October–May, rarities are sometimes found. Franklin's is most likely, but vagrant Black-headed and Little Gulls have also been seen. (The willow-riparian area across the river looks inviting, but birding there may be dangerous because of its transient *human* population. This area has been designated Talbert Park and will be opened in the future.)

To reach another access point for Fairview Park, turn right out of the parking lot onto Hamilton Avenue, cross the Santa Ana River (street name changes to Victoria Street), and turn left at the first signal, Pacific Avenue (0.5). Drive to the end of the street (0.5) and park. As soon as you enter the field ahead, you will be atop the bluff where hawks soar.

Return to the signal at Victoria Street and turn left, then right at the very next signal, Canyon Drive (0.1). Go two blocks to Sea Bluff Drive and park as close to the corner as you can. On your left, between the access road to the plant nursery and the driveway to the apartment complex, you will see a sign reading "No Vehicles Beyond This Point." This is the rear entrance to **Canyon Park**, another natural park in the City of Costa Mesa. The alder grove in front of you has the greatest birding potential, but the entire park is worth exploring. The alders are good for warblers, vireos, flycatchers, and other insectivores, especially during migration. This area also has hosted a large number of rarities.

Returning across the Santa Ana River to Brookhurst Street, drive south to Pacific Coast Highway (2.4). If you want to visit the mouth of the Santa Ana River, enter **Huntington Beach State Beach** at this point (the fee covers entry to all state parks visited on the same day), turn left, and drive as far as you can. Continue walking in the same direction to the river. On your right is a California Least Tern Sanctuary, active only during summer months. It has also attracted nesting Snowy Plovers. Return via the ocean shore and you can probably find Snowy Plovers any time of year.

Return to Pacific Coast Highway and turn right. Turn right onto Balboa Boulevard (1.7) and follow it onto the Balboa Peninsula. Here there are two more piers, the **Newport Pier** (1.1) and the **Balboa Pier** (1.6). Signs direct you to each one. Continue on to the end of the peninsula (1.3), bearing left at every Y-intersection. Park on the street and walk to West Jetty Park. From there you can view the entrance to Newport Harbor.

The entire peninsula should be avoided during the summer, especially on weekends, but the birding is best in the winter anyway. The expected birds are much the same as those listed for Huntington Beach Pier.

Retrace your route along Balboa Boulevard, but at the Newport Pier fork right onto Newport Boulevard. At Pacific Coast Highway (0.7), turn right (sign reads To San Diego). Turn left at the first signal light onto Riverside Avenue (0.4). At the stop sign at the top of the hill, continue straight ahead, now on Cliff Drive, to Irvine Avenue (0.5 from the highway). Turn left and go to 16th Street (0.6). Turn right and park in the second parking lot past the stadium (0.3), which belongs to the Newport-Mesa School District. Here you have access to the **Environmental Nature Center**, a gem of a spot established by the biology teachers at Newport Harbor High School. Plants from various California habitats attract a wide variety of birds.

To continue the tour, turn right out of the parking lot, then make an immediate right onto Dover Drive (0.1). At Pacific Coast Highway (0.4) turn left. Turn left again at Jamboree Road (1.0), then left once more onto Back Bay Drive (0.2). Shortly after passing Newport Dunes Aquatic Park (RV camping), the road becomes one-way and meanders along the shore of **Upper Newport Bay** for 3.3 miles.

Upper Newport Bay (sometimes called Back Bay) is the largest estuary in Southern California and one of the easiest to bird. It is most famous as a wintering ground for shorebirds and waterfowl, but should not be overlooked in the summer. Fall migration for shorebirds starts almost as soon as the last of them have gone north in June, and by the latter half of July is in full-swing. From then until the end of October is a wonderful time to study the birds in their breeding and juvenile plumages and in various stages of molt to their winter garb.

The most famous bird here is the "Light-footed" Clapper Rail (R. l. levipes). Well over half of the members of this subspecies residing north of the Mexican border are found right here. Listen for their loud choruses, and look for them along the shores of the channels at low tide or when the highest high tides force them up out of the cordgrass. Other rails at the bay include Virginia and Sora. Black Rails are reported with much more regularity than their numbers here warrant. All too many birders, whose judgment is distorted by abundant wishful thinking, mistake Soras, Clapper Rail chicks, and even Song Sparrows for these birds. Marsh-loving passerines common to this Southern California coastal habitat, such as Marsh Wrens, Common Yellow-throats, and "Belding's" Savannah Sparrows, are also found along the drive.

At the junction with San Joaquin Hills Road (1.0 from Jamboree Road) stop to look at the ducks. In winter there are usually a few Blue-winged Teal and occasionally a Eurasian Wigeon among the flocks of other more common dabbling ducks. The road now circles a large area of open water, where the common diving ducks and other common deep-water birds including grebes, pelicans, and cormorants occur.

Rounding the point, with a high cliff on the right, you will come to the Big Canyon parking lot, near which masses of shorebirds can be found most of the year. At high tide they will usually be napping on the small island just north of the parking lot and perhaps on the shore right in front of you. About an hour after a good high tide is the best time to arrive to study them. The most regular wintering species are American Avocet, Willet, Long-billed Curlew, Marbled Godwit, Western and Least Sandpipers, Dunlin, and Short-billed Dowitcher (with perhaps a few Long-billeds). Other regular shorebirds at the bay, which you may find here or elsewhere, include Black-bellied and Semipalmated Plovers, Killdeer, Black-necked Stilt, Greater Yellowlegs, Spotted Sandpiper, Whimbrel, and Ruddy Turnstone. Fourteen additional shorebird species have made an appearance at one time or another.

Terns of several species are often found fishing or resting on the distant sandbars. In winter, they will most likely be just Caspian and Forster's, but during the rest of the year there is the possibility of Elegant, Common (not in mid-summer), and Least—plus Black Skimmer. Royal Terns are possible in fall and spring, rare in winter. Wintering gulls of several species are also likely. Ring-billed and California are most common, but Bonaparte's, Herring, Western, and Glaucous-winged would not be unexpected. This is also a good place for the commonly occurring herons and egrets.

Across the street a little boardwalk leads to a freshwater pond. Here you will find many of the same ducks you encountered at the foot of San Joaquin Hills Road, but also some new ones. Canvasbacks are present most winters, but you might also find Gadwall, Redhead, Ring-necked Duck, or Hooded Merganser. Common Moorhen and Black-crowned Night-Heron are present all year.

The brush on the south side of the pond is another place for California Gnatcatcher. If you don't find these birds here, walk either direction along Back Bay Drive and listen for them. They might be anywhere in the brush along the cliff face. Look for Cactus Wrens in the thick stands of cactus.

If your taste for land birds has been piqued, continue up the Big Canyon trail on the south side of the pond. In the open area where the California Gnatcatchers reside, you should also find common birds like Say's Phoebe (winter), Loggerhead Shrike, and Savannah Sparrow (*P. s. nevadensis*). These species are also possible in similar habitat anywhere along Back Bay Drive.

In the willows and along the bluffs farther up the trail, the most-likely species found all year are Spotted Dove, Anna's and Allen's Hummingbirds, Northern Flicker, Black Phoebe, Bushtit, Bewick's Wren, Northern Mockingbird, California Towhee, Red-winged and Brewer's Blackbirds, Brown-headed Cowbird, House Finch, and Lesser and American Goldfinches.

Winter visitors include Ruby-crowned Kinglet, Blue-gray Gnatcatcher, Hermit Thrush, Orange-crowned and Yellow-rumped Warblers, Spotted Towhee, and Lincoln's, Golden-crowned, and White-crowned Sparrows. Some summer visitors are Black-chinned Hummingbird, Cassin's and Western Kingbirds, and Hooded and Bullock's Orioles.

Spring and fall migrations bring the possibility of Rufous and Allen's Hummingbirds, Olive-sided Flycatcher, Western Wood-Pewee, Willow, Hammond's, Pacific-slope, and Ash-throated Flycatchers, Swainson's Thrush, Cassin's and Warbling Vireos, Nashville, Yellow, Black-throated Gray, Townsend's, MacGillivray's, and Wilson's Warblers, Yellow-breasted Chat (rare), Western Tanager, Black-headed Grosbeak, and Lazuli Bunting.

Return to your car and drive the remainder of the road. There are no new habitats to be found, but you may still find additional species. Park along the road wherever you can to scope the mudflats and marsh, or work the bushes along the roadside for land birds.

Raptors are extremely mobile and can be found anywhere. The most frequently observed are Turkey Vulture, Osprey, White-tailed Kite (rare), Northern Harrier, Sharp-shinned (winter), Cooper's, Red-shouldered, and Red-tailed Hawks, and American Kestrel. Golden Eagle is rarely seen here, as are Merlin and Peregrine and Prairie Falcons in winter. No owls are observed commonly, but the list of possibilities includes Barn, Great Horned, Burrowing (on the opposite side of the bay, rare), and Short-eared in winter (rare).

The road finally climbs to Eastbluff Drive. Although it is difficult to do so without making an illegal U-turn, there is one last area which should be checked. It is the view north from the top of the bluff to your left. Here you can see man-made islands which were established to encourage nesting Least Terns. So far, predation has kept the area from living up to its potential, but small numbers of terns (Least plus other species) and Black Skimmers have nested there. The area also serves as a high-tide resting area for just about all the gulls and shorebirds of the bay.

This concludes the tour of Upper Newport Bay. Access to the opposite shore is possible at a number of spots. You may wish to get a street map and figure them out. Several of the access points present the possibility of lovely walks away from the traffic.

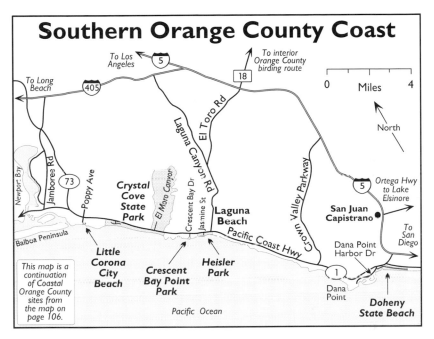

Southern Orange County Coast

From the north end of Back Bay Drive, turn right onto Eastbluff Drive and go to Jamboree Road (1.1). Turn right and return to Pacific Coast Highway (1.6). Turn left and go to the signal light at Poppy Avenue in Corona del Mar (2.1), then right to where the street ends at Ocean Boulevard (0.3). Park wherever you can and walk back to the corner and down the hill to the beach at **Little Corona City Beach**. This area is better covered on weekdays or early in the morning on weekends. At other times, people and dogs scare the birds away. Avoid it also at high tide or in the early summer, when the number of bird species is minimal.

Corona del Mar marks the dividing line in Orange County between sandy beaches to the north and rocky coastline to the south. An earthquake fault nearby accounts for the sharp transition.

A number of shorebirds preferring the oceanfront, which are uncommon or missing at Upper Newport Bay, include Wandering Tattler, Spotted Sandpiper, Whimbrel, Ruddy and Black Turnstones, Surfbird, and Sanderling.

Because water from Buck Gully enters the ocean at Little Corona, large numbers of wintering gulls gather here to drink. It is perhaps the best place in the county for wintering Herring, Thayer's, and Glaucous-winged Gulls. In addition, you should find Heermann's, Ring-billed, California, and Western. The Western Gulls will be mostly of the darker *wymani* subspecies, but occasionally a paler *occidentalis* reaches here from northern California. To compound the problem, Western x Glaucous-winged hybrids are also just as likely. The nice thing about this spot is that the birds will usually stand there patiently while you figure them out—or frustrate you until you give up!

Out in the water of the little cove you can expect three species of loons. (Red-throated Loons are the most likely right in the breaking surf.) Other birds which you looked for from Newport and Balboa Piers should also be expected. From the beach you can scope Arch Rock (better in the afternoon) and sometimes see all three of California's resident cormorant species.

Return via Poppy Avenue to Pacific Coast Highway and turn right. As soon as you leave Corona del Mar, you will come to **Crystal Cove State Park** (fee, or use the same-day permit from Huntington Beach State Beach). There are a number of parking lots between the highway and the ocean where you can park and walk down to the beach. The birds here are much the same as at Little Corona. The coastal sage scrub atop the bluff is home to a number of land birds, including California Gnatcatchers.

From the first parking lot (1.2 miles from Poppy Avenue), you can walk to a point which is a fairly good place from which to observe distant migrating seabirds (March–May, August–October). Loons, shearwaters, Brants, scoters, and alcids are possible.

Crystal Cove State Park (2,791 acres) also has an inland portion, El Moro Canyon, where you can hike for miles through coastal sage scrub, grassland, and willow-oak-sycamore riparian habitats. Turn left at the signal with a sign reading "School-State Park" (1.9 miles from the first parking lot). Double back past the school parking lot and turn right at the stop sign. Parking for the inland trails is at the end of the road (0.3), as is the park interpretive center.

Some of the more interesting land birds seen throughout the year in Crystal Cove State Park include Northern Harrier, Cooper's Hawk, California Quail, Greater Roadrunner, Barn Owl, White-throated Swift, Costa's Hummingbird (rare in winter), Nuttall's Woodpecker, Cassin's Kingbird (uncommon in winter), Cactus Wren, California Gnatcatcher (possible near El Moro Canyon parking lot, but more common on the ocean side of the highway), Wrentit, California Thrasher, Hutton's Vireo, Spotted and California Towhees, and Rufous-crowned Sparrow. A few summer visitors, most of which are confirmed or possible breeders, are Common Poorwill (may be present in winter, but inconspicuous), Western Wood-Pewee, Ash-throated Flycatcher, Phainopepla, Blue Grosbeak, Lazuli Bunting, and Black-chinned and Grasshopper Sparrows. This area has not proved to be a hotspot during migration, despite its proximity to the coast.

Two other locations for rocky-coast shorebirds and cormorants are in Laguna Beach. Return to Pacific Coast Highway and turn left. Continue southbound and watch carefully for Crescent Bay Drive (1.7 miles from "School-State Park" signal). Turn right and go to the end of the street (0.1), where there is a small viewpoint at Crescent Bay Point Park. View the rocks below for shorebirds and the offshore seastack (tall rock) for cormorants and California Sea Lions.

Return to Pacific Coast Highway, turn right, and go to Jasmine Street (0.7). Turn right, go one block to Cliff Drive, and park anywhere. (Parking meters require quarters; change machines are available.) Heisler Park runs along this stretch of coastline, another good place for birds of the rocky coastline.

The final stop on the tour is **Doheny Beach State Park**. Continue south to the signal at Dana Point Harbor Drive (8.6). Turn right to the park entrance (0.1), then left into the park (fee). If you visited Huntington Beach State Beach or Crystal Cove State Park the same day, your pass still will be good. Park in the last parking lot before the narrow bridge across San Juan Creek (0.2). The trees in the picnic area have attracted an amazing variety of vagrant landbirds during fall migration, and many have over-wintered. Walk toward the ocean and around the fence to view the mouth of San Juan Creek—an excellent place for shorebirds, terns, and especially gulls. This is probably the best place in the county for gulls. Besides the abundant wintering Ring-billed, California, Heermann's, and Western Gulls, you should also find Mew, Herring, Thayer's, Glaucous-winged, and Bonaparte's. The rare Glaucous, super-rare Lesser Black-backed, and outrageously rare Ivory (California's only—bizarre—record) Gulls have occurred here.

The gulls move back and forth from the creek mouth to the sandy beaches south of it. To get to these beaches, continue on the park road, crossing San Juan Creek and bearing right at the Y on the other side. After you pass the campground you will come to about a mile of day-use parking next to the ocean. Gulls can be anywhere, either on the dry sand or at the edge of the water.

To return to the tour's starting point, retrace your route to where you left Pacific Coast Highway at the signal. Turn right and follow the signs to Interstate 5 northbound (1.5). Interstate 405 eventually branches off (14.0) and will take you back to your starting point at Highway 55 (8.5).

From Doheney Beach State Park you can travel south on Interstate 5 to the San Diego County birding areas, or go inland on Interstate 5 for a few miles to the start of the Lake Elsinore trip at Highway 74 in San Juan Capistrano.

There is RV camping at Newport Dunes Aquatic Park, car camping at Doheny Beach, and abundant motels along the route.

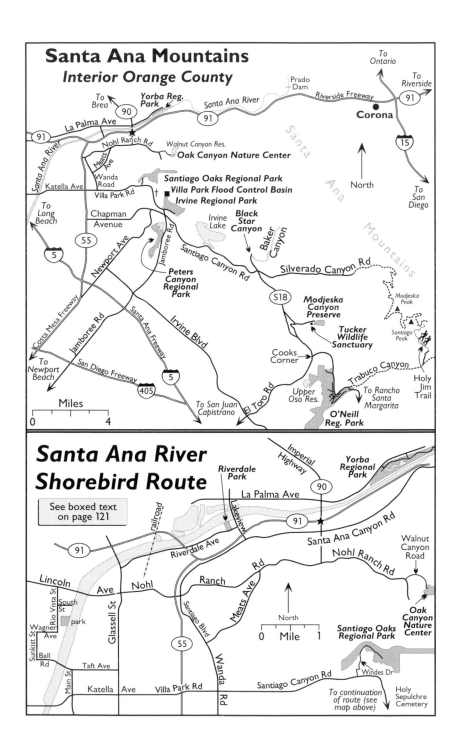

Santa Ana Mountains
Interior Orange County

To Ontario
To Riverside
91
Prado Dam
Riverside Freeway
Santa Ana River
Corona
15
To Brea
Yorba Reg. Park
90
La Palma Ave
91
91
Santa Ana River
Nohl Ranch Rd
Walnut Canyon Res.
Oak Canyon Nature Center
Meats Ave
Wanda Road
Katella Ave
Villa Park Rd
Santiago Oaks Regional Park
Villa Park Flood Control Basin
Irvine Regional Park
North
To San Diego
To Long Beach
Chapman Avenue
Irvine Lake
Black Star Canyon
Baker Canyon
Santa Ana Mountains
5
55
Newport Ave
Jamboree Rd
Santiago Canyon Rd
Silverado Canyon Rd
Peters Canyon Regional Park
S18
Modjeska Canyon Preserve
Modjeska Peak
Santiago Peak
Costa Mesa Freeway
Jamboree Rd
Santa Ana Freeway
Irvine Blvd
Tucker Wildlife Sanctuary
To Newport Beach
San Diego Freeway
5
Cooks Corner
Trabuco Canyon
Holy Jim Trail
405
El Toro Rd
To San Juan Capistrano
Upper Oso Res.
To Rancho Santa Margarita
O'Neill Reg. Park
Miles
0   4

Santa Ana River
Shorebird Route

Imperial Highway
Yorba Regional Park
Riverdale Park
La Palma Ave
90
See boxed text on page 121
railroad
Lakeview
91
Santa Ana Canyon Rd
Walnut Canyon Road
91
Riverdale Ave
Nohl Ranch Rd
Oak Canyon Nature Center
Lincoln
Ave
Nohl
Ranch
Rd
Meats Ave
Rio Vista St
South St
park
Glassell St
Santiago Blvd
North
0   Mile   1
Wagner Ave
Sunkist St
Ball Rd
Main St
Taft Ave
Katella   Ave
Villa Park Rd
Wanda Rd
Santiago Oaks Regional Park
Santiago Canyon Rd
Windes Dr
To continuation of route (see map above)
Holy Sepulchre Cemetery

SANTA ANA MOUNTAINS

Saddleback, the most prominent feature of the Santa Ana Mountains, can be seen from almost any point in Orange County. Not only do its twin peaks (Modjeska and Santiago) dominate the skyline, but also its presence is reflected in the names of many schools, motels, and other buildings. Its numerous canyons, ridges, and peaks are fun to explore. This trip will take you to a few of them.

Out-of-state birders should keep in mind the fact that most of Orange County typifies Southern California's image of suburban sprawl. Local chambers of commerce will boast that Orange County is one of the fastest-growing areas in the nation, but birders may view these pronouncements with a jaundiced eye. Not long ago the orange tree was king, but the main crop today is houses—tracts and tracts of them. Despite all this, Orange County still offers some fine birding in urban parks and large natural reserves, and its position on the southern California coast ensures an annual supply of vagrant birds during migration. Whether you are here on vacation or for a business trip, the sites noted below are well worth your birding time. You may have a weekend to do the entire route—if you move fast—or only a few hours to visit one of the local parks noted below.

The starting point is the intersection of the Riverside Freeway (Highway 91) and Imperial Highway (Highway 90) northeast of Orange. From this intersection go north on Imperial Highway across the (rarely dry) Santa Ana River and turn right immediately across the river onto La Palma Avenue. Drive 1.8 miles to **Yorba Regional Park** (fee); do not be distracted and enter the baseball section of the park en route. Yorba Park is a typical green urban park with lakes, but its location along a mile of the Santa Ana River where it leaves Santa Ana Canyon has brought it more than its share of vagrant species. Sections of the park are left unmowed to enhance wildlife habitat. It is especially good during migration and for wintering birds. Wintering ducks should include Cinnamon Teal, American Wigeon, Redhead, Ring-necked Duck, Wood Duck (resident), and Lesser Scaup. Lark and Savannah Sparrows, Western Meadowlark, and Lesser and Lawrence's Goldfinches (rare) are also present at this season. Spring and fall bring western migrants and the occasional vagrant.

Though the park is a worthy birding spot on its own merits, it also provides several access points to the **Santa Ana River**. Prado Dam in Riverside County to the east (see Other Good Birding Spots chapter) gradually releases water throughout the year to allow percolation to recharge groundwater levels. There are always pools in the riverbed for this reason, but they tend

119

to change their levels with regularity and no definitive statement can be made as to which area has the best birding pools on any given day. The pools are good for ducks in winter, of course, but it is the shorebirds that draw local birders to the Santa Ana River. Save for the short lull in shorebird migration in mid-to-late June, almost any time from April through October can produce good shorebirding here. See the Boxed Text on next page for a discussion of good access points.

Return from Yorba Regional Park to the intersection of Imperial Highway and Riverside Freeway (Highway 91).

Go south on Imperial Highway to Nohl Ranch Road, turn left, and follow past the golf course to Walnut Canyon Road (1.7) on the left. Turn here to **Oak Canyon Nature Center,** open 9 AM–5 PM daily (0.5). This 58-acre park offers six miles of trails through a variety of habitats of chaparral and oak woodlands with a small stream, all set in the Anaheim Hills. Stop at the visitors center for a trail map.

A partial list of the birds regularly seen here includes Cooper's, Red-shouldered, and Red-tailed Hawks, Anna's Hummingbird (Costa's and Black-chinned in summer), Acorn and Nuttall's Woodpeckers, Ash-throated Flycatcher (summer), Oak Titmouse, Cactus, Bewick's, and House Wrens, California Thrasher, Phainopepla (summer), a good variety of western warblers in migration (late March through April are particularly lively), Black-headed Grosbeak (migration and summer), Western Tanager (migrant), Spotted and California Towhees, "Oregon" Dark-eyed Junco ("Slate-colored" and "Gray-headed" are rare, winter only), and summering Bullock's Oriole. Scan Walnut Canyon Reservoir from the top of Roadrunner Ridge Trail for wintering diving ducks.

Return to Nohl Ranch Road, go past Imperial Highway, and turn left on Meats Avenue—this is not a misprint (1.2 miles past Imperial). Then turn left onto Santiago Boulevard (1.7). Bear right onto Wanda Road (0.6), and turn left onto Villa Park Road (0.3). This soon becomes Santiago Canyon Road (Route S18). Turn left onto Windes Drive (2.6) to **Santiago Oaks Regional Park** (fee) on the left. Santiago Creek, lined by California Sycamores, Coast Live Oaks, and coastal sage scrub, runs through the park.

Santiago Oaks Regional Park is one of the most interesting birding spots in Orange County when searching for coastal California's resident land birds. Although sharing many of the same species with Oak Canyon Nature Center, the habitats are in such close proximity here that you can sample them all in a 2-mile-long walk. Besides the various riparian habitats and coastal sage scrub, there is a large area dotted with exotic trees once planted in conjunction with plans for a mansion that never materialized. From the parking lot walk up the trail to the interpretive center and pick up a bird list. Among the *permanent residents* in the park are California Quail, Greater Roadrunner, Western Screech-Owl (night), White-throated Swift, Acorn and Nuttall's Woodpeckers, Western Bluebird, California Thrasher, Hutton's

Santa Ana River Shorebird Spots. Below the pass after which Southern California's infamous seasonal east winds were named, the Santa Ana River travels through Orange County to the Pacific Ocean. If you are in interior Orange County and are looking for a good shorebirding location, you will want to work some of the spots along this river. Start in the morning by birding **Yorba Regional Park**, noted at the beginning of this chapter, and then travel to the river-access points as detailed in the following instructions.

After birding Yorba Regional Park, exit and turn left onto La Palma Avenue. Continue across Imperial Highway to Lakeview Avenue, 1.6 miles past Imperial Highway. Turn left (south) on Lakeview, then immediately after you cross the river turn right onto Riverdale Avenue (0.4). Shortly after the turn you will come to Riverdale Park on the right. This free city park provides restrooms and parking for the Santa Ana River Bike Trail. If the river is flowing swiftly during your visit, the birding probably will be mediocre—don't get run over by bikers on the bike path; they are always flowing swiftly.

From Riverdale Park, turn right and continue on Riverdale Avenue, cross Tustin Avenue, and stop at the railroad tracks (1.6). A small dirt parking lot here and an opening in the fence provide access to the bike path—and the river. Going farther on Riverdale Avenue, stop and park near Riverdale's intersection with Glassell Street (0.6). Walk north on Glassell Street 100 yards to the river trail/bike path.

Next, drive south on Glassell Street to Lincoln Avenue (0.5), where you will turn right (west) to a small dirt parking lot on the right just before the bridge (0.6). This is one of the best areas for birds along the river trail. You can walk beside the bike trail, but perhaps even better is to walk across the main river channel on the Lincoln Avenue bridge (watch the traffic!), then down the bank to the dirt road on the dike. This dike runs between the main river channel and the settling ponds, and you can walk it for miles in either direction. This far downriver from Prado Dam the water in the main channel is usually petering out, and the resultant mudflats are excellent for shorebirds. The settling ponds here may be full (good for waterfowl), drying out (good for shorebirds), or dried out completely (good for nothing).

Cross the Lincoln Avenue bridge to Rio Vista Street (0.5). Turn left to South Street (0.3), where you will turn left again and go to the end of the street. Walk up the dirt path onto the dike. On the left is a deep-water pond, and on the right is its exit spillway where water may be flowing into a shallow channel. If the water is flowing, you will have the impressive spectacle of scores of herons and egrets lined up along the banks waiting for fish drawn to the aerated water. A short way ahead the trail intersects the dike road mentioned in the preceding paragraph, so this spot can serve as an alternative access point for that venue.

Return to Rio Vista Street and turn left. You will shortly come to a grassy park on the left. Scope the large settling basin through the fence. At the end of the street turn right on Wagner Avenue (0.5 from South Street), then left on Sunkist Street (0.5). Turn left on Ball Road—which becomes Taft Avenue at the river—(0.5) and cross the river again. Parking can be a problem in this area, but if you see birds in the channel as you cross the bridge, you can find a spot and walk back.

Just past the river bridge, turn right on Main Street (0.7 from Sunkist). Turn right on Katella Avenue (0.4) and park on the right in the insurance company parking lot just short of the river bridge (0.4). Take one last look at the river from here. This is the last place where there is likely to be any water short of the tidal influence of the ocean many miles distant.

Vireo, California Towhee, and Rufous-crowned Sparrow. In winter, Hutton's Vireo is often confused with the much more abundant Ruby-crowned Kinglet. Watch for the heavy black mark beneath the lower wingbar (the upper bar may be virtually invisible) on the kinglet, and the lack of this mark combined with the heavier head, bill, and prominent off-white lores of the vireo. *Summer visitors* include Black-chinned Hummingbird, Pacific-slope and Ash-throated Flycatchers, Black-headed Grosbeak, Black-chinned Sparrow, and Hooded Oriole. *Winter visitors* include Red-breasted Sapsucker, Blue-gray Gnatcatcher, Hermit Thrush, Cedar Waxwing, and Golden-crowned Sparrow. Rock Wrens are sometimes found at Villa Park Dam at the far end of the park. White-throated Swifts nest in crevices in the large cliff above the dam. In breeding season take the trail leading to the cliff-top from which you can watch the swifts as they fly to and from their nest crevices.

When leaving, turn left onto Santiago Canyon Road. In a short distance you will see Holy Sepulchre Cemetery on the left—continue on to Chapman Avenue (1.8). Turn left on Chapman Avenue to **Irvine Regional Park** (fee), which is just around the bend.

Dedicated by James Irvine II in 1897, the expansive central portion of Irvine Regional Park is turfed and planted with a wide variety of giant native and introduced trees that attract great numbers of both birds and people. Crowds typically remain reasonable on weekdays, but weekend/holiday birding becomes nearly hopeless after about 9:30 AM. At sundown during the spring and summer, Lesser Nighthawks may be seen and Common Poorwills heard along Santiago Creek at the park's east end. This park is, perhaps, Orange County's most convenient and reliable place to find Barn and Great Horned Owls, plus Western Screech-Owls; search the large oaks and sycamores after dusk. Golden Eagles are occasionally among the raptors seen soaring over the hills to the north and east. Breeding birds, found mainly in native habitats and weedy edges that surround the developed portion of the park, include those noted above for Oak Canyon and Santiago Oaks, plus California Gnatcatcher (rare), American Robin, Blue Grosbeak, Lazuli Bunting, and Lark and Grasshopper Sparrows (rare to uncommon). To search for nesting Bell's Vireos, Yellow-breasted Chats, and other species that require extensive willow woodlands, hike into the Villa Park flood-control basin located northwest of the park. During late fall and winter, Irvine Regional Park is known for sapsuckers (mostly Red-breasted), large flocks of sparrows—including Chipping, Lark, Lincoln's, White-crowned, and Golden-crowned—and, rarely, a Varied Thrush.

Exit the park onto Jamboree Road, cross Santiago Canyon Road/Chapman Avenue, and proceed south to Canyon View Avenue (0.5). Turn right and go to the parking lot for **Peters Canyon Regional Park** (0.2) (fee). This medium-size park built around Peters Canyon Reservoir includes good examples of coastal sage scrub, willow forest, freshwater marsh, and open-water habitats. Upon arrival, quickly check the reservoir for wading birds, Ospreys, grebes, and ducks. During spring and summer, keep an eye on nest boxes lining the reservoir for Tree Swallows and Western Bluebirds. This is one of the county's premier parks for finding such willow-associated breeding species as Black-chinned Hummingbird, Downy Woodpecker, Bell's Vireo, Yellow Warbler, Yellow-breasted Chat, and Blue Grosbeak. In season, search for these species in the large patch of willows located immediately east of the parking lot. Continuing through the willows to the south side of the reservoir, you will encounter coastal sage scrub vegetation that supports resident California Gnatcatchers, Cactus Wrens, California Thrashers, Rufous-crowned Sparrows, and other birds typical of this habitat. Complete the loop around the reservoir, checking emergent vegetation along the water's edge for Sora, Virginia Rail, and Common Moorhen.

Return to the corner of Jamboree Road and Chapman Avenue/Santiago Canyon Road, from which you may choose to turn left on Chapman Avenue and head back toward Los Angeles, Riverside, the beach, or many other destinations via Highway 55.

To continue the Santa Ana Mountains Loop (and perhaps bird some actual mountains!), turn right onto Santiago Canyon Road and continue east toward Irvine Lake. Irvine Lake has essentially the same waterbirds discussed at ponds and reservoirs above, as well as an exorbitant entry fee—it is best to keep going.

At the next intersection (3.0) you have a choice of three roads. The road to the left goes up **Black Star Canyon** and is worth exploring for the first 2 or 3 miles. You can park your car at the gate and walk through (unless the area has been closed by the fire marshal). A side road, **Baker Canyon**, can also produce most of the breeding species mentioned above, as well as Blue-gray Gnatcatcher and Rufous-crowned and Black-chinned Sparrows along the slopes. Winter occasionally brings one or two Lewis's Wood-peckers; watch for them on the utility poles or roadside sycamore snags.

The road straight ahead goes up **Silverado Canyon**, which is well-settled and rather poor for birding for its first couple miles. From the end of the paved road, however, a rocky, dirt road winds 13 miles to the top of Santiago Peak (El. 5,687 ft). This road is closed during fire season and also when storms make it impassable. Hiking above the gate, when it is locked, is productive at any time of year, but especially in spring when it can make a great trip with lots of birds, flowers, and magnificent views. The farther up the road one goes, the greater the divergence in the bird list from that noted thus far. Species regularly found breeding in this canyon (and in other high-elevation canyons containing comparable forested slopes) include Mountain Quail, Band-tailed Pigeon, Northern Saw-whet Owl (rare), Common Poorwill, Hairy Woodpecker, Olive-sided Flycatcher (rare), Western Wood-Pewee, Pacific-slope Flycatcher, Violet-green Swallow, Mountain Chickadee, White-breasted Nuthatch, Western Tanager, Black-headed Grosbeak, Lazuli Bunting, Black-chinned Sparrow, Dark-eyed Junco, and Purple Finch. Regular wintering species include Golden-crowned Kinglet, Townsend's Solitaire, and Fox Sparrow ("Sooty", "Slate-colored", and "Thick-billed" forms) among the more abundant visitors; some winters produce such irruptive species as Red-breasted and Pygmy Nuthatches, Varied Thrush, Red Crossbill, Pine Siskin, and Cassin's Finch. If the road to the top is open and passable, you may drive up the ridge and follow the road southeast along the Santa Ana Mountain crest to Falcon and Blue Jay (one assumes *Aphelocoma californica*) campgrounds—see the Lake Elsinore trip. Otherwise, to continue this route, descend Silverado Canyon to Santiago Canyon Road and turn left.

Bear left onto Modjeska Canyon Road (2.7), named after Madame Modjeska, a famous Polish actress formerly living in the canyon. There is a historical marker (1.5) on the right, but her home is not visible from the road nor is it open to the public.

You may wish to stop by the **Dorothy May Tucker Wildlife Sanctuary** (El. 1,350 ft) (0.4) (open 9 AM–4 PM; donation requested) farther up the canyon to watch hummingbird feeders or take a hike into interesting chaparral habitat up Harding Canyon. There are always a number of Anna's Hummingbirds about the feeders, augmented by Black-chinned and Costa's in summer, and by Rufous and Allen's in migration—especially March–April and late July through August.

Return to the mouth of the canyon (1.0) and turn left on Modjeska Grade Road toward O'Neill Park. Birding along Modjeska Grade Road in the summer routinely produces Black-chinned Sparrow. If, by the time of your visit, however, the region has been "improved" after the Orange County standard, you may as well drive on. After going over the steep ridge, you will rejoin Santiago Canyon Road (1.3), where you should bear left. At Cook's Corner (1.2), turn left onto Live Oak Canyon Road (Route S19) toward O'Neill Park. The visiting traveler should know that Cook's Corner is an immensely popular biker bar. If you are here on a weekend, you may wish to stop in for some liquid refreshment and local color while gaping at the sight of many tons of chromed, throbbing metal. Recovering from the scene, continue uphill to the summit, beyond which you will enter Live Oak Canyon, a good area for Hutton's Vireo—although there is usually too much traffic here to stop safely.

Set in Trabuco Canyon among miles of expansive oak-sycamore woodlands, **O'Neill Regional Park** (3.2) (fee) is a very popular camping spot during summer and many weekends, when there may be too many people for great birding. During the week or in off-seasons, however, the birding is fine and birders may wish to car-camp here. Breeding raptors include White-tailed Kite, Cooper's and Red-shouldered Hawks, American Kestrel, Western Screech-Owl, and Barn and Great Horned Owls. Other expected resident species include California Quail, Band-tailed Pigeon, Acorn and Nuttall's Woodpeckers, White-breasted Nuthatch, Oak Titmouse, Western Bluebird, and Hutton's Vireo; White-throated Swifts nest at the lowermost end of the park under the Oso Parkway bridge. The list of wintering birds here parallels those noted for Santiago Oaks and Irvine Regional Parks.

If equipped with a high-clearance vehicle and an adventurous nature, you may wish to continue on Live Oak Canyon Road 1.0 mile past the entrance to O'Neill Park and take Trabuco Creek Road, which proceeds 5.8 miles up the bottom of the Arroyo Trabuco and enters some of Orange County's most gorgeous landscape. Surprisingly large and noisy weekend crowds appear in this seemingly remote area, but problems generally don't start until around mid-morning, so just make sure to get an early start, or visit during the week—the birding should be great. This road is routinely closed after wet weather.

The first two miles of the road pass through a wide alluvial plain vegetated with dry scrub, but as the canyon narrows rapidly, lush carpets of Wild Grape foreshadow the majestic sycamore-alder riparian forests and oak-conifer woodlands beyond. Birding is best in April and May, when impressive numbers of nesting and migratory species can be found in roadside riparian forest habitat. You will find the large parking area for the Holy Jim Trail—and a surprising number of cabins—at 4.4 miles. This wonderful trail follows and crosses the perennial creek for about one gently-rising mile, then forks. The right arm proceeds only another quarter-mile to Holy Jim Falls, while the main trail heads off to the left, leaves the creek bed, and proceeds another four steep miles to the lush alder-oak-conifer forest of Bear Spring, located barely into Riverside County along the Main Divide of the Santa Ana Mountains. Birds found along the upper portion of Holy Jim Trail are comparable to those identified previously for upper Silverado Canyon.

Another option is to continue 1.4 miles past the Holy Jim parking area to the trailhead at the end of Trabuco Creek Road. From here, the Trabuco Canyon Trail continues another five miles through alternating riparian forests and dry scrub to extensive oak-conifer woodlands, ending at the Main Divide. Again, the expected species are similar to those described for upper Silverado Canyon, but upper Trabuco Canyon also harbors small numbers of Spotted Owls rather than Northern Saw-whets.

If you decided to bird the O'Neill Regional Park area, when you have finished return to Cook's Corner and turn left onto El Toro Road, which plows through the suburban madness to Interstate 5. From here you may wish to go south to San Juan Capistrano to link up with the Lake Elsinore tour, or wherever else your schedule may take you.

There are campgrounds in O'Neill Regional Park. The Laguna Hills, Lake Forest, El Toro area near the intersection of Interstate 5 and El Toro Road has many motels and provides a convenient lodging base for the Santa Ana Mountains route.

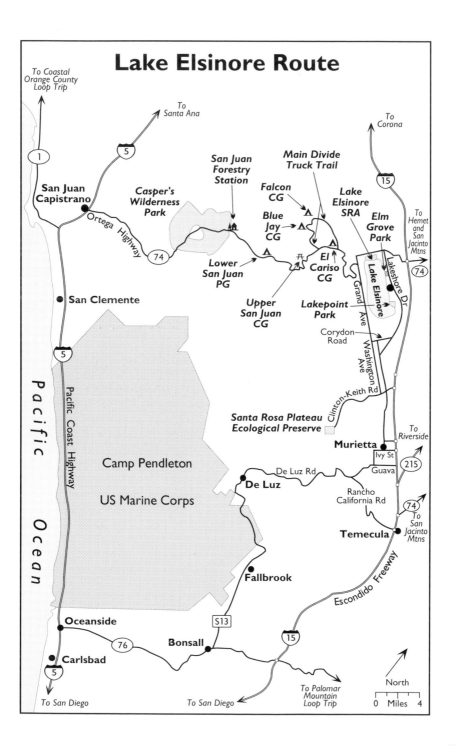

Lake Elsinore Route

LAKE ELSINORE

On a clear day after a heavy rain or a Santa Ana wind, the view from the Elsinore Escarpment is magnificent. From this high vantage point you can see the boats and swimmers on the lake a thousand feet below. The skyline is a ring of mountains. Nearly all of the major mountain peaks of Southern California are visible, especially in winter when their snow-capped summits stand out like huge bird-rocks in a sea.

A clear day is all too rare an occurrence in Southern California. In summer you may find the smog so thick that even the lake will not be visible from the escarpment. However, you should still find numerous birds and, in spring, blankets of wildflowers. Birding is at its best in winter and spring—and this is fortuitous since the smog density is typically lower then. The flowers are thickest In March and April.

The starting point is the junction of the San Diego Freeway (Interstate 5) and the Ortega Highway (Highway 74) in San Juan Capistrano. The Mission is one block to the west and is well worth a visit for anyone interested in California history (open 9 AM–5 PM; fee). Cliff Swallows have not nested here in twenty years (newspaper accounts of the swallows' return typically show pictures of flying White-throated Swifts, Rock Doves, European Starlings, or House Sparrows—never Cliff Swallows), but the beautiful grounds abound with Anna's Hummingbirds. The swallows have moved to the suburbs to be closer to the fields.

Go east on the Ortega Highway toward Lake Elsinore. For the first few miles, the road is bordered by houses, and birds are few. At San Juan Creek (2.3) the water attracts Lesser and American Goldfinches, California Towhee, and sparrows. Black Phoebes often nest under the bridge, and Bullock's Orioles nest in the California Sycamore at the end of it. White-tailed Kites, notoriously irruptive in their abundance, can sometimes be seen hovering over the grassy hillsides.

Farther inland, stands of Coast Live Oak become common. Check here for Acorn Woodpecker, Oak Titmouse, Bushtit, Hutton's Vireo, Black-headed Grosbeak (summer), and at night, Great Horned Owl and Western Screech-Owl. At the start of the rainy season in November, you may find the woods alive with California Newts, small dull-red salamanders.

The dry hillsides are covered in places with Prickly Pear cactus, which often shelters a Cactus Wren or covey of California Quail. In winter, here as elsewhere in California, White-crowned Sparrows are abundant. If you look hard enough, however, you may find other kinds of sparrows. During

127

the dry season you will want to stop at windmills and stock tanks to check for birds coming to these rare water sources.

Casper's Wilderness Park (7.6) (fee; picnicking and camping) is an excellent place to bird due to its wide variety of habitats—5,500 acres of fertile valleys and running streams. It also has a visitors center and trails. (Some camping areas may be closed due to periodic Mountain Lion scares.)

White-tailed Kite
Shawneen E. Finnegan

During the rainy season, when the roads in the Cleveland National Forest are open (Forest Adventure Pass required), you will want to drive the road behind the **San Juan Forestry Station** (4.9) on the left. Not only is the birding good, but also this road will enable you to get away from some of the traffic. Along this short road you will find a variety of habitats ranging from chaparral-covered hillsides to streamside woodlands. Birds to be found here include the typical suite of chaparral birds. In spring look for Black-chinned and Costa's Hummingbirds, Ash-throated Flycatcher, Western Wood-Pe-wee, Swainson's Thrush, Phainopepla, Warbling Vireo, Yellow Warbler, Hooded and Bullock's Orioles, Black-headed and Blue Grosbeaks, and Lazuli Bunting. In winter you may find Red-naped Sapsucker, White-breasted Nuthatch, American Robin, Hermit Thrush, Ruby-crowned Kinglet, Yellow-rumped Warbler, Purple Finch, Dark-eyed Junco, and Chipping, White-crowned, Golden-crowned, Fox, and Lincoln's Sparrows.

Beyond the forestry station on Highway 74, the canyon walls become steeper and rockier, good habitat for Canyon Wrens. **Lower San Juan Picnic Ground** (3.8) and **Upper San Juan Campground** (2.3) are worth checking. The birdlife is about the same as behind the forestry station.

If you like to hike, try the San Juan Loop Trail (0.8) or the Main Divide Truck Trail (2.4). The latter is open to motor vehicles at times during the non-fire season. It is an exciting road that runs along the crest of the mountains, but it is likely to be rough and muddy or dusty.

El Cariso Campground (1.2) near the summit of this highway is worth checking. Varied Thrush sometimes winters here. Beyond this point, the chaparral is very lush and productive. Check for any birds that you might have missed in this habitat. The sticky, bright-orange filament draping the chaparral is Dodder, a parasite.

Turn left (0.2) onto a paved road to the Falcon (4.3) and Blue Jay (0.5) Campgrounds. (These can also be reached by taking this loop road from its other end, the Main Divide Truck Trail, mentioned previously.) The camp-grounds are well off the highway, and during the week are not crowded. They also boast the best oak-woodland habitat along the Ortega Highway. Western Bluebirds and White-breasted Nuthatches nest here, as do most of the birds listed for the lower elevations.

Return to Ortega Highway and continue toward Lake Elsinore. After you pass the summit, look on the left for a viewpoint (1.2) from which you can see a good part of Southern California on a clear day. Most of the major mountain peaks are visible. On the far left is Mount Baldy (El. 10,064 ft) in the San Gabriel Mountains. The next peak to the right is San Gorgonio (El. 11,502 ft) in the San Bernardino Mountains. This bare, rounded mass is the tallest peak in Southern California. San Jacinto Peak (El. 10,786 ft) in the San Jacinto Mountains is nearly due east. Almost hidden from view to the right of this is Santa Rosa Mountain (El. 8,046 ft). In the distance to the far right, you can see the Laguna and Palomar Mountains. The shiny dome of the

Palomar Observatory is visible if you look hard enough. A thousand feet below is Lake Elsinore (El. 1,274 ft).

Wind your way down the mountain to Grand Avenue (4.4). The north end of the lake is accessible at the **City of Lake Elsinore Recreation Area** (camping; fee). To get there, turn left and follow Highway 74 (1.7). The park is heavily grown with willows and ornamental shrubs which may harbor migrants after a good flight-night, especially in spring. Ducks may be numerous here or elsewhere around the lake in winter. Loons, scoters, and Brant are rare winter visitors, adding spice to Riverside County birding. Locals also carefully watch the wintering gulls anywhere on Lake Elsinore; Herring Gulls show up occasionally among the Bonaparte's, Ring-billeds, and Californias—and other gulls rare this far inland appear infrequently.

Continue to the traffic-light at Lakeshore Drive (0.7) and turn right. At a public parking lot (1.6) stop to scan the lake. Keep right at the fork (0.2) as you continue on. At **Elm Grove Park** (0.3) you can get a general view of the south end of the lake. Continue south and turn left on Poe (0.2), then right onto Limited Avenue one block later, then right again on Main to go around the boat launching area. Turn left at the end of Main back onto Lakeshore Drive. Turn right into **Lakepoint Park** (1.1) and walk to the back fence from which you can view the south shore of the lake; bring your telescope if you have one with you. Returning to Lakeshore Drive, continue south to Corydon Road (3.4). The dry pasture on the right may have Horned Larks in winter. Check for longspurs (very rare) among the Horned Larks, because all three species have appeared here in the past. Turn right on Corydon Road and look in the fields for these birds as well as Vesper and Savannah Sparrows in season. At Grand Avenue (1.5) turn left. The street trees here are olives and California Pepper (fern-like leaves), common Southern California ornamentals.

Continue on Grand Avenue to Clinton-Keith Road (3.7). If you have plenty of time, turn right at Clinton-Keith Road to visit the Santa Rosa Plateau Ecological Preserve (3,100 acres acquired in 1984 by The California Nature Conservancy). There is a nice visitors center here. Varied habitats of grassland, chaparral, and oak woodland of Coast Live Oak and the rarer, threatened Engelmann Oak are in the preserve. There are also some riparian zones of sycamore and willow. Birds to be expected in the oak woodlands include Band-tailed Pigeon, Acorn Woodpecker, Phainopepla, and Red-shouldered Hawk. The chaparral produces such birds as California Quail, California Thrasher, and Wrentit. In the grassland look for White-tailed Kite and, in spring, Grasshopper Sparrow.

The creekbeds throughout the preserve contain deep holes called tenejas (*ten-AY-haas*) which hold water throughout the rainless summer months. Some of California's last vernal pools which may support some wintering waterfowl are found on top of the level mesas.

Return to Clinton-Keith Road and drive east to Palomar Street (3.5), which becomes Washington Avenue, and turn right. You will soon come to Murrieta. At the southern edge of town, turn right on Ivy Street (3.6), go just beyond the flood-control channel, and turn left onto Hayes Avenue (0.5). You will come to De Luz Road (1.0), where you turn right (if you turn left, the road is named Guava Street). This road (which starts out paved for 0.8 mile, but becomes gravel for the last 1.4 miles) leads up the escarpment and becomes good, paved De Luz Road (2.2), leading you through De Luz Canyon. (De Luz Road can be reached, avoiding the gravel part, by taking the Rancho California Road right [west] from Interstate 15 at the Temecula-Rancho California exit.) This is an excellent road to explore if you have the time. It leads 11.3 miles to De Luz and then on another 11.0 miles to Fallbrook (see Other Good Birding Spots chapter). During very wet weather, the road may not be passable where it fords the stream several times. When it is open, this is a beautiful drive through grasslands, chaparral, and oak woodlands. It is excellent in spring for wildflowers, in fall for autumn colors, and at all seasons for birds. Phainopeplas, in winter, are often found in large numbers, and during migrations the area can be alive with birds. From Fallbrook continue south on S13 to Highway 76 at Bonsall and turn right to Oceanside.

Although you may not want to drive De Luz Canyon, you may still want to follow the instructions toward De Luz Road, taking little side roads, birding the pastureland for raptors, flycatchers, sparrows, and other surprises. This is best in spring and winter when birds are abundant. You can then return to Ivy Street for the continuation of your adventure.

If you choose not to go toward De Luz Road, turn left on Ivy Street to Interstate 15 and consider several choices. You can return to San Juan Capistrano by taking I-15 north to Highway 74 (13.0) and driving back over the Ortega Highway. Or you may turn right on I-15 to Highway 76 (12.0) and right to Oceanside, following the San Luis Rey River westward. At Oceanside you can go north on Interstate 5 to return to the starting point at San Juan Capistrano, or begin the Palomar Mountain Loop, which starts at Oceanside. Other options present themselves as well. Get a map of the area and be creative. San Diego is forty minutes to the south, Anza-Borrego Desert State Park is 1½ hours east, Mexico is an hour away. Think of the possibilities!

You may camp at the Forest Service campgrounds on the Ortega Highway or at Lake Elsinore; many motels are available in San Juan Capistrano and Elsinore.

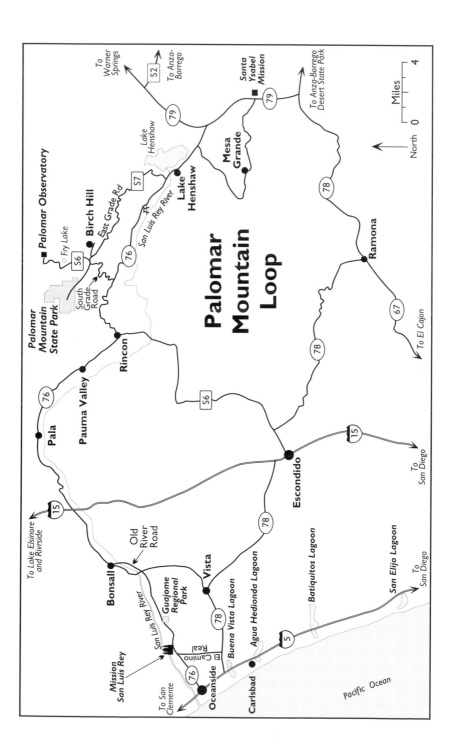

PALOMAR MOUNTAIN LOOP

This loop offers a wide variety of habitat types with an impressively long list of species en route. Most people are aware that Palomar Mountain is home to one of the world's largest telescopes. Rising to almost 6,000 feet in altitude, the mountain is also home to many species of western montane birds. The route takes you from coastal lagoons through oak groves and chaparral to the mountain's summit—a pleasing transect of northern San Diego County. It is best to give two days to the loop—one for the coastal lagoons and chaparral, the other for the mountain itself. Although it is possible to drive the entire loop in one day, it would not be possible to bird all areas most efficiently that quickly.

Palomar Mountain can be reached conveniently from the Anza-Borrego, Laguna Mountains, Lake Elsinore, Salton Sea, San Diego, or San Jacinto trips, and the reader is encouraged to review travel plans carefully, looking for opportunities to mix and match among these tours for productive and enjoyable birding opportunities.

The housing booms, freeways, and shopping centers that are so typical of Southern California have overwhelmed the western half of this excursion (creating significant light-pollution problems for the giant telescope). You can, however, still enjoy birding some coastal lagoons with contiguous chaparral habitat. As you progress eastward from the heavily populated western portion of the route you will travel through an increasingly rural countryside until arriving at the mountain itself. Although not as productive as the higher mountains to the north, Palomar is convenient for San Diego-based birders. You should be able to compile an impressive list of birds here at any season, though the higher reaches of the mountain itself will be far less productive in winter.

The loop starts at the intersection of the San Diego Freeway (Interstate 5) and the Vista Freeway (Highway 78) just south of Oceanside. (If you are coming from San Diego, start at San Elijo Lagoon and work your way north to this intersection.) Drive east on the Vista Freeway toward Vista. At the first exit, get off on Jefferson Street (0.6) for a drive around **Buena Vista Lagoon**. As soon as you leave the freeway, and before crossing the bridge, turn right onto the little road along the north side of the lake.

Buena Vista Lagoon was once the gem of northern San Diego County coastal lagoons. Its eastern segment was "improved" by the construction of a regional shopping mall in the sixties, however, and subsequent siltation of that which remained diminished its attractiveness to non-human species.

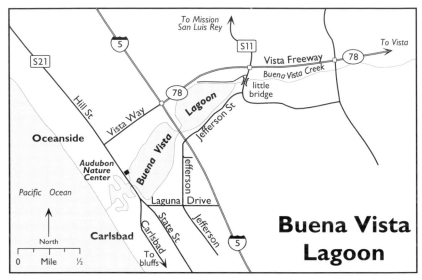

Buena Vista Lagoon

Tolerant flocks of ducks and a few shorebirds still winter on the lagoon. Most leave in summer, but a few stay to nest. In winter you should be able to find Mallard, Gadwall, American Wigeon, Northern Pintail, Green-winged and Cinnamon Teal, Northern Shoveler, Redhead (nests), Ring-necked Duck, Canvasback, Lesser Scaup, Bufflehead, Ruddy Duck (nests), and Red-breasted Merganser. You should also see Great Blue and Green Herons, Black-crowned Night-Heron, Great and Snowy Egrets, American Bittern (winter), Double-crested Cormorant, and numerous gulls and terns. Check the patches of tules for Common Moorhen, Marsh Wren, Common Yellow-throat, Song Sparrow, and Least Bittern (it is best to familiarize yourself with this bird's call before looking for it).

April and May often bring large flocks of swallows and swifts overhead, especially on cloudy days. Exceptional days have produced six species of swallows and three species of swifts all coursing about overhead at once. This same phenomenon can occur over the other north county coastal lagoons.

To check the western section of the lagoon, return to Jefferson Street and turn right across the little bridge. Go over the freeway (0.8) and turn right onto Laguna Drive (0.5) and right again onto State Street (0.3). This will take you back to the lagoon at Carlsbad Boulevard. Buena Vista Audubon Society has constructed an informative nature center on Carlsbad Boulevard on the northwestern bank of the lagoon. Stop here to learn about the local habitat and its birds and to bird the trails through the tules. This section can be good for Least Bittern, frequently heard, although these secretive birds are difficult to see. Redheads and Ruddy Ducks nest in this section of the lagoon.

If you cross the lagoon and turn right at the light on Vista Way (0.6), you will return to the starting point. However, you should bird more of the coastal lagoons and may want to scope the ocean before heading for the mountains. If so, turn around and go south on Carlsbad Boulevard. After passing through the town of Carlsbad, you will come to bluffs overlooking the ocean (0.8). Although not a hotbed of pelagic activity here, inshore birds and wintering loons, grebes, and scoters will be visible from this overlook.

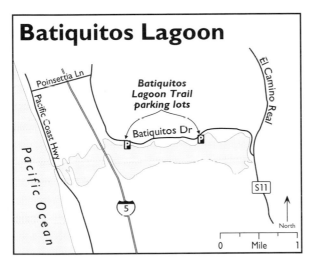

Batiquitos and San Elijo Lagoons to the south are less impacted by development than Buena Vista Lagoon and are therefore of significant interest. The chaparral-clad hillside south of San Elijo Lagoon is good for California Gnatcatcher as well as the common chaparral species one finds everywhere in the coastal region. The lagoon itself harbors the same species noted for Buena Vista above, and in greater numbers. Batiquitos Lagoon boasts a pleasant nature trail along the central section of its northern shore from which the species noted above can be seen, in season, as well as a representative sampling of passerines.

To reach **Batiquitos Lagoon Trail** continue south on Carlsbad Boulevard (S21, or Pacific Coast Highway) from the bluffs to Interstate 5. Travel south on Interstate 5 to the Poinsettia Lane off-ramp (1.5). Turn left on Poinsettia and right onto Batiquitos Drive (0.3) following it south and east. Park at the second Batiquitos Lagoon Trail parking lot on the right (2.0)—graced by the bronze statue of a female jogger—and walk downhill along the trail and then to the west. Bird the lagoon and the vegetation along the trail. A telescope is useful here as it is at the other lagoons.

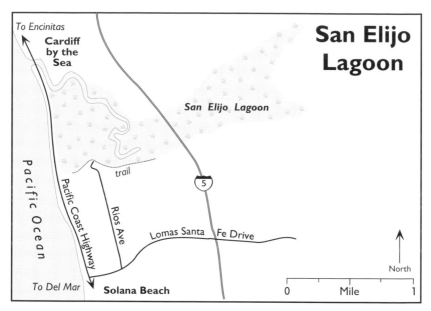

To bird the San Elijo Lagoon area, return to Interstate 5 and travel south to Lomas Santa Fe Drive in Solana Beach (6.7). Take the Lomas Santa Fe off-ramp, turning right at the traffic light, traveling west. Turn right onto Rios Avenue (0.7), which is approximately 0.2 mile east of Pacific Coast Highway—an alternate north-south route along the coast. **San Elijo Lagoon Sanctuary** is at the end of Rios (0.8). A good trail leads through willows and chaparral along the lagoon to the east, while the western leg leads you closer to shallow ponds. Check for waterbirds and shorebirds on the lagoon and, along the trail, for Anna's Hummingbird, Nuttall's Woodpecker, Cassin's Kingbird, California Gnatcatcher, Wrentit, and California Towhee. White-tailed Kite and Northern Harrier often cruise the marsh edges.

Retrace your way to Interstate 5 and drive north to the starting point, where you want to turn inland on the Vista Freeway (Highway 78). Get off at the second exit and go left (north) on El Camino Real (1.5) toward Mission San Luis Rey. Turn right onto Mission Avenue (Highway 76) (3.0). The mission (0.8) is on the left. Farther along on the right, you will see some ponds (3.0) which are part of Guajome Regional Park. This can be a good spot in winter and during migration. A White-tailed Kite often hunts over the marsh. As you climb the hill, watch for Cassin's Kingbirds in the Canary Island Pines. Vermilion Flycatcher has been found here several times, but is always a rarity anywhere in San Diego County.

Just past the turn-off to Vista (3.0), Highway 76 turns left across the San Luis Rey River, but you should make a little jog and continue straight ahead on **Old River Road** along the south side of the river. Rufous-crowned Sparrows frequent the brushy hillsides here, and you may find hummingbirds in the patches of flowering Tree Tobacco. (This is an exotic—a spindly greenish-gray somewhat willow-like plant with yellow tubular flowers about an inch long.) Anna's Hummingbirds are common all year; Black-chinned and Costa's are present in spring and summer, and Rufous Hummingbirds may be numerous during migration. Blue Grosbeaks like Mexican Elderberry along the stream in summer; look for Bell's Vireo—a rare bird in Southern California, but increasing due to consistent local trapping of Brown-headed Cowbirds. Yellow-breasted Chat and Hooded and Bullock's Orioles are present in summer.

At Country Club Road (2.2), turn left, cross the river to Bonsall, and rejoin eastbound Highway 76. Beyond Interstate 15 (5.3) the hills become steeper and the chaparral thicker. Golden Eagles are regular in this area. Watch on the left for the Pala Mission (6.6), which is small but interesting.

Birders are not welcome on Pala Reservation land, so make sure that you are well past it before walking the chaparral-edged washes. This area is good for Lazuli Bunting during the breeding season; also watch for the usual chaparral birds and Western and Red Diamond-backed Rattlesnakes. You will next pass through the Pauma Valley (*POW-mah*) (El. 840 ft) (2.0). At Rincon (1.8) bear left with Highway 76. The road climbs rapidly now and is bordered by groves of lemons and avocados. Red-shouldered Hawk and California Thrasher are among birds of the roadside here.

The road next enters an area of Coast and Engelmann Oaks. Engelmann Oak has light-gray bark and bluish leaves. Watch here for Acorn Woodpecker and Oak Titmouse. At the top of the grade, check the open area for Western Bluebird, Lark Sparrow, and Lawrence's Goldfinch.

Turn left onto Highway S6 (South Grade Road) (5.3) toward Palomar Mountain. (If you are pulling a trailer, continue on 10 miles to less-steep Highway S7, East Grade Road.) The road now climbs steeply through oak groves and tops out at Summit Grove (El. 5,202 ft) (6.8). You are suddenly in a different world. Here, on top of the mountain, the principal tree is the Jeffrey Pine of the Transition Zone. You will also find White Fir, Incense Cedar, Black Oak (deciduous), Canyon Live Oak, and White Alder.

Some of the birds that might be encountered on top are Mountain Quail, Band-tailed Pigeon, Northern Flicker, Hairy and White-headed (rare here) Woodpeckers, Steller's Jay, Common Raven, Mountain Chickadee, White-breasted and Pygmy Nuthatches, Brown Creeper, American Robin, and Dark-eyed Junco. In summer there also may be Olive-sided Flycatcher, Western Wood-Pewee, Violet-green Swallow, Cassin's Vireo (rare here), Western Tanager, Black-headed Grosbeak, Lawrence's Goldfinch, and Chipping Sparrow. In winter Purple Finch and Fox Sparrow are to be expected. If you work hard enough at night, you may find Great Horned, Spotted, Northern Saw-whet, and Western Screech-Owls.

There are three main areas on top of the mountain, and you should explore them all. **Palomar Mountain State Park** (fee for day-use, camping, or hot showers) is 3 miles to the left on Highway S7. On clear days stop at any of the various overlooks toward the west for a remarkable look at western San Diego County. Pishing at the chaparral downslope should produce Wrentit and various chaparral sparrows, while Red-tailed Hawk, White-throated Swift, and Common Raven are commonly seen overhead in any season but winter. The state park is a great area with meadows, forests, and a few little lakes. Spotted Owls have been found right in the campground. The view from Boucher Lookout on a clear day is magnificent.

Palomar Observatory (open 8 AM–5 PM) is 5 miles ahead on Highway S6. You only are able to look *at*, not through, the telescope, but it is still impressive and there are many exhibits. There is excellent birding all along this road, so you can stop almost anywhere and find something. One of the better spots is tiny **Fry Lake**. It is about 2 miles ahead on the right, just before the entrance to the Observatory Campground. Birds often come here to drink, and it is a good area for Spotted Owls at night. Check the picnic grounds below the parking lot at the telescope before visiting the observatory. Birds regularly seen here include Anna's Hummingbird, Acorn Woodpecker, Steller's Jay, Oak Titmouse, Western Bluebird, and Chipping Sparrow.

Many of the cabins in the housing area on **Birch Hill** have feeders, where you can occasionally find White-headed Woodpeckers. To reach the hill, turn right onto Highway S7 and then left onto the first little road.

After exploring the mountain-top, return to Summit Grove and go east on Highway S7 for the trip down the mountain. Traffic is not as heavy on this road, so you can stop frequently to bird. In a couple miles you will reach the grasslands, where Mountain Bluebirds often winter along with the more numerous Westerns. Also watch for Horned Lark, Lark Sparrow, and hawks.

Eventually, **Lake Henshaw** (El. 2,727 ft) (9.0) comes into view. This shallow lake resides on a plateau many score square miles in extent, most of which is grassland. Continue on S7 to its end just below the Lake Henshaw dam at Highway 76 and turn left. It is worth birding the lake at any time of year, but you will want to avoid duck-hunting season. In fall and winter the east end of the lake hosts large numbers of ducks and some geese. You may see wintering Bald Eagles hunting them singly or in tandem, then flying to the east shore to feast and be harassed by Common Ravens and Coyotes. Stop at turn-outs on Highway 76 opposite the east edge of the lake and unlimber your telescope (required here). An interesting aspect of spring weather can bring avian surprises here. Brief, violent storms have been known to ground migrating Common Loons, Brant, and Surf Scoters on the lake.

Public access to the east side of the lake is intermittent and a bit puzzling. It is usually possible to walk the shoreline from the boat docks to the east side. One or more of the turn-outs along Highway 76 may have turnstiles for access to the eastern shore. If possible, walk across the pasture to the east shore to check it for shorebirds in spring and fall migration. Whatever the status of access, always conform to landowner requirements.

If visiting in winter you have two productive options from Highway 76: the first is to continue east on Highway 76, turning left (north) on Highway 79 around the lake through miles of pastureland toward Warner Springs. You have a reasonable chance of seeing Ferruginous Hawk, Rough-legged Hawk (rare) in flight winters, resident Golden Eagle, and wintering Merlin and Prairie Falcon. Western Bluebird breeds nearby and Mountain Bluebird is a frequent winter visitor. Spring migration may produce scores of Western Kingbirds on the fence wires.

The second option is to look for wintering Lewis's Woodpeckers in the vicinity of Mesa Grande. Mesa Grande Road can be reached either from Highway 76, 1.8 miles west of its intersection with Highway 79, or from Highway 79 at 5.1 miles south of the intersection. The woodpeckers are usually seen around the old store at the site of Mesa Grande itself, or between this site and Highway 79. If you are at the intersection of Highway 79 and Mesa Grande you should drive a short distance south on Highway 79 to investigate the grounds of the small Santa Ysabel Mission on the left. Red-breasted Sapsuckers winter among the Siberian Elms below the church (look for the numerous horizontal rows of pits in the bark), and others of the "yellow-bellied" group are occasionally seen here, as well. Spring at the mission produces Western Kingbird, Black-headed Grosbeak, and Hooded and Bullock's Orioles. Lawrence's Goldfinch is fairly regular.

Retrace your route to Highway 76 and pass Lake Henshaw, traveling west down the mountain, following the San Luis Rey River. This riparian and oak grove route downhill is a good birding area at any season. In winter it is alive with Hermit Thrushes and sparrows, and in summer with Yellow-breasted Chats and Lazuli Buntings. The woods around the **San Luis Rey Picnic Area** downhill on the left about 1.5 miles below the dam are especially productive. A major nesting colony of Willow Flycatchers is here, and breeding pairs of Yellow Warblers are common.

Continuing west on Highway 76, you can retrace your way to Oceanside or you may want to intersect Interstates 15 or 5 and go anywhere in Southern California. Other routes lead back to the coast, of course, and all of them are beautiful, particularly in the spring. Another alternative is not to return to Highway 76, but to continue on Highway 79 to S2, 4.3 miles north of Highway 76, and take it east to Anza-Borrego Desert State Park, or hook up with the Laguna Mountains Loop. Yet another option is to continue north on Highway 79 for 27.6 miles past its junction with Highway 76 to its intersection with Highway 371 at the bustling metropolis of Aguanga. You can turn right on Highway 371 and conveniently join the San Jacinto Loop, travel to Palm Springs, or continue on to any of a variety of points in the desert to the east.

There are campgrounds on Palomar Mountain and two private camps along the San Luis Rey River. There are no motels in the recreational area, although motels are numerous in the lowlands of western San Diego County and cabins are available at Lake Henshaw.

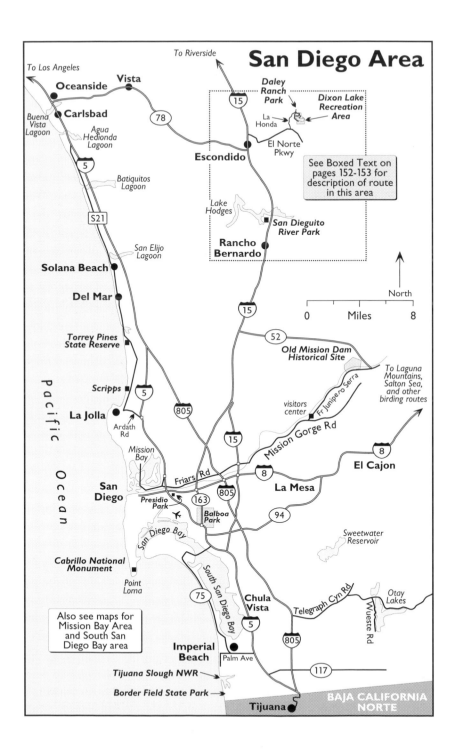

San Diego Area

To Los Angeles

To Riverside

Oceanside • Vista

Carlsbad

Buena Vista Lagoon

Agua Hedionda Lagoon

78

Daley Ranch Park

15

La Honda

Dixon Lake Recreation Area

El Norte Pkwy

Escondido

See Boxed Text on pages 152-153 for description of route in this area

5

Batiquitos Lagoon

S21

Lake Hodges

San Dieguito River Park

San Elijo Lagoon

Rancho Bernardo

Solana Beach •

Del Mar •

15

North

0   Miles   8

Torrey Pines State Reserve

52

Old Mission Dam Historical Site

Scripps •

5

visitors center

To Laguna Mountains, Salton Sea, and other birding routes

La Jolla •

805

15

Fr Junipero Serra

8

Ardath Rd

Mission Gorge Rd

Pacific Ocean

Mission Bay

Friars Rd

San Diego

Presidio Park

163

805

8

La Mesa

El Cajon

Balboa Park

94

San Diego Bay

Sweetwater Reservoir

Cabrillo National Monument

Point Loma

South San Diego Bay

75

Chula Vista

Telegraph Cyn Rd

Otay Lakes

Wueste Rd

Also see maps for Mission Bay Area and South San Diego Bay area

5

805

Imperial Beach

Palm Ave

117

Tijuana Slough NWR →

Border Field State Park →

Tijuana

BAJA CALIFORNIA NORTE

SAN DIEGO AREA

San Diego is a popular destination for Southern California birders. One might ask why: the coastal plain is blanketed by housing, mountain birding in the eastern county is below the standard of the San Bernardino or San Jacinto Mountains, and pelagic birding is average at best. The answer for the Californian is the probability of eastern vagrants in fall migration, as well as the occasional oddity from the south, and numerous accessible desert, water, and shorebird sites. Birding the coastal lagoons during migrations and in winter is always interesting.

For the out-of-state birder in San Diego on business with some free time, or the visiting traveler passing through, San Diego can be outstanding. The proximity and accessibility of different habitat types is most impressive, while the moderate weather ensures good birding days. When combined with a visit to the Salton Sea 2½ hours east, San Diego is, indeed, a fancy birding destination. There is *always* something to see in the San Diego area.

If you are planning a birding adventure in San Diego, set your itinerary only after consulting all the related chapters (Anza-Borrego, Laguna Mountains, Palomar Mountain, and Salton Sea) in this book. You may wish to create your own loops by combining, for instance, the northern county coastal lagoons from the Palomar Loop with Point Loma from this loop on a given day—and then Lake Hodges with Mount Palomar for a subsequent day(s). Many productive combinations are possible, given the geography. Always remember, however, that passerine birding is most productive in the morning, while waterbirds and shorebirds will be visible all day—so plan accordingly.

When coming to San Diego from the north on Interstate 5, the starting point is the intersection of the San Diego Freeway (Interstate 5) and the Sea World Drive exit. (See *Mission Bay Area* map on following page.) Take Sea World Drive to the **San Diego River** (0.7) and exit onto the old road on the north side of the river by taking the first left after the Friars Road intersection. Although productive at any time of day, this area is best birded within an hour on either side of high tide. Known as California's likeliest site for easily seeing Little Blue Heron, the list of herons, ducks, shorebirds, and gulls here is impressive—as are their numbers.

For eons the San Diego River meandered across this area, etching out Mission Bay on the north and San Diego Bay to the south. It is now strait-jacketed along this canal and can only flow meekly out to sea. However, the backwater along the channel is still an excellent refuge for waterbirds. This location really is a must for the visiting birder.

141

Mission Bay Area

If you are coming from the south on Interstate 5, or from the east on Interstate 8, go north on I-5 to Sea World Drive and follow the directions above.

Continue on Sea World Drive to Ingraham Street, taking it north about one-quarter mile to the next exit, where the road makes a loop and crosses over Ingraham Street. You are now on West Mission Bay Drive. After making the loop, take the first left turn, Quivira Road (0.5). Immediately turn left again and follow this road as its name changes to Quivira Way until it ends on the banks of the channel. This is Hospitality Point, where a walk out on the jetty can be productive. Also check for birds in Mission Bay Channel and the Quivira Basin, which is good in winter for Red-throated, Pacific, and Common Loons as well as Western and Clark's Grebes.

When you leave the river, go back up Quivira Way and take the first little road to the right, which is unnamed. Immediately turn right again onto Sunset Cliffs Boulevard going south across the river. After passing the Ocean Beach Freeway (I-8), bear right toward Ocean Beach. Turn right (west) onto West Point Loma Boulevard (2.0), then right onto Bacon Street to parking areas at Ocean Beach Park. Although Tricolored Blackbirds are less frequent here than formerly, check grassy areas for them and then the adjacent flood control channel for shorebirds and Brant. This is an excellent place to see terns, including—in season—Royal, Elegant, Common (migration only), and Least. Return to Sunset Cliffs Boulevard and drive south until you reach the rocky cliffs (1.3). (Now, consult North San Diego Bay Area map on following page.)

By stopping at all of the little turn-outs along the cliffs, you should find Western and Heermann's Gulls, Double-crested and Brandt's Cormorants, and a few shorebirds. In winter there also should be other kinds of gulls as

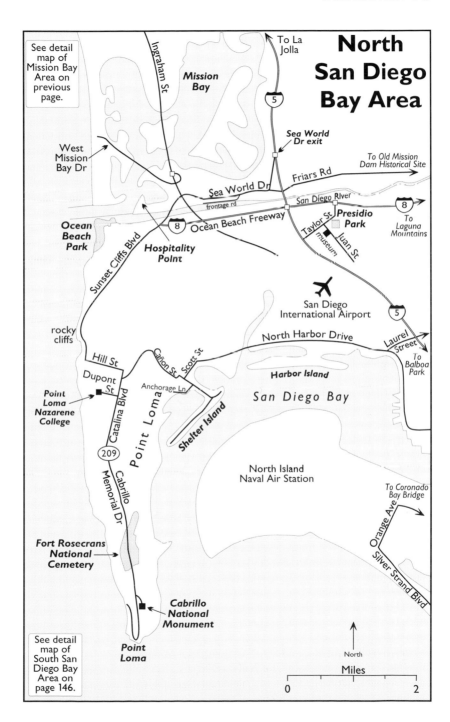

North San Diego Bay Area

See detail map of Mission Bay Area on previous page.

To La Jolla

Mission Bay

Ingraham St

5

Sea World Dr exit

West Mission Bay Dr

To Old Mission Dam Historical Site

Friars Rd

Sea World Dr

frontage rd

San Diego River

8

To Laguna Mountains

Ocean Beach Park

Sunset Cliffs Blvd

8

Ocean Beach Freeway

Taylor St

Presidio Park

museum

Juan St

Hospitality Point

San Diego International Airport

5

rocky cliffs

North Harbor Drive

Laurel Street

To Balboa Park

Hill St

Cañon St

Scott St

Harbor Island

Dupont St

Anchorage Ln

San Diego Bay

Point Loma Nazarene College

Catalina Blvd

Point Loma

Shelter Island

209

Cabrillo Memorial Dr

North Island Naval Air Station

To Coronado Bay Bridge

Orange Ave

Fort Rosecrans National Cemetery

Silver Strand Blvd

Cabrillo National Monument

Point Loma

North

See detail map of South San Diego Bay Area on page 146.

Miles

0   2

well as Pelagic Cormorant, Black Turnstone, a few Surfbirds, and Wandering Tattler.

At Hill Street (0.6) turn left and follow the scenic-route arrows toward Cabrillo National Monument. Turn right onto Catalina Boulevard (Highway 209) (0.7), which leads down the **Point Loma** ridge. This is the best migrant land bird locality in the area, and one of the best in the state. You may find American Robins, Red-breasted Nuthatches, and other mountain birds nesting in the conifer plantings here—a rarity on the immediate coast of Southern California. Bird along any street or on the grounds of **Point Loma Nazarene College** to the right at the end of Dupont Street (0.6). Park and walk the trails running both north and south. This area is best in migration, with numbers of western migrants in late April through May and an interesting variety of vagrants from the East during September and October.

To reach the monument, you must cross a military reserve (0.4), which is open only from 9 AM–5 PM in winter and 8 AM–7 PM in summer. **Fort Rosecrans National Cemetery** (1.4), on the road to the monument, is an excellent migrant trap (April 15–May 30 in spring, September 1–November 15 in fall) and is usually worth checking at any season. Many rare birds (mostly eastern vagrants) have shown up here over the years. The area is best for migrants in the morning and when the skies are overcast or foggy.

Continue on to the old lighthouse (1.0) at **Cabrillo** (*Cah-BREE-yo*) **National Monument** (fee). This viewpoint is one of the official observation stations for monitoring the migration of Gray Whales from December to March—the whales are, however, distant. Check the ornamental plantings around the parking lot, visitors center, and along the footpath to the old lighthouse for migrants in spring and fall. Flowering Bottlebrush attracts many hummingbirds in April, occasionally including Calliope. Check the brush along the hillsides for California Quail, California Thrasher, Bewick's Wren, Wrentit, Bushtit, Spotted and California Towhees, and several kinds of sparrows, including Golden-crowned in winter. White-throated Swifts usually dash about recklessly overhead.

The sea cliffs north of the new lighthouse are also productive. These can be reached by turning left onto Cabrillo Memorial Drive about a block after leaving the visitors center. Go down the hill and then bear right to the end of the road (2.0). Along this rocky shore in winter you can find Black Turnstone, possibly a Surfbird, and Wandering Tattler. Double-crested, Brandt's, and a few Pelagic Cormorants frequent the cliffs. Black-vented Shearwaters can be seen off the point at this time of year.

When you leave the monument, retrace your way north on Catalina Boulevard to Cañon Street (3.2) and turn right. In winter you may want to continue to the end of the street and turn left onto Anchorage Lane to check for any birds that may be there. Go one block to Shelter Island Drive and turn right for a loop around the island. Stop to check the fishing pier. You will probably see more naval ships than birds, but there are loons, grebes, and sea ducks on the bay in winter. Check the gulls and terns for a possible rarity and the lawns for Whimbrels and Black-bellied Plovers. Return to Shelter Island Drive and turn right at the traffic-light on Scott Street (0.4). You will pass the Point Loma Sport Fishing Pier, where you can arrange to go on a fishing or whale-watching boat to see pelagic birds. (See Pelagic and Island Birding chapter.) Turn right onto North Harbor Drive (1.1) for a scenic look at the bay and its various tourist attractions.

After checking the harbor area, continue on around the bay on North Harbor Drive until you reach Laurel Street at the end of the San Diego International Airport (3.2). Bear left onto Laurel Street and follow it east, as its name changes to El Prado, until it ends at Balboa Park. Birding in the park can be good in winter, while spring migration may present many common western species. You might want to visit the Museum of Natural History and the world-famous San Diego Zoo (open 9 AM–5 PM, fee), both excellent. Moreover, the blooming eucalyptus and other plantings at the zoo have yielded some interesting wintering passerine rarities in recent years, such as Greater Pewee and Dusky-capped Flycatcher.

When you are ready to leave Balboa Park, go south on Highway 163 (Cabrillo Freeway) to southbound Interstate 5 and follow it about 12 miles to the Palm Avenue (Highway 75) exit in South San Diego. (Switch to *South San Diego Bay Area* map on the following page.) Follow Palm Avenue to Seacoast Drive (3.0) and turn left. Watch on the right for the **Imperial Beach Pier** (0.3), an excellent observation station for birds of the inshore ocean. Loons, grebes, gulls, terns, scoters, and California Sea Lions are usually common in winter.

Continue south on Seacoast Drive past Imperial Beach Boulevard (0.2) to **Tijuana Slough National Wildlife Refuge**, one of the best saltmarshes remaining in Southern California. Numerous herons, egrets, and shorebirds usually can be found here. High tide may produce a Clapper Rail for your examination. Walk past the end of the road southward along the beach to the outlet of the Tijuana River. *Stay below the high-tide line to protect nesting Snowy Plovers and Least Terns during their breeding season.* At the river mouth look across to a sandbar where gulls and terns are usually resting (this is the location of the Belcher's Gull sensation of 1997–1998). Elegant Terns and an occasional Gull-billed Tern are often in this group in summer. Gulls and terns of the season roost here all year long. The slough behind often has a heron from the south in amongst the resident California species.

If you arrive in summer and could not find a parking place on Seacoast Drive, try the usually-less-crowded south end of 5th Street, which is accessible from Imperial Beach Boulevard at the Wildlife Refuge headquarters. By walking south along the fence-line to Ream Field (heliport), you will reach the river mouth, where large numbers of American Wigeons can be found in winter, including an occasional Eurasian Wigeon. "Large-billed" (*P. s. rostratus*) Savannah Sparrows (uncommon) winter here. This may also be the best place

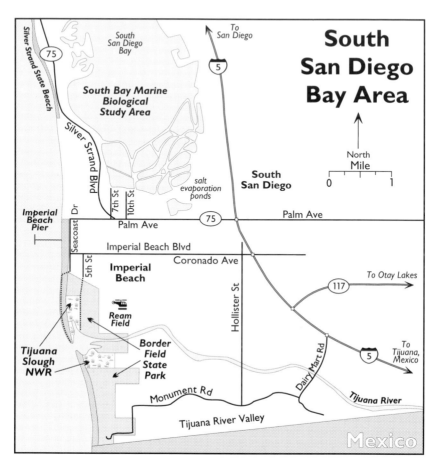

in the state to find a stray Reddish Egret or Tricolored Heron. Little Blue Herons are regular, but can be hard to see.

Return to Imperial Beach Boulevard (which soon becomes Coronado Avenue) and turn right. At Hollister Street (2.3), turn right toward the **Tijuana River Valley**, a famous (but declining) area for rare and unexpected birds. By closely checking all of the habitats, you may find something unusual in this valley, especially during fall migration (September and October).

Although much less productive than twenty years ago when the fields were alternately plowed, planted to tomatoes, and fallow, one may still find interesting birds here with diligent searching. Bird the Tamarisk rows and any weedy patches or wet spots encountered for lurking migrants and the occasional unexpected bonus.

At the south end of Hollister Street is Monument Road (2.3), which parallels the Mexican border. To the right is **Border Field State Park**.

The weedy fields between Hollister Street and the park are usually good for California Quail, Lesser Goldfinch, and, in winter, Short-eared Owl. You should be able to spot a White-tailed Kite somewhere in the area. Check the brushy hillsides along the road to the park for California Thrasher, Wrentit, California Gnatcatcher, and Golden-crowned Sparrow (winter) and the patches of Tree Tobacco and Bladderpod for Anna's, Black-chinned, Costa's, Allen's, and Rufous Hummingbirds. Lawrence's Goldfinches are occasionally found in March and April, although one has a better chance for this enigmatic bird on San Diego County's interior trips.

As you enter the park, you can make only a left turn. Drive as far as you can to the extreme southwest corner of the 48 States. This is an excellent place from which to view the marshland at the south end of Tijuana Slough by walking up the beach. Look out over the ocean to the Los Coronados islands in Mexican waters. For anyone keeping a Mexico list, this is an easy way to pick up some northwestern Mexican oceanic birds.

After you have worked the valley from one end to the other, go east on Monument Road to Dairy Mart Road (2.8). Turn left to Interstate 5 (1.2). Just before you reach the interstate, check the ponds—intermittently water-filled—and riparian growth along the river on both sides of Dairy Mart Road. This can be a most productive area, especially when the ponds are filled with water. Least Bitterns and Great-tailed Grackles both nest, and Northern Waterthrush has been found in winter. From here take Interstate 5 north toward San Diego.

At this point you may want to take a side trip to visit the **Otay Lakes** to the east. (Return to *San Diego Area* map, located at the beginning of the chapter.) To find the lakes, turn east onto Highway 117 (1.0) to Interstate 805 (2.0), drive north to Telegraph Canyon Road (4.0), and right (east) to the lakes (8.0).

Turn right onto Wueste Road (3.6) to reach Lower Otay Lake, which usually has more fishermen than ducks. However, you should be able to compare Western and Clark's Grebes, which both occur here. You should also be able to find Western and Cassin's Kingbirds and Bullock's Orioles (spring, summer) in the eucalyptus trees and Lark Sparrows along the fence-line. Otay Lake County Campground is located at the end of the road (3.0).

Return to the junction and turn right. In one-half mile the road curves back south between the two lakes, and, at mile 4.5, you will find a pull-off where you should park. Walk carefully through the chaparral toward the lake on your right. This entire area has numerous California Gnatcatchers. *(Remember, use of taped calls is inappropriate for this species.)* Check the reeds at the lake for Virginia Rail and Sora. You will notice that this has become a predictable site for resident Great-tailed Grackles—a bird first recorded in the county near here in 1977.

When you are ready to continue the loop, return to northbound Interstate 5, and exit at Palm Avenue (Highway 75) (1.4). (Now consult the *South San Diego Bay Area* map.) Drive west to where this broad highway curves north, becoming Silver Strand Boulevard. The best birding spot on the Silver Strand, the **South Bay Marine Biological Study Area** (3.5), is at the south end of San Diego Bay to your right. Gull-billed, Caspian, Elegant, and Least Terns, along with Black Skimmer, can be found nesting on the dikes here—however the dikes are closed to the public. They are best birded with a telescope from pull-outs alongside the northbound strand, or from the ends of 7th and 10th Streets in Imperial Beach—these can be reached by turning north on them where they intersect Palm Avenue. The diked ponds of South Bay Marine Biological Study Area are usually full of shorebirds during migration and in winter. Black Skimmers are year-round residents, and "Large-billed" Savannah Sparrows (*P. s. rostratus*) "winter" here (August–February). Note that the very dark, resident race of Savannah Sparrow—the "Belding's" Savannah Sparrow—is common here.

Continue north on Highway 75 along the Silver Strand. The State Beach (2.0) (camping; fee) is kept too clean for birds, but there are often resting flocks of gulls. You should be able to pick out Glaucous-winged, Heermann's, and Mew Gulls in winter, while Thayer's are uncommon, but possible.

You will see Coronado City Hall on your right (4.0). Stop in its parking lot and walk behind the National Guard building. In winter there are usually loons and grebes offshore. It is always worth checking through the large number of Surf Scoters on San Diego Bay for an occasional White-winged or Black Scoter, or an Oldsquaw. As of 1998, both White-winged and Black Scoters had become very scarce here, even to the point of being outnumbered by the relatively rare Oldsquaw! Check the rocky fill for Black Turnstone and Spotted Sandpiper. The landmark Hotel del Coronado (built in 1888) is three blocks north on the left. The beach in front of the hotel is good in winter for Mew Gull. Follow Highway 75 across the San Diego-Coronado Bay Bridge (toll) and turn north onto Interstate 5 (4.2).

At the junction of I-5 and I-8, you have several options. (Back to the *San Diego Area* map.) The closest birding area is **Presidio Park** in San Diego's Old Town. To reach it turn east onto I-8. Exit immediately at Taylor Street, which skirts the park. Turn left onto Juan Street and follow the signs for Serra Museum. You should find lots of birds if you wander around among the beautiful trees and down the hill behind the museum early in the morning—*do not* bother trying to bird this area at any other hour.

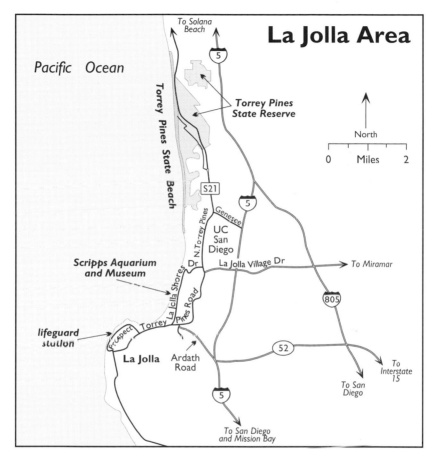

Your second choice from the intersection of I-5 and I-8 is to explore **La Jolla and Torrey Pines**. Even locals get lost in La Jolla and the traffic can be terrible, but it is productive—especially in winter. The rocky shoreline is not only very scenic, but also can be good for shorebirds and gulls. To reach La Jolla, drive north on Interstate 5, exiting at Ardath Road (6.8). By following the arrows for the scenic route, you easily can find the rocks and coves near the downtown area. Park at the lifeguard station just south of Point La Jolla; from the rocks there you may be able to see pelagic birds flying by offshore during high westerly winds.

Deep water just off the La Jolla coast makes it the best location in the county for observing seabirds. In winter you periodically can see large numbers (up to 1,000) of Black-vented Shearwaters from here along with occasional Northern Fulmar, Red Phalarope, Pomarine and Parasitic Jaegers, Black-legged Kittiwake (irruptive and irregular), Common Murre, and Rhinoceros Auklet. Although both Sooty and Short-tailed Shearwaters have been recorded from this location, beware—separation of these two species is more difficult than commonly understood, rendering identification at a distance through a telescope virtually hopeless (see Specialties section). All three species of both loons and cormorants are common at the appropriate times of year, as are Royal Terns. The rocky shore attracts Wandering Tattlers, Black Turnstones, Surfbirds, and even an occasional Black Oyster-catcher. Magnificent Frigatebirds (rare) have been seen around the boats fishing close to shore in July and August. Sabine's Gulls are somewhat regular here in September.

When you get to Torrey Pines Road, drive eastward until you can turn north onto La Jolla Shore Drive, again following the scenic-route arrows. There is a new aquarium at Scripps Institute of Oceanography (1.3) on the left, and also a very good bookstore. A Black-crowned Night-Heron nesting colony is at the opposite (south) end of the building complex. After visiting Scripps Institute, bear left onto North Torrey Pines Road (1.2) and left again onto the Pacific Coast Highway (S21) (1.2 miles).

Torrey Pines State Reserve (4.3) (fee) was set aside to protect the rare pine that grows only here and on Santa Rosa Island. It is a good area for chaparral birds. You should be able to find Western Scrub-Jay, Wrentit, California Thrasher, and Spotted and California Towhees without much trouble. Rufous-crowned Sparrow is resident around the lower parking lot and visitors center. Down the beach to the south and out of the park is one of the few official nude beaches in the nation. Judging from the number of binoculars seen in use along the cliffs, this must be a popular birding area.

If you have time to visit only one San Diego Area location away from the coast, make it the riparian woods at **Old Mission Dam Historical Site** on the San Diego River about 9 miles east of Interstate 5. This location is much more diverse than the Torrey Pines State Reserve above, and hence of more interest to the birder. Here, among the California Sycamores and Frémont Cottonwoods, you should find Nuttall's Woodpecker, Red-shouldered Hawk, Cassin's Kingbird, and American and Lesser Goldfinches, while White-throated Swifts dash about over the canyon. In summer look for Costa's Hummingbird, Pacific-slope and Ash-throated Flycatchers, Bell's Vireo (a resurgent population due to the consistent local trapping of Brown-headed Cowbirds), Yellow-breasted Chat, and Hooded and Bullock's Orioles. Can-yon Wrens and Rufous-crowned Sparrows are found on the rocky hillsides. The grassy fields have breeding Grasshopper Sparrows in spring and summer. The energetic may wish to walk the mountain trails across the river where "Bell's" Sage Sparrow, and, in winter, Golden-crowned and several races of Fox Sparrow can be found. During migration, you might find anything.

To reach the dam site, go east on Interstate 8, exiting at northbound Interstate 15. After approximately one-half mile turn right onto Friars Road and continue right (east) to Mission Gorge Road, a mile farther along, where you turn left. Continue on Mission Gorge Road to Father Junipero Serra Trail (4.2 miles east of I-15) where you turn left into Mission Trails Regional Park—a natural park in Mission Gorge. You should stop at the impressive visitors center on your left (it, and the one-way road into the canyon, are open at 8 AM), orienting you to the natural history of the area, after birding the canyon in the morning. (If you arrive before 8 AM, see directions below.) Follow the one-way road downcanyon, birding from pull-outs, to the dam-site parking lot on your left about 1.5 miles from Mission Gorge Road. From here you may walk trails along the river or up into the canyon and chaparral. Driving Father Junipero Serra Trail farther upstream (it becomes a two-way road at the dam parking lot) brings you parallel with Lake Kumeyaay across from the intersection with Bushy Hill Drive. Construction in the field between the intersection and the lake in 1998 made access routes questionable at that date, but this will be determined locally in the future. There is a trail around the lake and lush riparian habitat, also giving access to chaparral beyond. Least Bittern has been seen on the pond margins, while Common Moorhen is resident, a variety of ducks is present in winter, and an interesting array of swallows overhead and passerines in the willows is present in spring and summer.

If you arrive in Mission Gorge before 8 AM, continue east on Mission Gorge Road over the hill to its base eastward where Father Junipero Serra Trail loops back to it after going through the canyon. Turn left here and proceed west to the lower end of the one-way segment that began westward at the Nature Center, where there will be a locked gate. The parking lot for the old mission dam is here and you can bird this habitat early, before the influx of the day.

If your next birding stop is the Laguna Mountains area, retrace your route to I-8 and get onto the freeway eastbound. To return to the starting point in San Diego, westbound I-8 and northbound I-5 will take you there.

There is one public campground on this loop at Silver Strand State Beach; motels are numerous. Check at the Mission Bay Information Station, call the Chamber of Commerce, or look in the Yellow Pages or the AAA Camping Guide for the location of private camping and trailer facilities. One such facility that has camping for tents, trailers, and RVs is located on the north side of Mission Bay.

SAN DIEGUITO RIVER PARK AT LAKE HODGES

Adjacent to the community of Rancho Bernardo, approximately 20.2 miles north of the intersection of Interstate 8 and Interstate 15 in San Diego, this park provides unusual access to fine coastal sage scrub and lakeside birding. Many Southern California specialties can be found here with minimal effort. Morning is best, of course, and weekdays have fewer people—and their unrestrained dogs—on the trails. (It is a mystery why otherwise well-mannered people ignore the "Leashed Dogs Only" signs and let their pets run loose in a nature reserve.) This is a worthwhile stop any time of year, although spring and winter are probably best.

One reaches San Dieguito River Park, whether north- or southbound on Interstate 15, by taking the West Bernardo Drive/Pomerado Road exit and proceeding west on West Bernardo Drive. About one-half mile west of Interstate 15 you will find a signal-light and a sign pointing right toward Rancho Bernardo Community Park. Turn right and park one-quarter mile ahead near the tennis courts at the park.

Walk the trail across the street from the Senior Center. A few miles of trail winds around and over two chaparral-clad granite hills at the edge of Lake Hodges. The hill farthest from the interstate is recommended because it will have less highway noise. California Gnatcatcher is resident here, as are California Quail, White-throated Swift, Cassin's Kingbird, California Thrasher, and California Towhee. Blue-gray Gnatcatcher is found during winter and migrations, so look and listen carefully. Western and Clark's Grebes are common on the lake from fall through spring—listen for the difference in their single- and double-noted calls (the latter, Western Grebe) at these times. Golden Eagle used to nest in oaks near the lakeside. Although they have been displaced here due to an over-abundance of *Homo sapiens*, San Diego County still has the densest nesting population anywhere in California, and they are occasionally seen overhead here. White-tailed Kite is often seen hovering over grassy slopes in quest of voles. Both Rufous-crowned and "Bell s" Sage Sparrow are resident. Look for them anywhere in the sage scrub, but particularly along the trail in the saddle between the two hills.

Winter brings an assortment of waterbirds and the usual passerines wintering in Southern California. This is a very pleasant place to bird the unique chaparral/coastal sage scrub hills of western San Diego County.

From here you can travel south to San Diego or go north on Interstate 15 to Riverside, the San Bernardino and San Jacinto Mountains trips, or continue on to the Eastern Kern County Loop and the Mojave—indeed, to the Owens Valley east of the Sierra Nevada outside the range of this guide if you care to. Just 5.4 miles north of West Bernardo Drive, Highway 78 returns you toward the coast at Oceanside if you want to travel the coastline. From this junction there are also nearby alternate routes to Mount Palomar, the Laguna Mountains, and Anza-Borrego State Park to the east. Consult a AAA map of San Diego County for a larger picture of this area.

Just over a mile north of the Interstate 15/Highway 78 interchange, El Norte Parkway leads to another gem of native chaparral habitat in a City of Escondido park. Turn off I-15 at the El Norte Parkway exit and turn right onto the parkway (east). Turn left after 3.1 miles onto La Honda and follow it to its end 1.3 miles later at **Daley Ranch Park**. A trail winds through heavier chaparral than exists at San Dieguito River Park, although many of the birds resident here are the same. This is a more peaceful location than the latter, although it lacks the riparian habitat—with a consequently smaller bird list. Highly recommended for chaparral birds, it is a botanist's paradise.

Dixon Lake Recreation Area (fee) is immediately adjacent to Daley Ranch Park. The entry fee is collected only on weekends and holidays. The lake is good for waterfowl in winter and the chaparral is birdable year round. There are camping facilities at Dixon Lake, while motels abound in the Rancho Bernardo/Escondido area.

Cassin's Kingbird
Shawneen E. Finnegan

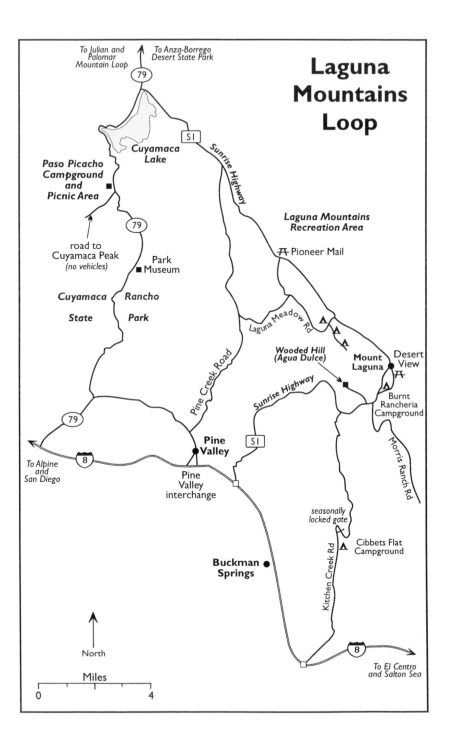

Laguna Mountains Loop

To Julian and Palomar Mountain Loop

To Anza-Borrego Desert State Park

79

S1

Sunrise Highway

Cuyamaca Lake

Paso Picacho Campground and Picnic Area

79

Laguna Mountains Recreation Area

Pioneer Mail

road to Cuyamaca Peak (no vehicles)

Park Museum

Cuyamaca

State

Rancho

Park

Laguna Meadow Rd

Wooded Hill (Agua Dulce)

Mount Laguna

Desert View

Pine Creek Road

Sunrise Highway

Burnt Rancheria Campground

79

Pine Valley

S1

8

To Alpine and San Diego

Pine Valley interchange

Morris Ranch Rd

seasonally locked gate

Cibbets Flat Campground

Buckman Springs

Kitchen Creek Rd

North

8

To El Centro and Salton Sea

Miles

0   4

LAGUNA MOUNTAINS LOOP

Two major north-south mountain ranges separate the Pacific coast from the deserts of interior San Diego County. Both ranges have peaks over 6,000 feet in elevation. The Laguna Mountains, the easternmost of the ranges, has a more arid climate since cool, wet air coming from the Pacific Ocean loses much of its moisture to the westernmost range, the Cuyamaca Mountains (quee-yah-MAH-cah).

Although the birder visiting Southern California would be well advised to center their montane birding on the higher ranges to the north (see the San Gabriel, San Bernardino, San Jacinto, and Mount Pinos chapters), those based in San Diego will find these mountains interesting. The trips into and out of the mountains here provide numerous opportunities to explore Coast Live Oak and chaparral habitats. Anyone with botanical or geological interests will be impressed.

Chaparral, oak-pine woodland, and grassy meadows comprise the predominant vegetation types in the Laguna Mountains. Rocky outcroppings, intermittent streams, and scattered small lakes and marshy areas add variety as they punctuate the landscape. Summers are pleasant, mostly sunny and warm. In autumn the nights turn cooler, and winter brings the occasional snow after November and most of the year's rain.

Begin at the junction of Interstate 8 and Route S1 (Sunrise Highway), 40 miles east of the intersection of Interstates 8 and 15 in San Diego. Go north on S1, stopping at the Meadow Information Station (6.0), located where the road climbs into the woodlands. Birds typical of this habitat include Western Bluebird, Steller's Jay, White-breasted and Pygmy Nuthatches, and Dark-eyed Junco. Drive on, and when you reach open meadow, stop to look for Western Meadowlark, Western Bluebird, Lark Sparrow, and Lawrence's Goldfinch. In winter it is possible to find Lewis's Woodpecker and Cassin's (scarce) and Purple Finches here. You soon reach Kitchen Creek Road (1.5).

You may start this tour differently, depending on the time of year and whether you want to search for the elusive, breeding Gray Vireo. The alternate route is not open the entire distance from late fall through early spring, but making a portion of the drive might still be productive.

To take the alternate route, leave the freeway at **Kitchen Creek Road**, 7.6 miles east of the Sunrise Highway exit, and go north. The lower, more-open areas will have typical grassland birds, while the middle section of the road traverses rocky, chaparral habitat containing Gray Vireo and Rufous-crowned and Black-chinned Sparrows. At Cibbet's Flat Campground

(4.6) you'll find a running creek, large oaks, and associated shrubs surrounded by thick chaparral. Stop at a parking area (1.7) and walk in either direction along the creek. Mountain Quail can be found here.

A gate just beyond the end of the tarred road (0.1) is locked from late fall through early spring, but you can walk up the irregularly-maintained dirt road for several miles to look for Mountain Quail, Gray Vireo (April through June), and Black-chinned Sparrow in spring and summer. During April and May, Gray Vireos are singing, and they might be found anywhere in the first two miles above the gate. Their song is said to be sweeter and more liquid than that of Cassin's Vireo. If the gate is open, continue on to the junction with Route S1 (11.8), looking for "Bell's" Sage Sparrows along the way.

The next stop, Wooded Hill (1.2), has two campgrounds and a dirt road leading to Agua Dulce Creek, an area known to have Spotted and Northern Saw-whet Owls. Check Burnt Rancheria Campground (1.4). The hamlet of **Mount Laguna** (0.2) has a ranger station, a restaurant, and a small market.

The cluster of campgrounds at Mount Laguna offers a sampling of habitats in a small area, increasing the variety of species you might see. The bird list is similar to that of Palomar Mountain. A partial list of birds seen here includes California and Mountain Quail, Band-tailed Pigeon, Anna's Hummingbird, Nuttall's Woodpecker, Red-breasted Sapsucker, Steller's Jay, Western Scrub-Jay, Oak Titmouse, Mountain Chickadee, White-breasted and Pygmy Nut-hatches, Brown Creeper, Western Bluebird, Hermit Thrush (winter), Wrentit, California Thrasher, Hutton's Vireo, Ruby-crowned and Golden-crowned Kinglets (winter), Spotted and California Towhees, and White-crowned and Golden-crowned Sparrows in winter. Fox Sparrow (*P. i. stephensi* presumably), Purple Finch, and Lesser Goldfinch are resident. In summer you might also see Olive-sided Flycatcher, Western Wood-Pewee, Violet-green Swallow, Black-chinned Sparrow, and Bullock's Oriole. Several coniferous-forest species—White-headed Woodpecker (very local, scarce), Mountain Chickadee, and Pygmy Nuthatch—reach their southernmost limits for California in this area.

Mount Laguna and environs are particularly valued for such species as White-headed Woodpecker, Williamson's Sapsucker (rare, winter), Purple Martin (summer), and Evening Grosbeak (rare, winter).

Desert View Picnic Area (0.3) and nearby Vista Point (0.1) offer wonderful views of the desert to the east. Laguna El Prado Campground (2.4) and the Laguna Meadow Road (left turn) access an area where Evening Grosbeaks and Pinyon Jays have been found in winter. Pioneer Mail Campground is (4.0) a pleasant picnic area.

Soon the woodland is left behind as the road drops in elevation, first into thick chaparral, and then into the wide and rolling, grassy fields north of Cuyamaca Lake. The landscape is punctuated by large live oaks and criss-crossed by fence-lines. In summer this habitat normally produces Turkey Vulture, Red-shouldered Hawk, Golden Eagle, American Kestrel, Acorn

Woodpecker, Horned Lark, Violet-green, Cliff, and Northern Rough-winged Swallows, Loggerhead Shrike, Black-headed Grosbeak, Lazuli Bunting, Lark Sparrow, Western Meadowlark, and Lesser and Lawrence's Goldfinches. In fall and winter look for Bald Eagle (Cuyamaca Lake), Northern Harrier, Ferruginous and Rough-legged (rare) Hawks, Merlin, Prairie Falcon, Mountain Bluebird, Black and Say's Phoebes, American Pipit, Vesper (uncommon) and Savannah Sparrows, and Cassin's Finch (uncommon).

The Sunrise Highway (S1) ends at Route 79 (7.4). *If you wish to end the loop here, you can reach Anza-Borrego Desert State Park by turning north onto Highway 79 to Julian (5.8), then right onto Highway 78 to Yaqui Well (18.2). Or continue north and west on Highway 79 at Julian, ending up at Lake Henshaw on the Palomar Mountain Loop (18.7).*

To continue this loop, go left onto Highway 79 and skirt the western shore of **Cuyamaca Lake** (El. 4,635 ft) on your way into Cuyamaca Rancho State Park. The lake's water level fluctuates widely and can produce excellent or poor birding. It is good for ducks in winter (a telescope is useful) and for American Robin and Western Bluebird at any season. Check the grassy flats around the lake in winter for American Pipit and Mountain Bluebird.

The state park encloses large areas of chaparral, oak woodland, and coniferous forest. Birding is good at almost any stop, and, depending on habitat, you may expect to find the same species listed previously. The best campground for birding is the **Paso Picacho Campground and Picnic Area** (4.9). Acorn Woodpeckers and Steller's Jays abound.

Green-tailed Towhees can be found in the brushlands well above the campground along the fire road (0.1) leading south from the campground to Cuyamaca Peak (El. 6,515 ft). Farther up this road (you are not allowed to drive the fire road to the summit) you should find Band-tailed Pigeon, Nuttall's and Hairy Woodpeckers, Olive-sided Flycatcher, Violet-green Swallow, Steller's Jay, Mountain Chickadee, Pygmy Nuthatch, and other mountain birds. Mountain Quail are found in the brushy terrain among Ponderosa Pines on the higher slopes. White-headed Woodpecker, very scarce anywhere in San Diego County, is most reliably found in the pine forest near the peak.

You may wish to stop at the Park Museum (2.7) to gain a further appreciation of the area on your way back to Interstate 8 (8.0).

If you are heading west toward San Diego, turn onto westbound I-8 and continue to the junction of Interstates 8 and 5. If you are on your way to the Salton Sea Loop, travel east on I-8 for 77 miles to El Centro, then north on Highway 86 to Brawley (15.9) to begin that loop. You may also choose to drive another 56 miles east to Yuma, Arizona, to do the Imperial Dam Loop.

You have a good choice of campgrounds on this loop, and of a few motels in the small mountain communities.

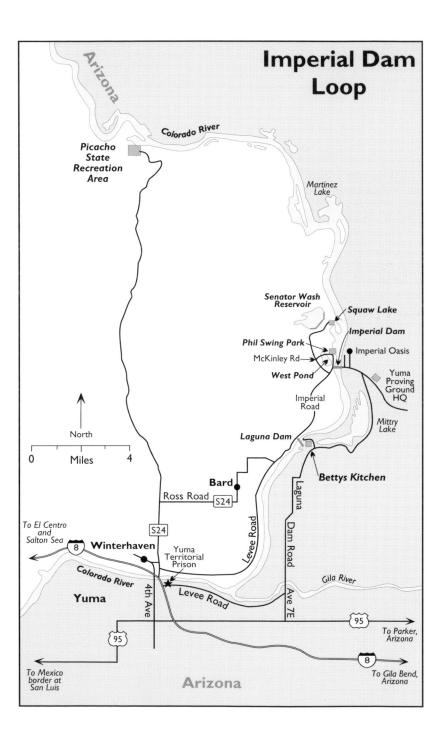

Imperial Dam Loop

Arizona

Colorado River

Picacho State Recreation Area

Martinez Lake

Senator Wash Reservoir

Squaw Lake

Imperial Dam

Phil Swing Park

McKinley Rd

Imperial Oasis

West Pond

Yuma Proving Ground HQ

Imperial Road

Mittry Lake

North

0 Miles 4

Laguna Dam

Bettys Kitchen

Bard

Ross Road S24

Laguna Dam Road

S24

To El Centro and Salton Sea

Winterhaven

Yuma Territorial Prison

Levee Road

Colorado River

Yuma

4th Ave

Levee Road

Ave 7E

Gila River

95

To Parker, Arizona

95

8

To Gila Bend, Arizona

To Mexico border at San Luis

Arizona

IMPERIAL DAM LOOP

The long, green oasis created by the Colorado River has been used for countless centuries as a migration route by both men and birds. Almost all of the native riparian vegetation that used to cover the broad floodplain has been replaced by cropland. Therefore, in addition to the migrants, you will now find many wintering species that didn't use the area before.

Most birders come during the mild winters, when waterfowl and other wintering species concentrate. The best times to see migrants are in late April and early May and from late August through October. A few hardy souls brave the summer heat, for this area is near the western limit for several breeding birds, such as Inca Dove, Crissal Thrasher, Lucy's Warbler, and Bronzed Cowbird. In late summer there is always a slim chance of finding a rare straggler from Mexico, such as a booby or a Roseate Spoonbill. Late-summer monsoon storms have been known to blow in such wildly-out-of-range species as Laysan Albatross, various storm-petrels, and Brown Pelicans.

Begin in Winterhaven, turning northward onto Picacho Road (S24). Cross a canal and then jog left (0.2) under the railroad tracks following the signs for Picacho State Recreation Area. The road crosses farmlands, usually empty of birds unless the fields are being irrigated. Wherever you find water in the desert, you will find birds. During migration, shorebirds may congregate by the hundreds on irrigated fields. Follow the main road (S24) as it swings right onto Ross Road (3.6) toward Bard.

If you have the time and inclination, you can follow Picacho Road straight ahead to Picacho State Recreation Area (19.0). The road is sometimes rough and always dusty. It passes through a barren but beautiful land of rocky canyons and multi-colored mountains. The park, located on the bank of the Colorado River, is small with few facilities; it is a delightful place to camp.

As you travel through the Bard Valley you will notice groves of citrus trees and date palms. They offer nesting sites for Gila Woodpecker, Gilded Flicker (rare), Barn Owl, White-winged Dove, Hooded Oriole, and the ever-present European Starlings and House Sparrows. The side roads in this area are worth exploring at any time of year. Resident species include Common Ground-Dove, Inca Dove, Greater Roadrunner, and Phainopepla. Ruddy Ground-Dove (very rare) has occurred here in winter. However, if you're in a hurry, stay on S24 as it winds its way toward the river.

Laguna Dam (9.7) was the first of many dams across the Colorado River. The brushy river valley between it and Imperial Dam can be entered by several dirt roads. The conifer-like Tamarisks, native trees of Asia, are abundant

159

here, along with Palo Verde and willow trees. Scan the area for the reintroduced Harris's Hawk (see Southern California Specialties section), Ladder-backed Woodpecker, Crissal Thrasher, Verdin, Black-tailed Gnatcatcher, Phainopepla, Lucy's Warbler, and Abert's Towhee.

The wetlands surrounding the Imperial Irrigation District's All-American Canal Section headquarters (3.4) are a good spot to look for the hard-to-see Black Rail. Turn into the headquarters, bear left, and park out of the way. Walk along the S24 right-of-way and listen for the rails, which call at any time of day or night. They prefer shallow wetlands dominated by bulrushes.

At Senator Wash Road (0.3) turn left. After crossing the All-American Canal (0.3) you will see **West Pond** on your right with several dirt roads leading to it. This small lake can be good for Black Rail, Least Bittern, other freshwater-marsh species, and sometimes a rarity or two.

At McKinley Road (1.0) turn right toward Imperial Dam. Another entrance to West Pond takes off at 0.5 mile. Imperial Dam is at the end of McKinley Road at Phil Swing Park (0.75), a little spot with tables, restrooms and drinking water. Part of the lake above the dam is visible from here. Most of it is silted in and supports a vast stand of cattails. The few date palms are also worth checking. The first California records of Great-tailed Grackle (now common) and Rufous-backed Robin were of birds that wintered in these trees. At dawn and dusk listen and watch for Lesser Nighthawk, Least Bittern, "Yuma" Clapper Rail, and Sora.

After checking the little park, return to Senator Wash Road. Turn right and go past Senator Wash Reservoir and over the dam (2.3). Below the dam is an inlet of the Colorado River known as Squaw Lake. There is a nice campground here and a few birds.

Return to Imperial Road (3.6), turn left, and cross the Colorado River to the Arizona side. (If you keep state lists, you will have to shuffle them a few times on this loop.) After crossing the river, turn left (0.8) onto a paved road and follow it to where it ends at the base of the dam (0.6). There is a small lake with picnic tables and grills. Check the lake and canals for herons, egrets, and waterfowl. Return to the main road, turn left, and (after crossing another bridge) turn left onto a paved road (0.1). This road ends at Hidden Shores RV Village after crossing the Gila Irrigation Canal. There are always a few Gambel's Quail running around the trailer park, and you may find an active bird-feeder or two. Check the open water behind the dam for loons in winter, waterfowl, and egrets.

Leaving Hidden Shores the way you came in, you will again cross over the Gila Irrigation Canal. Next, turn left onto the levee road and drive along the canal. Watch for birds on the sides of the canal on the left and in the marsh and the stand of mature cottonwoods on your right. Cross the paved highway (1.0) near the Yuma Proving Grounds headquarters and continue on the west levee of the canal.

Follow the levee through **Mittry Lake Wildlife Area**. The extensive marsh on the right contains large concentrations of waterfowl in winter. At wide points in the road stop to check the tules for Common Moorhen, Red-winged and Yellow-headed Blackbirds, and in summer for Least Bittern. The endangered "Yuma" Clapper Rail can be found here, along with Black and Virginia Rails and Sora. The easiest way to entice them from the thick tule growth is to play a tape of their calls, *sparingly*. In summer look for Brown-crested (rare), Ash-throated, and Vermilion Flycatchers, Phainopepla, Blue Grosbeak, Bullock's Oriole, and, rarely, Cassin's Kingbird. Check the mesquite for Verdin and Lucy's Warbler. In migration, you may find anything.

As you approach the Arizona side of Laguna Dam, turn right at the sign for **Bettys Kitchen Wildlife Interpretative Area** (6.1). Follow the signs to the parking area (0.2). There are picnic tables, restrooms, and a nature trail. During migration this is an excellent place to see flycatchers, vireos, warblers, tanagers, buntings, sparrows, and orioles. A dock overlooking the back of Laguna Dam can provide good views of Green Heron, Common Moorhen, and Spotted and Least Sandpipers.

Walk or drive west, past the parking area, to some irrigated fields (0.1). Keep going west along the south edge of the fields to a grove of trees surrounding an abandoned house and apiary. You are now in California again. Check the area for Harris's Hawk (reintroduced with marginal results), Greater Roadrunner, Abert's Towhee, Hooded Oriole, and several kinds of sparrows. The river is to the north on the other side of the fields.

Return to Mittry Lake Road and turn right. Soon the road—now called Laguna Dam Road—is again paved and passes through irrigated farmland. Stay on this road as it winds to the south, crossing what is left of the Gila River (7.4), and coming to the south levee of the Colorado River. If you are tired of dirt roads, continue south on what is now called Avenue 7E to US-95 (2.0). Turn right toward Yuma. At Interstate 8 (4.0) you can turn right to return to the starting point.

Otherwise, turn right onto the south levee of the Gila River. The river is on your right, and a concrete-lined canal will be on your left. Shortly (2.5), the road jogs and continues with the canal, now on the right side. Greater Roadrunner, Burrowing Owl, quail, and doves are plentiful. The levee ends at the infamous Yuma Territorial Prison State Historic Park (6.6). During migration the trees at the park may contain some good birds. A backwater of the Colorado River on your right at the end of the levee road often has American White Pelicans, egrets, herons, White-faced Ibis, Clapper Rail, Common Moorhen, and others. Interstate 8 will take you back to the start.

To reach Brawley and the Salton Sea Loop, drive west on Interstate 8 to the Highway 86 exit in El Centro (56.4), taking it north to Brawley (15.9).

The only improved campground is at Squaw Lake, but there is plenty of open space in which to camp. Motels and RV parks are abundant in Yuma.

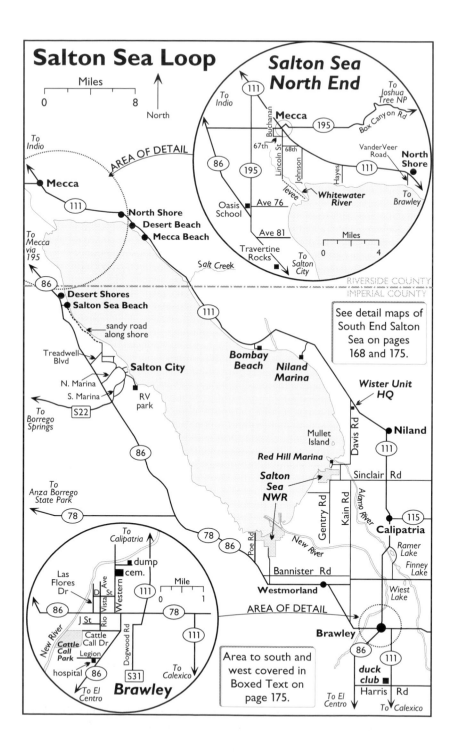

Salton Sea Loop

Miles
0 — 8
North

Salton Sea North End

To Indio — 111 — Mecca — 195 — Box Canyon Rd — To Joshua Tree NP

Buchanan
67th — Lincoln St — 68th
86 — 195 — Johnson — Hayes — VanderVeer Road — North Shore — 111

Oasis School — Ave 76 — Levee — Whitewater River
Ave 81 — To Brawley
Travertine Rocks — To Salton City

Miles
0 — 4

To Indio
AREA OF DETAIL
Mecca — 111
To Mecca via 195

North Shore
Desert Beach
Mecca Beach
Salt Creek

86
Desert Shores
Salton Sea Beach
sandy road along shore

111

RIVERSIDE COUNTY
IMPERIAL COUNTY

See detail maps of South End Salton Sea on pages 168 and 175.

Treadwell Blvd
Salton City — Bombay Beach — Niland Marina
N. Marina
S. Marina — S22 — RV park

To Borrego Springs

Wister Unit HQ

86

Mullet Island
Red Hill Marina
Salton Sea NWR

Davis Rd
Niland
111
Sinclair Rd

To Anza Borrego State Park
78

Gentry Rd — Kain Rd — Alamo River
New River
115
Calipatria
Ramer Lake
Finney Lake

To Calipatria
dump
cem.
Las Flores Dr
Rio Vista Ave — Western — 111
D St
J St
New River
Cattle Call Dr
Cattle Call Park
Legion
hospital — 86
To El Centro
Dogwood Rd
S31
Brawley

78 — 86
Poe Rd
New River
Bannister Rd
Westmorland
AREA OF DETAIL
Wiest Lake

Mile
0 — 1
78
111
To Calexico

Area to south and west covered in Boxed Text on page 175.

Brawley
86 — 111
duck club
Harris Rd
To El Centro
To Calexico

SALTON SEA LOOP

by Stacy Peterson

The Salton Trough, extending from Palm Springs south into the Gulf of California, is part of a rift valley created by the movement of tectonic plates and subsidence along the numerous north-south faults underlying the region. Millions of years ago the delta of the Colorado River created a dam across the gulf, isolating the trough. The basin has since been dry or filled with intermittent lakes, depending on the vagaries of the river. The last great lake to fill the basin was Lake Cahuilla, about 160 miles long and 35 miles wide. It lasted for roughly 450 years until A.D. 1500.

In the 1880s, the feasibility of bringing water from the Colorado River to irrigate the dry, fertile basin (the sediments are over 8,000 feet thick!) was recognized. By 1901 a 40-mile canal had been opened along an old course of the river; soon 300,000 acres were under cultivation. In 1905 a flood, one of the many which occurred on the river before the dams were built, caused the channel to shift until the entire river was diverted into the canal. Some 63 billion gallons of water a day poured into the dry lake bed. After 18 months, the river was finally turned back, but a lake 35 miles long and 15 miles wide had been formed. The Salton Sea was born! Birds and birders have been drawn to it since.

Excess water from irrigation projects continues to run into the lake; what was once a land of burning sand is now a lush valley filled with birds.

Currently the Sea is California's largest inland body of water, covering approximately 360 square miles (Lake Tahoe is 192 square miles) with an average depth of 20 feet. It is 48 feet at its deepest point at the south end. The temperature of the water fluctuates from the 50s to the 90s depending on depth and season.

The soils surrounding the Salton Sea are alkaline, and farmers leach out the salts by allowing fresh water to run over their fields. This salt-laden water runs into the Alamo, New, and Whitewater Rivers and then into the Salton Sea, which gets saltier every year. This over-abundance of salt and other contaminants threaten to make it a dead sea. The only loss of water from the Sea occurs through evaporation, further concentrating the salts and toxins.

Of the numerous fish that were introduced, only Orange-mouthed Corvina, Gulf Croaker, Tilapia, and Sargo have successfully survived, and some

163

of these are declining. Periodic fish die-offs due to algal blooms, and the recent outbreak of avian botulism which killed thousands of birds in 1997—including endangered California Brown Pelicans—is further evidence of the Sea's illness. Efforts to clean up Salton Sea are currently being debated in the United States Congress, and one hopes that such debates will result in a long-term, environmentally sound solution to the complex problems troubling this unique region.

First-time visitors to Salton Sea should prepare for an experience quite unlike any other. Although the birding is often extraordinary, the environment can be quite a shock to the uninitiated. Summer at the Sea brings a whole new meaning to the phrase "hot birding." Temperatures are consistently above 100 degrees, and days of 120 degrees are not uncommon. These are "in the shade" temperatures—and there is no shade. The humidity can be high as well, particularly close to the Sea. The stench resulting from algal blooms, dead fish, and other factors can be overpowering in spots. Flies can be a major nuisance, while the hundreds of dead or dying fish along the shoreline can add to the unpleasantness. Birders who are prepared for such experiences can find the birding spectacular, and the Sea remains at the top of many a Californian's list of "where to bird" during the summer months. Just remember to fill your gas tank, ensure that the car's cooling system is in order, take lots of water, sunscreen, water, a hat, water, and snacks. Did we mention water?

The infrequent winter rains bring about their own hazards, as the once dusty roads can become very slippery. Even four-wheel-drive vehicles have problems on some roads, and birders unfamiliar with the region are well-advised to stick (pun intended) to well-traveled roads when wet weather arrives. The roads into and around Finney and Ramer Lakes, and stretches of Davis Road, are especially likely to be impassable in wet weather.

All of these cautionary notes, however, should not deter you; the Salton Sea is an outstanding birding locale. It simply needs to be approached with appropriate preparation. The list of resident birds in the area is testimony to this fact, among the more enticing of which are Western and Clark's Grebes, American White Pelican, Cattle Egret, White-faced Ibis, Gambel's Quail, "Yuma" Clapper Rail, American Avocet, Black-necked Stilt, Costa's Hummingbird, Say's Phoebe, Common Ground-Dove, Greater Roadrunner, Burrowing Owl, Gila and Ladder-backed Woodpeckers, Black Phoebe, Verdin, Cactus and Marsh Wrens, Black-tailed Gnatcatcher, Crissal Thrasher, and Abert's Towhee.

Spring-through-summer specialties include Fulvous Whistling-Duck, Gull-billed Tern, Black Skimmer, White-winged Dove, Lesser Nighthawk, Black-chinned Hummingbird, Western Kingbird, Blue Grosbeak, and Yellow-headed Blackbird. Late June through July brings an influx from Mexico—Wood Stork (confined to the south end) and Yellow-footed and Laughing Gulls. Magnificent Frigatebirds are seen every year (though they can be difficult to relocate), while Brown and Blue-footed Boobies show up sporadically in late summer and fall. Roseate Spoonbill was also an infrequent visitor to the south end in the 1970s and 1980s, but has not been seen there for many years.

In winter up to a half-million ducks of 15 species are in the valley, as well as some 30 to 50 thousand geese, including Snow, Ross's, and Canada. Shorebirds are common, and landbirds are easy to find. A few of the more interesting wintering birds are Ferruginous Hawk, Sandhill Crane, Mountain Plover, Long-billed Curlew, Mountain Bluebird, Orange-crowned Warbler, and Brewer's and Sage Sparrows. Each year a few eastern warblers are found wintering in settled areas near the south end.

During migration, particularly in spring, millions of birds pass through the valley. Swallows sometimes line the telephone wires by the thousands. Irrigated fields may be covered by hundreds of egrets, shorebirds, and gulls. American White Pelicans can be seen in large flocks, and during some years more than one million Eared Grebes form huge rafts on the Sea. If you hit just the right day in spring, every tree and brush-pile may be brightly colored with warblers, tanagers, grosbeaks, buntings, and orioles. When faced with such a mass of birds, you may find a vagrant which chases you to the nearest coin phone (see the Rare Bird Alert telephone numbers in the Introduction).

Birders wishing to see some of the more irregular birds of the region should call the local RBA reports. San Bernardino Valley Audubon Society sponsors an RBA providing consistent coverage of this region. The San Diego RBA periodically reports very rare birds, too.

Many Audubon chapters in Southern California take field trips to the Sea—at all seasons. Visitors may join these trips and enjoy great birding with local, knowledgeable leaders. To find out if a trip will coincide with your visit, access the Audubon in Southern California web page (http://www.audubon.org/chapter/ca/SoCal/index.html), and go to the field trip link.

Birders wanting to cover this loop in its entirety should plan to spend at least two days—it is a three-hour non-stop drive around the Sea alone. However, by carefully planning your route to maximize habitat and target birds, a full day can easily net over 100 species in spring and summer. If time is limited, you can still produce dozens of birds for your list in just a couple of hours. The travel time to the closest portion of the Sea will then be the limiting factor.

Although this tour is designed as a loop, where you choose to start will depend on the direction from which you arrive, which birds you most want to see, and the position of the sun as it affects viewing conditions. Ambitious birders, or those already familiar with the region, may attempt to cover the entire loop—a round-trip of over 250 miles.

If you arrive on Interstate 10 from the north, take the new expressway (Highway 111) from Indio to the north end of the Sea. Just follow the signs for Highway 111 south toward Mecca and Niland. Birders traveling from the Los Angeles area may be tempted to take the regular Highway 111 south in Palm Springs, but this route goes through town, taking much longer.

We begin the loop from the end of the Highway 111 expressway at its intersection with Highway 195 at the north end of the Sea. From here proceed west away from Mecca for one block to Buchanan Street, where you turn left. If arriving in the morning, you can sometimes hear and see Crissal Thrashers in the desert scrub in this area. At the end of Buchanan (0.5), you may quietly bird the Tamarisk trees along the road. The residence here is known as Rattlesnake Ranch; birders should be wary of a few noisy dogs running loose. The Tamarisks can be good in migration, and the cottonwood grove and stand of palms along 67th Avenue just east of the residence also can be good for migrants. A Red-shouldered Hawk often hangs out in the cottonwoods. Check the palms for Hooded Oriole in spring and summer. The few records for Western Screech-Owl in the valley have been from this location. *Bird only from the road.*

Continue east on 67th Avenue to Lincoln Street (0.9) and turn right. At the St. Anthony Fish Farm (0.4) you will see a number of ponds on your left. This is private property (the owner and his progeny have been known to be very hostile to birdwatchers), so scan the ducks and waders *from the road. Do not (i.e., do **not**) trespass!*

Continue on Lincoln Street to where the pavement ends at the Whitewater River Levee (2.1), heading left. Although all the old "No Trespassing" signs have been removed, the actual permitted access routes to the end of the **Whitewater River delta** change periodically. As of this writing (1998), the Coachella Valley Water District has placed dirt berms over the dike roads to limit vehicular traffic in an attempt to control illegal dumping at the delta. CVWD is willing to remove the berms for official groups or tours, so the roadblocks may or may not be there when you arrive.

Prior to this development, the first dike road on the left inside the gate had been open fairly consistently; birders, duck hunters (October through January), and fishermen had been able to access this area easily. Depending on which access route is open (there is often another route paralleling the river), the road can be sandy and overhanging brush may scrape your car. If you choose to walk in, be aware that it is over one mile to the delta tip: take water! The delta looks southeast; morning arrival, therefore, requires maneuvering to achieve a good viewing angle from the sun. Early morning, however, can be very productive at the delta. During hunting season you should bird very cautiously here, or not at all.

The shallow water of the Whitewater River delta is good at any season, but may be best during spring migration when ducks and shorebirds often bank up before moving north. This locale has the distinction of being one of the best spots for finding rarities in all of Southern California. The dead tree snags provide perches for Osprey, Bald Eagle (very rare in winter), and—in late summer—for Brown Booby (very rare), Magnificent Frigatebird (irregular), and Brown Pelican. Blue-footed Booby, which never perches in trees (but will perch on telephone poles), has also been seen here. The reed-lined river channel near the delta is one of the most consistent spots at the Sea for

Least Bittern. Gull-billed Tern, Black Skimmer, and several species of gull are often seen. All three species of jaeger have been seen here, especially after storms from the south. Yellow-footed Gull, primarily a summer visitor from the Gulf of California, may be found here, but is much more common along the western shore.

Return to Lincoln Street and go north. Turn right at 68th Avenue (2.1), just past the St. Anthony Fish Farm. Continue to Highway 111 (0.9) and turn right. Quickly turn right again onto Johnson Street (0.2) and go to where water over the road prevents you from driving farther. A ditch, which is good for Green Heron, Common Moorhen, Gull-billed Tern, and Belted Kingfisher parallels the road on the right side. Look straight down the road from your stopping point; you can see the delta of the Whitewater River. Scope the snags in the water for Ospreys and frigatebirds. The island in front of you is a good place to find Black Skimmer in summer. All manner of unusual birds have been seen in the waters offshore—especially in summer. You should find numbers of ducks, waders, and shorebirds. Remember the cautionary note about birding this area during duck season.

Return to Highway 111 and proceed south. If you have time you can scope the Sea at Hayes Road (2.2) or Vander Veer Road (5.4). Eventually you will come to the Salton Sea State Recreation Area headquarters (2.3) (fee; visitors center with historic documentary about the Salton Sea open in winter 9 AM–4 PM; pick up a checklist). This area used to be a magnet for swimmers, water-skiers, and boaters, but the Sea's reputation has apparently warned all but fishermen and birders to stay away. The campground (with pay showers) can be good for migrants in season, and the old swimming area is a haven for roosting gulls and terns. At least ten species of gull have been found here, including Little, Heermann's, Mew, Lesser Black-backed, Thayer's, and Yellow-footed. Although these are not to be expected in any given year, such records illustrate this location's potential.

Continue south along Highway 111 to Mecca Beach State Campground (1.6) (fee unless you paid at the headquarters earlier), another part of the State Recreation Area. Birding generally has not been as productive here, but the trees in the campground hold potential for migrants. You probably will have noticed that the landscape along Highway 111 is getting very desolate, and the next several miles are not much different. County listers will need to pull out another checklist at the Imperial County line (6.2).

If time permits, you can investigate all the side roads down to the beaches and check the shore. The better spots are Bombay Beach (8.0) and Niland Marina (5.8). These two places have fair numbers of "Large-billed" Savannah Sparrows in winter (*P. s. rostratus*—another sparrow future-split-candidate, most common November through January). Check the *Salicornia*-like vegetation (*Allenrolfia* spp.) that grows very close to the shore—these birds do not stray more than a few yards from water and seem to prefer this habitat.

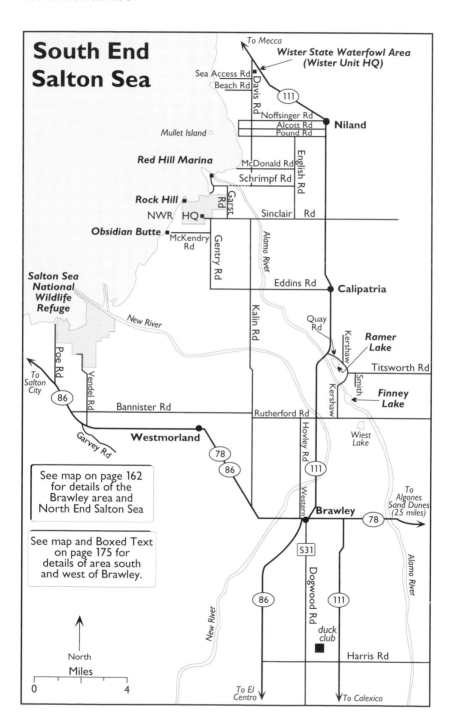

South End Salton Sea

To Mecca

Wister State Waterfowl Area (Wister Unit HQ)

Sea Access Rd
Beach Rd

Davis Rd

111

Noffsinger Rd
Alcott Rd
Pound Rd

Niland

Mullet Island

Red Hill Marina

McDonald Rd
Schrimpf Rd

English Rd

Rock Hill

Garst Rd

NWR HQ

Sinclair Rd

Obsidian Butte

McKendry Rd

Gentry Rd

Alamo River

Eddins Rd

Calipatria

Salton Sea National Wildlife Refuge

New River

Poe Rd

Vendel Rd

Kalin Rd

Quay Rd

Kershaw

Ramer Lake

Titsworth Rd

To Salton City

86

Kershaw

Smith

Finney Lake

Bannister Rd

Rutherford Rd

Garvey Rd

Westmorland

78

86

Hovley Rd

111

Wiest Lake

See map on page 162 for details of the Brawley area and North End Salton Sea

To Algones Sand Dunes (25 miles)

Brawley

78

See map and Boxed Text on page 175 for details of area south and west of Brawley.

S31

Western

Dogwood Rd

Alamo River

86

111

duck club

North

Harris Rd

Miles

0   4

To El Centro

To Calexico

Continue south on Highway 111 to the Wister State Waterfowl Area (6.7) on the right. Better known among birders as **Wister Unit**, this is at the north end of Davis Road and the beginning of arguably the most productive segments of the Sea. Park near the outhouse and information kiosk, and sign in. It is good to register so others will recognize the value of this region to birders and ecotourism. The trees and shrubs before the end of the pavement can be productive for flycatchers, warblers, tanagers, and orioles during migration. A nature trail and overlook (with wheel-chair access) are on the west side of this row of trees across from the small residential area. Gambel's Quail, Verdin, Black-tailed Gnatcatcher, and Abert's Towhee are resident. During spring and fall migrations, many Audubon Society field trips start here at dawn. If you are an early riser, you may choose to do so as well.

Davis Road leads south through some great duck and shorebird habitat. Because this is a State Waterfowl Area, you should be careful here during duck season—this is what is known as a "multiple use area." Several of the assorted access roads and dikes heading west toward the Sea's shore, as well as almost all of the freshwater impoundments along Davis Road, are off-limits during hunting season. They are generally well worth a drive at any other season, however, as long as you are prepared to back up for a quarter-mile or more to get out of some of them. Good roads to check include Sea Access Road on the right just as the pavement ends (0.5), Beach Road (1.0), Noffsinger Road (2.1), Alcott Road (0.5), and Pound Road (0.5).

As you approach the southern end of Davis Road, you will notice that the shoreline comes right up to the road. Depending on the water level and the prevailing winds you may find the road inundated—or you may see a vast expanse of mudflats covered with shorebirds. If Davis Road is flooded, you simply can turn east on any of the named county roads and drive to English Road. Turn south and pick up the route again at Schrimpf Road.

A cluster of old adobe buildings at the intersection of Pound and Davis Roads is an excellent place to stop. These buildings were once part of a mineral-water spa and dry-ice plant. A number of hot springs used to be here, but the geothermal source is now being tapped for energy at several hard-to-overlook facilities. This location is a fine place for studying shorebirds, being the spot where a number of the area's Semipalmated Sandpiper reports have originated in spring. Stilt Sandpiper is regularly seen in migration and winter. Snowy and Semipalmated Plovers are consistent, as well.

Look toward the Sea and you will see Mullet Island, a protected nesting area for large numbers of Double-crested Cormorants. It is also the site of recent Brown Pelican nesting attempts.

Watch the telephone poles along Davis Road for Peregrine Falcon. Be sure to take a right onto McDonald Road (1.0), which dead-ends at some impoundments near the Sea. In summer large flocks of Wood Storks used to roost in old snags just off the beach. Although these snags were recently removed by the landowners, Wood Storks may still be seen in the vicinity. Brown Pelican, Gull-billed Tern, Black Skimmer, and other waterbirds are common. Blue-footed Booby has been seen near here. Search the flocks of Bonaparte's Gulls for Little Gull, which has been found in this area many times.

Back on Davis Road, continue south. You will come upon several large termite mound-like structures in the field on your left. These are a few of the remaining mud pots that have not been inundated by the rising Sea. At the end of Davis Road (1.5) check on your right. For years a gate here was open; you could drive west on Schrimpf Road until you came to the bridge over the Alamo River, saving yourself several miles and passing some nice habitat and Gull-billed Tern nesting areas. Recently the property owners have closed the gate to minimize the disturbance at their adjacent duck club during duck season, but this situation might not be permanent. If the gate is up, you must turn left on Schrimpf Road, then right on English Road (2.1), then right on Sinclair Road (1.5).

The detour above is not a total waste of time because this area is typically attractive to the Round-tailed Ground Squirrel and its guest, the Burrowing Owl. Watch both the concrete-lined canals (they use burrows between the concrete and the dirt) and the larger dirt ditches along almost any road in the valley. The agricultural fields, when flooded, can be filled with gulls, Long-billed Curlews, and White-faced Ibises.

Turn right at Garst Road (3.1) toward Red Hill Marina. Park at the end of Garst (1.6) and walk up the berm and over the old bridge over the **Alamo River**. (If the Schrimpf Road gate is open as noted earlier, this is the road's end.) Clark's Grebe can often be found near the bridge. A flock of birds on the seashore frequently contains Yellow-footed Gull and assorted shorebirds. Both species of pelican, Gull-billed Tern, and Black Skimmer can be found regularly in this area. The vegetation to the east along the river often has contained some wintering eastern warblers. You can walk down the dike to the west to reach the Alamo River delta with its vast accumulation of gulls.

Return to your car and head west to **Red Hill Marina** (0.7). In the shallows of the causeway ponds and on the Sea (El. currently minus 226.4 ft), you should find numerous ducks, gulls, terns, and shorebirds. The mouth of the Alamo River is the best area on the Sea to find Wood Stork in summer. The campground is not deluxe, but it is adequate (phone 760/348-2310 for camping information). The sign at the end of the road indicates that there is a day-use fee, but birders have been allowed to bird the area around the hill southwest of the entrance road for short periods of time at no charge. Go left from the stop sign and proceed clockwise around the hill. As you return east from the backside of the hill, park your car near the picnic tables and grills and walk up the road to your left. The view overlooking the Alamo River delta and Red Hill Marina is expansive, but the large flocks of roosting gulls seen from this vantage point are a bit distant for effective study. You will likely see a small flock of escapee flamingoes somewhere around the delta.

Retrace your way to Sinclair Road and turn right. The **Salton Sea National Wildlife Refuge** headquarters (906 West Sinclair Road, Calipatria, CA 92233; phone 760/348-5278; open sunrise–sunset) is located at the end of Sinclair Road at its intersection with Gentry Road (1.1). The refuge personnel are very courteous and can be helpful in locating some of the 384 species on the Salton Sea National Wildlife Refuge checklist (visitors center open 7 AM–3:30 PM Monday–Friday and weekends as volunteers are available). A checklist and information about which areas are open to birding are available at the bulletin board. When the NWR was formed in 1930 it contained nearly 38,000 acres. The Sea has since risen until all but 1,785 acres are under water. Check the bird report sheet at the covered picnic area to see what birds are being reported.

Many resident birds, including Abert's Towhee, can be seen in the bushes and trees around the buildings, and the observation tower is a good place from which to observe the area beyond for waterfowl. In spring migration, the area teems with birds. In winter the refuge hosts thousands of ducks and geese, primarily Ross's and Snow. During the hunting season, you can often see great flocks right behind the headquarters, where they are safe. Many visitors enjoy sorting through the flocks of geese, attempting to read the numbers on the colored neckbands on geese banded near the Arctic Circle (report the numbers and details of banded birds to the bird banding laboratory at Patuxent, Maryland; phone 800/327-BAND; e-mail bandreports@patuxent.nbs.gov).

Walk west past the headquarters for one-half mile on Seaside Trail to Rock Hill. From here you can view a portion of the south end of the Sea and the many ducks usually present. As you turn right to begin this walk, check the ponds and reeds at the corner for Least Bittern. These freshwater ponds formed naturally behind dikes of washed-up barnacles. The barnacles were introduced accidentally into Salton Sea by the floats of seaplanes conducting training activities here during World War II. Some of the larger ponds provide nesting-sites for Clark's and Western Grebes. During July and August watch for Laughing Gull, Gull-billed Tern, and Black Skimmer. Look to the southwest and you will see **Obsidian Butte** and Cove.

As of this writing, you can drive to Obsidian Cove and around the butte by taking Gentry Road south from headquarters and turning right onto McKendry Road (0.5). *In the future, access may be restricted to foot traffic only* in order to protect endangered California Brown Pelicans which have recently begun nesting just west of the butte. If allowed access, birders should observe the birds from the road with a spotting scope instead of walking down to the shoreline. In spring and fall scan the rocks just offshore behind the butte for Blue-footed Booby, which occasionally perches here among the numerous Brown Pelicans. This is a good area for Yellow-footed Gull in summer, and in winter—when it is rare anywhere at the Sea. Several "Large-billed" Savannah Sparrows have been seen near the brackish water along the entry road just southeast of the butte.

Return to Gentry Road and turn right. The drive to Eddins Road (3.1) should give you ample chances to see Burrowing Owls if you happened to miss them earlier. In winter, watch for Ferruginous Hawk. Go left on Eddins to Highway 111 in Calipatria (6.0) (El. minus 184 ft), "the lowest-down town in the Western Hemisphere." The people of the town built the world's highest free-standing flagpole so the flag would fly above sea level. You can't miss seeing it along the left side of the road just before you reach the highway.

Continue south on Highway 111 to the State Waterfowl Area Finney - Ramer Unit (2.9) on your left. (There is a convenient rest-stop to the left of Highway 111 just across the river if you miss the turn). Just off the highway toward the lake is a patch of mesquite that usually yields Abert's Towhee and, perhaps, Crissal Thrasher.

Proceed to the sign-in kiosk (0.6) northeast of the maintenance compound along **Ramer Lake** and sign in. You can drive clockwise around the lake, including a shortcut over a levee. This is a good place to see Fulvous Whistling-Duck and Clark's and Western Grebes. The shrubbery at the southwest end of this levee contains a large heron and egret rookery. Watching many hundreds of squabbling Cattle Egrets, White-faced Ibises, and assorted herons here in April is a remarkable experience. One of the few Salton Sea records for Tricolored Heron was from this rookery during nesting season.

Once you have made the loop and ended up where you began near the kiosk, turn right (east) over the railroad tracks—following the sign to Finney Lake—to Kershaw Road (0.2). Turn right and travel to Titsworth Road (0.6). Turn left on Titsworth to Smith Road (0.2). Another right will take you toward **Finney Lake**. Bear right at the T-intersection (0.6), then make a quick left over the canal. Finally, go counter-clockwise around the shrubs in front of you, and sign in at the kiosk. The Tamarisk grove in the (very) primitive camping area can be full of warblers in migration. Keep an eye out for Barn Owl and Lesser Nighthawk in summer. Several vagrant passerines have wintered in this area, so it could be worth a stop at any season.

Continue through the primitive camping area on the east shore of the lake to a high spot from which you can look over the tules. Explore the network of dirt roads and dikes around the numerous ponds. Except during the hunting season (October to January), ducks—apparently knowing better—frequent the site. Fulvous Whistling-Duck, Wood Stork (post-nesting visitor), and Black Rail (rare) may be found here in summer, along with the more numerous herons, egrets, and Common Moorhens. Be sure to work the patches of saltbush and Honey Mesquite for White-winged Dove, Gambel's Quail, Crissal Thrasher, and other resident land birds. Crissal Thrashers are easiest to find early in the morning when they are more vocal. To reach a consistent spot for these birds, continue south on the dirt road from the bluff overlooking the lake until you cross a canal with a paralleling road bearing the descriptive (in some years) name of Mayflower Drive (0.6 from the kiosk). About 0.1 mile south of the intersection the desert opens up into a parking area. Listen for the thrashers in the early morning along the edges of this area, and back along Mayflower Drive as it extends east along the canal.

Return to Kershaw Road the way you came in and turn left. At the T-intersection with Rutherford Road (2.3) you can't help but notice what the atmosphere has already announced—a large cattle pen, teeming with blackbirds. Red-winged, Brewer's, and Yellow-headed Blackbirds are regulars, Brown-headed Cowbirds are numerous, and Cattle Egrets are seen here frequently. Check beside the grain elevators along Kershaw Road for Common Ground-Doves. Great-tailed Grackle, also present in large numbers, was unknown in California until the first female was found at West Pond near Imperial Dam along the Colorado River on June 6, 1964. By 1969 they were at Finney and Ramer Lakes, nesting nearby a year later. Today they are abundant at certain sites around the south end of the Sea, and frequently are seen beside the road among agricultural fields.

Weist Lake has a good campground, and you can bird Weist Lake Imperial County Park (fee) a few miles to your left if you wish—flocks of Black Terns occur here in migration—but the bird life is often minimal there, so our loop turns right onto Rutherford Road. Just before you reach Highway 111 (0.8) you will cross over the old Colorado River channel, formed when the river flowed into the Salton Basin, spawning the Salton Sea, nearly 100 years ago.

There are local rumors that Highway 111 will be moved eastward to avoid downtown Brawley at some point in the future, but until that time just head south on Highway 111 to its intersection with Highway 78 in **Brawley** (5.6) (El. minus 113 ft). Birding the Brawley area can be rewarding, especially in winter months (October–March). To find some good birding spots go right (west) to Rio Vista Avenue (1.0) and turn left (south) to J Street (0.3); then park and walk. This residential area is often good for Gila Woodpeckers, most easily found by their noise. A number of birds unexpected in winter, such as Cassin's Vireo, Yellow and Black-throated Gray Warblers, American Redstart, Hooded Oriole, and even Red Crossbill, have been known to over-winter. This is a most productive area in April and early May when flowering Bottlebrush attracts many hummingbirds, including Calliope.

Continue driving south on Rio Vista to Cattle Call Drive (0.2) and turn right to **Cattle Call Park** (0.2). This area, too, is good for Gila Woodpecker and Common Ground-Dove. Bronzed Cowbird is regular in summer, and Cactus Wren is often found near the rodeo grounds.

If you are visiting in summer and you can't find Bronzed Cowbirds at Cattle Call Park, return to Cattle Call Drive and proceed east to Highway 86 (0.4). Turn right, then right again onto Legion Road (0.8) at Pioneer Memorial Hospital. The residential areas just west of the hospital often have a few Bronzed Cowbirds about the yards.

Finding Sandhill Cranes south of Brawley is a special winter treat. To reach a roost site (current 1998), drive south on Highway 86 to Harris Road

(7.3 miles south of Highway 78/86, 4.0 miles south of Pioneer Memorial Hospital).

Turn left (east) to Dogwood Road (2.1). Plan to arrive at least one hour before sunset. The cranes might be feeding in any of the fields in this area and sometimes fly to a duck club set back in the field on the northeast corner of Harris and Dogwood. Large flocks of White-faced Ibises, egrets, and gulls may fly in, too.

If you arrive early, you might search for the cranes feeding in any of the fields nearby. While their exact location is dependent in part on the condition of the fields, your chances are probably best north of Harris along Dogwood between Highway 111 (east of you) and Highway 86—although they could be anywhere in the valley. Stop every half-mile or so to listen for their noisy calls. Flocks of 250 birds can be quite noisy! The San Bernardino Valley Audubon Society RBA often has updates on recent locations of these birds, if they are being reported.

When you have completed your crane search, return to Highway 86. From this point you may choose to return to Brawley and bird the Las Flores Drive area, continuing north from there, or to continue farther southwest to yet more productive areas. (See *Boxed Text* on following page.)

If you wish to go to Las Flores Drive now (a highly recommended location regardless of the way you structure your trip), return to Highway 86 and drive north to its intersection with Highway 78 in Brawley. (See inset map on page 162.) Go left to **Las Flores Drive** (0.6), turn right, and proceed one block to West D Street. Park in the vacant lot at the northeast corner of the intersection and walk into the small, sunken date palm grove to the north. This area virtually guarantees Gila Woodpecker and many other desert birds such as Common Ground-Dove, Verdin, Cactus Wren, Black-tailed Gnatcatcher, and Abert's Towhee along with the more common species. Check the residential area around the grove for Inca Dove, which can often be heard calling *no-hope* from the yard of the house immediately west of the parking area. *Do not trespass in any of the yards, or into the signed area behind the house west of the grove.*

Proceed east on West D Street to Western Avenue (0.5) and turn north. The **Brawley Cemetery** (0.7) on your right can be good year round, although it is best known for migrants—including the occasional vagrant—and wintering passerines (gate closes at 4 PM). For those uncomfortable birding residential areas, this is one of the most productive areas in Imperial County. Although a small area, it is worth a look at any time of the year.

Leave the cemetery and head north briefly on Western Avenue to the first road on your right, just before the New River crossing. Turn onto this unnamed road and drive to any vantage point overlooking the **Brawley Dump**. Lesser Black-backed, Thayer's, and Glaucous-winged Gulls all have been seen here in winter. Most activity is during the day when the dump is

South and West of Brawley. Go to the intersection of Dogwood and Keystone (S 27) Roads and turn west, traveling 6½ miles to Forrester Road (S30). Turn left onto Forrester to Edgar Road (1.8), turn right, and drive a quarter-mile to the entrance of Sheldon Reservoir. Check here for loons, grebes, ducks, and terns. Following this, drive a quarter-mile farther, parking by the drop on the Westside Canal. Walk south, birding the Palo Verde and Tamarisk trees. This is an excellent area for migrants, Lesser Nighthawk, Crissal Thrasher, and other desert birds. Continue west on Edgar Road, turning left at the end onto Pierle Road, and right at the end of Pierle onto Wheeler Road. Turn left onto Erskine Road a mile farther. The whole Pierle-Wheeler-Erskine-Roads area is the best location in Imperial County for Mountain Plover; flocks of 300 or more are not uncommon. It is also excellent for winter raptors, Prairie Falcon, and wintering Mountain Bluebirds.

Continue south on Erskine Road to its end at Worthington Road. Turn right (west) 1.3 miles to Huff Road, on which you will turn left to Evan Hewes Highway (S80) (4.2). At the crossroads of Huff and Evan Hewes, turn left onto Evan Hewes, driving a mile east to Derrick Road. Turn right (south) on Derrick, crossing Interstate 8, until you reach **Fig Lagoon** on the east side of Derrick. Almost all of the lagoon is readily visible from the dirt roads that run around the bluffs. This lagoon is worth a visit at any time of the year, and is a magnet for vagrants. Rarities such as Blue-footed Booby, Magnificent Frigatebird, Neotropic Cormorant, Yellow-crowned Night-Heron, Roseate Spoonbill, and Sabine's Gull have all turned up here in the past. Least Bittern, "Yuma" Clapper Rail, and many other resident species may be seen here throughout the year.

After birding Fig Lagoon, continue south on Derrick to Diehl Road, turning left to Drew—at this point you are approximately six miles north of the Mexico border. Turning left onto Drew starts you northward again. Drive 3.2 miles north of Diehl Road, crossing Interstate 8 again, to Sunbeam Lake County Park at the southeast corner of Drew Road and Ross Road. This park holds migrant waterfowl and land birds, and is good to check at any time of year. When finished birding at Sunbeam Lake you will go north to Evan Hewes (S80) and turn right, traveling east seven miles to Highway 86. Turn left on 86, going 13.3 miles north to Highway 78 in Brawley. Turn left on Highway 78 to reach Las Flores Drive (0.6).

operating, but in late afternoon in winter a large number of gulls come in to roost.

Continue north on Western Avenue (which becomes Hovley Road) until you get to Rutherford Road (3.8; if this sounds familiar, you were on this road when you crossed the old Colorado River channel earlier in the day), then turn left. The agricultural fields in this region (as well as those near the Salton Sea NWR headquarters) have often contained Mountain Plovers in winter. One hopes that the sign-up sheet at headquarters or the local RBAs would have alerted you to their presence.

Right on Kalin Road (2.1) and left on Bannister Road (0.5) will take you to Vendel Road (7.7). Turn right on Vendel and watch for Burrowing Owls at any season and in winter for Mountain Plover and Mountain Bluebird along the way. The road ends at the observation overlook Unit 1 of the **Salton Sea National Wildlife Refuge**. Part of this area of man-made ponds and fields is open all year (no hunting), while other sections are heavily hunted in season. A walking trail takes you through endangered "Yuma" Clapper Rail habitat, and patient photographers may even get its picture from the photo blind. Other birds you may encounter include Least Bittern (uncommon), Cinnamon Teal, Redhead, Ruddy Duck, and Black Rail (very rare). Songbirds will be found in the Tamarisks and cattails. In winter look for Stilt Sandpiper (annual) among the large number of Long-billed Dowitchers. You can also expect White-faced Ibis along with many Snow, Ross's, and Canada Geese.

Return to Bannister Road and continue west to Highway 86 (0.8). Drive north to Poe Road (2.8) and turn right to the southern shore of the Salton Sea. Yellow-footed Gulls are found here consistently, and the assorted shorebirds should be looked through.

Continue north on Highway 86 which will take you through some very barren desert, usually out of sight of the Sea.

To visit **Salton City**, the next stop, turn right on North Marina Drive (21.9). Johnson's Landing on your left (0.4), and the area near an abandoned round yacht club building, accessed by turning left off Marina Drive onto Yacht Club Drive (0.4), provide good vantage points from which to scope the Sea and shoreline. You may wish to explore several other roads down to the Sea.

Shorebirds, waders, pelicans, and gulls may be numerous here. In Salton City you will notice that many buildings were abandoned as the water level rose in recent years. This is a good place to find Yellow-footed Gull in summer, with a few usually present year round. North Marina Drive becomes South Marina Drive, which will eventually take you back to the highway opposite the road (S22) leading west to Borrego Springs. If you wish to bird Anza-Borrego Desert State Park, S22 is the route you will take to access it from the Sea.

To continue the Salton Sea loop, return to the intersection of North Marina Drive and Highway 86 and continue north to Salton Sea Beach (5.7) and **Desert Shores** (2.5). Both offer good vantage points from which you can look over the shore and the Sea. Among the gulls in summer, you should be able to pick out a Yellow-footed. Always keep an open mind as to what other waterbirds might occur. Such outstanding Salton Sea rarities as Laysan Albatross, Pomarine and Parasitic Jaegers, and Sooty Shearwater have all been seen from Desert Shores and vicinity.

Continue north on Highway 86. Notice the cliffs along the mountain on the left where traces of the ancient waterlines of previous lakes are still visible. You can see them very clearly on Travertine Rocks, near the road. There are several more places at the northwest end of the Sea from which to scan the shoreline, including Avenue 86 (1.7; switch back to your Riverside County checklist again) and Avenue 81 (3.3). Surf Scoters and other interesting seabirds are periodically spotted from these vantage points.

At the Y with Highway 195 bear right toward Mecca, continuing to the Oasis School on the left (0.6). Across the highway from the school is Avenue 76, which parallels the south side of a drainage ditch, ending at the Sea just south of the Whitewater River delta. This is a good vantage point for viewing the north end of the Salton Sea, and as of this writing it is not posted. Watch for large flocks of shorebirds, including Wilson's and Red-necked Phalaropes, as well as assorted herons and egrets, American White Pelican, and gulls. In late summer and fall, Blue-footed Boobies (rare) have been seen perched with Brown Pelicans on the partly submerged telephone poles.

Continue north on Highway 195 to the stop sign (5.0), where the highway turns right (east) to Mecca. You will rapidly approach our starting point, the Highway 111 expressway (1.1). Depending on your stamina, the amount of available daylight, and access issues, you might opt to return to the White-water River delta by continuing to South Lincoln Street (0.8), then turning south. Evenings at the delta can often produce a completely new set of birds.

If you wish to travel northeast to nearby Joshua Tree National Park, continue on to Mecca where you will follow Highway 195 east from town. This road eventually joins Interstate 10 at a point immediately south of the southern entrance to Joshua Tree National Park. Or, you may wish to travel northwest back to Los Angeles or immediately west to the San Jacinto Mountains loop via Highway 111.

There are motels in Brawley, El Centro, North Shore, Salton City, Calipatria, and Indio. Campgrounds range from the primitive ones at Finney Lake and the Wister Unit of the State Waterfowl Area to the Wiest Lake Imperial County Park and the ones at Salton Sea State Recreation Area. The primitive campground at Red Hill Landing may smell of fish, but it is close to the best birding area. A good improved campground is located at Salton City.

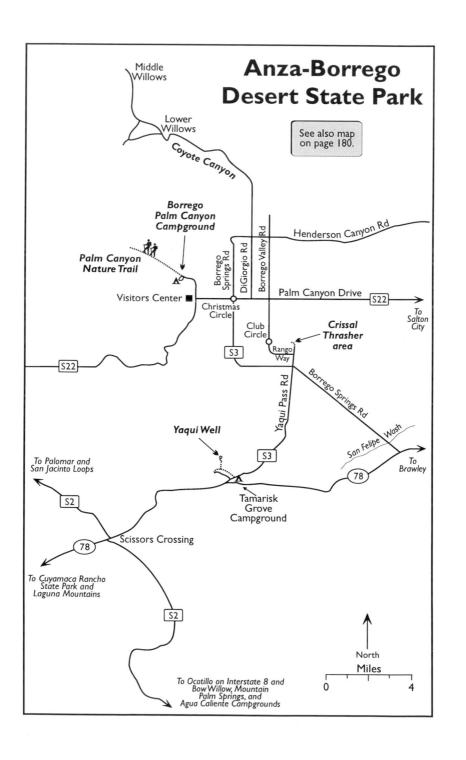

Anza-Borrego Desert State Park

See also map on page 180.

Middle Willows

Lower Willows

Coyote Canyon

Borrego Palm Canyon Campground

Palm Canyon Nature Trail

Visitors Center

Christmas Circle

Borrego Springs Rd

DiGiorgio Rd

Borrego Valley Rd

Henderson Canyon Rd

Palm Canyon Drive — S22

To Salton City

Club Circle

Rango Way

Crissal Thrasher area

S3

S22

Yaqui Pass Rd

Borrego Springs Rd

Yaqui Well

San Felipe Wash

To Palomar and San Jacinto Loops

S2

S3

To Brawley

78

Tamarisk Grove Campground

78

Scissors Crossing

To Cuyamaca Rancho State Park and Laguna Mountains

S2

North

Miles

0   4

To Ocotillo on Interstate 8 and Bow Willow, Mountain Palm Springs, and Agua Caliente Campgrounds

ANZA-BORREGO DESERT STATE PARK

Anza-Borrego Desert State Park is one of those rare Southern California locations relatively unchanged since European contact. Although it has some private in-holdings, a few improved campgrounds, and is transected by roads, it essentially remains a place of unusual plants, dry washes, rugged mountains, and solitude (with the exception of holiday weekends). Fascinating to botanists and geologists, it also has a great deal to offer the visiting birder. Its migrant traps are not so productive of eastern vagrants as those farther east in the desert, but during migration one still approaches the rare pockets of green with the feeling that just about anything is possible. Its breeding birds include many southwestern desert specialties, while winter brings an interesting assortment of avian visitors as well. All-in-all, Anza-Borrego Desert State Park is a beautiful corner of Southern California.

Over 600,000 acres in extent, this largest of California's State Parks is 80 miles east of San Diego and 25 miles west of the Salton Sea. Seventy miles long and 32 miles wide, Anza-Borrego offers many nooks and crannies to explore. Its varied terrain includes mountains, flatland, dry lakes, creosote scrub, palm groves, and a few riparian areas, each with its representative assortment of plant and bird life. Over 230 species of birds have been found here.

If you are looking for sanctuary from the frenetic world of Rare Bird Alerts and mind-numbing weekend blitzes to hot stake-outs, the Anza-Borrego Desert is your refuge. Visitors not under time constraint should not be slavish in their adherence to exploring only the locations noted in this chapter; there are many canyons, washes, and mountain tracks worthy of investigation due to their scenic and natural history values. Take the time to explore this rich area and any of its side roads that your vehicle is competent to enter. As with all desert travel, you must remember to carry extra water and to avoid washes and narrow canyons during storms in the fringing mountains. The rangers at the State Park visitors center update their knowledge of local conditions regularly.

Although this short chapter serves as a "bridge" between the Salton Sea and Joshua Tree National Park loops, it could just as easily link up with the Palomar Mountain Loop, the San Jacinto Mountains Loop, or with the nearby short Laguna Mountains Loop. Whether bridge or not, it is worth visiting in its own right for its bird life and abundant natural history values.

If starting this loop from the coast, you should look at a San Diego County map (AAA's is very good) to decide how you want to enter **Anza-Borrego Desert State Park**. The approaches via Highway 78, or S2 from Highway 79, are wonderfully scenic and productive of the representative suite of California birds expected in the habitats they traverse. Entering from the east through rugged desert is less productive of birds (unless, of course, you bird the Salton Sea), but the scene of rugged mountains ahead is impressive.

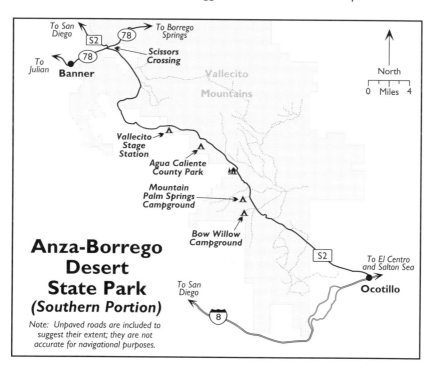

If you enter the park by way of Highway S2 from Ocotillo on Interstate 8, several campgrounds (all on the south side of S2) offer good birding en route—especially during migration. Bow Willow has Rock Wren and offers an opportunity for Le Conte's Thrasher and Brewer's Sparrow (winter). At Mountain Palm Springs you may find Western Bluebird and Scott's Oriole in winter. The mesquite in and around the campground at Agua Caliente County Park (fee) is one of the best migrant traps in the region, attracting a wide variety of birds including both migrants and the resident desert species. The county rangers there may have useful local birding information. If you stop at the old Vallecito Well stage station, note that any dark thrasher you see is a California Thrasher. The only place in the Anza-Borrego region with Crissal Thrasher is at a specific site in the Borrego Sink near the town of Borrego Springs, as noted below.

Our loop tour of Anza-Borrego Desert State Park officially starts in the town of Borrego Springs, population 3,000, doubling during the winter season. A stop at the State Park visitors center is recommended for its attractive exhibits and invaluable area information. From Christmas Circle in the heart of town, go west on Palm Canyon Drive to the end (1.75). You can get maps, a bird list, and other information about the park at the visitors center. Some birds found in the vegetation just outside include Costa's Hummingbird, Ladder-backed Woodpecker, Verdin, Cactus Wren, and Phainopepla. Return east on Palm Canyon Drive to the first road on the left (0.3), which leads to **Borrego Palm Canyon Campground.** Here, and on the Palm Canyon Nature Trail, you should be able to find Gambel's Quail, Greater Roadrunner, Rock and Canyon Wrens, and Black-throated Sparrow. Bell's Vireos and Hooded Orioles nest here. Desert Bighorn Sheep—lending the town, campground, and the state park half of its Spanish name—are sometimes seen coming down off the precipitous canyon slopes to water near the palms.

If you drive north from Christmas Circle on Borrego Springs Road, you can bird the fringes of the citrus groves from the road. Greater Roadrunner, Gambel's Quail, Common Ground-Dove, Verdin, and Black-throated Sparrow can be found along the roadsides. In the open desert, where the bushes are few and far between, look for the Le Conte's Thrasher. Even though the cover is sparse, they are hard to find unless you hike around a bit. A good place to look for the thrashers is the sharp right turn where Borrego Springs Road becomes Henderson Canyon Road (3.3). They can also be found along the dirt road that leads up Coyote Canyon from the north end of DiGiorgio Road (1.0) (closed to visitors June 16–September 15 to allow Bighorn Sheep undisturbed use of the water). High-clearance vehicles are sometimes necessary here; check road condition at the visitors center. At Lower Willows along Coyote Creek look for resident Virginia Rail and wintering Sora. This is a good place for migrating warblers in spring, and you should see White-winged Dove, Yellow-breasted Chat, and Blue Grosbeak, as well.

In winter it may be worthwhile to check out Club Circle on Borrego Valley Road about 2 miles south of its intersection with Palm Canyon Drive. Look for wintering Scott's Orioles here; desert rarities such as Harris's Hawk and Lewis's Woodpecker have been found in this area.

One of the park's signature breeding birds, Scott's Oriole, is most abundant in spring in the higher desert and rock hills in the western portion of the park. Its ethereal song in the still morning air is one of nature's delights. Early spring also brings the possibility of seeing a kettle of Swainson's Hawks—rare anywhere in Southern California—as they move slowly through, feeding on caterpillars among the new growth on the desert floor. You will be more likely to see this event in the Borrego Valley than in other parts of the park, but you will be lucky to see it at all.

The Borrego Sink, in which Borrego Springs is located, is the only area for Crissal Thrasher in the park. Take Borrego Springs Road south from Christmas Circle to its junction with Yaqui Pass Road (5.0). Turn left (north) onto **Yaqui Pass Road**, and drive to the dead-end (1.1), where it is possible—although difficult—to find Crissal Thrasher in the mesquite. (See the Salton Sea and Imperial Dam loops for more predictable sites for this species.) This area may also produce Brewer's and Sage Sparrows (pale migratory race of Sage, probably *nevadensis*) in winter; breeding birds include Costa's Hummingbird, Verdin, Bewick's Wren, Phainopepla, Lucy's Warbler (the westernmost population of this species), and Black-throated Sparrow. Here, as elsewhere, migrating warblers are drawn to insects in the mesquite. Park by the side of the road at the end and walk into the mesquite straight ahead, taking care not to enter private property on either side of the road.

San Felipe Wash to both sides of Borrego Springs Road is a good place (among many in the park) for desert-floor birding. From the junction of Borrego Springs Road and Yaqui Pass Road, go east on Borrego Springs Road for approximately 5 miles where it descends steeply into the broad wash. There are a few sandy roads (walk these roads, do not attempt to drive them unless you are driving a high-clearance four-wheel-drive vehicle) leading into the wash at various places on both sides of the wash. Le Conte's Thrasher is a breeder here but, as always, is usually difficult and requires considerable walking and patience.

Retrace your route south to Yaqui Pass Road (Highway S3) and turn left to **Tamarisk Grove Campground** (6.8), or continue through San Felipe Wash, turning right onto Highway 78. Drive west on Highway 78 for 8.5 miles to S3 and turn right. The campground is obvious less than one mile on the right. Long-eared Owls are known to nest in the trees here (February–April); ask the ranger for help locating the owls. The Tamarisks form a windbreak for campers, and also surround clumps of creosote bush in the campground. The Tamarisks, the blooming creosote bush, and a mesquite tangle just west of the campground are all good birding during fall and spring migration. Many eastern vagrants have turned up here along with western migrants and resident White-winged Dove, Verdin, Bewick's Wren, California Thrasher, and Phainopepla. Both the campground and nearby Yaqui Well occasionally produce Lawrence's Goldfinch. On leaving Tamarisk Grove, continue one block (just short of Highway 78) and turn right (west) up the dirt road to unimproved Yaqui Well Campground (free). This road can be soft after a rain, so before entering check for signs of recent travel. If in doubt, walk. You can also reach the spring on a trail leading there from Tamarisk Grove Campground. **Yaqui Well**, one of very few wet spots in the park, is up a short trail northeast of the campground.

This little spring attracts a nice variety of birds, particularly in migration. Look for California Quail, Greater Roadrunner, Ladder-backed Woodpecker, Rock Wren, California and Sage (migration) Thrashers, Black-tailed and Blue-gray (winter) Gnatcatchers, Phainopepla (numerous, especially in winter around Ironwood Trees with mistletoe clumps), House Finch, and (in winter) sparrows. In migration, you can expect almost anything. The canyon behind the spring can be very good at times. February through April the air is filled with the bullet-like zings of Costa's Hummingbirds making their courtship dives about the Chuparosa bushes. Anna's Hummingbirds also breed here.

Note that you are close to many other trips included in this guide while traveling in Anza-Borrego Desert State Park. You may wish to join the Salton Sea or Joshua Tree National Park loops by traveling east on Route S22 from Borrego Springs to Salton City (29.0). From here you can travel north on Highway 86 to Highway 111 (24.7), east to Interstate 10 (8.2), and east to the Highway 62 exit (21.1) to reach Joshua Tree National Park. You may join the Salton Sea Loop at the intersection of S22 and Highway 86 and go either north or south. Alternatively, you can travel to the rich mountain avifauna in the high-altitude portion of the San Jacinto Mountains Loop by joining S2 at Scissors Crossing and traveling northwest to Highway 79. Travel 23.3 miles northwest on Highway 79 to Highway 371 at the Aguanga Junction. Follow Highway 371 approximately 21 miles to its junction with Highway 74, turning left toward Idyllwild to reach the high mountains. Whether joining another route or merely extending your Anza-Borrego birding adventure, the Lake Henshaw area on Highway 76, just south of the S2-Highway 79 junction, is highly recommended—especially in winter (see the Palomar Mountain Loop). Lake Henshaw, only about 25 miles from Scissors Crossing on the desert floor, offers much of interest. From here you can easily join the Palomar Mountain Loop, the Laguna Mountains Loop to the south, or travel back to the coast via Highway 76.

You will find motels in the town of Borrego Springs and a good selection of campgrounds along the birding route.

Scott's Oriole
Shawneen E. Finnegan

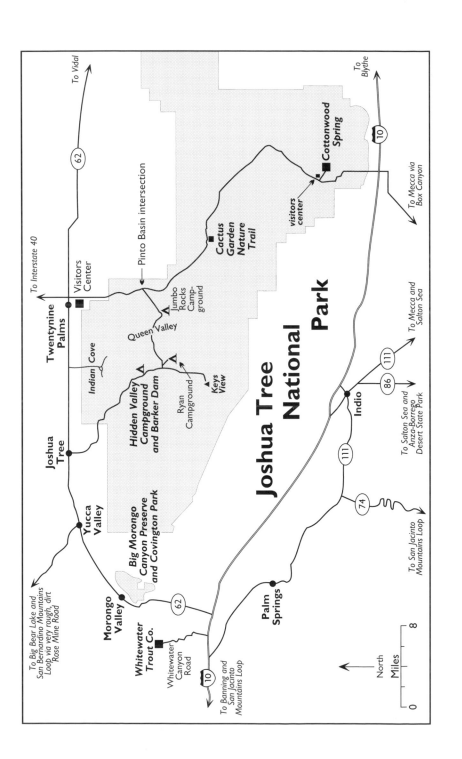

Joshua Tree National Park

JOSHUA TREE NATIONAL PARK

Joshua Tree National Park lies north of Palm Springs and the San Andreas Fault in a wondrous array of rocks, arid slopes, and superb desert vegetation. Its sandy washes drop as low as 500 feet above sea level in the Colorado Desert, while its austere peaks rise to over 5,000 feet along the ridge of the Little San Bernardino Mountains in the Mojave Desert. The park is particularly interesting because it is at the conjunction of two different deserts, defined by altitudinal differences, with the resultant variation in plant communities. Although it may look barren and forbidding, it has a strange magnetism that will draw you back again and again to explore its treasures.

You will not be alone. The granite outcroppings in the northern half of the park are very popular with rock climbers; Joshua Tree (as the park is generally known) holds over 3,000 named climbs.

Herpetologists and botanists might find more of interest in this 575,934-acre wonderland than birders, but there are oases where birds are sometimes numerous. For a greater appreciation of this varied area, read *Lives of Desert Animals in Joshua Tree National Monument* by Miller and Stebbins.

Most birders come during the cooler months, but many area specialties can be found at any season. Gray Vireo and Scott's Oriole are rare summer residents here, best looked for in April, May, and June. White-crowned, Vesper, and Brewer's Sparrows are winter visitors from October to May. During migration look for Bendire's and Sage Thrashers as well as the flycatchers, western vireos, warblers, icterids, and sparrows normally found at desert oases. An occasional anomaly—like the sight of a migrating Osprey overhead—can add an unexpected touch to the desert experience. Permanent residents of interest include Prairie Falcon, Mountain Quail (higher elevations), Greater Roadrunner, and Le Conte's Thrasher (sandy washes). Phainopepla and Verdin are common.

The starting point is the intersection of Interstate 10 and Highway 62, some 16 miles east of Banning. The entire route is driveable in a day, dependent on the birding and your schedule. Go north on Highway 62 toward Twentynine Palms. The road climbs rapidly from the low, barren Colorado Desert (El. 1,000 ft), through the Little San Bernardino Mountains, to the Mojave Desert at Morongo Valley (El. 2,600 ft).

Turn right at East Drive (10.5) and go 3 blocks to the *best birding spot* on the loop, BLM's 29,000-acre **Big Morongo Canyon Preserve** (free; open 7:30 AM–sunset daily). This oasis has a fine grove of Frémont Cottonwoods, a permanent stream, and thick stands of brush. Over 200 species of birds have been found here, mostly during migration. (Web surfers can see the list online—see Resources in the Introduction.) California birders are particularly attracted to the preserve because it is one of the few places in the state where one can find nesting Brown-crested and Vermilion Flycatchers, Lucy's Warbler (uncommon), and Summer Tanager. You may also be attracted by nesting Gambel's Quail, White-winged Dove, Long-eared Owl (rare), Nuttall's Woodpecker, Costa's Hummingbird, California Thrasher, Phainopepla, Yellow-breasted Chat, Scott's Oriole, and Lawrence's Goldfinch. This is an excellent place for migrants and has proven a good spot for eastern vagrants (April–May and September–early November).

Adjacent to the preserve is tiny **Covington Park**, which you should also check. Vermilion Flycatchers like the area around the baseball field, and Brown-crested Flycatchers usually nest in the tall cottonwoods.

Continue to the town of Yucca Valley (8.0), where you may want to visit the Hi-Desert Museum, one block left (north) off 29 Palms Highway on Dumosa Street. The next town is Joshua Tree (8.0), gateway to **Joshua Tree National Park**. The turn-off to the park is marked by a small sign about midway through this drawn-out town. Watch for a sign on the right at Park Boulevard, where you will turn right. Top off your gas and pick up a Joshua Tree National Park map at the entrance kiosk (fee).

As soon as you enter the monument (5.2), the Joshua Trees seem to get bigger and more contorted. To really appreciate these strange lilies, take a walk among them. Some of the 30-foot giants may be over 200 years old. They play host to a variety of birds, including Ladder-backed Woodpecker, Cactus Wren, Black-throated Sparrow, House Finch, and Scott's Oriole. You may find bats flying around the flowers at night, feeding on Yucca Moths—the chief pollinators of the Joshua Trees.

Hidden Valley Campground (9.0) is the first of several dry camps. Mammals here include Coyote, Desert Cottontail, Antelope and California Ground Squirrels, and Merriam's Chipmunk. Scan the massive rocks for Golden Eagle (rare), Red-tailed Hawk, Prairie Falcon, and Rock Wren.

Adjacent to Hidden Valley Campground is **Barker Dam**, reached by following a road north of the campground (look for the sign near the campground entrance) to the Barker Dam parking lot. The dam, about one-half mile distant, sometimes has water behind it, especially in spring, and the place can be teeming with migrants.

Return through the campground and continue east on the park road until you reach Keys View Road (1.4), where you turn right. Go one block, and stop for the **Cap Rock Nature Trail**. Here you can learn to identify most of the desert plants. Keys View (El. 5,185 ft) (5.6) offers an excellent overlook of the Colorado Desert toward the Salton Sea. Return to the main road and turn right toward the city of Twentynine Palms just outside the park.

Continuing eastward you will pass Sheep Pass Campground, entering the Queen Valley. A few pairs of Bendire's Thrashers breed in the Queen Valley area, between Jumbo Rocks and Hidden Valley; sites vary each year.

Park headquarters is located in the **Twentynine Palms Oasis** on the left at the bottom of the long hill. After viewing the exhibits, walk the nature trail to see what is left of the original 29 palms. Gambel's Quail, Phainopepla, and Verdin can be abundant here. This is a good migrant trap for passerines. Check with the rangers about other birding areas. If you like to hike, ask about the Fortynine Palms Trail.

Retrace your route to Pinto Basin intersection and bear left toward Cottonwood Spring. The Cactus Garden Nature Trail (10.0) will help you to identify the plants of the lower desert. Reptiles seem more abundant here. In spring you might even see a Desert Tortoise. You should at least see the speedy little Zebra-tailed Lizard, which darts across the road with its banded tail curled over its back. Your chances of seeing snakes are better if you drive the roads at night. You may also spot a Black-tailed Jackrabbit, Bobcat, Kit Fox, or Coyote.

Continue toward Cottonwood Spring and the Cottonwood Visitors Center near the south entrance to the park. Although badly overrun, **Cottonwood Spring** (21.0) still attracts numerous birds, but there are usually hordes of people about. The campground here is the most popular in the park. Check the Frémont Cottonwoods for flycatchers, warblers, tanagers, and grosbeaks during migration. The area is also good for wintering birds.

Lost Palms Oasis, reached by a rather rough 4-mile trail that starts at Cottonwood Spring, can be a good birding area; it is a beautiful place. Here, among the 110 California Fan Palms nestled in a deep canyon, you can find Hooded and Scott's Orioles, Ladder-backed Woodpecker, Ash-throated Flycatcher, Bell's Vireo, and numerous migrants. Water levels vary both here and at Cottonwood Spring, affecting the number of birds. Even if you do not see many birds, it is a nice hike.

Continue south out of the park to Interstate 10 (8.0). Turn right on Interstate 10 to return to the starting point at its intersection with Highway 62 some fifty miles west. Highway 243 and the start of the San Jacinto Mountains Loop intersect the interstate in Banning, 17 miles farther west. If you want to visit the Salton Sea now, continue straight ahead on Highway 195 to Mecca via Box Canyon.

There are numerous dry camps in the monument, so be sure to take plenty of water. Some require reservations. Call Park headquarters for information at 760/367-5500. All of the cities along Highway 62 have motels; accommodations can likewise be found south of Joshua Tree National Park in Indio and the Palm Springs area.

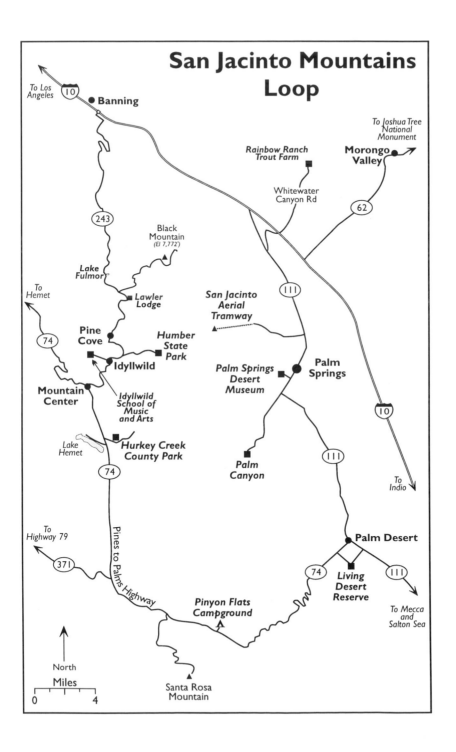

San Jacinto Mountains Loop

To Los Angeles

10 ● Banning

To Joshua Tree National Monument

Rainbow Ranch Trout Farm

Morongo Valley

Whitewater Canyon Rd

62

243

Black Mountain (El 7,772')

Lake Fulmor

To Hemet

Lawler Lodge

San Jacinto Aerial Tramway

111

74

Pine Cove

Humber State Park

Idyllwild

Palm Springs Desert Museum

Palm Springs

Mountain Center

Idyllwild School of Music and Arts

10

Lake Hemet

Hurkey Creek County Park

74

Palm Canyon

111

To Indio

To Highway 79

371

Pines to Palms Highway

Palm Desert

74

Living Desert Reserve

111

Pinyon Flats Campground

To Mecca and Salton Sea

North

Miles

0   4

Santa Rosa Mountain

SAN JACINTO MOUNTAINS LOOP

From the summit of Mount San Jacinto at 10,786 feet, one can look almost straight down to Palm Springs, at an elevation of 450 feet. Most birders will never reach the summit, but this trip will take you all the way around it. Because of the great changes in elevation, you will cross four life zones and many habitats. This is one of the most scenic trips in Southern California.

To reach the starting point, take the 8th Avenue exit off Interstate 10 in Banning (El. 2,250 ft). Continue south one block to Lincoln, turn left, and proceed 1.4 miles to San Gorgonio Avenue (Highway 243). Turn right onto San Gorgonio Avenue. Very quickly the road begins to climb, presenting a magnificent view from every turn.

The chaparral of the Upper Sonoran Life Zone is the dominant vegetation for the next 10 miles. It has been called the elfin forest. In spring when every bush bursts into bloom, it is indeed a fairyland. Stop anywhere and do a little squeaking and you should see Western Scrub-Jay, Wrentit, California Towhee, and perhaps a Black-chinned Sparrow. After passing the 4,000-foot marker, the road dips into a stand of Coast Live Oaks where you may find Band-tailed Pigeon, Acorn and Nuttall's Woodpeckers, and Oak Titmouse. The red-stemmed manzanita has now become prominent in the chaparral, in places forming dense thickets. Its little bell-shaped flowers attract hummingbirds, particularly in April, when Calliopes may be abundant.

Lake Fulmor (14.8; requires Forest Adventure Pass, as do most of the stops in this loop), when not crowded, is worth checking. Owls at this elevation include Flammulated, Western Screech-Owl, Northern Pygmy-Owl, Spotted, and Northern Saw-whet. All are rare here; *taping is strongly discouraged*. In response to recent vandalism here at night, Forest Service personnel often stop by to question birders after dark.

As the road climbs beyond the lake, Incense Cedar and Sugar Pine (very long cones) become noticeable. Look for the well-marked dirt road on the left (1.9) to **Black Mountain** (may be closed in winter). Along this road to Boulder Basin Campground (5.3) or Black Mountain Lookout (0.3) you can find Mountain Quail, Acorn, Nuttall's, Hairy, and White-headed Woodpeckers, White-breasted and Pygmy Nuthatches, Western Bluebird, Cassin's Vireo, Black-throated Gray Warbler, and Purple Finch. The area around the campground has been good for White-headed Woodpecker, Red-breasted Sapsucker, and Cassin's Finch. Flammulated Owl has been found near the

189

campground most summers for several years, although they are heard much more often than seen. Back on Highway 243, Lawler Lodge (0.9) and vicinity is a good vantage point from which to look for Black Swifts in summer.

Most of the dirt roads that branch off from the highway are not particularly outstanding for birds. The moist canyons are far better. One such is Dark Canyon, signed "North Fork of the San Jacinto River" (0.4). Look for Western Wood-Pewee, American Dipper, Hermit Thrush, Pine Siskin, and other birds.

Continue up the highway a couple miles to the community of Pine Cove, the highest point on this highway (El. 6,300 ft), turning right at the gas station onto Pine Cove Road. If feeders are out in summer, some hummingbirds may be found within the first half-mile in the town. Most are Anna's and Black-chinned, but Calliope, Rufous, and Allen's may occur. Other birds such as White-headed Woodpecker, Western Tanager, Black-headed Grosbeak, and Purple, Cassin's, and House Finches are found. Even in midwinter there is often something around. Return to the highway to continue with the loop.

On the way to **Idyllwild**, you will be treated to fine views of Mount San Jacinto, Tahquitz Peak, and Lilley Rock. Check the meadow opposite the Buckhorn Camp (1.5) in summer for Lawrence's Goldfinch and the manzanita thickets in the Idyllwild County Park (0.6). The nature center at this park (fee, only open Saturday–Sunday 10 AM–4 PM) is definitely worth a stop when it is open. Woodpeckers, including Acorn, Hairy, and White-headed, as well as both White-breasted and Pygmy Nuthatches come to the suet feeders on the back balcony. Band-tailed Pigeons appear to be omnipresent.

There are two campgrounds at Idyllwild (0.7) (El. 5,394 ft); both are good for camping and birding. Mount San Jacinto State Park (fee) is on the right as you enter town. Idyllwild County Park (fee) can be reached by turning right one block past the State Park onto Maranatha Drive. Immediately bear left on (Lower) Pine Crest Avenue, proceed to County Park Road (0.3), then turn right to the park (0.2). If uncrowded, **Humber State Park** can be productive—it offers spectacular views in any case. It can be reached by returning to Highway 243, going right a few feet, then quickly making a weird turn left up the hill onto (Upper) Pine Crest Road (the local road signs don't note "Upper" or "Lower" Pine Crest Roads, but local-area maps do). Continue to South Circle Drive (0.7), following the strategically placed signs to the park. Continue straight onto South Circle Drive to Fern Valley Road (0.1). Turn left to the park (1.9). This is the starting point for the Devil's Slide Trail to the summit of Mount San Jacinto (9.0 miles). Even a short walk up the trail is impressive, but the hike to the top is really rewarding with spectacular views and a chance to bird the Boreal Life Zone. (A permit may be required.)

You should find White-headed Woodpecker, White-breasted and Pygmy Nuthatches, Mountain Chickadee, and on summer nights, Flammulated Owl (uncommon) in the immediate vicinity of the park. Also look for Mountain Quail. Higher on the trail there should be Clark's Nutcracker, Red-breasted

Nuthatch (rare), and Townsend's Solitaire. Black Swift has been found above the Tahquitz Trail, which branches off the main trail.

Another good birding area is along the road to the **Idyllwild School of Music and the Arts**. To reach that, return to Highway 243, continue south, and turn right onto Tollgate Road (0.8). Anywhere along this road may be good. Lincoln's Sparrow and Lawrence's Goldfinch can often be found in the meadows along the streams near the campus, 1.3 miles along the road.

Beyond Tollgate Road, Highway 243 soon leaves the cool basin and quickly descends the warm south side of the mountain. The brush here is dominated by Ribbonwood, easily identified by its shedding red bark and airy clusters of light-green leaves. Birds are fairly numerous here on the sunny slopes.

Check the dead tops of tall trees in summer for Olive-sided Flycatcher. Its song is a rousing *Quick, three beers!*

At Mountain Center (3.7), turn left onto the Pines-to-Palms Highway (Highway 74). **Hurkey Creek Campground** (fee) (El. 4,400 ft) (3.5) is a favorite of birders in all seasons. Birders can gain walk-in access, by-passing the gate and continuing on the road signed to Pine Springs Ranch, crossing the creek, and parking along the roadside next to the pedestrian access in the fence on the left. Look among the pines for Band-tailed Pigeon, White-headed Woodpecker, Steller's Jay, Clark's Nutcracker (winter), Mountain Chickadee, Oak Titmouse, Pygmy Nuthatch, Lawrence's Goldfinch, and with luck in fall and winter, Evening Grosbeaks. A flock of Pinyon Jays often wanders noisily around the picnic tables. By hiking up the dirt road beyond the west end of the camp, you can find Mountain Quail, Dusky Flycatcher (summer), Spotted Towhee, and when the manzanita is in bloom in April and early May, Calliope Hummingbird.

Ducks can usually be found on Lake Hemet (0.3) in the winter, but they leave at the start of the fishing season. Common Snipe and other shorebirds like the wet meadows at the upper end of the lake near the highway. A Golden Eagle sometimes makes passes at the American Coots on the lake. Bald Eagles regularly winter here too, sometimes remaining into late April and early May. In the dry, open pine forest around the lake you can also find a flock of the noisy Pinyon Jays in any season. Check the hillsides along the entry road for Black-chinned Sparrow and Lawrence's Goldfinch.

Beyond the lake, the highway enters an area of open pine forest, an excellent area for birds. Birds to watch for here are Band-tailed Pigeon, White-headed Woodpecker, Pygmy Nuthatch, Brown Creeper, Brewer's Blackbird, Pine Siskin, and, in summer, Western Wood-Pewee, Violet-green Swallow, Western Bluebird, Western Tanager, Black-headed Grosbeak, and Lawrence's Goldfinch. In winter, Clark's Nutcrackers and Mountain Bluebirds may be found.

If the Pinyon Jays were not at Hurkey Creek, they should be somewhere along the next 5 miles of road. They travel in flocks, and when they go by, you are bound to see or hear them. If you miss them the first time, it is often worthwhile to drive through the pines again.

Past Highway 371 (9.0) the birds seem to fizzle out, so scoot along. If you are adventuresome, try the Santa Rosa Mountain Road (5.3). It is a rough, dirty, 10-mile climb to the summit, but the view is magnificent. On the road up look for Mountain Quail. The area around the summit has produced many interesting summer records (Zone-tailed Hawks, rare anywhere in California, even nested here from 1978 to 1982) With a lot of luck, you might see Desert Bighorn Sheep on the route. If you decide not to take the climb, you might want to check the area below Highway 74 at the junction of Santa Rosa Mountain Road. This area has produced Gray Vireo.

The campground and housing area at **Pinyon Flats** (3.7) are worth checking. Most of the jays here among the One-leaf Pinyons, California Junipers, and Parry's Nolinas will be Western Scrub-Jays, but you might find a Pinyon. They often visit the feeding-stations around the cabins, when these are maintained. In summer, watch for Gray Vireo (rare) and Scott's Oriole.

Within the next 13 miles, the road drops 4,000 feet to the low desert and the Lower Sonoran Life Zone. In this scenic section of rocks, cactus, and sand, you may find only an occasional Ladder-backed Woodpecker, Rock Wren, or Black-throated Sparrow. However, it is a rich area for reptiles. Try your luck scoping for sheep at the Bighorn Sheep Overlook.

At Haystack Road (14.5) in Palm Desert (see map on page 194), turn right to Portola Avenue (1.3). Turn right for a visit to the **Living Desert Reserve** (0.2) on your left (fee). This self-supporting natural history institution has live-animal exhibits and a botanic garden with nature trails. All this gives one an intimate view of the Colorado Desert. The reserve is open daily 9 AM–5 PM, but is closed during the months of June, July, and August. Common Ground-Doves, Cactus Wrens, and Black-throated Sparrows can all be seen here, and more importantly, it is a good place to check for migrants.

Leaving the Living Desert Reserve, go north on Portola to Highway 111 (1.5). Turn right and proceed through what some consider the business conference center of California, easily determined by immaculately manicured lawns and luxurious motels. As you enter Indio you will notice the scenery begin to change. A fun place to stop for a date shake (and dates themselves) is Shields Date Gardens (6.6). Continue east on Highway 111 until you come to Auto Center Drive (3.6). Turn left to Avenue 45 (0.6), then proceed right to the **Coachella Valley Wild Bird Center** a mile or so down the road on the left, just past the sewage treatment plant. (The road will change names to Van Buren here, but don't worry about that). The Wild Bird Center is a recent addition to the birding community of the valley, and as an active bird rehabilitation center can be an interesting visit at any season. Winter is particularly good, with many species of ducks using the sewage ponds adjacent to the center. When landscaping is completed around the outbuildings, assorted marshlands and ponds associated with the treatment plant will be worth a check. Fulvous Whistling-Duck has already been reported from the property. Large cottonwood trees on the grounds of the center provide cover for owls and raptors, and may contain vireos, warblers, and orioles in season.

Return to Auto Center Drive and turn right to Interstate 10 (0.4). Go west on I-10 to the Washington Street exit (6.3). Go north (right) on Washington Street, soon heading out in the middle of nowhere. The wildflowers in spring can be beautiful on this stretch. Soon you will come to Thousand Palms Canyon Road (5.1). Turn right to The Nature Conservancy's **Coachella Valley Preserve** (2.1 miles; 760/343-1234). This preserve contains one of the few remaining stands of California Fan Palm and the Thousand Palms Oasis centerpiece is a migrant magnet during spring. Preserve personnel lead frequent field trips through the preserve, and eastern vagrants as well as typical migrants are often found.

Return to Washington Street and turn right. This road becomes Ramon Road, and will cross over I-10 again. However, for our route, you will make a trek on this road until you come to Palm Canyon Drive (13.0). Go south on this one-way road to the fork at South Palm Canyon Drive (1.2), where you should bear right. This will lead you to the Aqua Caliente Indian Reservervation (2.8 miles; fee; open 8 AM–5 PM year round).

A visit to this well-preserved desert reserve is well worth the admission fee. Nearly all of the birds, mammals, and reptiles of the desert can be found here among the rocks and lush desert vegetation. Gambel's Quail, Rock Wren, Phainopepla, and Black-throated Sparrow are common. You should also see Antelope and California Ground Squirrels, Black-tailed Jackrabbit, and lots of lizards.

The main attraction is another large stand of California Fan Palms. These shaggy old trees, nestled in the bottom of the wild, rocky canyons, are but a remnant of a forest that once covered the area. Their fronds shelter nests of Hooded Orioles in summer. The clear stream at their feet is important to the many thirsty denizens of this arid land. It is also the home of the Canyon or Desert Treefrog. Be sure to check the hummingbird feeders at the Trading Post.

In late winter, Costa's Hummingbirds zoom in courtship dives over every clump of Chuparosa, with its little, red, tubular flowers. In January and February, you should find the hummingbirds easily on the reservation or along the road just before reaching the gate. Later in the spring, they move up the mountain to the yellow-flowered stalks of the Desert Agave or the red-flowered canes of the Ocotillo. When the really hot weather arrives, they will have nested and gone.

Return to Highway 111 and continue north on Palm Canyon Drive into Palm Springs. Notice something different? There are no gaudy billboards; all

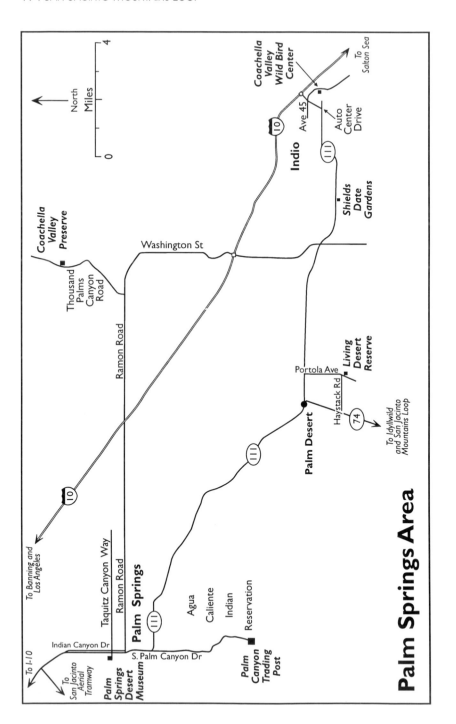

Palm Springs Area

of the signs are flush against the buildings. Even the street lights are hidden in the palm trees.

When the highway splits into one-way Indian Canyon Drive (0.9), continue to Tahquitz Canyon Way (0.6) and turn left. Turn right on Museum Drive (0.2). The **Palm Springs Desert Museum** is on your left (760/325-0189; fee, closed Mondays and major holidays). It has very good exhibits on the natural history and Indians of the area. The bookstore always has books on local subjects.

Return to Indian Canyon Drive and continue north. If you wish to ride up the Palm Springs Aerial Tramway, stay in the left lane and watch for a left jog that will return you to two-way Palm Canyon Drive (0.6), where you will soon make your way out of town heading north. On the northern edge of town you will see the road leading to the Palm Springs Aerial Tramway (2.2; 760/325-1391). This is an expensive but easy way to reach the Boreal Life Zone; it is also the jumping-off place for the 5-mile hike to the summit of Mount San Jacinto. Limited amounts of camping equipment are allowed on the tram, which can take 80 passengers up the 5,873-foot vertical climb in approximately 14 minutes.

In lieu of the tram ride, or after returning from it, continue north on Indian Canyon Drive to Interstate 10 (5.2). Proceed west, passing very close to some of the many wind turbines which generate significant amounts of electricity for the growing population in this area. If you wish to visit Big Morongo Canyon Preserve (760/363-7190), a part of the Joshua Tree National Park route, it is a few minutes north of the interstate, reached by taking Highway 62 (3.2) north to East Drive (10.5) in Morongo Valley.

If you bypass Morongo, or upon your return from it, continue west on I-10 to Whitewater Canyon Road (2.5). (See map on page 183.) Head north, jog east, then quickly north again and proceed on Whitewater Canyon Road to a trout farm (4.1). The Tamarisks and cottonwood trees around the ponds can be loaded with birds during spring migration. It is usually not worth the drive at other seasons, although fall and early winter may produce some birds of interest.

You are now near many other routes in this guide. You can continue west to the San Bernardino or San Gabriel Mountains, or to western Riverside County. You may turn south to the Salton Sea and its connections with the Anza-Borrego Desert and thence to San Diego. In any event, there are numerous motels in Idyllwild in the San Jacinto Mountains where campgrounds are also plentiful, and a full range of accommodations is available in the Palm Springs region.

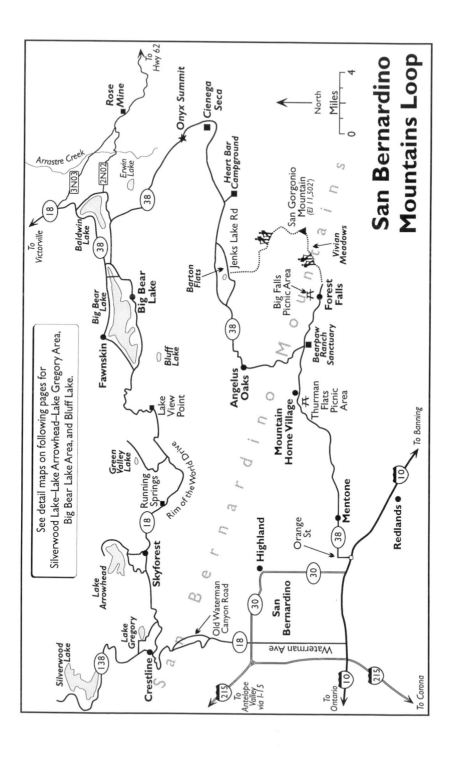

San Bernardino Mountains Loop

See detail maps on following pages for Silverwood Lake–Lake Arrowhead–Lake Gregory Area, Big Bear Lake Area, and Bluff Lake.

San Bernardino Mountains Loop

The San Bernardino Mountains are California's highest range south of the Sierra Nevada. Approximately sixty-five miles long and up to thirty miles wide, placed in the eastern segment of the Transverse Ranges, the San Bernardinos contain over 1,000 square miles of forests, lakes, streams, valleys, and lofty peaks. Elevations vary from about 1,000 feet in the sage-covered foothills to 11,502 feet atop the barren summit of San Gorgonio Mountain. Most of the land in San Bernardino National Forest is public domain (Forest Adventure Pass required), although about one-third of it is privately-owned and has been developed into resorts and cabin sites, making this the most densely-populated of Southern California's mountain areas. As you would expect, the privately-owned part tends to center on highland lakes and these are the most heavily-developed areas, rendering the most popular—Arrowhead and Big Bear—less attractive for the birder. This is not to say that they do not have birds, but rather that access diminishes with development, while at the same time the habitat itself is impacted.

Do not be deterred by these disclaimers regarding the largest lakes. The San Bernardino Mountains are beautiful, include wonderful forests and birds, and are easily accessible from the urban centers. Explore them—on weekdays if possible—and relax in the crisp mountain air amongst an interesting avifauna. Simply be aware that it is most productive to spend the majority of your time away from the resort centers.

The entire area is crossed by an all-weather road named Rim of the World Drive in an earlier era when, on any given day, the view seemed unbounded; on Sunday afternoons nowadays it seems as if most of Southern California travels it. Rim of the World Drive should really be named "Rim of the Basin Drive," given its location on the northeast crest of the metropolitan basin—a location guaranteeing heavy traffic. It is wise either to plan your trip for a weekday or to get an early start on the weekend. This loop can easily put 150 miles on your car—and they will be slow miles due to the winding roads and numerous stops, traffic excluded. The rewards, however, can be substantial in these lovely mountains.

The starting point is the intersection of Interstate 215 and Highway 18 in San Bernardino (El. 1,040 ft). Leave Interstate 215 at the exit for Highland / Mountain Resorts (East 30) and follow the signs for the mountain resorts and Highway 18. Turn left onto Highway 18 at the Waterman Avenue freeway

197

exit (2.4), also signed Highway 18-Crestline-Lake Arrowhead, which becomes Rim of the World Drive.

The road quickly begins to climb through the brushy foothills. To check for this habitat's birds, turn right onto unmarked but well-paved **Old Waterman Canyon Road** (3.3), the first right after entering San Bernardino National Forest. Patches of chaparral may yield California Quail, California Thrasher, Wrentit, Bewick's Wren, and California Towhee. Check the Canyon Live Oaks for Band-tailed Pigeon, Acorn and Nuttall's Woodpeckers, Bushtit, Oak Titmouse, and House Wren. Farther up the canyon, in the groves of White Alder, Western Sycamore, and Black Cottonwood, you may find Swainson's and Hermit Thrushes, Downy Woodpecker, and American and Lesser Goldfinches. California Ground Squirrels abound.

Continue upcanyon to rejoin Highway 18 (3.0), which climbs higher and higher, offering increasingly better views of the valley, if the smog is not too thick. Take the Crestline exit (Highway 138) (4.2) and proceed to the town of Crestline (El. 4,700 ft), where Steller's Jays frequent seed-feeders. In the center of town you have a choice. If you stay on Highway 138, you can visit **Silverwood Lake State Recreation Area** (9.3). Mountain Quail are often observed along the road in early morning or evening. Until the lake was drained recently, it had a few ducks and, in winter, Bald Eagles. Water is now being returned to the lake, so the birding may improve again. During migrations many passerines are found among the trees, especially in the group-camping area.

If you decide not to go to Silverwood Lake, or upon your return from it, continue straight ahead on Lake Drive to Lake Gregory (1.1). Turn right to cross the dam on Lake Gregory Drive. Along this road you will find good stands of yellow (a common name denoting both Jeffrey and Ponderosa Pines in the same way that calidrids are collectively called peep) and Sugar Pines, Incense Cedar, and Goldcup and Black Oaks. Stop anywhere to look for Mountain Chickadee, White-breasted and Pygmy Nuthatches, Brown Creeper, Pine Siskin, and other common mountain birds.

When you eventually reach Highway 18 (2.3), turn left. Baylis Park Picnic Area (0.6) is a pleasant place to stop to bird for typical mountain species. Farther up the road you will see a turn-out (0.3) from which the view of the valley is superb. On a clear day, this really does seem to be the rim of the world. The mellow *wook* of Mountain Quail can often be heard in the brush below, but the bird is difficult to see. At the community of Rimforest (1.3) look for White-headed Woodpecker in mature yellow pines.

Lake Arrowhead's popularity comes from its status as a resort community rather than as a birding destination. You may get lucky, however, and find a few ducks on its surface. Turn left at Highway 173 (2.0) for Lake Arrowhead. To reach the only place on the lake where birders can get a relatively unobstructed view through the iron fence, turn right at the traffic-light at the bottom of the hill in Lake Arrowhead Village (1.6). Stay on this road (Highway 173) as it twists its way to the dam at the east end of the lake (2.5), where you can park alongside the road and overlook the marina. It is possible, of course, to pay an entry fee for access to the lake at the main recreation area—but this would not be worthwhile from a birding perspective.

Retrace your route to Kuffel Canyon Road (2.1), turning sharp left onto it to rejoin Highway 18 at Skyforest (1.2). Turn left and continue on Highway 18 toward Big Bear Lake. For the next ten miles the highway passes numerous resorts. As you go, you will find many places to pull off to look for birds, including Heaps Peak Arboretum (1.4). One resort worth checking is **Green Valley** (7.6). Watch for Mountain Quail around patches of Buckthorn along the road to the lake (3.3). At the lake and around the campground (1.2) beyond, you may find Common Nighthawk and Williamson's Sapsucker in summer, and resident mountain birds. At night, look and listen for Spotted Owl. This is a good place to camp. In winter the campground is closed and the Cross Country Ski Center is in the ascendant.

Beyond the Green Valley turn-off along Highway 18, the highway climbs higher until it reaches the summit near Lake View Point (El. 7,207 ft) (4.6) overlooking Big Bear Valley. The habitat here changes from pine forest to high-mountain brushlands of scrub oak and *Ceanothus*. This is nesting habitat for Dusky Flycatcher, Black-throated Gray Warbler, Green-tailed Towhee, and "Thick-billed" Fox Sparrow. If you do a little squeaking near the brush-patches, they will usually come out into view. In late summer and fall, Clark's Nutcrackers may be common.

A side trip here leads to **Bluff Lake** (El. 7,900 ft), a place many birders claim is the finest montane birding in Southern California. Even though it is situated only 1.5 miles south-southeast of Lake View Point, the drive to this area is about eight miles. It is most accessible from May through October.

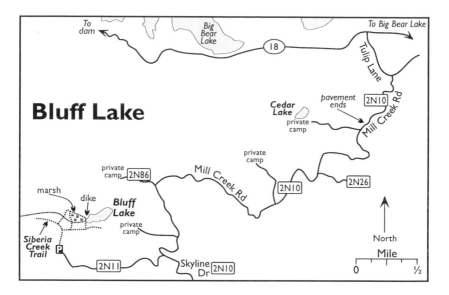

There are a number of locally uncommon species which may be reliably found at Bluff Lake between mid-May and July, including Common Nighthawk, Williamson's Sapsucker, Dusky Flycatcher, and Calliope Hummingbird. Most of the San Bernardino's breeding species are likewise found in the area. Other species present in the breeding season, but not necessarily breeding, include Virginia Rail, Sora, Lazuli Bunting, and Red Crossbill. Hermit Warbler may be seen here during fall migration along with several other migrant warbler species. Golden-crowned Kinglets are regular in fall. The World Champion Lodgepole Pine is a local celebrity—the largest specimen on the West Coast.

To reach Bluff Lake, continue along Highway 18 to the west end of Big Bear Lake (5.4). Cross the dam, staying on Highway 18 until Tulip Lane (2.9) opposite the stables. Turn right onto Tulip Lane and go to Mill Creek Road (Route 2N10) (0.5); turn right again. Where the rough pavement ends (0.8), continue on the main (now dirt) road, bearing left. Turn right at the T-intersection (0.8) (which is still Route 2N10). At the next major intersection (0.65) turn right (still the main road). At the next T (1.55), turn left. The right turn is marked 2N86 Dead End. Next you will come to a sign for Bluff Lake YMCA Camp (0.45). Continue past this sign to another T-intersection (0.3). Turn right onto Route 2N11, crossing two small fords (one is about 14" deep), to the parking lot (1.05).

The trail to the Champion Lodgepole Pine and Siberia Creek Trail is marked by a plaque at the edge of the parking lot. Birding is best along the Siberia Creek Trail, about 300 yards farther. At the T-junction with this trail follow Siberia Creek Trail to the left for about one-quarter mile through prime coniferous forest and meadow habitat. Retrace your steps to a trail leading left (north) from a Forest Service sign. This trail takes you past the 110-foot-tall World Champion Lodgepole Pine. Continue along the trail to a T-intersection at the marsh. Turn left and cross over the foot-bridge.

In 200 feet bear right at the fork; 300 feet farther along you will approach the dike at the west end of Bluff Lake. The entire lake is posted, so you must retrace your route to the parking lot. Find your way back to the intersection of Tulip Lane and Highway 18 (following the trail of whole-grain bread crumbs you would have been wise to drop on the outward journey).

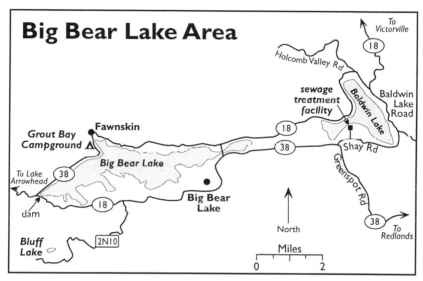

You may continue east on Highway 18 along the south side of the lake through the town of **Big Bear Lake**. To continue the loop, however, return to the dam (1.5) and turn right onto Highway 38 to skirt the north shore of the lake. Waterfowl and Ring-billed Gulls can be found here at any season, and during migration there may be large flocks. Concentrations of over 200,000 American Coots have been recorded, if not welcomed. A few linger into winter, which is also the time to look for the Bald Eagle, a regular visitor with up to 25 birds present some years.

Grout Bay Campground (2.9) (closed in winter to protect the eagles) is popular with birders. Look among the pine trees for the typical forest species, and at night for Flammulated and Western Screech-Owls. The meadows across the road can offer good birding as well. The wilder areas just north of Fawnskin are good for Spotted and Northern Saw-whet Owls.

East of Fawnskin (0.6) the land becomes more arid. The vegetation changes from yellow pine to Western Juniper, One-leaf Pinyon, and sage. More extensive areas of this habitat may be found by following the self-guided Gold Fever Trail (2.2) through Holcomb Valley. The sage flats are the summer home of Common Poorwill, Green-tailed Towhee, and Black-chinned,

Brewer's, Lark, and Sage Sparrows. Nocturnal birders find Holcomb Valley of great interest because of its Spotted Owls.

Past the end of Big Bear Lake, Highways 18 and 38 cross. Highway 38 turns south, and you will eventually follow it to complete the loop, but right now you should continue straight ahead on Highway 18 toward Victorville.

When it has water, **Baldwin Lake** (1.0) attracts many birds. It hosts the second-largest breeding population of Eared Grebes in Southern California (Salton Sea has the largest). In late summer and fall shorebirds and ducks may be common. Cinnamon Teal are present throughout the summer and probably nest. Continue around the lake past Holcomb Valley Road (2.8) and turn right onto Baldwin Lake Road (0.3). If you miss the turn, you will soon top the ridge overlooking the Lucerne Valley far below in the Mojave Desert.

After leaving the highway, you will cross an arid area of sagebrush, where nesting Green-tailed Towhees and sparrows may be common. Up to nine different species of sparrows, towhees not included, may be found here or close by. Sparrows breeding here include Savannah, Vesper, Lark, Sage, Chipping, Brewer's, Lincoln's, and Song, as well as "Oregon" Dark-eyed Junco.

If you are here in summer, turn left on Arrastre, left on Minnow, and right on Pioneertown (see map on page 196). Watch for Forest Service road signs (you should be on 2N02). Stay on 2N02 for just over 3 miles, when it crosses Arrastre Creek (the first sizable creek crossing). This area has had nesting Hepatic Tanagers some years and is quite reliable for Calliope Hummingbird. Surrounding Pinyon Pine-covered slopes have even had nesting Plumbeous Vireos. From Arrastre Creek continue east to a prominent road junction at Rose Mine (where 2N02 and 3N03 join). The area right around the Rose Mine junction is the most reliable spot in the San Bernardinos for Gray Vireo. By taking 3N03 (locally called Smarts Ranch Road) northwestward, there are more opportunities for Gray Vireo within the next 2 miles, as well as more crossings of Arrastre Creek, where you can investigate the good riparian areas. Passenger cars will find this road slow going, but passable in dry weather. Observe desert-travel precautions, for there appears to be little traffic on week-days. Beyond Rose Mine you will enter a valley with Joshua Trees rivaling those in the National Park.

To continue the loop follow Baldwin Lake Road around the lake, entering an open stand of large old yellow pines, where Mountain Bluebirds and Pinyon Jays can usually be found at any season. Cliff Swallows have, in the past, built their mud nests on the trunks of large pines under the shelter of the larger limbs. This unusual choice of nesting sites has not been observed elsewhere, and is apparently irregular here, so watch for an occurrence.

Baldwin Lake Road merges with Shay Road. Shay Road begins where Baldwin Lake Road makes the 90-degree right turn after crossing the bridge, 3.8 miles from Highway 18. At Palomino Drive, 0.3 mile farther, turn right and proceed to the end of the road. Here you will find the Palomino substation of the Big Bear Area Regional Wastewater Agency, open 8 AM–4:30 PM Monday–Friday (best in winter and migration). Ask permission at the office to bird the impoundments for ducks and gulls. Return to Shay Road and continue west to where it ends at Highway 38 (Greenspot Boulevard) (0.5). If you have time, continue straight ahead to explore the villages along the south shore of the lake. Pinyon Jays are often seen and heard in this general area.

To reach another good spot for these noisy corvids, continue south on Greenspot Boulevard toward Redlands to Mann Drive (0.3). Turn right and slowly drive the residential area. Watch for bird feeders, which often attract the jays.

Return to Greenspot Boulevard and continue south. You will soon enter forests of Jeffrey Pines. Look-alike Ponderosa and Jeffrey Pines can be separated accurately by their cones. Simply remember "gentle Jeffrey and prickly Ponderosa"; Jeffrey cone spines are gently decurved on the tips of the scales, while those on Ponderosa cones point outward and are prickly. Although it is true that Jeffrey Pines have a richer vanilla/butterscotch smell when one's nose is thrust into the crevices in the bark (a highly recommended olfactory experience, but a vulnerable position—best done when others are not nearby), this varies with air temperature and other factors. Your nose may vary.

As the road climbs up from the valley, these pines give way to Western Juniper and One-leaf Pinyon. The brushy area around the Greenspot Picnic Ground (El. 7,500 ft) (3.5) can be good in summer for Dusky Flycatcher, Black-throated Gray Warbler, and Green-tailed and Spotted Towhees. In the vicinity of Onyx Summit, you will see a few stunted White Firs.

Onyx Summit (El. 8,443 ft) is the highest point on the highway—it is the divide between the Colorado River drainage to the east and the Santa Ana River to the west. Water flowing down the eastern slope is swallowed by the Mojave, but to the west there is ample winter and spring flow into the Santa Ana, the largest river in Southern California—though much of the flow is underground. Park at the pull-out for Onyx Summit and walk the dirt road to the top. Clark's Nutcracker, Townsend's Solitaire, and Cassin's Finch may be seen here with other mountain species.

The highway leaves the summit to skirt the edges of massive San Gorgonio Mountain and cross Barton Flats Recreation Area (8.5). This very popular vacation spot has several public campgrounds and many private organizational camps. It is no place to go birding on a summer weekend, but can be good during the rest of the year. One of the best places to stop is **Heart Bar Campground** (6.0). The main attractions in summer are both Whip-poorwill and Common Poorwill, which can sometimes be heard after dark on the hillside south of the campground, plus Red-breasted and Williamson's Sapsuckers and White-headed Woodpecker, which are fairly common. Notice the numerous half-inch-diameter holes that they drill in the trunks of the larger pines.

Turn left onto Jenks Lake Road (4.1). Common Nighthawks are sometimes heard on June evenings about 100 yards or so off the highway. Jenks Lake Road leads to a small lake (3.0) and also to the road to Poopout Hill, the jumping-off place for the hike up San Gorgonio Mountain. A permit is required for the hike, but you may find good birding around the parking lot, including Northern Saw-whet and Flammulated Owls at night. The steep, rugged, 8-mile trail to the summit crosses the **San Gorgonio Wilderness** and passes through forests of pine and fir and by delightful lakes and meadows. If you reach the summit at 11,502 feet, you will be in the largest Alpine-Arctic area in Southern California. Here the blue of the sky is matched only by the blue of the numerous Mountain Bluebirds. Jenks Lake Road returns to Highway 38 (1.8).

Many people at Angelus Oaks (5.4) maintain bird feeders, particularly for hummingbirds. In summer, Anna's, Black-chinned, and Calliope Hummingbirds are fairly common. In late summer, they are joined by hordes of Rufous and some Allen's; Costa's seldom gets this high, being more common among the sages at lower elevations. Summer evenings sometimes bring the explosive call of the Whip-poor-will (rare and local) from the hillside.

Slow down and make a very sharp left onto Forest Falls Road (5.2) to drive up **Mill Creek Canyon**. Immediately on your right, look for a small sign pointing to **Bearpaw Ranch Sanctuary**, a new 70-acre wildlife sanctuary run by San Bernardino Valley Audubon Society. The dirt entry road is very rough and steep as it leaves Forest Falls Road, but can usually be navigated by a passenger vehicle. The faint of heart may wish to park at the wide spot at the top of the entry road and walk in. Depending on recent rains and the condition of the creek, this may be your only option, even with four-wheel drive. The pleasant walk to the sanctuary is only one-quarter mile. An electric gate crosses the road (0.2) to keep ORVs out, but birders who drive in can call ahead (909/794-0509) to get the pass code. It's a good idea to call ahead anyway, if possible, to alert the manager that you will be coming; a message to that effect left on the answering machine will suffice. The pass code is also kept on the SBVAS RBA (909/795-5599, option 6) for those times when the sanctuary manager is unavailable. Birds seen here are similar to those up the canyon, but this place can be a godsend when it appears that the entire population of Southern California is trying to enjoy the picnic grounds at Forest Falls. Watch for American Dippers as you cross the stream if it is flowing briskly. Black Swifts nest in Monkeyface Falls—on the high cliffs on the north side of Valley of the Falls Drive, just opposite the Bearpaw Ranch entry road—so watch for them overhead with White-throated Swifts. White-headed Woodpecker is here, too. A small pond near the parking lot attracts migrants and residents during the warm season, much to the enjoyment of photographers. In winter check the bird feeders behind the manager's residence. Evening and Rose-breasted Grosbeaks (rare) have been known to join the usual Golden-crowned Sparrows and other expected birds here in winter. When the berries are plentiful, watch for Varied Thrush (rare) among the American Robins. Picnic tables and restrooms are available near the Audubon barn below the manager's residence. Several self-guided nature trails begin near the parking lot.

Return to Valley of the Falls Drive. **Big Falls Picnic Area** (El. 5,560 ft) (4.2) is situated in a grove of large Incense Cedars and Black Oaks at the end of the road. Take the short trail across the river to the falls, where Black Swifts can be found among the more numerous White-throateds. American Dippers are also found at the falls. By hiking upstream a short way, you can reach **Vivian Meadows**, an excellent spot for Townsend's Solitaire, Cassin's Finch, and Spotted Owl (night). This is also the starting point for the 7.2-mile Big Falls Trail to the top of San Gorgonio Mountain.

Return to Highway 38 and continue down the mountain. Near Mountain Home Village (2.3), turn left onto Old Mill Creek Road, jog left, turn right onto Sycamore Road, and follow it through the little settlement. There are large numbers of birds around the cabins. Fox and Golden-crowned Sparrows are abundant in winter. You might want to try Thurman Flats Picnic Area farther down the road (1.1), which is also good for sparrows.

Follow Highway 38 through Mentone to Redlands. Here there are Spotted Doves, European Starlings, House Sparrows, and other city birds if you care to look. Turn left at the traffic-light on Orange Street (11.0) to join the freeway (Interstate 10) going west. This will join Interstate 215 (6.7) to take you north back to San Bernardino.

To visit nearby San Bernardino County Museum (fee), continue straight at the Orange Street traffic-light on Lugonia Avenue to California Avenue (2.4). Turn left for one block to Orange Tree Lane, where you turn left again. The museum drive is a short distance ahead on the left. Here you can examine the large egg collection, excellent bird exhibits, and shop at the bookstore. The museum is open 9 AM–5 PM Tuesday–Sunday; closed Mondays and national holidays. Annual passes are available, as are group discounts (2024 Orange Tree Lane; phone 909/307-2669).

You are very close to the starting point of the Western Riverside County route. To reach it, follow Interstate 215 south to Highway 91 (10.9).

There are 29 public campgrounds in the San Bernardino Mountains and numerous motels and lodges. Some of the campgrounds are on a reservation system in summer. If you are interested, write to the San Bernardino National Forest, 144 North Mountain View Avenue, San Bernardino, CA 92408, and they will tell you the procedure for making reservations.

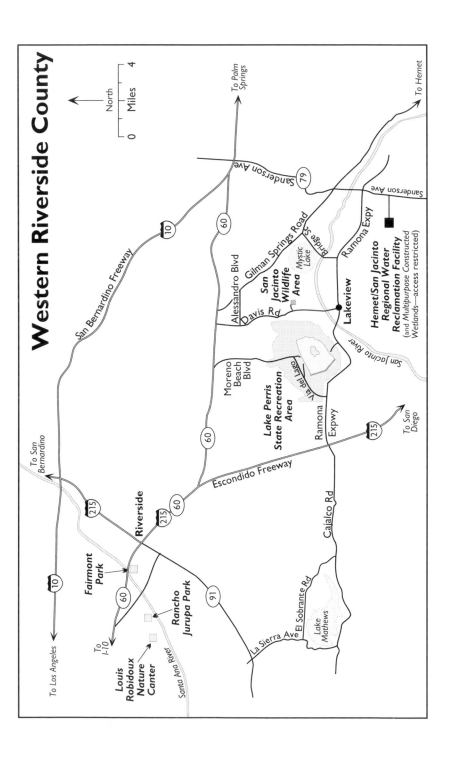

Western Riverside County

North — 0 to 4 Miles

To Palm Springs

To Hemet

San Bernardino Freeway

Sanderson Ave

79

Sanderson Ave

Ramona Expy

Hemet/San Jacinto Regional Water Reclamation Facility (and Multipurpose Constructed Wetlands—access restricted)

10

60

Alessandro Blvd

Gilman Springs Road

Bridge St

San Jacinto Wildlife Area

Mystic Lake

Davis Rd

Lakeview

San Jacinto River

Moreno Beach Blvd

Lake Perris State Recreation Area

Vía del Lago

60

Ramona Expwy

215

To San Diego

To San Bernardino

215

Riverside

215

60

Escondido Freeway

Caialco Rd

To Los Angeles

10

Fairmont Park

60

Rancho Jurupa Park

91

El Sobrante Rd

La Sierra Ave

Lake Mathews

To I-10

Louis Robidoux Nature Center

Santa Ana River

WESTERN RIVERSIDE COUNTY

by Chet McGaugh

Although it is one of the fastest developing areas in California, and the scene of continuing struggles between the Endangered Species Act and economic forces, western Riverside County offers excellent opportunities for birdwatchers. Some of the most extensive riparian forests remaining in Southern California are found along the Santa Ana River. Huge man-made reservoirs, including Lake Perris, Lake Skinner, Lake Mathews (virtually unbirdable), and the soon-to-be-filled, as-of-yet unnamed, mega-reservoir in Domenigoni Valley (near Winchester) provide habitat for waterfowl, loons, grebes, gulls, and other waterbirds. The San Jacinto Valley offers some of the best inland winter birding in the United States, including an exciting variety of raptors.

Western Riverside County is located just south of the San Gabriel and San Bernardino Mountains trips, and west of the San Jacinto Mountains route. It will be easy for you to connect to one of these high-mountain routes from western Riverside. Look at a highway map of Southern California and examine the spatial relationships in order to best plan your birding expedition.

The trip begins at the **Louis Robidoux Nature Center**. (Refer to map on following page.) From Highway 60, 2.7 miles west of the junction of Interstate 215 and Highway 91, take Rubidoux (the city and the nature center are spelled differently—strange, but true) Boulevard south to Mission Boulevard (0.6) and turn right. Turn left onto Riverview Drive/Limonite Avenue (0.3), and left again, following Riverview Drive as these two roads diverge (0.6). Follow Riverview Drive to the Louis Robidoux Nature Center (1.2). The Nature Center building, on the left behind a pecan grove, is visible from the road. If the gate is locked, park on Riverview Drive and walk in.

Trails from the Nature Center lead to a variety of habitats: riparian, marsh, pond, orchard, scrubby field, and to the Santa Ana River. Although an entire day is easily spent birding here, even an hour or two can be good. Nesting species include Cinnamon Teal, Red-shouldered and Red-tailed Hawks, Great Horned Owl (often nesting in the pecan grove), Anna's and Black-chinned Hummingbirds, Nuttall's and Downy Woodpeckers, Western Kingbird, Ash-throated Flycatcher, California Thrasher, Loggerhead Shrike, Yellow Warbler, Common Yellowthroat, Yellow-breasted Chat, Black-headed and Blue Grosbeaks, California Towhee, Song Sparrow, and Bullock's

Riverside Area

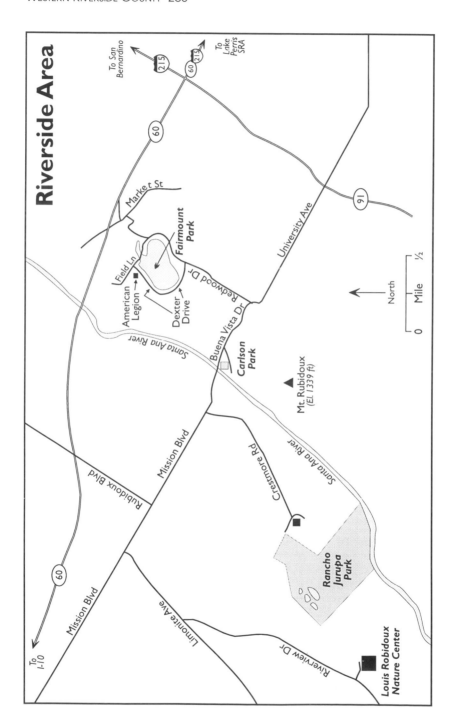

Oriole. Listen for the quizzical song of "Least" Bell's Vireo, an endangered subspecies, which was formerly common in willow thickets along the Santa Ana River.

From October to April the fields and thickets are full of sparrows (Savannah, Fox, Song, Lincoln's, Golden-crowned, White-crowned, and rarely Green-tailed Towhee, Swamp, White-throated, and Harris's Sparrows), the trees are full of Yellow-rumped Warblers, and the marsh is home to Virginia Rail, Sora, and (often) American Bittern. Flocks of Canada Geese may be seen loafing on sandbars in the river, along with myriad ducks and shorebirds (Black-necked Stilt, Greater Yellowlegs, Spotted, Western, and Least Sandpipers, Long-billed Dowitcher, and Common Snipe). Sharp-shinned and Cooper's Hawks forage in the riparian thickets and dense scrub. White-tailed Kite, Northern Harrier, Ferruginous Hawk, Merlin (rare), and Prairie Falcon (increasingly rare due to urban sprawl) hunt the more open terrain. The air over the river is a bird highway: flocks of ducks, geese, shorebirds, and gulls move up and down the river, visiting favorite feeding and roosting spots. Big Day teams birding the river *on foot in January* have tallied over 100 species!

During migration, look for Olive-sided Flycatcher, Western Wood-Pewee, Hammond's and Pacific-slope Flycatchers, Cassin's, Plumbeous (uncommon), and Warbling Vireos, Black-throated Gray, Wilson's, Nashville, Townsend's, and Hermit Warblers, and Western Tanager. Recent rarities include Virginia's and Blackburnian Warblers and Summer Tanager.

Return to the intersection of Riverview Drive/Limonite Avenue and Mission Boulevard. Turn right (east) and proceed to Crestmore Road (1.0). A right turn here will take you to **Rancho Jurupa Park** (1.2)(fee). As you drive down Crestmore you will be paralleling the Santa Ana River (to your left), but you will be unable to see it. Rancho Jurupa Park, which is also accessible by trail from the Robidoux Nature Center, has a fishing-lake and small ponds that are often full of wintering ducks (American Wigeon, Redhead, Ring-necked, Ruddy, and others). A trail leads to the river and to areas of dense riparian habitat. Watch for Phainopeplas. Gray Flycatcher occasionally winters in the vicinity of the small ponds.

Return to Mission Boulevard and turn right. You will cross the river and, as soon as you do, you'll see a small park on the right (0.4). From **Carlson Park** you can walk up and down the river or, if you're feeling energetic, you can hike one of the steep trails up Mount Rubidoux to look for White-throated Swift, Cactus Wren (in a cactus patch on the northeast side near the bottom), Rock Wren, and Rufous-crowned Sparrow. It's also a good vantage point for watching the thousands of birds that fly up and down the river on a winter's day.

From the park, proceed east on Buena Vista Drive (the continuation of Mission Boulevard), and turn left onto Redwood Drive (0.3). Turn left on Dexter Drive (0.5), drive around Lake Evans, and park at the American Legion Hall (0.4), across the street from the army tank. You are now in **Fairmount**

Park. This is a popular urban park, so exercise caution; however it can be an excellent place to study gulls—as many as a thousand may be loafing on the lake on a winter afternoon. Bonaparte's, Ring-billed, California, and Herring are the common species; Mew, Thayer's, Glaucous-winged, and Glaucous have been seen, too. Pied-billed Grebe, Double-crested Cormorant, Great Blue Heron, Great and Snowy Egrets, and Belted Kingfisher are usually present. Many species of waterfowl use the lake; Wood Ducks are fairly common in winter. Birding in the riparian thicket and the open parkland can be good, but be alert, heed the signs, and *don't go alone*. Winter rarities include Red-throated Loon, Lewis's Woodpecker, Williamson's Sapsucker, Bohemian Waxwing, Chestnut-sided Warbler, and White-throated Sparrow.

From the parking area, make a left turn to reach Field Lane (0.1), where you will turn right. At Redwood Drive (0.2) turn left. Follow Redwood Drive to the park's exit at Market Street (0.2), being careful to make a quick left so you don't enter the area marked "Do Not Enter." A left turn onto Market Street will take you to the eastbound Highway 60 on-ramp (0.1). Get on the 60 and head east, making sure to avoid the Interstate 215 split (5.9) going toward San Diego. Exit the freeway at Moreno Beach Boulevard (6.5) and go south until you reach Via del Lago (3.1). Turn left and enter **Lake Perris State Recreation Area**(1.1; fee).

Lake Perris should be avoided in summer. In winter, however, the crowds are gone and the birds have returned. Horned Grebes occur every winter, joining thousands of Eared, Western, and Clark's Grebes. Greater Scaup, and sometimes Tufted Duck, have been found in the large (but shrinking) Lesser Scaup flock that usually rafts near Lot 8. Pacific Loons, rare inland, are found on the lake almost every winter. An impressive list of winter rarities keeps turning up here.

Strategies for birding the lake depend on the amount of time you have. A walk out the dam (3.5 miles round trip) can be good, as can a walk around the east end of the lake where the riparian vegetation meets the water. Check the snags for Ospreys. Birders in a hurry can drive and stop at each of the parking lots to scope the little bays, and walk out the "peninsulas" to scope the open water.

The hills of coastal sage scrub around the lake are home to Costa's Hummingbird, Rock, Canyon, and Bewick's Wrens, California Gnatcatcher (rare), California Thrasher, California Towhee, and Rufous-crowned and Sage Sparrows. Be cautious in identifying gnatcatchers; Blue-gray Gnatcatchers are much more common than California Gnatcatchers during most of the year (see illustration in the Palos Verdes Peninsula chapter).

From the entrance station at the west end of the park (2.7), drive south to the Ramona Expressway (0.9) and turn left. The expressway takes you past the road to Bernasconi Beach (3.7), another access to Lake Perris and the surrounding hills. If you have time, check Bernasconi Beach, then continue to Davis Road (2.1) and turn left. You are now in the town of Lakeview in the San Jacinto Valley.

For birding purposes the vast, mostly flat San Jacinto Valley is defined by Alessandro Boulevard (north), Gilman Springs Road/Sanderson Avenue (east), the Ramona Expressway (south), and Davis Road (west). It is the winter home for an impressive number and variety of birds; the San Jacinto Lake Christmas Bird Count is consistently among the top inland CBCs in North America. Ducks and geese (including Greater White-fronted) fly back and forth over the valley, visiting agricultural fields, hunt clubs, and the San Jacinto Wildlife Area. Thousands of Horned Larks and, during most winters, small flocks of longspurs (McCown's, Chestnut-collared, rarely Lapland) forage in the fields. The "longspur field" changes locales based on weather and agricultural practices. Mountain Plovers winter in the valley, as do Mountain Bluebirds.

Drive north on Davis Road (it soon becomes dirt and may be impassable after a rain) to the turn-off for the headquarters of the **San Jacinto Wildlife Area** (2.2)(fee), on your right. Hunting season here stretches from mid-October to mid-January; hunt days are Wednesdays and Saturdays. Nonetheless, there are still many areas open to birders on those days. Watch the fences along Davis Road for Say's Phoebes and Mountain Bluebirds (winter) and Western Kingbirds (summer). Turn right and proceed 0.2 mile to the headquarters and entrance kiosk. Check with wildlife area personnel for information on recent bird sightings and road conditions, and pick up a map and checklist. The San Bernardino Valley Audubon Society Rare Bird Alert (909/793-5599) also has information on recent sightings.

San Jacinto Wildlife Area comprises 4,700 acres of wetlands, marshes, grasslands, and rocky hills of coastal sage scrub. It remains a refuge for the endangered Stephens' Kangaroo Rat, the "mouse that roars" at developers in western Riverside County, and is the first of the state's wildlife areas to use reclaimed water to re-establish wetlands sacrificed earlier in the century to flood control, agriculture, and development. *It is a birder's paradise.*

Wildlife Area personnel may be able to tell you if longspurs and/or Mountain Plovers have been seen, whether or not there are any Short-eared Owls in the vicinity, where the Long-eared Owls are, and whether or not Bald Eagles have been reported. There's something to see at all times of the year in the wetlands. Nesting species include Eared and Pied-billed Grebes, Mallard, Northern Pintail, Northern Shoveler, Gadwall, Redhead, Ruddy Duck, Virginia Rail, Common Moorhen, Black-necked Stilt, American Avocet, Killdeer, and Red-winged, Tricolored and Yellow-headed Blackbirds. Nesting Grasshopper Sparrows have been found occasionally in the scrubby fields. Sage Thrashers may be seen in winter and migration. Recent rarities include Tundra Swan, Oldsquaw, Red Knot, and Least Flycatcher.

In fall, the edges of the ponds, mudflats, and wet fields are visited by thousands of shorebirds on their way south; Solitary, Baird's, and Pectoral

Sandpipers are found among them by careful searching. Wintering shorebirds include Black-bellied Plover, Greater and Lesser Yellowlegs, Spotted Sandpiper, Long-billed Curlew, Western and Least Sandpipers, Dunlin, and Long-billed Dowitcher, along with the resident Killdeer, Black-necked Stilts, and American Avocets.

Head north on Davis Road until the pavement begins again (3.4), and continue straight to Alessandro Boulevard (0.1). This is a good place to stop to scan the telephone poles for Ferruginous Hawks (September–April). Turn right and drive east on Alessandro Boulevard, watching the poles, the ground (Ferruginous Hawks like to stand out in the middle of big, sparsely vegetated fields), and the sky for raptors. Be sure to check the poles (but don't turn) along the side road (1.0) that heads south from Alessandro Boulevard. At Gilman Springs Road (1.0) turn right. Turn right onto Bridge Street (5.0).

A unique phenomenon in the San Jacinto Valley is the appearance and persistence of Mystic Lake. During extremely wet winters (e.g., El Niño 1997-1998) a vast, shallow lake forms in the valley west of Gilman Springs Road and north of Bridge Street. The ephemeral lake may cover two to ten thousand acres and attract many thousands of birds. Over 1,000 American White Pelicans were there for the 1994 CBC! As the lake shrinks under the summer heat, mudflats are formed in time for the fall shorebird migration. Baird's Sandpipers are seen regularly in late summer, and rarities such as Hudsonian Godwit, Semipalmated, and Stilt Sandpipers have been found among the multitudes of "regular" shorebirds. Would you believe 22 Brown Pelicans and a Blue-footed Booby on appeared August 31, 1996? Access the lake from Gilman Springs Road, Bridge Street, and/or the San Jacinto Wildlife Area. Depending on the season, it can be a long walk, a short walk, a muddy drive, or there may be enough birds on Gilman Springs Road or Bridge Street to keep you interested!

The fields on both sides of Bridge Street can be good for Mountain Plover, Burrowing Owl, Mountain Bluebird, and longspurs. White-tailed Kite, Northern Harrier, Ferruginous Hawk, and Golden Eagle are often in the area. When Sprague's Pipits (very rare) have been found in the valley, they have been found here. Horned Lark, American Pipit, and Savannah Sparrow may be here in abundance, depending on weather and land use. If you want to find longspurs, you must walk the fields. Do not cross "No Trespassing" signs or go through fences; the relationship between birders and property owners in the San Jacinto Valley is fragile.

If you are doing this trip in winter you should have an impressive list of raptors by now. You should also see Turkey Vultures (though you can't count 'em as raptors anymore; their closest relatives are the storks), and—if you're lucky—you may have seen a Bald Eagle, Rough-legged Hawk, Peregrine Falcon, or a Merlin. Six species of owls are possible: Barn, Western Screech-, Great Horned, Burrowing, Long-eared, and Short-eared. The staff at the wildlife area headquarters can usually give you information on owl locations. The San

Jacinto Valley, the Carrizo Plain, and the Antelope Valley are, perhaps, the best wintering raptor areas in Southern California.

After exploring the Bridge Street area, continue to follow the road as it crosses the usually dusty San Jacinto River (1.8) and ends at the Ramona Expressway (0.8). (*However, at the time of this revision, El Niño storms have destroyed the Bridge Street crossing and it is necessary to backtrack to Gilman Springs Road, turn right, proceed to Sanderson Avenue, then to Ramona Expressway. Be prepared for another possible scenario: Mystic Lake covering Bridge Street, as it did in the mid-1990s.*) Turn left (east) and follow the expressway to Sanderson Avenue (4.0). Turn right and proceed south on Sanderson until you see a large tan-colored sphere. This is the methane ball at the Hemet/San Jacinto Regional Water Reclamation Facility (1.7). Eastern Municipal Water District's Multipurpose Constructed Wetlands is approximately 1.5 miles to the west of the facility gates. At the present time, admission to the wetlands is by prior arrangement only. Arrangements can be made by contacting the Reclamation Facility staff at 909/654-2741, between 6 AM–3:30 PM daily. Enter by way of the front gate, stop at the front office, and sign in.

The **Multipurpose Constructed Wetlands** is a man-made wetlands supplied by the secondary treated effluent stream from the Reclamation Facility. In addition to water treatment, goals of the project include habitat creation, public education, and passive recreation. The ponds are the winter home of thousands of American Wigeons (and always a few Eurasian Wigeons) as well as all of the other species of waterfowl found in the valley. Pied-billed and Eared Grebes nest in the wetlands; Western, Clark's, and (occasionally) Horned Grebes are seen in winter. The marshes, mudflats, and shallows are used by a variety of large waders, including American Bittern, Great Blue Heron, Great and Snowy Egrets, Black-crowned Night-Heron, and White-faced Ibis (possibly nesting). Residents and regular migrants include the same shorebirds noted for other western Riverside sites.

The marsh is home to one of the largest Tricolored Blackbird colonies in Southern California. Other marsh inhabitants include Marsh Wren, Common Yellowthroat, Song Sparrow, and Yellow-headed Blackbird. During spring and fall, the sky over the marsh may be full of swallows—Tree, Violet-green, Cliff, Bank (rare), and Barn.

From the entrance to the Reclamation Facility, return to the Ramona Expressway (1.7), go left (west) back to Interstate 215 (15.0), then south on Interstate 215 back to its intersection with Highway 91 in Riverside (11.5). From here, you can retrace your steps to Rubidoux Boulevard (2.5) and the Robidoux Nature Center (2.7) to complete the loop, or continue on Highway 60 to begin the San Gabriel Mountains trip.

There are campgrounds at Rancho Jurupa Park and at Lake Perris State Recreation Area. Hotels and motels are abundant. There are entrance fees at Rancho Jurupa Park, Lake Perris State Recreation Area, and the San Jacinto Wildlife Area.

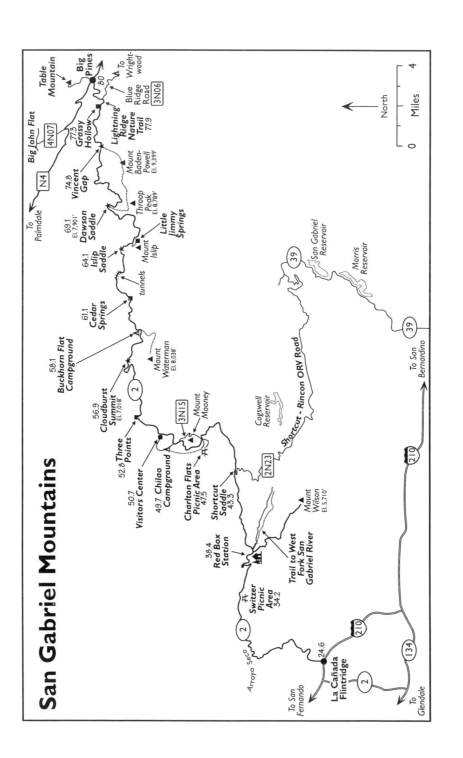

San Gabriel Mountains

Table Mountain — Big Pines — To Wrightwood

Big John Flat

4N07

Big John Flat

N4

To Palmdale

77.3 Grassy Hollow

80

Blue Ridge Road

3N06

Lightning Ridge Nature Trail 77.9

74.8 Vincent Gap

Mount Baden-Powell EL 9,399'

69.1 EL 7,901' Dawson Saddle

Throop Peak EL 8,789'

64.1 Islip Saddle

Little Jimmy Springs

Mount Islip

tunnels

61.1 Cedar Springs

58.1 Buckhorn Flat Campground

Mount Waterman EL 8,038

56.9 Cloudburst Summit EL 7,018'

2

52.8 Three Points

50.7 Visitors Center

3N15

Mount Mooney

49.7 Chilao Campground

Charlton Flats Picnic Area 47.5

Shortcut Saddle 43.3

2N23

Cogswell Reservoir

Shortcut – Rincon ORV Road

39

San Gabriel Reservoir

Morris Reservoir

39

To San Bernardino

38.4 Red Box Station

Trail to West Fork San Gabriel River

Mount Wilson EL 5,710'

Switzer Picnic Area 34.2

2

Arroyo Seco

To San Fernando

24.6

La Cañada Flintridge

210

210

2

134

To Glendale

North

0   Miles   4

SAN GABRIEL MOUNTAINS

by Thomas E. Wurster

The San Gabriel Mountains are aligned in an east-west direction atop the San Andreas fault line, separating the greater Los Angeles basin from the high desert to the north. The mountains rise abruptly from the coastal plain, reaching elevations of just over 10,000 feet. They are a relatively young range, still wearing many of the sharp features of their birth. There are no idyllic meadows and valleys in these raw mountains, and precious little level ground. Deep canyons and steep slopes cut their rugged flanks, making most of the range inaccessible except by trail.

The Angeles Crest Highway (Highway 2) is the primary access route to the heart of the range and provides the backbone of this tour. It enters the mountains from the community of La Cañada Flintridge on the mountains' southwestern flank. The road quickly climbs the slopes of the Arroyo Seco drainage to Red Box Station, then turns north along a ridge that connects with the main divide. Beyond Chilao, the road turns east and is continuously above 6,000 feet as it meanders along the north flanks of the higher peaks and the saddles between. Dawson Saddle (El. 7,901 ft) is the highway high-point, and Mount Baden-Powell (El. 9,399 ft) immediately to the east is the highest peak along the route. Beyond Vincent Gap the highway shifts to south-facing slopes and climbs above 7,400 feet, where it crosses the Blue Ridge Divide. Highway 2 then descends steeply to Big Pines and the resort community of Wrightwood (El. 5,931 ft).

The tour is loosely structured around major recreation sites in Angeles National Forest. These facilities, roadside stops, and adjacent trails provide access to excellent birding habitat in all elevation ranges.

A Forest Adventure Pass is required for all vehicles parked along roadways within National Forests. Passes are sold year round at several gas stations and stores in La Cañada Flintridge. They are also sold in Wrightwood for those who enter the mountains from the other end of the route. You risk a substantial fine if your car is parked within the National Forest without displaying this pass.

Don't limit your birding to the developed recreation sites named in this chapter, which were selected for convenience factors as much as for birding opportunities. The San Gabriel Mountains are a popular destination; the major recreation sites are crowded on weekends and holidays, especially during the warm season. Birding opportunities can be excellent anywhere along the route. Include stops at one or more of the less-developed sites mentioned, or simply make roadside stops at points of your own selection; you will be surprised by the number of birds seen or heard from the roadside.

You can't miss when you leave the highway and crowded, noisy recreation areas behind and hike even short distances on any of the many trails that cross the highway. Fifteen to twenty-five bird species are likely to be found in brief stops in any habitat. You will experience the mountains and forests more intimately, and can accumulate an impressive species list by simply making a series of stops at varying elevations along the highway.

Throughout this account, stops and turn-offs are referenced by mileage designations. These refer to the mileage marked on large white highway markers posted regularly to mark the shoulder of the highway, or mileage that is interpolated from nearby mileage markers. They are especially useful because *the posted mileage is independent of your direction of travel.* Use it to calculate your distance and direction between destinations along the highway. Three simple considerations need be observed. First, note that the mileage posted on these markers is the distance from a reference point outside the tour; *it does not represent mileage from the starting point of this tour.* Second, mileage posted on highway markers increases as you enter the mountains from La Cañada Flintridge, and decreases as you return. Third, the mileage posted for a particular destination is the same on marker signs read from *either* direction of travel.

For example, the mileages for Charlton Flat and the Chilao Visitor Center turn-off are respectively 47.1 and 50.2. You immediately see that Chilao is farther up the highway than Charlton Flat because the mileage for Chilao is higher. The distance between these locations, 3.1 miles, is easily determined by subtraction. Because mileage markers are posted several times per mile, they enable one to quickly determine distance and direction from any stop mentioned in the text. There is no need to track mileage on the car's odometer, and the system works regardless of your direction of travel.

The starting point is in La Cañada Flintridge (El. 1,300 ft) at the intersection of the Foothill Freeway (Interstate 210) and the Angeles Crest Highway (posted mileage 24.6). Carefully check the road-advisory sign for road conditions as you start up Highway 2 toward the mountains. The road is usually closed during winter in the high country from Islip Saddle (64.1) to the junction with Highway N4 at Big Pines (80). Closures may last until May in years with heavy snow.

Highway 2 quickly leaves the city behind and crosses the national forest boundary (27.0) just a couple of sweeping turns above La Cañada Flintridge. Early-morning stops at a major canyon turn-out in these lower elevations can be rewarding (especially between 28.0 and 30.0). On an active spring migration day you might encounter a wave of migrant warblers, tanagers, grosbeaks, and orioles swarming up the slopes. Listen for Northern Pygmy-

Owl, an uncommon resident on steep slopes luxuriantly clothed with Canyon Live Oak, California Bay, and tall, long-limbed Bigcone Douglas-fir. Carefully scan the swallows that circle among the snags high above at the head of the canyons. They usually are all Violet-greens, but you may occasionally see a Purple Martin, a localized and declining species in these mountains.

The slopes become drier and more exposed for several miles beyond 30.0. The stiff, aromatic brush is dense and impenetrable, but a brief stop at a roadside turn-out can still be productive. These slopes are home to all the local chaparral bird species including Costa's Hummingbird (spring and early summer) and Rufous-crowned Sparrow. You may see a Greater Roadrunner cross the road or perhaps hear its soft cooing or bill clatter from a hidden spot on the slopes.

Turn off the highway at **Switzer Picnic Area** (34.2), following the road downhill about one-half mile to the parking area in the canyon bottom (El. 3,302 ft). Coast Live Oak, California Sycamore, and White Alder line the stream bottom of this deep, narrow gorge. Switzer is a cool and delightful spot to escape the scorching summer heat, but on a winter day the shaded portions of the canyon are often cold and birdless. The bird list for the area is lengthy and includes species from riparian, chaparral, oak woodland, and pine-oak habitats. A sampling includes Acorn, Nuttall's, and Downy Wood-peckers, Pacific-slope Flycatcher (summer), White-breasted Nuthatch, Oak Titmouse, Hutton's Vireo, Warbling and Cassin's Vireos (summer), Yellow Warbler (summer), Black-headed Grosbeak (summer), and Spotted Tow-hee. Wide-ranging species such as Band-tailed Pigeon, and birds more common at higher elevations such as Hairy Woodpecker, Western Wood-Pewee, Steller's Jay, and Western Tanager (summer), are also found here. Most are easily found in the picnic area or along the trail that follows the stream. Be sure to arrive early because parking is limited. Latecomers have to park on the highway above and walk down the steep road to reach the canyon bottom.

Continuing up Highway 2 the upper reaches of the Arroyo Seco can be accessed from a trail that leads back down to Switzer. Look carefully for downhill traffic before crossing to park in a turn-out on the left side of the highway at 39.1. Walk up the highway 0.1 mile to the trail located where the highway makes a steep switchback turn. A locked gate marks the trailhead. Follow it 100 yards or so to get away from some of the road noise, and listen at dusk and dawn for Common Poorwill and owls. Great Horned Owl and Western Screech-Owl are often heard here, and Spotted Owl is a slim possibility from the steep slopes downcanyon. In winter "Sooty" Fox and Golden-crowned Sparrows frequent the dense thickets of scrub oak and chaparral covering the hillside.

The road to Mount Wilson Observatory intersects Highway 2 at Red Box Station (38.4). Note that the observatory and Skyline Park are open on weekends only, 10 AM–4 PM. The observatory makes an interesting side-trip, but provides only limited birding opportunities. Canyon Wrens can usually be heard from the vertical granite cliffs at Eaton Saddle trailhead (2.4), and the chatter of White-throated Swifts may fill the air as they chase one another madly through the airspace above and below your vantage point. Mountain Chickadee, White-breasted Nuthatch, Blue-gray Gnatcatcher (summer), and Black-throated Gray Warbler (summer) are some of the common species at the observatory summit (5.0). The steep north-facing slopes below the road are clothed with magnificent stands of Bigcone Douglas-fir, Canyon Live Oak, Big-leaf Maple, and California Bay, but the lack of broad turn-outs severely limits birding opportunities. Fortunately, the trail described below remedies this limitation.

Return and park at **Red Box Station**. Look for the unpaved Forest Service road (gated and locked) and trail that begin across the street from the station. The road and trail parallel one another and lead downhill and eastward into the West Fork of the San Gabriel River. A hike to the first river crossing in the canyon bottom (about one mile) is worthwhile. During spring and summer Western Tanagers and Black-headed Grosbeaks are conspicuous; their melodically-phrased songs can be heard throughout the day. Also look and listen for Olive-sided Flycatcher calling from a tall Douglas-fir. You'll find Black-chinned Hummingbird, Pacific-slope Flycatcher, Warbling Vireo, and Yellow Warbler patrolling the alders and sycamores lining the river bottom, while Costa's Hummingbirds and Black-chinned Sparrows occupy the drier and more open south-facing slopes near the canyon bottom. Ash-throated Flycatchers range over scrub and open wood-land, and Lazuli Buntings frequent brushy openings between the oaks. You may also find Cassin's Vireo in moist ravines and adjacent slopes where there is a good mix of conifers and broadleaf trees. At night, Western Screech-Owls may call from territories that are centered on the tributary streams that cross the roadway. The steep, densely forested ravines are prime Spotted Owl habitat, but you would be very fortunate to hear one.

Return to Highway 2 at Red Box Station and continue up the mountain. Listen for Mountain Quail and Black-chinned Sparrows from any turn-out in the next several miles (between 39 and 42). You'll be hard pressed to see Mountain Quail anywhere, but you will hear their loud *quee-ark!* call from every hillside throughout the spring. Look for Black-chinned Sparrows singing from the tops of the chaparral shrubs on the hot, exposed slopes. They are often found in extensive stands of chamise.

Take note of the gated and locked forest service road you pass on the right at mile 43.3. This is the **Short-cut Saddle to Rincon Station ORV Trail**. Travel on this road is regulated by the Forest Service. It offers a delightful, slow-paced alternative to highly trafficked Highway 2. It traverses a beautiful canyon and scenic ridges, providing access to a constantly changing mix of habitats in the 3,000–6,000-foot elevation range. Starting on the hot, exposed, south-facing chaparral slopes at Short-cut Saddle, the road descends through dry stands of Canyon Live Oak to an idyllic riparian corridor along the West Fork of the San Gabriel River. It then slowly climbs through a cool, moist, mixed forest of Canyon Live Oak and Bigcone Douglas-fir on the north-facing slopes, then follows the east-west trending ridgeline. The upper basins of several large canyons are filled with dense stands of oak and Douglas-fir and frame-alternating vistas of the Los Angeles basin to the west or the main ridge and peaks of the San Gabriel Mountains to the east. The road then descends along ridges clothed in Coast Live Oak and chaparral to join Highway 39 near Rincon Station.

This route provides a unique vehicle-based opportunity to penetrate an isolated section of the mountains. You will experience a degree of quiet and solitude that is unattainable on or near the highway. The pace is slow, and opportunities for quality birding abound. Inquire with the Forest Service Ranger Station at Oak Grove in La Cañada Flintridge for road reservations and road conditions. They offer a limited number of vehicle permits (free) when road conditions are safe. A high-clearance vehicle and a day with no other plans is all that is required.

Continuing on Highway 2, you enter the first significant stands of pines as you approach Charlton Flat (El. 5,393 ft). The rather open, airy, structured pine with long, stiff gray-green needles is a Coulter Pine. Its claim to fame is a huge cone which is the heaviest of all pine cones.

Turn left into **Charlton Flat Picnic Area** (47.5) and follow the road downhill. There is usually ample parking near the gate at the lower end. This is a productive stop at any season. In summer you are likely to see many Western Bluebirds and Violet-green Swallows before you even park the car. This is the first stop where you will find White-headed Woodpecker. Western Wood-Pewee is common in summer, and Pygmy Nuthatch and Mountain Chickadee can be annoyingly abundant. The latter two species will be your constant companions at all stops from here to Big Pines. Walk the road beyond the gate to the trail that follows the stream downcanyon. Nearly all the oak-woodland and transition-forest species can be found here. Over the years, several vagrant warbler species have been recorded.

You have a choice of routes when you return to the highway. You can continue up Highway 2 toward Chilao, or take an unpaved forest service road (Route 3N15) that begins immediately behind the trailer sanitary dump station located just opposite the entrance road to Charlton Flat Picnic Area. This alternate route winds over the east and north slopes of Mount Mooney, offering a pleasant alternative to the busy highway. It rejoins Highway 2 at mile 49.5, immediately south of the turn-off to Chilao Campground (49.7). Hutton's Vireo, Black-throated Gray Warbler, and Purple Finch breed in this area. Also listen for Northern Pygmy-Owl. It may call actively in early morning or late afternoon, often responding to whistled imitations of its call.

Otherwise, continue on Highway 2. Continue past the turn-off to Chilao Campground (49.7) and turn left for **Chilao Visitors Center** (50.7) (Note: the campground road loops back to Highway 2 near the visitors center.) The visitors center (El. 5,200 ft) is staffed irregularly (infrequently). When the feeders around the building are stocked, they attract droves of Band-tailed Pigeons, California Quail, a few Mountain Quail, and a variety of finches.

Chilao is a bird-rich area where virtually all species from lower elevation oak and chaparral habitats and most transition-zone species can be easily found. Lawrence's Goldfinch is one of the more localized species generally found here. Search for them in the willow riparian and meadow area. They frequently nest in the pines scattered across the meadow near the campground. After late June you might find Sage Sparrows (*canescens*) along the stream where there is a mix of Great Basin Sagebrush and willows. Northern Saw-whet Owls have been recorded along the stream near the visitors center, and Common Poorwill call regularly from the dry chaparral slopes near the campground. A fall or winter visit can also be rewarding. Species typical of higher elevations in summer such as Williamson's Sapsucker and Red Crossbill, and eruptive species such as Red-breasted Nuthatch and Evening Grosbeak (rare), are possible.

Return to Highway 2 and continue up the mountain. You'll immediately pass Newcomb Ranch Cafe (49.9). This is the only cafe between La Cañada Flintridge and Wrightwood, and it is usually crowded on weekends. The forest begins to show the aspect of higher elevation beyond Three Points junction (52.8). This is the beginning of Flammulated Owl country. A widespread but generally sparse population of these small migrant owls is scattered from here to Big Pines. Listening for a few hours from a series of roadside turn-outs in the 6,000–8,000-foot elevation range on evenings in June or July may produce several Flammulated Owls and an occasional Northern Saw-whet Owl. Unfortunately, both owls are notoriously difficult to spot, even when perched in a tree overhead.

The highway parallels the Pacific Crest Trail as it climbs the long western flank of Mount Waterman between Three Points and Cloudburst Summit (56.9); the trail is readily accessible from numerous turn-outs. Birding short segments of the Pacific Crest Trail can be very productive and has the advantage of being less crowded than the busy campground birding stops. The western approach to Cloudburst Summit (El. 7,018 ft) is the first area along the highway where Clark's Nutcrackers can be reliably found. Groups can often be located by listening for their loud and distinctive *kra-a-a* call. Dusky Flycatcher, Green-tailed Towhee, and *stephensi* "Thick-billed" Fox Sparrows generally make their first appearances at elevations near 6,500 feet.

Buckhorn Flat Campground (58.1) is a major stop in the 6,500-foot elevation range. You need to look carefully to find the left turn-off to the campground. This narrow one-way road follows a shaded stream and passes a magnificent stand of Incense Cedars before reaching the campground. Nearly all the higher-elevation species breed in this area. Although the campground area is noisy and crowded on summer weekends, you can easily avoid these distractions by working the broad north slope of Mount Waterman (El. 8,038 ft) from several trails and highway turn-outs.

Coverage should include the trail opposite the turn-off; it leads up to the ridge east of Mount Waterman's summit, the entrance road, the campground and willow thickets bordering it, and the stream crossing the highway at the exit road junction. Dusky Flycatcher, Green-tailed Towhee, and Fox Sparrow are usually easy on the knolls just above the turn-off. Hairy and White-headed Woodpeckers, Red-breasted Sapsucker, Olive-sided Flycatcher, Red-breasted Nuthatch, Brown Creeper, Cassin's Vireo, Yellow-rumped Warbler, Hermit Warbler, MacGillivray's Warbler, Cassin's Finch, and Pine Siskin are just a sampling of the birds likely in this area. At night Common Poorwill, Northern Pygmy-Owl, and Northern Saw-whet and Flammulated Owls are all possible.

There are many excellent birding stops in the 6–8,000-foot elevation range between Buckhorn and Big Pines. Diligent searching among the White Fir on the gentle slopes at Cedar Springs (61.1) can produce a Hermit Warbler. You may find MacGillivray's Warbler in the willow-lined seeps and drainages along the roadside beyond Islip Saddle (64.1). During spring and fall migration impressive numbers of Yellow-rumped, Townsend's, and Hermit Warblers move over these forested ridges in mixed flocks.

An excellent birding trail leads gradually up to **Little Jimmy Springs** on the north slope of Mount Islip. The trailhead is at Islip Saddle (64.1), but the hike can be shortened if you intercept the trail by hiking an unpaved forest service road (gated and locked) at 65.5. These slopes are forested with an impressive mix of White Fir and Jeffrey and Sugar Pines. The bird list is similar to the list for Buckhorn, but with increased opportunity for Red-breasted Sapsucker, Townsend's Solitaire, and Red Crossbill. Golden-crowned Kinglet (very local) is also possible.

Continue on Highway 2 to Dawson Saddle at 69.1 (El 7,901). A two- to three-mile hike on the **Throop Peak Trail** (El. 8,789 ft) provides the least strenuous route to the highest elevations along this route. Look for Williamson's Sapsucker in stands of scaly-barked Lodgepole Pine and White Fir. Opportunities for Clark's Nutcracker, Townsend's Solitaire, Red Crossbill, Cassin's Finch, and Pine Siskin are also excellent along this trail. More adventurous hikers can continue on to the summit of Mount Baden-Powell (El. 9,399 ft). A more popular, more strenuous, trail to the summit of Mount Baden-Powell starts from Vincent Gap (74.8). This trail switchbacks it way to the summit of Mount Baden-Powell and offers similar target birds.

Continue on Highway 2 to **Grassy Hollow Visitors Center** (77.3). Birding can be very productive here, and the open forest and gently sloping terrain makes birdfinding easy. Look for Chipping Sparrow and Cassin's Finch on the ground in the picnic area. A flock of Red Crossbills once entertained watchers by hopping on the upper sides of downed pine cones, thereby nimbly rolling the cone to get at pine nuts on the other side!

Parking for the Lightning Ridge Nature Trail is on the left at 77.9, just beyond Grassy Hollow. This short loop trail winds through a beautiful stand of the deciduous Black Oak. Look for White-breasted Nuthatch and Brown Creeper working the trunks and limbs. Western Wood-Pewees and Dusky Flycatchers patrol the openings, and Orange-crowned Warblers abound in the brushy thickets. Also search for Nashville Warblers, which nest on the ground beneath the oaks in some years. Study them carefully so as not to overlook a Virginia's Warbler. One year, a pair of out-of-range Virginia's Warblers attempted to nest here.

Black-chinned Sparrow, Green-tailed Towhee, and *stephensi* "Thick-billed" Fox Sparrows are abundant on the surrounding brushy slopes and ridge. Listen carefully to the songs of the latter two species, which are very similar and are easily confused. However, their call notes are distinctive. The Green-tailed Towhee has a cat-like-mew call note, while Fox Sparrow call notes sound very similar to the *chink* note of California Towhee.

Forest Service Road 3N06 leading to Blue Ridge Campground (El. 7,900 ft) begins on the right side of Highway 2 at 77.9, opposite the Lightning Ridge Nature Trail parking area. Birding the roadside or the Pacific Crest Trail which closely parallels the road here can be very rewarding. Habitats include extensive brush thickets on exposed south-facing slopes, a few Black Oak groves on the north slope just below the ridgeline, extensive stands of mixed pine and White Fir intermixed around brushy openings, plus ski run clearings. Mountain Quail, Northern Pygmy-Owl, Red-breasted Sapsucker, Dusky Flycatcher, Olive-sided Flycatcher, Townsend's Solitaire, Chipping Sparrow, Cassin's Finch, and Pine Siskin are just a few of the species you find. Violet-green Swallows are also abundant, offering close-up viewing opportunities as they swoop repeatedly across the ridge at eye-level.

Highway 2 descends rapidly toward Big Pines (80) and Wrightwood where the tour ends. This area provides opportunities to find several bird species that are either uncommon or localized in the San Gabriel Mountains. The dense willow thickets lining the north side of the highway below Mountain High Ski Resort offer chances for Calliope Hummingbird. MacGillivray's Warbler is regularly seen here, and Wilson's Warbler is possible. Park along the roadway and walk any of the dirt roads that wind through the willows.

Whip-poor-will and Common Nighthawk have been recorded in this area. Several years generally pass between sightings, and any new sightings should be reported. Listen for Whip-poor-will from turn-outs on the first two miles of the Big Pines Highway (N4) immediately downhill from the junction with Highway 2. They are occasionally heard calling from the oak-and-pine-covered slopes in the upper part of this canyon. Common Nighthawk has been reported from the Table Mountain area.

A small population of Gray Flycatchers has been found in Pinyon Pine woodland in this area. Take Forest Service Road 4N07 to Big John Flat. There should be Gray Flycatchers anywhere along the first mile of this dirt road. They are also suspected to be in the Table Mountain area (but never confirmed—make a contribution!). Take the road from Big Pines toward

Table Mountain Campground. Halfway to the top, a forest service road heads off to the east. The road is well graded initially as it winds through stands of Black Oak and pines, but deteriorates and requires high-clearance 4-wheel-drive vehicles beyond the first Pinyon Pines. Gray Flycatchers should be looked for on the desert-facing slopes along the eastern ridge of Table Mountain.

After completing this route you have many options. You are approximately 44 miles southeast of Palmdale (all services available) in the Antelope Valley chapter, and roughly the same distance from the start of the San Bernardino Mountains route—consult your highway map. To reach Palmdale, continue north on Highway N4 to Highway 18 and turn west until joining Highway 14, turning north there toward Palmdale. In Palmdale you are immediately south of Mojave in the Eastern Kern County loop. To reach San Bernardino, go south on Highway 138 to Interstate 15, turning south to San Bernardino.

Motels and services are available in abundance in the lowlands at the beginning of this route; there are some in Wrightwood at the end, as well.

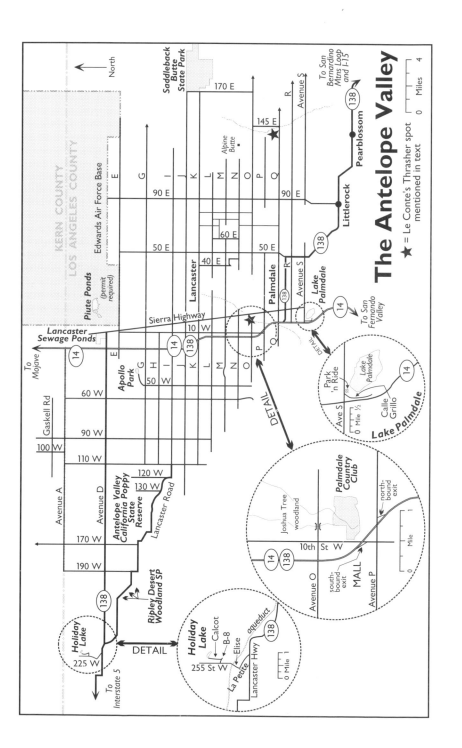

The Antelope Valley

★ = Le Conte's Thrasher spot mentioned in text

THE ANTELOPE VALLEY

by Charles Hood

Located in the Mojave Desert about an hour's drive northeast of Los Angeles, the Antelope Valley hosts a few specialty species easier to find here than elsewhere. Once a mixture of Joshua Trees, junipers, prairie grasses, saltbush, and artesian springs, now it offers alfalfa farms, housing tracts, aerospace plants, and miles of abandoned fields. The water table has dropped drastically and the human population has soared—one reason there are no Pronghorns left in the Antelope Valley—but in many isolated places native habitat endures, offering new visitors their first California Poppies (the state flower), California Quail (the state bird), Cactus Wrens, Sage Sparrows (A. b. canescens here), and Ladder-backed Woodpeckers. In other places agriculture attracts wintering Ferruginous Hawks and Mountain Bluebirds, while terminally optimistic birders comb through thousands of Horned Larks each winter hoping to find a few Lapland Longspurs. This is also a test-flight area, so birders keeping a "plane list" should watch overhead for stealth bombers, stealth fighters, the SR-71 Blackbird, the B-2, and planes so secret nobody in Congress even knows they are being built.

As a general rule, fall and winter are the best times to bird. In these seasons rainfall is rare, seventy-five-mile views are common, and temperatures, while dipping below freezing in the morning, usually warm rapidly during the day. Spring from mid-April onward often means heavy winds, which can blow day and night without end. Unlike Arizona's deserts, the Antelope Valley receives virtually no monsoon thundershowers, so mid- and late-summer visitors should be prepared for daily highs of 100–115 degrees (and nil cloud cover—bring hat, canteen, and sunscreen).

Usual access is via Highway 14, a freeway connecting Los Angeles with US-395, the two-lane road that runs north through the Owens Valley past the eastern Sierra Nevada to Reno, Nevada. (Birders continuing to Yosemite from Southern California may want to consider this route, as the Mono Lake and Tioga Pass areas reached from US-395 make a good circle route into the park, with a return through the Central Valley or San Francisco.) Access to the Antelope Valley from Palm Springs, Joshua Tree National Park, or Riverside is via Highway 138 off of Interstate 15. Highway 138 is also the same road to watch for if you're headed into the Valley southbound on Interstate 5 from the Bay Area.

Once here, navigation is simple. Starting at the Kern County / Los Angeles County line, east-west avenues proceed alphabetically from Avenue A in Rosamond to Avenue S in Palmdale, with each letter spaced one mile apart. North-south streets are numbered and also grid out at mile intervals—every ten digits equates to one mile (e.g., 10th Street to 20th Street is one mile in distance). Streets are divided into east and west components roughly in line with the freeway. If a street you're on ever dead-ends, just jog left or right to pick up a parallel route—something is bound to go through. The accounts below *do not always list mileages*, as individual routes will vary. *You can always estimate distance by using the street numbers and letters as a guide.*

There is no standardized birding route; instead, people will visit species-specific sites depending on the birds they wish to find. Directions below describe places most of interest to visiting birders. Sites covered during the Lancaster Christmas Bird Counts (including sod farms, golf courses, small hunt clubs, and private stock ponds) which are not generally open to the public have not been listed. When birding from public roads, park off the pavement as much as possible, since local traffic may be going thirty miles an hour faster than the posted 55 mph speed limit. Yet you must also remember to test all berms first before pulling off, since the sand on some shoulders can be quite soft, especially after rain.

Motels, fast food, and gas stations can be found adjacent to the freeway on Avenues K, J, and I in Lancaster and at Palmdale Boulevard in Palmdale. Gas up before leaving town; you will not find services in the rural areas.

BIRDING SPOTS AND SPECIES LOCATIONS EAST OF THE 14 FREEWAY

Lake Palmdale is the large reservoir visible on the right from the 14 as you drop out of the mountains. Surrounded by cottonwoods, it is a private hunt club that does not welcome birders. *Do not trespass.* (It is listed here first only because it is the first spot most birders come to as they head out from Los Angeles.) To scope the lake for Western and Clark's Grebes, exit at Avenue S, go east a few yards to the first street (Calle Grillo), and turn right. Bird along the access road overlooking the lake. If that hasn't worked, go a bit farther east on Avenue S to the Park 'n Ride lot and scope from near the handicap parking spaces by the signal-light. The grebes are a long way out, so you'll need a good telescope or a vivid imagination.

Birds in the scrub around the fence include Brewer's Blackbird, House Finch, White-crowned and occasionally Sage, Brewer's, and Lark Sparrows, the odd Say's Phoebe or two, and if you're really lucky, a Greater Roadrunner with a snake in its beak or an accipiter flushing California Quail. Both Nuttall's and Ladder-backed Woodpeckers occur by the lake, and any thrasher seen will almost certainly be a California Thrasher, as Avenue S marks the edge of their range. Overhead will be the ubiquitous ravens and a steady flow of

California Gulls going back and forth to a nearby landfill. In winter there are ducks on the lake (including decoys) and an occasional loon. Sabine's Gulls are seen some falls, but are more reliable (and more easily seen) at the Lancaster Sewage Ponds.

Geologists may enjoy knowing that when looking at Lake Palmdale they are looking at (and standing on) the San Andreas Fault. Good photos of folded bedrock can be taken at the road-cut where the 14 slices through a small hill immediately north of Avenue S; this accordianed cross-section has been featured in several geology textbooks, although Caltrans improvements have recently made the face less sheer.

Palmdale Country Club (**Le Conte's Thrasher Site #1**) can be reached from the Avenue P exit of the 14 (by Wal-Mart). If northbound, go left from the freeway on Avenue P one-third mile, turn right (north) at the first street (10th Street West) for one mile, and then turn right onto Avenue O. From the southbound lanes of the 14, exit at 10th Street West (by the Antelope Valley Mall), go left (north), and then right on Avenue O. Once on Avenue O drive 0.6 mile and park by the low bridge over the sandy wash. Here, as elsewhere, remember that you will be in fragile habitat—no matter how sere it may look—and the ABA Code of Birding Ethics exists for situations like this.

Le Conte's Thrashers occur both in the treeless scrubby area between the road and the country club and in the denser Joshua Tree woodland on the north side of the road. Sometimes they are found in five minutes, sometimes in five hours, and sometimes never at all. Certainly these elusive birds are missed more often than seen. Do not use tapes; this is a heavily visited site. (Try not to trample the low vegetation, also.) February can be better because sometimes they sing then; if the thrashers are not singing, then you'll have to walk them out. Look low, between shrubs—you are watching for a mockingbird-sized grayish bird with tan undertail coverts running away lickity-split. Sometimes it helps to imagine that you're looking for a mouse, not a bird. In winter the country club's grounds may harbor sapsuckers (all three possible, but Red-naped most likely), along with large flocks of White-crowned Sparrows (watch for the odd Golden-crowned among them) and other montane species (Dark-eyed Juncos, for example). Look over the fence into the grounds, but do not trespass.

Le Conte's Thrasher Site #2 is some distance from town but offers a quiet desert walk if you're tired of sitting in the car. From Avenue P and the 14 (see above) head east on P to 50th Street East. Go left (north) to Avenue O, turn right (east), and drive to 145th Street East. Turn right (south) and, at the T-intersection with Avenue Q, park. Walk in the wash north, watching the brush along the sides. You may need to walk a mile. Do not use tapes. As with the above site, this can be hit or miss; in recent years birders have enjoyed a higher success rate looking for Le Conte's Thrashers in Jawbone Canyon, Kern County. One of the mysteries of this bird is why it isn't more common, when so much habitat seems suitable. It is currently listed as a California species of special concern. At both this and the previous site, also watch for Ladder-backed Woodpecker, Verdin, Black-throated Sparrow (mainly April–September), and Scott's Oriole (March–August).

Mountain Plover, Mountain Bluebird, and wintering raptors can usually be found from November to February somewhere in the agricultural areas between 40th Street East and 90th Street East, and Avenue K and Avenue N. If present, the plovers can be on bare earth or in alfalfa stubble; the bluebirds prefer irrigated alfalfa. Longspurs (in order of probability, Lapland, Chestnut-collared, and McCown's) are possible, but rare. Raptors could include Golden Eagle (uncommon), Red-tailed, Ferruginous, and Rough-legged (rare) Hawks, American Kestrel, Merlin, Prairie Falcon, and Northern Harrier. Turkey Vultures can be abundant migrants in spring and fall. Swainson's Hawks have nested, but generally are seen only as migrants. Great Horned and Barn Owls are widespread but uncommon permanent residents. Long-eared Owls winter, but rarely in the same places twice. Dense, isolated Tamarisk or other tree clusters (such as one finds around abandoned homesteads) are preferred. If this bird is a goal, check every stand of trees like this in the entire valley. Eventually you might find one (or even six or seven, since in winter they sometimes roost communally).

Saddleback Butte State Park at 170th East and Avenue J has camping, hiking, Rock and Cactus Wrens, Verdin, Ladder-backed Woodpecker, Black-throated Sparrow, and a few Scott's Orioles (March–August).

BIRDING SPOTS AND SPECIES LOCATIONS WEST OF THE 14 FREEWAY

Westside Raptors and Burrowing Owl Site. The same raptors from the east side list can be found on the other side of the Antelope Valley along Avenue D (here also called Highway 138) between 60th Street West and Interstate 5; it can be productive to explore north and south from here as well. Burrowing Owls were formerly widespread throughout the Antelope Valley, but feral cats, habitat destruction, and a reduced insect fauna have caused the population to crash. Some occasionally are seen around 120th Street West and Avenue I (which becomes Lancaster Road), or at the homestead ruins at 110th Street West and Avenue G. Sometimes Mountain Plover and Mountain Bluebird are found here in winter, while Horned Larks can be extremely abundant. This also is a good place to keep an eye out for Prairie Falcon and Golden Eagle. If you notice somebody out here unloading an old sofa at the end of a dirt road or target shooting at abandoned cars, pay no mind—they're just engaging in the local Antelope Valley custom of trashing the environment. If you're wondering where all the vegetation went that originally grew in this area, the answer is a five letter word: sheep.

The Antelope Valley California Poppy State Reserve (on Lancaster Road between 130th West and 170th West) is managed to maximize the reproduction of the native California Poppy. April is the best month; although densities vary, every year there are always at least some fields of poppies. In peak years the hillsides are ablaze with carpets of orange flowers visible from across the entire valley. The poppies are not limited only to the preserve—sometimes they even grow along the freeway berms. For current reserve information, call 805/724-1180.

Good Scott's Oriole habitat occurs at **Ripley Desert Woodland State Park** at 205th West and Lancaster Road, just west of the aqueduct. Cactus Wren, Verdin, California Quail, and Ladder-backed Woodpecker are permanent residents. Equally good is the section 0.5 mile north on Lancaster Road. This is what the Antelope Valley used to look like.

Holiday Lake (see inset map on page 224) often hosts breeding Tricolored Blackbirds, if the water company which manages this pond has not done one of its periodic brush and cattail clean-outs. This is private property, but public access remains unrestricted so far. From Highway 138 between Gorman and Neenach watch for La Petite, a small street on the north side of the road 0.5 mile west of the aqueduct. From La Petite go right on Elise (0.7) (which will become 255th Street West), go right on B-8 (1.1), and left on Calcot (0.2). Park by the gate and walk the circle around the pond. In addition to quail, migrant warblers, and winter ducks, you might see an owl (Great Horned or Barn, and very rarely Long-eared or Burrowing). Check among the Lesser Goldfinches to be sure that none are Lawrence's—advice that applies everywhere in the Antelope Valley. There is a pay phone by the water district office in case you find something so rare it deserves to be called in to the Southern California Rare Bird Alert. Mountain Plovers have been found in the fields around 100th Street West and Gaskell Road, north of Avenue A.

Apollo Park (50th Street West and Avenue G, east of the airfield) is a public park where the artificial ponds are stocked with fish; fall and winter are the best times to bird. Once In a while the water attracts something out of the ordinary such as a Pacific Loon or a Ross's Goose or a pair of White-winged Scoters. Most gulls here are Californias, with a few Ring-bills and the occasional Herring. Brewer's Blackbird and Cactus Wren are permanent residents. Trees around the perimeter can be good for migrants. If rushed for time, skip this spot, which can often be dead.

BIRDING SPOTS AND SPECIES LOCATIONS IN THE NORTH-CENTRAL VALLEY

Due to expansion and modification, the **Lancaster Sewage Ponds** (Avenue D and the 14 freeway, just west of Sierra Highway) may not be what they once were, but over the years they have attracted a long list of good birds, including California's only Gray-tailed Tattler. They are open 7 AM–3 PM seven days a week. To sign in, turn up the obvious entrance adjacent to the freeway and drive several hundred yards to a cluster of buildings on the right. After the first processing tanks, and before coming to a maintenance shed, there is a small tan unmarked office on the corner of a small intersection. Try the door closest to the intersection; there is a sign-in log inside. Once permission has been granted, drive the dikes (carefully!), stopping to scope the ponds. Do not drive your car through the concrete dips that join some ponds, where a flash flood could definitely spoil your day. In the past, the northernmost pond on the freeway side was the most productive, but it recently has been reconfigured, so this may change. Red-necked and Wilson's Phalaropes stop over during spring and fall migrations, and in winter hundreds of Northern Shovelers and other ducks fill the impoundments. Migrant shorebirds include Snowy and Semipalmated Plovers, Killdeer, Least, Western, and Baird's Sandpipers, Whimbrels (spring), Long-billed Curlews, Marbled Godwits, and even Ruddy Turnstones. A few California Gulls are always around, with an occasional spring Franklin's Gull, a passing flock of Bonaparte's Gulls or Black Terns, or (in September) a few juvenile Sabine's Gulls. Look for American Pipits along the perimeter. In high winds the sewage forms whitecaps and sloshes over the sides of the dikes, adding an aromatic yet maritime aspect to desert birding. The adjacent unit of the sewage ponds (east of Sierra Highway) is closed to birders, which is probably why it always looks like it has all the birds in it.

To find Sage Sparrow, take a walk in the saltbush flats between the sewage ponds and the freeway. The sparrows often can be found here (especially in winter), and even if you don't find any on your visit, you now know what habitat they like. Look for a gray sparrow with a long tail, running among the low brush, or teed up singly on its tops. As with Le Conte's Thrasher, this bird is widespread but often hard to find, making one wonder why they are not more abundant. If you're going to Galileo Hill for migrants and/or Chukars, there are Sage Sparrows there, too. The *canescens* race (species?) breeding in the Antelope Valley is supplemented by *nevadensis* birds in winter.

Local birders check **Piute Ponds** during shorebird migration to study Baird's and other sandpipers. (Rarities have included Ruff, Red-necked Stint, and Sharp-tailed and Curlew Sandpipers.) This is an artificial marsh on Edwards Air Force Base property. The Clark's Grebes, White-faced Ibises, Cinnamon Teal, Redheads, Northern Harriers, and Yellow-headed Blackbirds which breed are easier to see than the Soras, Virginia Rails, and muskrats also found here. Le Conte's Thrasher, Sage Sparrow, and Burrowing Owl are

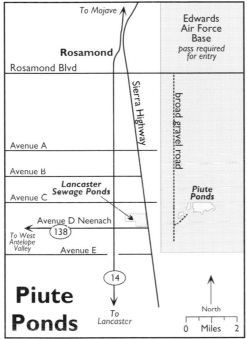

possible; large numbers of ducks over-winter. This is the single "birdiest" spot in the Antelope Valley. *Permission to visit this site must be requested in writing at least three months in advance*; give the number of people in your party, ask for specific dates and times, and list alternate dates in case the marshes are closed for test flights or hunt days. *Under no circumstances give in to a temptation to trespass*—security personnel armed with automatic weapons patrol regularly. To request a day-use permit, write to the Natural Resources Management Office, 5 East Popson Avenue, Edwards AFB CA 93524-1130. Request their new checklist of birds when you write for permission. If you need more information, call the office at 805/277-1401.

To reach the main ponds, exit Highway 14—pass in hand—at Rosamond Boulevard and turn right (east), heading toward the base. A quarter-mile past the "Welcome to Edwards Air Force Base" billboard look for a broad gravel road on the right, just past a row of utility poles. Take this road south five miles and watch for a small spur road going left. Park and walk the dikes.

When finished birding the Antelope Valley you can continue north on Highway 14 sixteen miles past its intersection with Highway 138 to Mojave and the Eastern Kern County loop, travel to the mountain loops by following Highway 138 east from Palmdale to Littlerock, turning south on the N6 road to the San Gabriel Mountains route, or continue to Interstate 15 south to reach the San Bernardino route.

Camping is available at Saddleback Butte State Park, and motels are numerous in Palmdale and Lancaster.

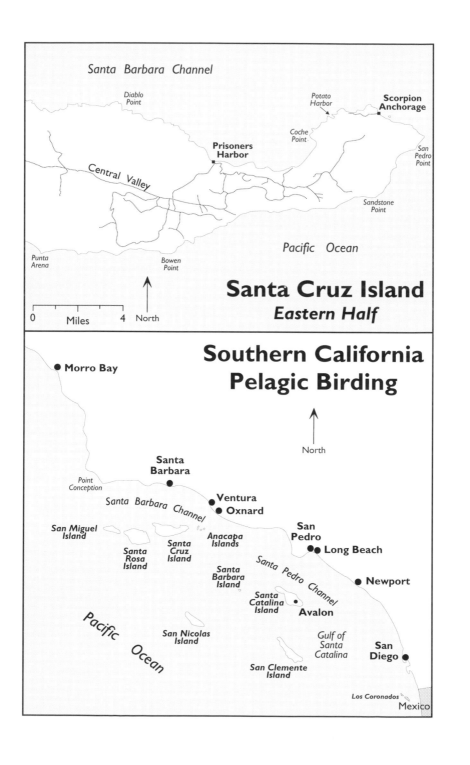

Santa Cruz Island
Eastern Half

Santa Barbara Channel

Diablo Point

Potato Harbor

Scorpion Anchorage

Coche Point

Prisoners Harbor

San Pedro Point

Central Valley

Sandstone Point

Punta Arena

Bowen Point

Pacific Ocean

0 Miles 4 North

Southern California Pelagic Birding

North

Morro Bay

Point Conception

Santa Barbara

Santa Barbara Channel

Ventura
Oxnard

San Miguel Island

Anacapa Islands

Santa Rosa Island

Santa Cruz Island

San Pedro

Long Beach

Santa Barbara Island

Santa Pedro Channel

Newport

Santa Catalina Island

Avalon

San Nicolas Island

Gulf of Santa Catalina

San Diego

Pacific Ocean

San Clemente Island

Los Coronados

Mexico

PELAGIC AND ISLAND BIRDING

More than 35 pelagic species can be found off the coast of Southern California, but there is little hope of seeing them unless you take a boat to their offshore habitat—vagrants to the Salton Sea notwithstanding.

The best plan is to sign up for a pelagic birding trip scheduled by local birders. These trips are reasonably priced and well-conducted by experienced leaders. They are very popular, however, and are often booked solid for weeks or even months in advance. Be sure to make your inquiries and reservations early (see Resources in the Introduction for a listing of RBAs and web-sites containing field trip information). A beginning pelagic birder is well-advised to take the first several trips in the company of birders experienced with the territory.

Pelagic birding seems to alternate between two extremes: crushing boredom (offering plenty of time to regale others, and be regaled, with stories of past pelagic triumphs) and moments of panic. A third possibility, despair, is dealt with elsewhere (see Poe, *The Raven*). When things do happen, they happen quickly. There simply may be no time to consult your field guide before another life bird wheels by. Do your homework *before* getting on board (Stallcup's *Ocean Birds of the Nearshore Pacific*, 1990, was written specifically to help pelagic birders hone their skills; see also Harrison, 1983), assume that you will get seasick and take the precautions proper for you, and park yourself at the rail within earshot of one of the trip's leaders. Once you've learned to recognize the more common species, keep on trying to identify each bird you are able to get in your binoculars. Eventually you will turn up something new and different.

Los Angeles Audubon Society (7377 Santa Monica Boulevard, Los Angeles, CA 90046-6694; phone: 213/876-0202) runs several trips a year from a variety of ports. The itinerary varies with the season, often involving trips toward Santa Barbara and San Nicholas Islands, Arguello Canyon west of Point Conception, Rodriguez Seamount, and the like. Their bird tape (213/874-1318) will apprise you of any last minute changes in trip schedules or cancellation due to weather.

Morro Coast Audubon Society (PO Box 160, Morro Bay, CA 93443-0160; phone 805/528-7182 RBA, will include field-trip info) has a fall trip annually off Morro Bay, and occasionally a spring or winter trip as well. The fall trip is typically very productive. Contact them in advance for details.

Western Field Ornithologists (4637 Del Mar Avenue, San Diego, CA 92107; or via their web site listed in Resources in the Introduction) schedules

233

very popular trips in May and September departing Mission Bay in San Diego. Tour groups of various sizes often book for these trips well in advance, making early inquiry on your part desirable. These trips may head out as far as possible for a one-day trip or, alternately, may search the waters around San Clemente Island hoping for Red-billed Tropicbird.

Shearwater Journeys (PO Box 190, Hollister, CA 95024-0190; phone 408/637-8527) concentrates its busy pelagic trip schedule in the waters around Monterey Bay and to Cordell Bank off Bodega Bay to the north. Although these trips are outside the geography of this guide, they should be noted as they are consistently among the best pelagic birding California has to offer. Shearwater Journeys occasionally schedules a trip from Monterey to Davidson Seamount, off northern San Luis Obispo County, in search of *Pterodromas* and other rarities.

Another option is a luxury trip on the steamer or ferry to **Santa Catalina Island**. This route can be good for pelagic birds, but it varies. On a typical trip in fall and winter you should see Black-vented Shearwater, and if it is a good year for Northern Fulmar (irregular), you should be able to find one or more. Other pelagic species you could see are Parasitic and Pomarine Jaegers, Black-legged Kittiwake (irregular), Common Murre, and Rhinoceros Auklet. You may see Black Storm-Petrel in summer and early fall, and Sooty and Pink-footed Shearwaters in late spring and summer. Xantus's Murrelet is possible in the spring. Catalina cruises leave daily from San Pedro and Long Beach. The San Pedro terminal is under the Vincent Thomas Bridge; the trips from Long Beach leave from 320 Golden Shore Boulevard. There are at least a few trips a day starting from either location, but the schedule changes seasonally and on weekends. Make reservations at any ticket office, or phone 310/519-1212. (For details on birding onshore on Santa Catalina Island, see the end of this chapter.)

A good way to find pelagic birds is to go out with the fishermen, but careful inquiries and planning are required to make sure that you get on the best boat for your needs. Birds often follow schools of fish, and fishermen follow the birds to these movable fishing locations. Nearly every pier and marina along the coast has a landing where you can buy tickets for deep-sea fishing boats. Costs vary, but birders are often able to buy discounted tickets because they are only "along for the ride." Make sure that the boat is going to the islands or well offshore. *Half-day trips to the kelp beds a mile or so off the beach are a waste of money.* Ports housing fishing boats for this venture include: Point Loma Landing at Shelter Island in San Diego, the landings along Quivira Drive in Mission Bay, out of SEALanding at Santa Barbara, and Bob's or Virg's in Morro Bay. Albacore season in late summer can be a very good time for a birder to get aboard a boat. These small tuna are found well offshore and feed on bait fish, which also attract pelagic birds.

You can take boats from many locations, but most go to the same select fishing areas. Those docking farther away from these areas just take longer to get there. In order to save money and have more time in the good birding waters, arrange to board a boat docking closest to the area you wish to visit. Boats to **Los Coronados Islands** and the **Baja California Fishing Banks** should be taken from San Diego; both of these destinations are in Mexican waters. For **San Miguel** and **Santa Rosa Islands**, take a boat from Santa Barbara Harbor—where you may also find a boat to **Santa Cruz Island** on a Nature Conservancy-sponsored trip on an irregular basis (see below). For regularly scheduled trips to **Santa Cruz** and **Anacapa Islands**, leave from the Ventura Marina.

Channel Islands National Park, comprising Anacapa, Santa Cruz, Santa Rosa, San Miguel, and Santa Barbara Islands, may also be reached through a private concessionaire, **Island Packers**. Their office is located next to the park headquarters (1867 Spinnaker Drive, Ventura, CA 93001; phone 805/642-7688 for recorded schedule and fare information or 805/642-1393 for reservations). Infrequent trips to The Nature Conservancy property on Santa Cruz Island leave from SEALanding in Santa Barbara (805/965-3564; see discussion of Santa Cruz Island at the end of this chapter).

Fishing boats out of Morro Bay via Bob's Sportfishing (805/772-3340) or Virg's Landing (805/772-1222) at the northern edge of this guide's coverage often yield good pelagic birds.

If you can schedule a trip to Anacapa Island only in the late fall or winter months, you should find such birds as Northern Fulmar (if it is a good fulmar year), Black-vented Shearwater (pretty well guaranteed), Red Phalarope, Pomarine and Parasitic Jaegers, Black-legged Kittiwake (irregular), Common Murre, and Cassin's and Rhinoceros Auklets. From May to September you should find Black and Ashy (less common) Storm-Petrels and a possible Least Storm-Petrel (late summer to early fall). You have an 80–100 percent chance of finding Xantus's Murrelet (late February to early July—although March to early June is best), which nests on the island. When your boat approaches to within three or four miles of Anacapa Island, start watching for pairs off the bow. Murrelets of all species are notorious for flying straight away at the boat's approach. Other breeding birds for the island include Brown Pelican, Double-crested, Brandt's, and Pelagic Cormorants, Black Oystercatcher, and Pigeon Guillemot.

The best regularly run boat trip for birders wishing to go to the National Park is an Island Packers pelagic trip to **Santa Barbara Island**, some 35 miles beyond Anacapa. Plan your trip from late spring through Labor Day; this trip is especially good from May through early June, and mid-August through mid-October. Because of the deeper water beyond Anacapa, you could find such birds as Black-footed Albatross, Flesh-footed Shearwater, Leach's Storm-Petrel, and South Polar Skua along with most of the above-mentioned species. Horned Puffins have been seen a few times in late spring, and Red-footed Booby and Brown Booby have occurred, also. Of course, these latter three species are casual visitors.

Whale-watching trips can be productive pelagic birding trips as well. Winter and spring are the seasons for Gray Whales. Some 6,000 or more of these huge creatures, up to 50 feet long, annually migrate from Alaska to the calving bays in Baja California and back. In Southern California the peak of the southward movement is reached in late December and January, and the northward movement peaks in late March and April. While their spouts may be seen from shore, the best way to see whales is from one of the whale-watching boats, which are operated out of nearly every marina and landing, including Island Packers out of Ventura Marina, the *Condor* out of Santa Barbara (also taking Humpback and Blue Whale trips farther into the Santa Barbara Channel in summer), and from Virg's in Morro Bay. Birding aboard whale-watching boats from these harbors can be quite productive. Whale-watching trips are typically for a half-day or less and can be a good way to break into pelagic birding. If you are interested in birding from a whale-watching boat in spring, be sure to inquire how far out the boat will travel; some springtime whale-watching excursions merely go out just a mile or so. These short trips are virtually worthless for pelagic birding.

There are several things to remember when taking boat trips (particularly when going out with fishermen):

1. Take the largest boat available. The higher you are above the water, the more birds you will see.

2. Make sure the boat is going well offshore. Unless you get out over 5 miles (except at Monterey), you are wasting your time.

3. If possible, talk to the captain before buying your ticket and tell him that you are going birdwatching. He will know if his trip is good for that purpose. Sometimes, you can get a reduction in price if you are not fishing. Also, ask for permission to get on the upper deck out of the way of the fishermen; you can see more from up there.

4. Take a warm coat, hat, gloves, sun block, and snacks (many are partial to the calming effect of soda crackers) at any time of year. Overcast days, usually providing the best light conditions, can also fry your face. Take the admonition to bring sun block seriously.

5. Tripod-mounted spotting scopes are not permitted (and are useless) onboard unless you are landing on an island.

6. Do not expect to find all species on one trip. Familiarize yourself with the seasonal status of pelagic species for an accurate assessment of your chances. To accumulate a large pelagic bird list requires many boat trips.

To find the greatest number of pelagic birds on one trip, you should probably go in the fall (from mid-August to mid-October). This is when most of the shearwaters, storm-petrels, jaegers, Sabine's Gulls, and Arctic Terns are moving by. Even then, you may see little, for pelagic birds are unpredictable. Winter is the time for Northern Fulmar and most alcids, while the rare Red-billed Tropicbird shows up in late summer and early fall. Check the

Southern California Specialties chapter to get an idea of which part of Southern California is best for specific birds.

Each January, the American Birding Association's newsletter *Winging It* has devoted an entire issue to detailing pelagic birding trip opportunities in the U.S. and Canada. Schedules, as well as lists of expected species (often broken down seasonally or for specific trips) are given. Call 800/634-7736 to inquire about getting a copy of this issue and information about the ABA's other activities and publications: American Birding Association, PO Box 6599, Colorado Springs, CO 80934.

SANTA CRUZ ISLAND

As you undoubtedly know, the taxonomy of North America's "scrub" jays changed when they were split from one to three species by the American Ornithologists' Union in 1996. Although the Florida Scrub-Jay is one of the few North American birds (north of Mexico) never to have occurred in California—nor is it expected—the other two jays affected are native here: Western Scrub-Jay of the oak and chaparral and Island Scrub-Jay, endemic to Santa Cruz Island off Santa Barbara. Island Scrub-Jay is notably larger than Western Scrub-Jay, has a noticeably larger bill proportionately, and is brighter overall—the blues deeper and more intense, the back rustier. It is strictly limited to Santa Cruz Island, where identification is not a serious problem—there are no records of Western Scrub-Jay from the island.

As you travel to the island, whether from Ventura or Santa Barbara, you will keep a watch for pelagic birds. Spring and fall migrations are the best times, of course, but interesting species can be seen in the channel almost any day of the year. April through June is the best time to see Xantus's Murrelet, endemic to islands and the open sea of Baja and southern California north to Monterey. Craveri's Murrelet is the more likely murrelet to be seen here from mid-August through early October. The spring migration of Pacific Loons up the Santa Barbara Channel, at its peak in April, is most impressive; some days will produce many thousands of these beautiful birds arrowing by in loose flocks. Both Red-necked and Red Phalaropes likewise may be seen in hundreds and thousands during this time. Shearwaters, jaegers, gulls, terns, and other alcids may be seen during migration. Albatrosses are accidental in the channel and are therefore unlikely.

Once you reach the island, watch for the nesting Brandt's and Pelagic Cormorants—Double-crested Cormorant, common inshore, occurs locally in small numbers on the nearer (e.g., Santa Cruz) channel islands. The rocky shores are good for rock-adapted shorebirds during migration and the winter months.

The eastern end of Santa Cruz Island is managed by the National Park Service and access is possible every weekend and six days per week during spring and summer via Island Packers, a private charter boat company operating out of Ventura Harbor. Landings are typically made via Zodiac at

Scorpion Anchorage. The habitat inland from the anchorage is much altered due to its history of ranching. Blue-gum Eucalyptus groves inland from the old ranch house contain campgrounds. They also frequently contain Island Scrub-Jays. In the unlikely event that you do not see the jay in the eucalyptus groves, hike farther inland—approximately one mile from the beach—to the oak grove canyon. Squeaking will usually produce these inquisitive birds. As landing time on day-trips is limited, unless you are staying to camp, it is best to head directly inland to the eucalyptus—or beyond if necessary—to find the jay. After this you can explore and bird at your leisure. Black Oyster-catcher and, in spring and summer, Pigeon Guillemot should be seen in the vicinity of the anchorage; Common Raven and House Finch will be conspicu-ous near the landing. Watch for migrants in the ornamental plantings near the house—but do not trespass inside the fence; this is a private residence.

The western 90 percent of Santa Cruz Island is owned and administered by The Nature Conservancy. Landings on this portion of the island are by permit only, as the organizaiton emphasizes restoration and preservation of fragile island habitat, and has no tourist facilities. Prisoner's Harbor, within the Nature Conservancy-administered portion almost due south of Santa Barbara, is possibly the best land-birding destination on the island. A stream enters the ocean here, its willows providing shelter to migrant and resident birds alike. The canyon inland along the stream harbors a fine grove of live oaks, and the hillsides are a botanist's dream. The contrast with Scorpion Anchorage is marked. The *Condor* out of Santa Barbara (and occasionally other SEALanding boats) takes trips to Prisoner's Harbor irregularly, when groups have arranged access with The Nature Conservancy (Santa Barbara office phone number: 805/962-9111). You may want to inquire about future plans by calling the *Condor's* dock, SEALanding at 805/965-3564. If you are able to attach yourself or your group to an island trip aboard the *Condor,* you will be amply rewarded.

Breeding birds on Santa Cruz Island include island sub-species of Allen's Hummingbird, Pacific-slope Flycatcher, Orange-crowned Warbler, and Rufous-crowned and Song Sparrows. Although these may not be candidates for future splits, their insular adaptation should be acknowledged.

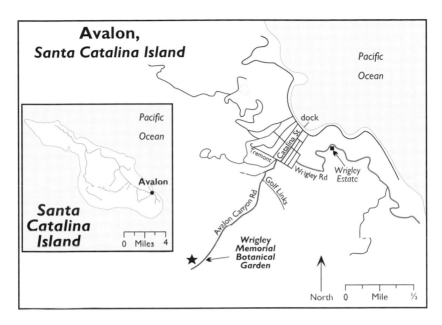

ONSHORE BIRDING AT SANTA CATALINA ISLAND

Although all species resident on the island can also be found on the mainland, you might want to explore the area around Avalon while waiting for the cruise ship to take you back to San Pedro or Long Beach. (See the beginning of this chapter for details on reaching the island.) From Crescent Beach Road on Avalon Bay, walk or ride a rental bicycle or golf cart uphill on Catalina Street for three blocks. Jog right one block at Tremont Street and turn left onto Falls Canyon Road. Avalon Canyon Road soon splits off to the left; follow it uphill past the golf course and farther (for a total of about 1.7 miles) to the Wrigley Memorial Botanical Garden. Most of Catalina's endemic plants are on display here, as well as a fine collection of succulents from around the world. In summer look for Allen's Hummingbird, Northern Flicker, Black Phoebe, Spotted Towhee, and Chipping Sparrow. Lost, out-of-range birds have also showed up in the gardens during migration. In winter you might see Bewick's Wren, Mountain Bluebird (on the ridgetops), Orange-crowned and Yellow-rumped Warblers, Golden-crowned and White-crowned Sparrows, and Dark-eyed Junco. If you have time, hike up Memorial Road (which begins right behind the Wrigley Memorial) to the ridge for a breathtaking view of the town. You'll have a view of the Palisades, a series of cliffs at the east end of Catalina—an occasional perching area for re-introduced Bald Eagles.

Custom tours to the island's varied habitats chaparral, coastal sage scrub, oak woodland, and riparian can be arranged.

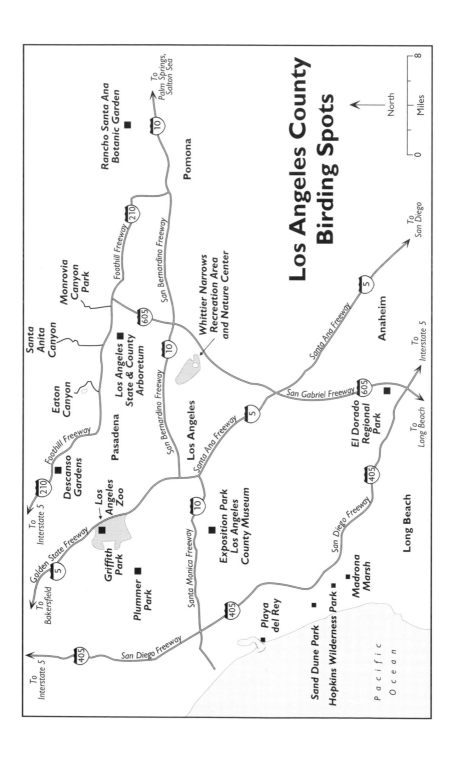

Los Angeles County Birding Spots

North

0 — Miles — 8

To Palm Springs, Salton Sea

Rancho Santa Ana Botanic Garden

Pomona

Foothill Freeway

San Bernardino Freeway

Monrovia Canyon Park

Santa Anita Canyon

Eaton Canyon

Whittier Narrows Recreation Area and Nature Center

Los Angeles State & County Arboretum

Pasadena

Foothill Freeway

Descanso Gardens

To Interstate 5

To Bakersfield

Golden State Freeway

Los Angeles Zoo

Griffith Park

Plummer Park

San Bernardino Freeway

Los Angeles

Santa Ana Freeway

Santa Monica Freeway

Exposition Park Los Angeles County Museum

San Diego Freeway

Playa del Rey

Sand Dune Park

Hopkins Wilderness Park

Madrona Marsh

Pacific Ocean

San Gabriel Freeway

El Dorado Regional Park

To Long Beach

Long Beach

San Diego Freeway

Anaheim

To San Diego

To Interstate 5

OTHER GOOD BIRDING SPOTS

Other good birding areas in Southern California that are not dealt with in the main text deserve your attention if they fit in with your travel plans. These are sites favored by local birders in Imperial, Los Angeles, Riverside, San Bernardino, and San Diego Counties.

IMPERIAL COUNTY

Cibola National Wildlife Refuge

This 12-mile-long refuge is located on the lower Colorado River, 20 miles south of Blythe. Its southern boundary adjoins Imperial National Wildlife Refuge. The main portion of the refuge is alluvial riverbottom with dense growths of Tamarisk, mesquite, and Arrowweed. The Colorado River flows through the refuge, in both a dredged channel and through a portion of its original channel. Some 2,000 acres of farmland and 785 acres of desert foothills and ridges are also included within refuge boundaries, for a total of 16,627 acres. Over the years, 232 species of birds have been found here, with 48 species nesting. Nesting species include Great Egret, Great Blue Heron, Black-crowned Night-Heron, Least Bittern, "Yuma" Clapper Rail, White-winged Dove, Greater Road-runner, Western Screech-Owl, Great Horned and Burrowing Owls, Lesser Night-

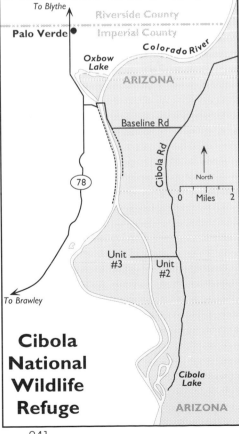

241

hawk, Common Poorwill, Gila and Ladder-backed Woodpeckers, Verdin, Cactus and Rock Wrens, Black-tailed Gnatcatcher, Crissal Thrasher (common), Phainopepla, Blue Grosbeak, and Abert's Towhee (common). Reintroduced Harris's Hawks have recently been added to the avifauna at Cibola. Many Canada Geese, ducks, and shorebirds winter here, along with good numbers of Sandhill Cranes.

To reach the refuge, drive south on Highway 78 from Interstate 10 at the western edge of Blythe. Continue through Palo Verde (16.3) into Imperial County. Palo Verde County Park on Oxbow Lake (1.8) is a good (free) place to camp. At the south end of the lake turn east and jog left and then right to cross the river. (At the jog is another free campground, Palo Verde Oxbow, operated by the BLM). (Also at this point, you can explore a dirt road leading south along the dredged channel for 4.8 miles.)

After crossing the river, turn right (south) to Baseline Road (1.0), then turn left to Cibola Road (2.7). (The road continuing straight ahead at the turn follows the left bank of the river for 5 miles.) Turn right (south) on Cibola Road to the headquarters of Cibola NWR (1.0). Pick up a checklist and a map. The road continues south to Farm Unit #2 (4.3), where you can cross the river to Farm Unit #3. Both units are good in fall and winter for Sandhill Cranes and shorebirds. Back at the junction, Cibola Road continues south to Hart Mine Marsh (good for bitterns, rails, and Common Moorhen) and Cibola Lake (4.0).

For information call 602/857-3253, or via the World Wide Web at http://www.gorp.com/gorp/resource/ us_nwr/az_cibol.html.

LOS ANGELES COUNTY

Descanso Gardens—(fee) Beautiful gardens with many common birds. Look for hummingbirds among the flowers and songbirds in the large stand of Coast Live Oaks. Check the bird observation station. There are bird walks on the second and fourth Sundays of the month. Open 9 AM–5 PM. (1418 Descanso Drive, La Cañada Flintridge 91011; phone 818/790-5571)

Eaton Canyon—The park and nature center are located in an area of chaparral and oak woodland, which can be very good for foothill birds (see web site information under Resources in the Introduction). California Condors nested in Eaton Canyon until 1910. H.T. Bohlman and W.L. Finley's famous series of California Condor photographs was made here in 1906. (1750 Altadena Drive, Pasadena 91107; phone 818/794-1866)

El Dorado Regional Park—(fee, but see below) Situated along the San Gabriel River in Long Beach the park offers several hundred acres of productive birding year round. There is a variety of habitats, including riparian, brushy meadows, and some oak woodland, along with eucalyptus, pine, alder, and sycamore groves.

The park is located off the 605 freeway between the 405 and 91 freeways. Heading southbound on the 605, exit at Spring Street, go west (right), and the entrance to the park is immediately on your right. Heading northbound on the 605, you will exit at Katella/Willow. Follow the ramp west (left) to Willow, (Katella becomes Willow), go to Studebaker Road, and turn north. Go to Spring Street and turn east. The entrance to the park will be about ¾ mile down on your right. Hours are from 7 AM–dusk year round.

During spring and fall migrations the park can be rich with western passerine migrants. Eastern vagrant species occasionally make an appearance. This is also a reliable spot to find many wintering species, including Osprey, many other raptors, Cassin's Kingbirds in large congregations, Black-throated Gray and Townsend's Warblers, and Bullock's Orioles. Wintering vagrants are often found here, as well. In summer, look for Ruddy Duck, Common Moorhen, Spotted Dove, Allen's, Black-chinned, and Anna's Hummingbirds, Downy Woodpecker, Ash-throated Flycatcher, Western Kingbird, Orange-crowned Warbler, Bullock's and Hooded Orioles, and most of the normal coastal Southern California passerines.

El Dorado Park Nature Center (7550 East Spring Street, Long Beach, CA 90815)—enter either from within the park by following the signs, or from (eastbound) Spring Street. The nature center offers several trails through a variety of habitats, two lakes, and plenty of birding potential. A park checklist and trail map are available. Nature center trail hours are Tuesday–Sunday from 8 AM–4 PM. Call 562/570-1745 for information.

Area 2—this section of the park is on the north side of Spring Street. Enter either from Spring Street or from within the park by following the road that turns left before the exit from the nature center. It has two lakes, pine, eucalyptus and sycamore groves, and is another good spot for wintering raptors, warblers, orioles, and other species.

Area 3—continue north through Area 2, following "Ranger Station" signs, under the bridge and into Area 3. This section of the park has open grass areas, two lakes, and stands of pine, sycamores, and eucalyptus. The area west of the rangers' station frequently has hosted substantial numbers of Cassin's Kingbirds and the occasional wintering vagrant.

Free Sections—Take Spring Street from the park exit, go west to Studebaker Road; go left (south) on Studebaker. There is a large, no-fee area of El Dorado Park on both the northeast and southeast corners of Studebaker and Willow with lots of pines, sycamores, and eucalyptus trees. Parking is plentiful and free; enter off Studebaker. These are productive areas to bird for waterfowl (winter) in the lake on the south side of Willow, winter warblers (occasionally including eastern vagrants), and migrants in spring and fall. These locations have produced some vagrants, as well.

Griffith Park—This is not only the home of the Los Angeles Zoo, but this large park also has numerous trails and a scenic road. The best birding is in the Ferndale area and along the road to the Griffith Observatory. This area can be reached from Los Felis Boulevard, one block east of Western Avenue. The park can be reached by city bus. *Do not linger after dark.*

Hopkins Wilderness Park—Located in Redondo Beach on Sepulveda east of Prospect (10 AM–4 PM, closed Wednesdays.) From the 405 Freeway, take the Crenshaw exit and go south on Crenshaw to 190th Street (0.4). Turn right (west) to Prospect Avenue (3.0). Go left again to Camino Real/Sepulveda (2.0) and turn right (Camino Real is on the south side, Sepulveda on the north). At the first light (0.1) turn left into the parking lot. Carefully bird the alders along the stream that runs through the park and the trees over the pond in the lower, back portion of the park. This park can be a great place for a wide variety of migrants, and is an especially good spot for *Empidonax* and other flycatchers. At one time or another, nearly every eastern warbler or vireo species that makes it to the west coast somehow winds up here. A Plumbeous Vireo and a Black-and-white Warbler or two are nearly always found here in fall among the Orange-crowned, "Myrtle", "Audubon's", and Townsend's Warblers. In most winters, montane and northern species such as Red-breasted Nuthatch, Red Crossbill, and Pine Siskin can be found, sometimes in remarkable numbers.

Los Angeles County Museum—Located in Exposition Park just off the Harbor Freeway, the museum has extensive exhibits and an excellent collection of birds for those interested in research. See web page address in the Introduction.

Los Angeles State and County Arboretum—(fee) This beautiful old estate at 301 North Baldwin in Arcadia has extensive gardens where birds abound. Many Peafowl have nested here for years and now roam all over town. They are beautiful, loud, and uncountable. The arboretum can be reached by city bus.

Madrona Marsh—This somewhat isolated spot in Torrance is very productive. Local birders and conservationists fought a pitched battle in the early 1980s to save this beautiful vernal (seasonal) marsh, and it was well worth it! The bird list is over 200 and constantly rising as excellent, regionally very scarce freshwater wetland and upland habitats are being restored. The best time to visit is after substantial rains have begun in November or December, until the water is nearly gone in July or August. From the 405 Freeway, take Crenshaw south to Sepulveda (2.7) and go right to Madrona Avenue (1.0). Turn right and—behold on your right the southwest corner of a lovely oasis in the middle of a highly urbanized area. Park to the right (pull off all the way to the fence; usually you can safely ignore the No Parking signs if you do so) and observe from outside the wrought-iron fence, or go through any of the gates, most of which are usually open. The official entrance is by the visitors center; to play it safe, get there by taking Madrona north from Sepulveda to Plaza del Amo (0.2) and go right. At the first opportunity, hang a U-turn and come back to the first driveway. Turn right and park in the visitors center lot, then proceed across the street to the main entrance, detouring via the visitors center to see the exhibits and pick up a bird list.

A trail loops through the park, but some of the best viewing can be done from outside the fence along Madrona Avenue (in this case, afternoon is best, since otherwise you will be looking east into the morning sun.) A wide assortment of ducks is the main draw here. Regularly seen are all three teals, Mallard, Northern Pintail, Northern Shoveler, Gadwall, American Wigeon, and Ring-necked and Ruddy Ducks. Also in the water are Pied-billed Grebe, American Coot, and if you check the reeds, Sora, Virginia Rail, Black-crowned Night-Heron (common) and other herons, Black Phoebe, Marsh Wren, Common Yellowthroat, Song Sparrow, and Red-winged and Tricolored Blackbirds. Check the mud at the edge of the reeds for Greater Yellowlegs, Long-billed Dowitcher, Common Snipe, and, increasingly, a good variety of shorebirds. Solitary Sandpipers seem to pass through regularly during migration, and sometimes stick for the winter! Regularly seen upland species include Red-shouldered Hawk and the other common Southern California raptors, Spotted and Mourning Doves, Anna's and Allen's Hummingbirds, Loggerhead Shrike, and Western Meadowlark. All the western swallows show up in migration, especially Northern Rough-winged, Cliff, and Barn.

At the southwest corner, along the central north-south trail, and in the north-central portions of the park are stands of willows that can be great for migrants, Orange-crowned Warblers, and Hooded and Bullock's Orioles. Before or after the rains, the dry brushy areas can be excellent for Lazuli Buntings (migration), sparrows, and goldfinches.

Playa del Rey—The rock jetties at the entrance to the harbor attract Brown Pelican, Double-crested and Brandt's Cormorants, gulls, terns, and, in fall and winter, Black Oystercatcher (rare), Wandering Tattler, Black Turnstone, and Surfbird. The middle jetty is usually the best. To reach it, go south on Lincoln Boulevard (Highway 1) past Marina del Rey and turn right onto Culver Boulevard, which soon merges with Jefferson Boulevard. At the end of this road, turn right onto Pacific Avenue and go as far as you can. Park (fee) and walk across the old bridge to the middle jetty, or to the Ballona Wetlands, upstream on your right, for other shorebirds.

Plummer Park—Los Angeles Audubon Society has its headquarters and bookstore in this park (7377 Santa Monica Boulevard, West Hollywood, 90046; phone 213/876-0202, Tuesday–Saturday). The monthly meetings are held here on the second Tuesday of the month, September–June.

Rancho Santa Ana Botanic Garden—A very fine collection of native plants located at 1500 North College in Claremont. It is at its best in April.

Sand Dune Park in Manhattan Beach—Especially considering its small size, this is an exceptional place for migrants and very good for eastern vagrants that have overshot the coast and found their way back to the only isolated green spot along a heavily urbanized coastline. Take the West Rosecrans exit off the 405 Freeway in Hawthorne. Go west to Bell Avenue (2.5), then left to the end of the street (0.2); park. Weekday mornings are best. Walk the trails up, down, and around the cliff to the right, just past the sand dune slope. Birds move in and out of the park from the trees in the adjoining neighborhood, so keep a (respectful) eye out for birds there.

Sand Dune is good in spring, even better in fall, and worth a visit in winter. This spot *always* has something interesting at these seasons, and is famous among the locals. There are usually a few interesting flycatchers, warblers, buntings, sparrows and more. Western Tanagers and orioles frequently winter here. This is a good place to see specialties like Spotted Dove, and Allen's Hummingbird, as well as Mitred Parakeet (uncountable), Western Scrub-Jay, Orange-crowned Warbler, Townsend's Warbler (winter), California Towhee, and others.

Santa Anita Canyon—This lush, wooded canyon, only a half-hour drive from the highrises of downtown LA, provides numerous opportunities for a large variety of birds. The 3-mile round-trip hike to 75-foot-high Sturtevant Falls from Chantry Flats crosses open slopes, then winds through a shaded canyon with a perennial stream. It is good for American Dipper and breeding Olive-sided Flycatcher, Western Wood-Pewee, Pacific-slope Flycatcher, Warbling Vireo, Yellow Warbler, and Western Tanager. The recently split Cassin's Vireo and most chaparral species can also be found. In mid-May a walk along the trails to Mount Wilson and Winter Creek—when the live oaks and Bigcone Douglas-firs are in fresh foliage—should produce migrating mixed flocks of Black-throated Gray, Townsend's, Hermit, and Wilson's Warblers.

This is one of the most reliable places in Southern California for Black Swift, most easily seen from the upper falls trail. Look for the Gabrielleno trail sign on the left, just past Cabin #42. Then go about 500 meters farther up the trail where you can look up to open sky. Best time for the swift is during the hour before sunset. Northern Pygmy-, Western Screech-, and Spotted Owls are all residents of the canyon, as are Nuttall's Woodpecker, Canyon Wren, Steller's Jay, and Hutton's Vireo. Northern Pygmy-Owl can often be seen during the day on exposed branches next to the trails. In spring look along the open slopes for Ash-throated Flycatcher, Black-headed Grosbeak, and Rufous-crowned Sparrow. Scan the mountain slopes for White-throated Swift, Purple Martin, and Violet-green Swallow in summer from any of the road turn-outs.

To reach the canyon take Interstate 210 east of Pasadena to Santa Anita Avenue, then north for about 6 miles to its terminus at Chantry Flats, the trailhead to Mount Wilson, Winter Creek, and Santa Anita Canyon. The trails are well marked and maintained, but be aware that the best birding is in the morning during the week and in early morning on weekends in order to avoid the throngs of people using this very popular trail. A US Forest Service Forest Adventure Pass is required.

Monrovia Canyon Park—Most of the species seen in Santa Anita Canyon are also found here along the gentle mile-long trail to Monrovia Falls. American Dipper is resident above the bridge from the main road into the park along the streamside forking right toward the dam. You can either pay the modest entry fee to the park and picnic area or use the parking lot at the gate free of charge. Parking your car there allows you to bird the riparian corridor next to the road. Monrovia Canyon is reached by Interstate 210 east of Pasadena to Myrtle Avenue. Drive north one mile to Foothill, right for one-half mile to Canyon Boulevard, and then left (north) for 3 miles to the park entrance.

Whittier Narrows Nature Center—This sanctuary is located along the west bank of the San Gabriel River about ten miles east of downtown Los Angeles. Its riparian habitat, several lakes, chaparral, and open fields have attracted over 260 species of birds. Wintering waterfowl rest and feed on the lakes, while shorebirds use the mudflats and sandbars along the river. Hawks and other landbirds are numerous during migrations, and many stay over the summer to nest. The locally introduced Northern Cardinal is now a rare resident here. Two other exotics may also be encountered—both uncountable—Orange Bishop and the diminutive Nutmeg Mannikin. The Center, open 9 AM–5 PM seven days a week, is located on Durfee Avenue and is easily reached from Highway 60's Santa Anita exit, just west of Interstate 605. Go south to Durfee Avenue (0.7) and turn left (east) to the Center (0.5) on your right. Pick up trail maps and a bird checklist.

RIVERSIDE COUNTY

Corn Spring—Approximately 9 miles east of Desert Center on Interstate 10 is the Chuckwalla Road turn-off (the AAA Riverside County map shows this route in detail). Turn south at the off-ramp, then left onto Chuckwalla Road. After 0.1 mile turn right onto dirt Corn Spring Road to the south. You will drive 7.1 miles of rough road to reach Corn Spring. Resident birds in the area include Gambel's Quail, Black-tailed Gnatcatcher, and Bendire's Thrasher. The vegetation around the spring is a classic desert migrant trap, and fall and spring days can be very productive. There are many eastern vagrant records from this location.

Desert Center—The Lake Tamarisk Golf Course area is always worth a visit during migrations and winter for landbirds. It is a classic migrant trap: an oasis of water, grass, and Tamarisk trees surrounded by seemingly limitless desert. Rare warblers, flycatchers, and thrushes have turned up among the western migrants here. The lake is interesting for waterbirds—check it for wintering geese and ducks, and its edges during migration for shorebirds. Be sure not to interfere with golfers and respect the privacy of residents—they have been kind to birders for years. Some two miles west of Desert Center is the Edmund C. Jaeger Nature Center. Not very birdy and difficult to reach, it can be found by following the road under the power-lines along the south side of the freeway, then turning south. This was the discovery site of the hibernating Common Poorwill.

Prado Basin—The Prado Flood Control Basin is just northwest of Corona, immediately northeast of the junction of Highway 71 and the 91 Freeway. The 11,000-acre site contains a 400-acre man-made marsh and the single largest stand of riparian woodland remaining in Southern California. Of the 274 bird species found in the basin, a remarkable 110 have been confirmed breeding. Such interesting species as the federally endangered "Least" Bell's Vireo (a Brown-headed Cowbird control program operates here), Yellow Warbler, Yellow-breasted Chat, and Blue Grosbeak are plentiful. Uncommon breeders include Common Ground-Dove, Greater Roadrunner, Belted Kingfisher, Pacific-slope and Ash-throated Flycatchers, California Thrasher, Hutton's Vireo, Lazuli Bunting, and Lark Sparrow. Yellow-billed Cuckoo, Willow Flycatcher, Swainson's Thrush, Indigo Bunting, and Lawrence's Goldfinch are present in very small numbers during the breeding season and are unlikely to be seen. Least Bittern and White-faced Ibis have recently bred in the marsh, and Little Blue Heron and Wood Stork (both are rare non-breeders here) have been seen on multiple occasions.

At present, access is limited in much of the basin. However, the Orange County Water District, controlling the site, recently has allowed guided walking tours of its extensive network of ponds and marshland. To arrange a tour, call 714/378-3323.

Additional birding opportunities exist at several other locales, such as at **Prado Regional Park** (along Euclid Street off Highway 71) in Chino. With two large lakes and extensive willow woodland edge, all expected riparian species can be seen. Adding spice to the locality, such rarities as Brown Pelican (rare anywhere away from the ocean or Salton Sea) and Scissor-tailed Flycatcher have been found here. Just north of Prado Park (along River Road in Norco), the Hellman Street crossing of channelized Mill Creek is always worth a look. Ruff and Sabine's Gull both have been seen here, and Lesser Yellowlegs can be surprisingly common in migration and winter. In nearby Corona, Rincon Road (off Lincoln Street, north of the 91 Freeway) traverses a long stretch of willow woodland. While traffic and parking can be problematic, birding nonetheless can be rewarding (a White-eyed Vireo in 1994 was a highlight). Lastly, check the nearby **Corona sewage ponds** from the corner of Butterfield and Smith Streets. Eared Grebes recently bred here; Surf Scoter, Franklin's and Little Gulls, and Black Skimmer have been recorded.

San Timoteo Canyon—When you are returning from the desert to Los Angeles on Interstate 10, this section of the old highway allows you to get off the crowded freeway for a few miles. The traffic cruises through at high speed and the area is largely private property, but it is better than freeway madness—provided that you have the time. The grassy hillsides along the canyon abound with Black-tailed Jackrabbit, Desert Cottontail, California Ground Squirrel, and mice that attract Golden Eagle, hawks, White-tailed Kite, and Long-tailed Weasel. In winter, also watch for Mountain Bluebird and perhaps a Prairie Falcon. Check the two trout-farm ponds at the RV park for ducks, Tricolored Blackbirds, and Black Phoebes (birders are welcome to free day-use). In summer look for Bell's Vireo (rare), Blue Grosbeak, Bullock's Oriole, and Lazuli Bunting in the trees along the stream.

To reach the canyon, go west from Beaumont past the intersection of Highway 60. Go another 1.3 miles and turn south at the well-marked exit

San Timoteo Canyon. When this road ends at Barton Road (16.3), turn left to Waterman Road (3.6), then right to the freeway.

Vidal Wash at the Colorado River—The Colorado River forms the eastern edge of Riverside County. The Tamarack tangle along the river's edge is home to a few breeding pairs of Northern Cardinals—the only reliable location known for a small, native, population of cardinals in the state. The river in the vicinity of the mouth of Vidal Wash (on the San Bernardino/Riverside County boundary) has been productive in recent years. The best time to find cardinals is in June and July. To get there, drive Highway 95 north of Blythe for 35.5 miles to Agnes Wilson Road, north of Lost Lake, on the right. Turn here, driving 2.5 miles to the dirt road on the left just before the bridge to Arizona. Drive north a few miles to where the broad mouth of Vidal Wash enters from the left. Park your car and walk the road in both directions from the wash, watching and listening for cardinals. They may be anywhere along the river, not being limited to the Vidal Wash vicinity. Their exact location may appear on the San Bernardino Audubon RBA; if not, and you find a cardinal, they would appreciate hearing about it.

Bird here early in the morning when it is merely uncomfortable; it gets beastly hot during the rest of the day. Common birds in the riparian thicket nearby include White-winged and Mourning Doves, Ladder-backed Woodpecker, Western Kingbird, Verdin, and Abert's Towhee.

SAN BERNARDINO COUNTY

Clark Mountain—From Interstate 15 east of Baker take the Cima exit, heading north on paved Kingston Road. (Watch for feral burros on the roads at night.) After about 9 miles you will reach a wide dirt track following between two sets of power lines. Follow this road east for about 6 miles, turning southeast (right) onto a rough dirt road (but passable in a passenger car). Follow this road for almost 3 miles as it winds toward the base of Clark Mountain. A four-wheel-drive vehicle is required to continue from this point to a primitive campsite a mile farther up the road to the southwest.

Camp overnight and start the hike up the mountain before dawn using a flashlight. You want to do this for two reasons; a) you need to get up into the White Firs in the amphitheater formed high on the mountain while the birds are singing, and b) it gets hot fast (which also quiets the birds). The hike is steep, very rugged, and will take about three hours. It is best to go up the right side of the slope toward the top, staying out of the creek bed. No one should attempt this hike unless they are in good physical condition. Carry plenty of water.

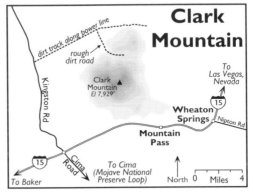

The mountain has an interesting list of birds, not all of which are found every year (indeed, birds like Red-faced Warbler are among the rarest of the rare in California). Previous birding trips to Clark Mountain in the breeding season have found Whip-poor-will, Flammulated Owl, Broad-tailed Hummingbird, Gray Flycatcher, Cordilleran Flycatcher, Plumbeous Vireo, Virginia's Warbler, Grace's Warbler, Red-faced Warbler, Painted Redstart, Hepatic Tanager, and Rose-breasted Grosbeak. Although nesting has not been confirmed for all these species on Clark Mountain, their presence, singing, in appropriate habitat during the breeding season, was provocative. There is no guarantee, however, that any of these species will be seen at the end of your grueling hike!

Mojave Narrows Regional Park and Wildlife Area—Accessible from Interstate 15 about three miles south of Victorville, Mojave Narrows is regarded by locals as one of the premier birding spots in San Bernardino County. Exit at the Bear Valley Cut Off. Go east to Ridge Crest Road (3.9) and turn left to the park entrance (2.6)(fee; camping). This 800-acre desert oasis has substantial groves of cottonwoods and willows along the river. Several small lakes and ponds with adjacent open meadows, farmland, and arid desert highlands all combine to make the area a most unusual habitat for a varied assortment of bird life. During migration, numerous warblers and other landbirds are found. In summer look for Black-chinned Hummingbird, Vermilion Flycatcher (scarce, but has bred here), Ash-throated Flycatcher, Brown-crested Flycatcher, Hutton's and Warbling Vireos, Yellow Warbler, Yellow-breasted Chat, Bullock's Oriole, Summer Tanager, Blue Grosbeak, and Lazuli Bunting. Yellow-billed Cuckoo and Bell's Vireo are rare, but regular. Resident birds such as Virginia Rail, Common Moorhen, six species of hawks, six species of owls, four woodpeckers including Ladder-backed, and eleven finches and sparrows are all here.

SAN DIEGO COUNTY

De Luz Canyon—Driving about 45 miles north from the junction of Interstates 8 and 15 in San Diego, turn off at the Mission Road (S13) exit. Proceed west into Fallbrook and turn right on De Luz Road (5.0). The road drops steeply down into the valley of the Santa Margarita River. Stay left at the bottom of the downgrade (6.2 miles from the I-15 exit). There is a parking area immediately on your right. This is now a county park. A rich variety of riparian birds may be found here in spring and summer including Bell's Vireo. Continuing on De Luz Road you will climb into the highlands, a mosaic of chaparral, oak woodland, coastal sage scrub, and agricultural land. Bird along De Luz Road, watching for raptors, Grasshopper and Rufous-crowned Sparrows, Blue Grosbeak, and Lazuli Bunting. At mile 14.7 from I-15 you will reach the old De Luz schoolhouse, now functioning as an elementary school environmental center. On weekends this is a good spot for a wide variety of woodland and chaparral birds. The center maintains feeders which attract many birds. At night, Western Screech-Owl is a good bet. Beyond the Riverside County line, the road is "iffy" during winter rains. New bridges and road improvements, though, make the San Diego County portion accessible year round. At 23.9 miles from the freeway, you want to turn right onto Rancho California Road. You reach Interstate 15 in Temecula at 29.0 miles from the original exit onto Mission Road. This is an excellent area for almost any lowland land bird you would hope to find in southern California.

Silverwood—This San Diego Audubon Society sanctuary is located in an area of fine chaparral and oak woodland. Some of the common birds are California Quail, Anna's and Black-chinned Hummingbirds, Northern Flicker, Nuttall's Woodpecker (Acorn is rarely seen in Silverwood), Pacific-slope and Ash-throated Flycatchers (breeding), Western Scrub-Jay, Oak Titmouse, Bushtit, Wrentit, House and Bewick's Wrens, California Thrasher, Western Bluebird, Lesser and American Goldfinches, Black-headed Grosbeak, Bullock's Oriole, and, in winter, Ruby-crowned Kinglet, Hermit Thrush, and numerous sparrows. Normally open to the general public only on Sundays; call the Society phone, 619/443-2998, for visitation hours; 13003 Wildcat Canyon Road north of Lakeside.

SUGGESTED ITINERARIES

The purpose of the following itineraries is to give the reader with little or no Southern California birding experience several suggested routes for sampling as much of the region as possible on a limited time budget.

If you are a visitor to Southern California—or are just wondering where to start—you may want to consider the sample itineraries below, taking you through selected sites from the guide's many chapters. Be sure to read the chapters appropriate to the following itineraries for more complete directions and bird information. In following these abbreviated routes, you will not be able to experience an area so thoroughly as when you are following a single chapter, but you will see much of Southern California and a representative group of its birds.

Your trip's pace and purpose are important elements in planning. Remember that this is a large area and that driving time must be carefully considered. It takes six hours of non-stop driving, for instance, from San Diego or the south end of the Salton Sea to San Luis Obispo under optimum conditions. Add two hours if going through the Los Angeles basin during commuting hours. The AAA map of California has an insert map showing projected driving times, as well as mileages, between cities. Consult this when planning your birding trip. Mileages are generally not included in the following sample itineraries—consult the individual chapters for local information, directions, and lodging options.

NORTHERN TRANSECT

Best in spring and fall, optimum in May and late September to early October, this route takes you through most Southern California habitat types and includes excellent migrant traps, oak savannah, montane forest, and chaparral birding, ending on Santa Cruz Island after a brief cross-channel pelagic trip. It does not include any chance for California Gnatcatcher, and covers approximately 400 highway miles. This route can be traveled and birded quickly—in as little as three days for one in a hurry (at this speed it will seem like three Big Days back-to-back), although a minimum of four is suggested, and this still may be too rigorous for some. More than one day can be profitably spent in any segment of this route.

Start at dawn in **Jawbone Canyon** (*Eastern Kern County Loop*), working for Le Conte's Thrasher. Following the Great Thrasher Quest, drive to nearby **Butterbredt Spring** and bird the cottonwoods and willows thoroughly for western migrants and eastern vagrants. Bird the canyon surround-

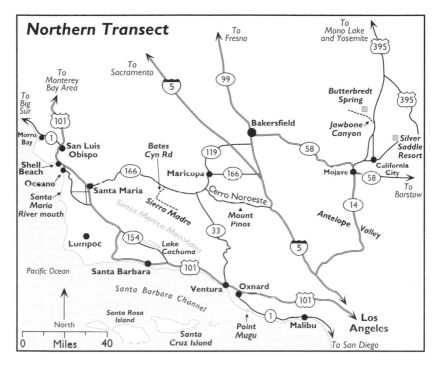

Northern Transect

ings for Brewer's, Black-throated, and Sage Sparrows and Scott's Oriole, all best seen in spring. Leave here by mid-morning and drive to the **Silver Saddle Resort** east of California City, carefully following the parking requirements and rules of etiquette for this *private* resort. After thoroughly birding this oasis, return to California City, and bird **Central Park**. By now it is the warmest part of the day and you may want to stay at a motel in nearby Mojave before traveling west, or repeat these locations the following day. If you plan to stay overnight, check into your motel during the heat of the day, enjoy the air conditioning, and return to Central Park in the late afternoon when it is more comfortable. A word of warning, however—the afternoon winds here can be ferocious, making birding a waste of time. It is best to bird the sites above before the wind rises (if possible).

Drive west from Mojave via Highway 58 through the Tehachapi Mountains to Highway 99 in the Central Valley. Turn south on Highway 99 for approximately 16 miles to Highway 166. Go west on Highway 166 to Cerro Noroeste Road—see *Carrizo Plain/Mount Pinos* chapter—and go south to **Mount Pinos**, following the birding directions in that chapter. Watch for birds all along Cerro Noroeste. Your goals on Mount Pinos include Mountain Quail, Red-breasted Sapsucker, White-headed Woodpecker, Pygmy Nuthatch, Cassin's Finch, Green-tailed Towhee, "Thick-billed" Fox Sparrow, and more. Mornings and late afternoons are best, of course. You could camp here overnight to do some owling. Retrace your path to Highway 166 and turn west. In the Cuyama Valley, follow the directions in the *California Condor Trip* chapter to **Cottonwood Canyon Road**. You may not wish to take the arduous road to the Sierra Madre crest, but the road as far as Bates Canyon Campground will give you good looks at Yellow-billed Magpie, Western Bluebird, and other oak-savannah species. On reaching the chaparral in the vicinity of the campground you will be able to find chaparral specialties such as California Quail, Wrentit, Oak Titmouse, California Thrasher, and Spotted and California Towhees.

Return to Highway 166 and continue west. When you reach US-101, drive 25 minutes north to **Shell Beach** for rocky-shore birds and, in spring and fall, Oceano Campground for Pacific-slope Flycatcher and migrants (see *San Luis Obispo-Morro Bay Areas* chapter). Return south on US-101 and follow the directions in the *Santa Barbara County* chapter to the **Santa Maria River mouth**. If the mudflats are not inundated, there will be many shorebirds to sort through in fall and summer and large numbers of Heermann's Gulls and Elegant Terns occur in the gull flock. Next, return east to Black Road to take a side-trip to the wastewater treatment plant on weekdays. Travel south on Black Road to its intersection with Betteravia. In fall scope the green pasture on the southeast corner for Pacific Golden-Plover (rare). Return to US-101 by driving east on Betteravia, then south on US-101 toward Santa Barbara.

Santa Barbara by itself is worthy of a weekend or more of birding. If you are here in spring or fall with limited time, you may want to confine your birding to **Goleta Beach, Lake Los Carneros County Park, Rocky Nook Park, East Beach**, and **Andree Clark Bird Refuge** on your way south to Ventura. Follow the directions to those locations in the *Santa Barbara County* chapter.

Reserve space on board one of Island Packers' day-trips to **Santa Cruz Island** (see *Pelagic and Island Birding* chapter) before starting this transect. The boat trip to the island can produce shearwaters, jaegers, gulls, terns, and alcids. Xantus's Murrelet is likely in spring, unlikely in fall—although fall may produce Craveri's Murrelet in its place—see Specialties and the bar-graphs. After your island experience with Island Scrub-Jay, you have a brief return pelagic trip to look forward to.

Following completion of this transect across northern Southern California you are within a few miles of US-101 with easy access to anywhere in the state.

If you are here in fall and you have another morning to bird before catching a flight in Los Angeles, stay overnight in Ventura. Read the portion of the *Santa Monica Mountains Loop* chapter regarding the area between Point Mugu and Oxnard. Stop at the sod farms on the Oxnard Plain to look for Pacific Golden-Plover and any rarities present (call the Los Angeles Rare Bird Alert for updates) via telescope from the road. After birding here you can continue south on Highway 1 through Malibu (not recommended during summer beach season) to Interstate 405 and thence to the airport, or return to US-101.

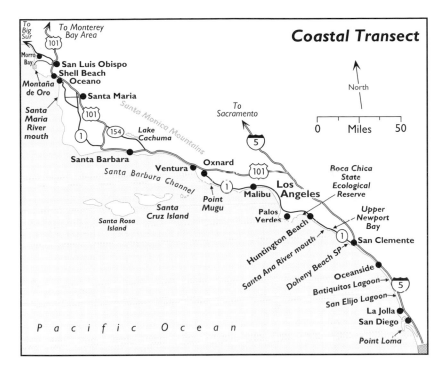

COASTAL TRANSECT

The coastal transect stretches from Morro Bay in the north to San Diego in the south, a distance of approximately 340 highway miles—it is good birding at any time of year. The route takes you to many fine shorebird habitats, coastal migrant traps, wintering waterfowl spots, coastal canyons, and chaparral habitats. It includes some of the most scenic examples of Southern California's remaining natural beaches. *Read the coastal chapters* and add or delete locations based on your available time and birding interests. Although it is possible to bird this itinerary in three days, such a quick dash through the habitats may be frustrating. Because this route takes one through the Los Angeles basin, it is most important to remember to time your drive through the coastal Los Angeles and Orange Counties freeway system so that you are not on the road during morning and evening commuting hours.

The passerine migrant traps can be very good in fall, not bad in spring, and rather pedestrian at other times. Lakes and bays are best in winter, and shorebirding is best in spring and late summer through fall. Winter also brings an influx of northern raptors, gulls, and sparrows. The trip to Santa Cruz Island is best done in spring when Xantus's Murrelet is present (make reservations ahead of time for a day-trip). Resident species are present year round, naturally. Summer months, especially July onward, produce good shorebirding along with the post-breeding influx of Heermann's Gulls and Elegant Terns in coastal estuaries. This time of year tends to be warm, however, and the resident chaparral species are quiet and difficult to find except in early morning and evening. Although the route can be started from either end, if you plan your trip in fall, start first thing in the morning at **Point Loma**, San Diego. Again, read the relevant chapter for local directions to the birding areas mentioned below, and call the San Diego Rare Bird Alert before going.

Bird the **Point Loma Nazarene College** campus before the gates to the Cabrillo National Monument open. Once the gates open, bird the cemetery and then the shrubbery around Monument headquarters. When finished (approximately 3 hours later, dependent on birding conditions) follow the directions to the **San Diego River** channel to bird the upper edge of the tidal flow for herons, ducks, gulls, terns, and shorebirds. Drive east to Interstate 5, driving north to **San Elijo Lagoon**. Bird the chaparral along the south edge for California Gnatcatcher and the lagoon itself for shore and marsh birds—bring your telescope. (The easiest place for the gnatcatcher is at the west end of Lake Hodges, a few miles inland. You may want to follow the directions in the *San Diego Area* chapter to this location—best birded in the morning—and then return to the coast.) During shorebird migration or in winter, you may want to bird **Batiquitos Lagoon** a few miles to the north, as well. Directions for both Batiquitos and San Elijo Lagoons are found in the *Palomar Mountain Loop* chapter. The San Diego locations can easily take a full day. You can conveniently overnight in San Clemente.

Continue north on Interstate 5 to Orange County (the following sites are all in the *Coastal Orange County* chapter). If you are running this route in late fall or winter, stop at **Doheny Beach State Park** to scope the thousands of gulls congregating on the beach for Thayer's and other wintering species. Your next stop will be **Upper Newport Bay** via Highway 1 through Laguna. Do not drive this stretch during commuting hours except as a last resort. Follow the directions for birding the upper bay; target birds include Clapper Rail and, in winter, Nelson's Sharp-tailed Sparrow. Continue up-coast on Interstate 405 to Brookhurst Street, turning to reach **Huntington Central Park** (best in the morning in fall or spring). The Orange County RBA will detail any rarities known to be present. Next, follow directions to **Bolsa Chica State Ecological Reserve**. The spectacle of nesting terns and Black Skimmers is a remarkable sight. Return to Interstate 405 and continue north to US-101 in the San Fernando Valley. Turn west on US-101 to Ventura (alternately, if it's fall and you have the time—come north on Highway 1 through Malibu, stopping in southern Ventura County to bird Big Sycamore Canyon, Point Mugu, and the Oxnard Plain on your way to Ventura).

Take the boat trip from Ventura Marina to **Santa Cruz Island** for Island Scrub-Jay and pelagics en route. Following this day's adventure you can either drive 30 minutes north to Santa Barbara for the night or, if you are here in fall, stay in Ventura for a morning spent birding the sod farms on the **Oxnard Plain** as noted in the *Northern Transect* above.

In Santa Barbara bird **Andree Clark Bird Refuge**, the outfall on **East Beach**, and the harbor. Bird **Santa Barbara Botanic Garden** (fee) for chaparral species, including California Quail, Wrentit, California Thrasher, and Spotted and California Towhees. Bird the riparian area in the canyon below for Pacific-slope Flycatcher, Hooded Oriole (spring and summer), and resident Canyon Wren. Continue to **Rocky Nook Park** for oak-grove species, including Acorn and Nuttall's Woodpeckers and Hutton's Vireo. Both areas can be good for passerine migrants in fall and spring. Continue up-coast on US-101 to Goleta. Take Highway 217 to **Goleta Beach** to bird the estuary entrance for gulls, terns, and shorebirds. If here in April or May, enter the UCSB campus (fee; parking restrictions) to bird the freshwater lagoon for lingering ducks, as well as the bluff-top at **Goleta Point**—best done on blustery west-wind afternoons. The spectacle of northbound Brant, scoters, phalaropes, and especially Pacific Loons, can be unforgettable at this time of year. Continue through campus and neighboring Isla Vista to **Devereux Slough**—telescope required. **Lake Los Carneros,** to the north across US-101, should be birded in fall for migrants, best done in the morning.

Return east on US-101 to Highway 154 to travel north over the Santa Ynez Mountains. Bird **Kinevan Road** in winter for Winter Wren, Golden-crowned Kinglet, and Varied Thrush, and in spring for Cassin's Vireo among numerous breeding species. Add East Camino Cielo for chaparral species including Rufous-crowned Sparrow. Continue north through chaparral into Valley Oak savannah and Coast Live Oak forests in the Santa Ynez Valley. In winter stop at the Bradbury Dam overlook of **Lake Cachuma**, scoping for many species of ducks, grebes, and the occasional look at an Osprey or Bald Eagle. Continue north through the valley, watching for the Yellow-billed Magpies resident here, usually seen at roadside—as are Western Bluebirds on the barbed-wire fences.

Take the Main Street (Highway 166) exit in Santa Maria, traveling west to the mouth of the **Santa Maria River**. June is the only month when little is happening here, and even then it is possible that a large flock of Sooty Shearwaters may be whirling by just offshore. Bird the river mouth; expect to see many species of gulls, terns, and shorebirds most seasons (consult the *Santa Barbara County* chapter and the bar-graphs for details). Bring your telescope and rubber boots.

If you are running this route in the fall, you will want to bird **Oceano Campground** on Highway 1 to the north, as outlined in the *San Luis Obispo-Morro Bay* chapter. This is a classic coastal migrant trap, best done in morning before the afternoon breeze. The trees around the campground and the pond can be filled with western migrants—especially warblers. Many vagrants have been recorded here, primarily in fall. Continue north on Highway 1 through Pismo Beach to the sea cliffs in **Shell Beach**. Bird the cliffs and offshore rocks from the tennis courts and Margo Dodd Park, and scope the waters offshore. Harbor Seals sprawl on the flat rock just offshore, and Sea Otters are seen routinely in the nearshore waters. Rock-loving shorebirds are regular in migration; Wandering Tattler, Black Turnstone, and Surfbird should be found at these times. Black Oystercatchers breed here, and Pigeon Guillemots are easily visible as they nest on the cliffs; watch for them from April through early August. The summer sight of hundreds of Brown Pelicans, Brandt's Cormorants, and Heermann's Gulls on the offshore rocks is most impressive.

Return to US-101 to continue north to San Luis Obispo, where you take the Los Osos Valley Road exit to reach **Montaña de Oro**. Consult the *Morro Bay* section for details on birding this location. Although birding the campground and willows in fall is by far the best time of year, the sea cliffs and tide pools are exceptional at any season. Proceed to nearby **Morro Bay**. The bay, its mudflats, estuary, shoreline, and Morro Rock are worth birding at any time of year, although the willows and the state park campground are best in fall. Consult the tidal chart—best shorebirding on the bay is within one hour either side of a high tide which pushes the shorebirds toward the edges. It is a beautiful, quiet location set amidst a small human population.

Although this ends the coastal transect, when in Morro Bay you are close to many fine birding locations. This is also true if you started in Morro Bay, reversing the order, ending in San Diego on Point Loma. Consult the chapters to construct your own trip as time, interests, and season dictate.

OCEAN, MOUNTAINS, AND SALTON SEA TRANSECT

This transect is another *Reader's Digest*-version of Southern California birding for those on a limited time budget. It starts at sea level, tops at over 6,000 feet in the San Jacinto Mountains, and concludes at the Salton Sea 226 feet below sea level. You will be able to see many Southern California endemics, an amazing sampling of habitat types, and a correspondingly diverse—and long—list of birds. The route is roughly 300 miles in length, depending on your creativity with side jaunts and sightseeing, and should take a minimum of three days. As usual, three days is a once-over-lightly approach; the more days you give, the greater your reward.

Best time of year is summer and fall; spring and winter are wonderful times too, but highland snows greatly reduce the high-country bird list. If you are birding this transect from winter through mid-April, you could bypass the high-mountain portion entirely and bird from San Diego to the Salton Sea via the Anza-Borrego Desert, as detailed below.

If here in fall or spring, start at **Point Loma** in the morning, following the regime noted for the *Coastal Transect*, above. In winter you should start at a coastal estuary, such as **San Elijo**, or the **San Diego River** channel south of Mission Bay. In summer you should start at the **South Bay Marine Biological Study Area** with its tern colonies and migrant shorebirds.

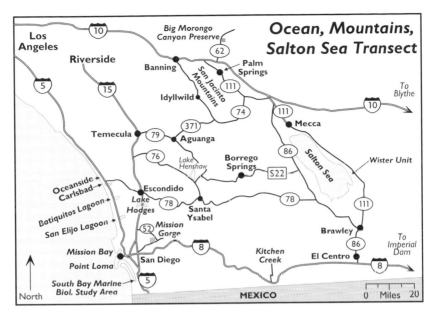

Ocean, Mountains, Salton Sea Transect

However you start, at whatever season, bird the San Diego River channel above the tide line and the coastal estuaries as objectives and time allow.

After birding the San Diego coast, proceed east on Interstate 8 to Interstate 15, turning north. Exit on Friars Road, following the directions in the *San Diego* chapter to **Mission Gorge** and the Old Mission Dam Historical Site. Bird the riparian habitat, the lakes, and the chaparral north of the lakes. The canyon has Canyon Wren and Rufous-crowned Sparrow; California Gnatcatcher and "Bell's" Sage Sparrow can be found on the chaparral-covered slopes. The riparian habitat is a magnet for western migrants; Bell's Vireos and Yellow-breasted Chats breed here as do Nuttall's Woodpeckers, Cassin's Kingbirds, and Hooded Orioles. Winter is good here, too.

Return to Interstate 15 via Highway 52 north of Mission Gorge. Drive north to **San Dieguito River Park** at Lake Hodges (see *San Diego* chapter). This is an outstanding place to make the acquaintance of local chaparral birds at any season, including California Quail, Gnatcatcher, Thrasher, and Towhee. The park's location on the southern edge of Lake Hodges makes it a fine place to see both Western and Clark's Grebes and a selection of shorebirds. Keep watch overhead for Golden Eagle, White-tailed Kite, Red-shouldered Hawk, and other raptors, as well as White-throated Swift. It is best in morning and evening. You may wish to spend the night nearby.

If you are pressed for time, after leaving the park, return to Interstate 15 and turn north. Travel the 32 miles to the junction with Highway 79 in Temecula, turning east on 79. Continue east 18 miles to Aguanga. Turn left onto Highway 371, following the directions below from that point onward. You will reach Aguanga in approximately one hour.

If you have time for a more leisurely, bird-rich drive, consult your map of San Diego County (AAA's is excellent) and notice that you can cross the freeway and continue east on Highland Valley Road 4 miles to Bandy Canyon Road. Turn left on Bandy Canyon to Highway 78 and turn right. You will follow Highway 78 to its end in the hamlet of Santa Ysabel. There are many places along this route where you might pull off to bird from the road (best done mid-week when the traffic is lightest). On reaching the rolling pasture-land west of Santa Ysabel, watch for Ferruginous Hawks in the winter (Red-tails are resident), Golden Eagles, and Western Kingbirds in the spring. Turn left onto Highway 79 at the intersection in Santa Ysabel. Drive almost two miles to small **Santa Ysabel Mission** on the right, turning into the parking lot (see *Palomar Mountain*). Siberian Elms and other ornamental trees on the lawn are host to sapsuckers in winter, and act as a small migrant trap during passerine migration. Continue north on Highway 79.

In winter consult the *Palomar Mountain* chapter for directions to the Lewis's Woodpecker wintering location near Mesa Grande a few miles away. Next, follow directions for birding Lake Henshaw and then travel to the S2 highway, descending into the Anza-Borrego Desert. Follow directions in the Anza-Borrego chapter to Borrego Springs, and thence to the Salton Sea. This route completely bypasses the high mountains, gives you alternate birding time in live oak groves on the way and in **Anza-Borrego Desert** (good in winter), while allowing you to rejoin this transect at the Salton Sea.

Bird **Lake Henshaw** and environs at any season (see *Palomar Mountain* chapter), return to Highway 79, and travel northwest to Aguanga where you will turn right, traveling north on Highway 371, which intersects Highway 74 approximately 21 miles later. Turn left on 74, driving the next nine miles to **Hurkey Creek Campground** through a beautiful valley meadow fringed with Jeffrey and other pines. Watch for Pinyon Jays along this stretch. Consult the *San Jacinto Mountains Loop* chapter for the list of high-mountain birds likely at Hurkey Creek, a fine birding spot. Drive north via Highway 243 to the town of Idyllwild, 3.4 miles farther, where you may overnight. *(If you are here mid-day, bird Humber State Park, and bird your way down to Banning for the night. Big Morongo Canyon Reserve is best in the morning.)*

Bird **Humber State Park** above town the following morning for mountain birds. Make sure to pack extra water for the desert ahead. Return to Highway 243, turning north. **Black Mountain Road** is a fine place to see montane species. Continue north, ultimately descending to Interstate 10 at Banning. *(Alternately, you may choose to travel 243 south to Highway 74, continuing on 74 all the way to Palm Desert on the spectacular Pines-to-Palms Highway. This will shorten your trip by at least ½ day, although you will miss Big Morongo Canyon Preserve—which may be the best choice in any season but spring and fall.)*

Turn south, driving 15.5 miles to Highway 62 where you will turn north to Morongo Valley, a well-known, productive migrant trap. This is one of those locations where anything can happen in spring or fall migration. Acquaint yourself with this site in the *Joshua Tree National Park* chapter. **Covington Park**, adjacent to **Big Morongo Canyon Preserve**, holds breeding Vermilion and Brown-crested Flycatchers mid-spring–summer.

Return to Interstate 10, driving east to the Highway 111 Expressway south toward the Salton Sea. Follow directions in the *Salton Sea* chapter to the **Whitewater River**, hoping that access is available during your visit; in any case, after investigating Whitewater River, continue south on 111 to bird the **Wister Unit** at the southeast corner of the Sea. Continue south from Wister on **Davis Road**, birding the waterfowl and shorebird spots along the way. Continue to Red Hill and bird the **Red Hill Marina**, and the **Alamo River Delta** looking for Yellow-footed Gull and Wood Stork in summer. Go south from the marina to Sinclair Road, turning right to its end at Gentry Road to headquarters for **Salton Sea National Wildlife Refuge**. Bird among the Palo Verde trees for residents and migrants and, in winter, bird the fields behind the headquarters for wintering geese. Return east on **Sinclair Road** to Highway 111, watching the roadside berms for Burrowing Owls. Turn south on 111.

Stop at **Ramer Lake** and **Finney Lake**; both are outstanding for wintering waterfowl, breeding herons, migrant passerines, and resident desert species including Verdin, Black-tailed Gnatcatcher, Crissal Thrasher, and Abert's Towhee. Drive south to Brawley, birding as you have time, and spend the night.

Bird **Brawley** in the morning; J Street, the cemetery, and Las Flores Drive (note details in *Salton Sea* chapter) are all good birding—you should see many desert species at any time (including Gila Woodpecker, Common Ground-Dove, and Inca Dove), interesting migrants in spring and fall, and wintering birds at that season. Following this you may want to return to San Diego via Interstate 8 to the south. In *winter*, bird your way to Interstate 8 by following the directions to the **Pierle, Erskine, Wheeler Roads** area for Mountain Plovers and wintering raptors. From here, drive to **Fig Lagoon** to the south at any time of year. You have now completed this transect.

If returning to San Diego (two hours west) in spring, you could stop at Kitchen Creek (see *Laguna Mountains* chapter) to try for Gray Vireo and Black-chinned Sparrow along the way. However you fashion your return, you have already experienced a major slice of Southern California's habitats and birds on this transect.

SOUTHERN CALIFORNIA SPECIALTIES

The definition of "specialty" employed below is rather broad. It includes those regularly-occurring species that travelers from other states might be most interested in seeing. It does not exclude birds found regularly in other states, but emphasizes those whose overall ranges or low population densities make Southern California one of the prime locations in which to find a given species. This can be arbitrary; our common Brown Pelican, for example, is included due to its status as a signature species in its habitat and uniquely coastal range—notwithstanding the Salton Sea population—while Western Scrub-Jay is not because it is abundant in appropriate habitat throughout most of the western states. Many of the comments below include locations where species may be sought. These are not meant to imply limits to their occurrence, but rather that the areas cited are among the more dependable or accessible areas for finding these birds.

Red-throated and **Common Loons**—Both are common winter visitors, found on the coast; most easily seen from piers and in harbors as noted below. When birding from a beach, you will usually find that Red-throated Loons are found among the sets of waves, diving in shallower water, while the Commons are a bit farther out—this is not diagnostic, merely indicative. Common Loons are uncommon on larger lakes inland.

Pacific Loon—Common winter visitor to coastal waters. It tends to be more offshore than other loons, but usually can be seen from piers such as those at Santa Barbara, Santa Monica, Seal Beach, Newport Beach, Oceanside, or Imperial Beach. The jetties at Playa del Rey and Corona del Mar are also good spots. Large migrating flocks in spring are seen regularly from coastal promontories in the northern part of the region. Point Mugu, Goleta Point, Shell Beach, Montaña de Oro, and the San Simeon Coast are especially good for spring passage, which sometimes numbers in the tens of thousands of birds per day. Although there is only one record of **Arctic Loon** for our area—and one record in northern Baja California, Mexico—and it should not be expected, its possible occurrence when Pacifics are present should provoke observers to carefully note the flanks of all Pacific-types as they float on the water. Arctic Loons will have obvious white flanks extending in an oval pattern well above the water-line—but beware of Pacifics turning on their sides while preening! See Birch and Lee, *Arctic and Pacific Loons*, in References.

Horned Grebe—Uncommon but regular winter visitor to coastal waters, bays, and—more rarely—large lakes. It usually can be found on San Diego or Newport Bays, Ventura and Santa Barbara harbors, and at the various piers along the coast. Quite rare at the Salton Sea, and uncommon on some inland lakes (e.g., Perris, Cachuma).

Western Grebe—Common winter visitor to coastal waters and larger, deep-water lakes. It can usually be seen anywhere along the coast, often in large rafts close to shore. It is also found regularly on large lakes such as Cachuma, Sherwood, Perris, Mathews, Hodges, and the Salton Sea.

Clark's Grebe—Uncommon winter visitor to coastal waters, a few usually appearing in large rafts of Westerns just beyond the surf; slightly more common on inland lakes, and significantly more common than Western Grebe at the Salton Sea. Paler than Western Grebe; the white of the face extends above and behind the eye, and the bill is more yellow-orange. Voice is a single *creet*, differing from the Western's two-note call.

Black-footed Albatross—Uncommon but regular visitor to offshore waters in late spring to early summer, rare in fall and winter. Usually seen well offshore, is more numerous north of Point Conception, and is rarely observed inshore of the Channel Islands.

Laysan Albatross—Rare but regular well offshore late fall to early spring in northwestern corner of the region—most predictably north of Point Conception; casual elsewhere. Six records for the Salton Sea area in the past twenty years. It is assumed that these birds, trapped in the northern Gulf of California, continue overland on their northward course, finding the Salton Sea. Some of the six records are of birds north of the sea, continuing on their course.

Northern Fulmar—Irregular winter visitor, usually rare to uncommon offshore, but may be common in flight years during which it can sometimes be seen from piers and jetties.

Cook's Petrel—Rare but regular far offshore north of Point Conception during fall–winter. Identification of the *Pterodroma* petrels is often subtle; see Harrison's *Seabirds*. Three genuine, but still incredible, July records for the Salton Sea.

Pink-footed Shearwater—Common mid-spring through fall well offshore; rare at other times. Sometimes seen from shore, e.g., Point Fermin, Point Dume, Point Mugu, Goleta Point.

Flesh-footed Shearwater—Rare spring and fall migrant offshore. A few records at other seasons farther north.

Buller's Shearwater—Uncommon to rare fall migrant well offshore; uncommon north of Point Conception, although appears in flocks some years. Fairly common north of this region, but seldom comes close to shore in Southern California. One record from the Salton Sea (1966).

Sooty Shearwater—Common to abundant offshore visitor from spring through fall, uncommon the remainder of the year. This is the shearwater most likely to be seen from shore (especially May–August north of Point Conception), frequently in amazing numbers. Eight records from the Salton Sea area.

Short-tailed Shearwater—Rare fall migrant and winter visitor (November–March) offshore. Great care should be taken in its identification—best told by its subtle pale-gray wash on the underwing (in contrast to the bold silvery-gray wing-linings in Sooty) combined with its abruptly sloping forehead (again in contrast to a typical Sooty) and smaller bill. Tends to follow boats closely and settle in the wake—but so does an occasional Sooty, so use this fact as a spur to careful scrutiny and not as an ID point.

Black-vented Shearwater—Regular fall and winter visitor to offshore waters. May be common to abundant at times. Regularly seen from coastal promontories from San Diego to San Luis Obispo Counties.

Fork-tailed Storm-Petrel—Casual visitor to offshore waters at all seasons, although most likely late winter–early spring. It occasionally irrupts in numbers all along the coast. Nests off northern California.

Leach's Storm-Petrel—Mainly a spring and fall migrant well offshore only; at times fairly common. Both dark-rumped and white-rumped forms occur off Southern California. The distinctive bounding, erratic flight is reminiscent of a butterfly as they bounce along on deep wing strokes. Nests in our region on islets off San Miguel Island. Two records for the Salton Sea.

Ashy Storm-Petrel—Fairly common to common summer-to-fall visitor in northern portion of the region; less common in the south and at other seasons. Nests on northern Channel Islands near which it is common May to October.

Black Storm-Petrel—Fairly common to common visitor offshore during spring, summer, and fall. More common in late summer. Has bred on an islet off Santa Barbara Island, the only known colony in the United States. Two records for the Salton Sea (more than 10 birds one time), and 100s at Lake Havasu in 1997 following Tropical Storm *Nora*.

Least Storm-Petrel—Irregular late August to mid-October visitor from Mexican waters. Seen most regularly off San Diego, but recorded offshore throughout. One record of several hundred birds from the Salton Sea (September 1976) following Tropical Storm *Kathleen*, two other records for the Salton Sea, and many at Lake Havasu in 1997 following Tropical Storm *Nora*.

Red-billed Tropicbird—Rare and irregular summer and fall visitor to offshore waters, especially off the southern Channel Islands. Many birds are immatures without the long tail. Immatures closely resemble Royal Terns, but are larger with a barred back and heavier red bill—and more rapid, stiff Roseate Tern-like wingbeats. Less consistent appearance off our coast than twenty years ago.

Red-tailed Tropicbird—Casual *well* offshore, especially late fall through the winter.

Blue-footed Booby—Rare and irregular late summer and fall visitor to the Salton Sea; casual on large lakes and the coast at other seasons. This bird is the least likely booby to be found on the coast. In late summer and early fall it may occasionally be found at the north end of the Salton Sea, at Salton City, or at the south end. Many years typically go by between occurrences. Most of the boobies stay one or two months before disappearing. Any Southern California booby occurrence will be noted on regional RBAs.

Brown Booby—Casual summer and fall visitor to the Salton Sea, the Colorado River, and on the coast. Probably the most frequently seen booby along the coast and offshore, but still extremely rare.

Red-footed Booby—Casual at virtually any season, usually well offshore. Although extremely rare in southern California waters and never an expected bird, it may be the most regularly occurring of the boobies far out at sea here—although Brown Booby is the booby most expected (if one can expect a casual bird) at sea generally.

Brown Pelican—Common permanent resident along the coast and on Channel Islands. Abundant coastally in summer and fall when population is augmented by Mexican birds. This bird has become common at the Salton Sea in summer and fall. **American White Pelican** usually winters on large inland lakes and year round at Salton Sea, where often abundant; not regular coastally except at Morro Bay where a flock winters annually.

Brandt's Cormorant—Abundant to common permanent resident on Channel Islands. Typically seen along the coast south of Point Conception in the nonbreeding season. Prefers rocky areas and cliffs such as at Point Loma, Point Fermin, and in the Santa Barbara area. It is abundant at all seasons north of Point Conception, and is *the* common cormorant over open ocean.

Pelagic Cormorant—Fairly common to uncommon permanent resident on rocky cliffs of Channel Islands and north of Point Conception. It regularly occurs coastally to the south in winter. Pelagics are much less common at sea than Brandt's Cormorants.

Magnificent Frigatebird—Rare, but almost annual, summer visitor along the coast and to the Salton Sea. Very rare north of Point Conception.

White-faced Ibis—Common transient and summer visitor, common to abundant permanent resident of Imperial Valley where tens of thousands flock in winter. Uncommon fall migrant in coastal marshes. Most often found in irrigated fields in Imperial Valley. Very uncommon in coastal marshes north of Point Conception.

Wood Stork—Uncommon post-breeding wanderer from Mexico to the Imperial Valley, and casually to the coastal marshes. Most common in late July, August, and September at the south end of the Salton Sea. Numbers have steadily declined to the point where rarely more than 50 birds summer.

Fulvous Whistling-Duck—Very uncommon spring and summer resident of freshwater lakes and flooded fields in the Imperial Valley. Ramer and Finney Lakes are best. Recorded sporadically elsewhere, numbers having declined greatly.

Greater White-fronted Goose—Uncommon winter visitor to Salton Sea and large inland lakes. More common as a spring and fall migrant, although unpredictable. Easiest to find at the Salton Sea, but local coastal RBAs usually have a wintering bird staked out.

Ross's Goose—Fairly common winter visitor to south end Salton Sea; rare elsewhere. Sometimes occurs with tame geese in city parks. The majority of these birds winter in the Central Valley of California; only a few drift south along the coast. Coastal RBAs often have a wintering bird staked out.

Brant—Fairly common winter visitor to the larger coastal bays and estuaries. Some winter at the mouth of the San Diego River, on San Diego Bay, and in large numbers at Morro Bay. More widespread in spring, March to May, when large flocks may be seen from coastal promontories, especially Santa Barbara north, in their northward migration; a small number over-summer. Regular at Salton Sea in spring (up to several hundred).

Tufted Duck—Rare fall through winter on lakes and ponds. Usually seen in company with Lesser Scaup and/or Ring-necked Ducks. Its known presence will always be noted on local RBAs.

Scoters—All three scoters winter along the coast. Surf is by far the most common, Black is rare, and White-winged is uncommon and irregular. Look for them just beyond the breakers on the ocean and on the larger bays. Can usually be seen from piers and jetties. Small numbers of Surfs over-summer. Surf Scoters are seen uncommonly during migration at the Salton Sea, White-winged is very rare there, and Black Scoter is casual. Surf Scoter is rarely seen on other inland bodies of water, and Black and White-winged Scoters are casual there.

California Condor—The US Fish and Wildlife Service's release of captive-bred California Condors started in 1992. As of 1998 there are 24 condors in the wild in California, with another 15 at the Vermilion Cliffs in Arizona. The captive breeding program's goal is to establish three stable populations of 150 birds each: one wild in California, one wild in Arizona, and the third the captive breeding stock. Your best chances of seeing free-flying California Condors in California is atop the ridge of the Sierra Madre in northern Santa Barbara County or—less predictably—at Castle Crags on the edge of the Machesna Mountain Wilderness Area in San Luis Obispo County. To reach these areas, see the California Condor Trip and San Luis Obispo chapters. Some of the released birds are being seen on Mount Pinos on the border of Kern and Ventura Counties, and you should check locally in Southern California for updates on their current movements.

White-tailed Kite—Uncommon to fairly common permanent resident of the coastal plain and inland valleys at lower elevations west of the deserts.

This is an irruptive species; it can be common one year and uncommon the next at the same location. Typically more common in winter when groups may gather nightly in large local roosts. Prefers areas of grassy hillsides or meadows which are bordered by densely-topped trees for nesting and perching. Usually productive spots include the grassy valleys east of Morro Bay, fields west of Lompoc, fields along US-101 north of Santa Barbara, the Oxnard Plain, along Interstate 5 at Camp Pendleton in northern San Diego County, and the Tijuana River Valley south of San Diego. It is often seen hovering over grassy freeway medians and edges, where they exist, from San Diego to San Luis Obispo. Rare in the vicinity of the Salton Sea.

Harris's Hawk—Formerly an uncommon resident in the Colorado River Valley and the south end of the Salton Sea. It was extirpated by the early 1960s. Efforts to reintroduce this bird along the Colorado River met with mixed results. A recent surge of wintering birds as far west as Borrego Springs in San Diego County and as far north as Victorville, San Bernardino County, corresponds with a widespread irruption in the desert Southwest and is likely a natural occurrence. One must always exercise caution regarding sightings of Harris's Hawks, however, due to numerous instances of escaped falconer's birds. Known locations for wintering Harris's Hawks, if any, will be on area RBAs.

Red-shouldered Hawk—Fairly common resident of woodlands and riparian areas west of the deserts. Quite common on roadside perches from Santa Barbara northward. Coastal lowland numbers increase somewhat in winter. Rare to uncommon fall migrant through desert regions where wintering birds are rare.

Ferruginous Hawk—Fairly common winter visitor to grasslands in interior valleys as well as grasslands and irrigated regions in the desert. Although decidedly uncommon coastally, individuals are regular in shortgrass pastures near the coast from Lompoc to Point Piedras Blancas north of Morro Bay.

Prairie Falcon—Uncommon permanent resident of rocky cliffs mainly in the deserts and grasslands. Ranges widely over open country when feeding and in the winter. More common and widespread in winter; a few are found along the coast. Always found in winter on the Carrizo Plain in eastern San Luis Obispo County, the Cuyama Valley of southern San Luis Obispo-northern Santa Barbara Counties, Antelope Valley of northern Los Angeles County, and adjacent Kern County to the north.

Chukar—Widely introduced in arid regions such as the Mojave Desert. Sometimes locally common. Fairly common in the brushy deserts and hilly country north of Mojave, especially at Galileo Hill adjacent to Silver Saddle Resort. Also seen in the desert hills at Calico and Yermo.

Blue Grouse—Possibly extirpated from Southern California. Occasional provocative feathers found, or third-hand reports, from the Mount Pinos/Mount Abel area above 6,500 feet on the north-facing slope. May persist in the Tehachapi and Piute Mountains. If found, should be documented and reported immediately.

Gambel's Quail—Common permanent resident of brushlands near water in the deserts, but *not* in the western Mojave. Can be seen about oases around the Borrego Valley, Twentynine Palms, Palm Canyon, Morongo Valley, Finney and Ramer Lakes, and near the Salton Sea. Common at Salton Sea National Wildlife Refuge headquarters and at Wister Unit.

California Quail—Common permanent resident of chaparral and riparian brushlands west of the deserts, and in western Mojave desert (e.g., Antelope Valley). This bird does occur commonly, however, in the Anza-Borrego Desert save the Borrego Valley—so beware. If you do much driving in the foothills of Southern California, you are sure to see a covey scooting across the road.

Mountain Quail—Fairly common permanent resident of brushy terrain in the mountains, mostly above 2,000 feet in elevation. Although widespread, these shy birds can be hard to find even though their territorial call—*quee-ark*—is commonly heard in appropriate habitat. They are perhaps easiest to find in late summer when the young have fledged; usually chanced upon along some back road. Consistently good places are the road leading to the top of Mount Pinos in summer and along the road between Crestline and Silverwood Lake in the San Bernardino Mountains. The Chilao area in the San Gabriel Mountains is also good.

Clapper Rail—Uncommon to rare and declining, depending on the location. Perhaps most easily seen in Upper Newport Bay, coastal Orange County. See chapters about Coastal Orange County, Imperial Dam, Salton Sea, and San Diego for specific locations.

Pacific Golden-Plover—Rare spring and fall transient, and winter visitor, on damp grassy fields near the coast. Usually not encountered until late August when fall migrants are seen on the Oxnard Plain and in their wintering areas. Some over-winter, especially in the pastureland in the Santa Maria area, but also at Seal Beach National Wildlife Refuge and occasionally the San Diego River mouth area. Occasional birds are seen as late as early June; conversely, those rare individuals seen in late June are probably early fall migrants. It is a casual transient and winter visitor at the Salton Sea. **American Golden-Plover** occurs less commonly in spring and regularly in much smaller numbers in fall at the same locations and is more likely inland than Pacific Golden-Plover.

Snowy Plover—Uncommon, local, and decreasing permanent resident of sandy beaches above the tide line. Fairly common at the Salton Sea where they are most easily found in shallow ponds along Davis Road and at the Sea's north end. Dunes and sandy beaches near river mouths or harbors from Morro Bay to San Diego consistently display these plovers.

Mountain Plover—Uncommon winter visitor on barren flats and smoothly-plowed fields of the dry plains and in the Imperial Valley. Find this bird by scanning newly-plowed fields in their favored locations; the bird blends very well with the soil and prefers fields that do not have large clumps of vegetation. Most easily found in fields in the Imperial Valley (where most numerous—see Salton Sea chapter), the Antelope Valley, and on the Carrizo Plain. Also regular in the San Jacinto Valley, Riverside County. The bird is irregular enough in other locations to appear on RBAs when present.

Black Oystercatcher—Common permanent resident on rocky shore of Channel Islands; breeds on the breakwater at Marina del Rey, occasionally seen on breakwaters at Ventura and Point Loma. Common on rocky shores north of Point Conception.

Black-necked Stilt—Common permanent resident of marshes, mudflats, and shallow ponds at lower elevations throughout the region save San Luis Obispo County where it is uncommon and irregular. Abundant and conspicuous at the Salton Sea.

American Avocet—Common permanent resident of marshes, mudflats, and shallow ponds at lower elevations throughout, less common in San Luis Obispo County. Easy to find at Mugu Lagoon, Upper Newport Bay, coastal San Diego County marshes, Salton Sea, Tecopa Marshes, settling ponds, and the like.

Wandering Tattler—Uncommon but easy-to-see migrant and winter visitor to rocky shores along the coast. Can be found at Point Loma, La Jolla, Laguna Beach, Corona del Mar, and rock jetties and shores northward. Casual at the Salton Sea.

Whimbrel—Common migrant and winter visitor on sandy beaches and less commonly on mudflats and fields. Mostly along the coast, but migrates through the Imperial Valley in large numbers, mainly in spring—likewise in the Antelope Valley.

Long-billed Curlew—Fairly common migrant and winter visitor to mudflats and fields along the coastal plain and at the Colorado River; very common in agricultural fields in the Imperial Valley during these seasons.

Black Turnstone—Fairly common migrant and winter visitor on rocky shores and jetties along the coast. Casual at the Salton Sea.

Surfbird—Uncommon and local winter visitor and migrant to rocky shores along the coast. Same areas as Wandering Tattler. Casual at Salton Sea.

Red Knot—Uncommon migrant and winter visitor on the mudflats along the coast, particularly in coastal Orange County (Bolsa Chica, Upper Newport Bay) and on San Diego Bay. Fairly common at the Salton Sea in spring; rare at other times.

Ruff—Rare but regular vagrant in fall, occasionally wintering. Usually found with dowitchers at water treatment plants and mudflats. Casual inland. If any are known to be present, they will be mentioned on local RBAs.

Wilson's Phalarope—Common to fairly common transient. Although regularly seen on migration in the coastal lowlands at water treatment plants and the like, it is most abundant at large bodies of water inland (e.g., Lancaster sewage ponds, Salton Sea) in spring and again in late summer.

Pomarine Jaeger—Common fall migrant in offshore waters. Uncommon in winter and spring. Often seen from shore in fall. Casual inland.

Parasitic Jaeger—Fairly common fall migrant in offshore waters—and the most expected jaeger inshore. Less common in winter and spring migration. Regularly seen chasing terns, and sometimes gulls, along the shore. Rare but regular fall visitor at Salton Sea.

Long-tailed Jaeger—Uncommon but regular fall migrant well offshore. Casual inland.

South Polar Skua—Rare spring and fall migrant to offshore waters. Single birds regularly seen off Morro Bay in fall and on May and early June pelagic trips out of Los Angeles.

Laughing Gull—Common in summer months at the Salton Sea post-breeding. Accidental along the coast.

Heermann's Gull—Common summer, fall, and winter visitor from Mexico to coastal beaches, river mouths, and Channel Islands. Harder to find in spring, although non-breeding birds are still fairly common. Casual at Salton Sea.

Mew Gull—Uncommon to common in winter along the coast; more common farther north. It is a regular habitué of sewage plants. Rare at the Salton Sea.

California Gull—Abundant fall and winter visitor along the coast, less common in early summer (non-breeder). Fairly common at the Salton Sea, and a transient elsewhere in the interior.

Thayer's Gull—Uncommon winter visitor along the coast and inland on the coastal slope. One has to look carefully through the gull flocks to find it (see Lehman, *The Identification of Thayer's Gull in the Field*, in References. The municipal dump in Santa Maria is one of the best spots; also the Santa Clara River mouth in Ventura and the beach at Doheny State Park in Orange County, but it is possible in any flock of large gulls at coastal congregating spots. Rare at Salton Sea.

Yellow-footed Gull—Fairly common summer visitor from Mexico to Salton Sea. Most numerous July to September. Best looked for in the Red Hill, Obsidian Butte, and Salton City areas. Rare at Salton Sea in winter. Casual to the coast of San Diego in early winter.

Western Gull—Abundant permanent resident along the coast and on the Channel Islands. Casual at Salton Sea (making it impossible to assume that all dark-backed gulls there are Yellow-footed).

Glaucous-winged Gull—Fairly common winter visitor along the coastal beaches. Rare at Salton Sea.

Black-legged Kittiwake—Irregular and irruptive winter visitor to offshore waters, sometimes rather common. Occasionally seen along the beaches and at piers and jetties.

Sabine's Gull—Regular, fairly common spring and fall migrant to offshore waters. Rarely seen near shore. A few are found inland every year, particularly at large bodies of water such as Salton Sea.

Gull-billed Tern—Fairly common summer resident at Salton Sea mid-March to early September. Several pairs breed on San Diego Bay.

Elegant Tern—Common post-breeding (July–October) visitor from Mexico along the coast. Nests on the dikes at the South Bay Marine Biological Study Area of San Diego Bay from March through June. Three to five thousand pairs nest at Bolsa Chica in Orange County.

Arctic Tern—Common fall, uncommon spring migrant to offshore waters. Casual at Salton Sea and on the mainland coast.

Least Tern—Uncommon and local breeding bird along the coast, casual at Salton Sea. Likely areas to search from late April to September include south San Diego Bay, coastal lagoons in San Diego County, Bolsa Chica, the lagoon at Point Mugu, and the Santa Ynez and Santa Maria river mouths.

Black Skimmer—Fairly common summer resident where it breeds at Salton Sea, San Diego Bay, and Bolsa Chica. Found on the coast in winter throughout the region, it is common in late fall and winter on beach near Santa Barbara pier; uncommon north of Santa Barbara.

Pigeon Guillemot—Common breeder on northern Channel Islands and on the cliffs from Shell Beach northward in San Luis Obispo County. Easily seen at its nesting cliffs in Shell Beach, Montaña de Oro State Park, and at Morro Rock from April through mid-August. Rarely seen on pelagic trips away from these locations.

Xantus's Murrelet—Uncommon spring and summer visitor to offshore waters. Very rare in fall and winter. Nests on Channel Islands. A boat trip to Anacapa Island, or to Santa Cruz Island for Island Scrub-Jay, from March through June offers a good chance to see this bird, as do March–June trips from Los Angeles to the Channel Islands. In order to see this bird, station yourself on the bow. Murrelets are small and difficult to pick out among swells and wind chop; they also have the disagreeable habit of diving or—more commonly—flying straight away from the boat low to the water as the boat draws near. Watch for the color of the underwing coverts as they fly: Xantus's are very white throughout, while Craveri's show only a bit of a grayish-silver cast, especially on the axillaries. There is some discussion concerning the possible splitting of *scrippsi* from *hypoleucus* Xantus's Murrelet subspecies into full species. The large split eye-ring and white lores of the more southern *hypoleucus* form makes its identification straightforward (for detailed ID information of Craveri's and Xantus's Murrelets see Zimmer, 1985).

Craveri's Murrelet—Rare to uncommon (although somewhat irruptive) migrant August to October from Mexico to offshore waters throughout the region. See Xantus's Murrelet above.

Ancient Murrelet—Rare to uncommon winter visitor, most often seen within a few miles of land.

Cassin's Auklet—Fairly common to common year-round visitor to offshore waters. Nests on northern Channel Islands, around which it easily can be seen in the breeding season.

Rhinoceros Auklet—Fairly common fall, winter, and spring visitor to offshore waters, occasionally inshore. Common some winters, especially in the northern part of the region.

Tufted Puffin—Rare winter visitor to offshore waters, occasional in fall; most records are in late spring.

Band-tailed Pigeon—Fairly common permanent resident of oak and pine woodlands in the mountains, foothills, and north coast, and locally in interior valleys (e.g., Los Angeles Basin, Riverside, San Gabriel Valley). Lower elevations in winter.

Spotted Dove—Common permanent resident of residential areas in Los Angeles and Orange Counties, local elsewhere. Introduced into Los Angeles and has spread to Santa Barbara, San Diego, and inland at least as far as Indio. Usually can be seen perched on telephone wires in residential districts with trees in the Los Angeles area, more difficult elsewhere; declining in Santa Barbara area.

Eurasian Collared-Dove—Uncommon to locally common along the coast from Port Hueneme to Cambria; perhaps most easily seen in the residential areas just north of the Ventura marina. The West Coast population is currently not "countable" per ABA listing standards.

White-winged Dove—Common summer resident along wooded stream-courses and in desert brushland, such as those at Yaqui Well in San Diego County, along the Colorado River, and the Salton Sea. A few occur in winter in the Anza-Borrego Desert and in other areas (e.g., rare along coast in fall and winter).

Common Ground-Dove—Fairly common permanent resident about farms and wooded watercourses in the Colorado Desert. Particularly common about feed-lots in the Imperial Valley. Expanding north and west and found in low densities in Fullerton, Corona, and in citrus orchards in Ventura County near Oxnard and Ventura and the Goleta Valley near Santa Barbara.

Ruddy Ground-Dove—Casual fall and winter visitor to low desert areas. Found at oases, such as Furnace Creek in Death Valley, in company with other ground-doves, if any. Will be on local RBAs if present.

Parrots—Red-crowned Parrots can be abundant in the San Gabriel Valley and urban Orange County, with smaller numbers on the Malibu coast and the northern San Fernando Valley. **Lilac-crowned Parrots** occur in small numbers in the same areas as the Red-crowneds. For a real parrot spectacle, look for aggregations of these amazons and other parrots in Temple City in the late afternoon in the area roughly a mile in radius from the intersection of Baldwin and Live Oak Avenues. **Yellow-headed Parrots** occur in small numbers in West Los Angeles and urban Orange County. **Yellow-chevroned** (recently split from Canary-winged) **Parakeets** are fairly common in the Los Angeles basin, including the Los Angeles Civic Center, Exposition Park, West Hollywood, Redondo Beach, and the Palos Verdes Peninsula; look for them around the large green pods of silk-floss trees (those exotic trees with the thorny green trunks); the related **White-winged Parakeet** is sometimes seen in Redondo Beach and Palos Verdes. **Mitred Parakeets** ("conures") occur in flocks in the coastal areas of Malibu, Redondo Beach, Long Beach, as well as in the Los Angeles basin and the San Gabriel Valley. Other "conures" occurring in small numbers are **Red-masked Parakeets** (mainly in Arcadia/Temple City) and **Blue-crowned Parakeets** (San Fernando Valley around Northridge). **Black-hooded Parakeets** ("Nanday Conures") are most often seen on the west side of Los Angeles from Brentwood and Pacific Palisades to Malibu. **Rose-ringed Parakeets** are found in small numbers from Malibu to Westchester on the coast, and in the San Gabriel Valley around Temple City. No California parrots are considered "countable" by the CBRC.

Yellow-billed Cuckoo—Rare summer resident along the Colorado River, the Kern River delta above Lake Isabella in Kern County, and the Prado Basin in Riverside County. It is a very rare transient elsewhere.

Greater Roadrunner—Fairly common (although declining along the coast) permanent resident of open brush in lowland areas from the coastal plain to the deserts. Most easily seen on the southern deserts, e.g., Imperial, Coachella, and Colorado River valleys.

Flammulated Owl—Uncommon, hard-to-find, summer resident of coniferous forests and high-mountain oaks and pines. Has nested at Palomar Mountain, in San Bernardino Mountains, the San Gabriel Mountains, Black Mountain in the San Jacintos, on Mount Pinos, the Tehachapi and Greenhorn Mountains, and at Big Pine Mountain in interior Santa Barbara County. Your best chance to see it is to be in mature Ponderosa or Jeffrey Pine forest from April to June at midnight and follow-up on its mellow single-noted call. *A word on owling in Southern California: we strongly discourage the playing of taped calls at the locations noted in this guide because of their popularity as birding destinations; birders will not want to be the cause of nest abandonment due to harassment.*

Western Screech-Owl—Fairly common to common resident of live oak and riparian woodlands throughout the region. Absent from open desert and heavily forested highlands.

Northern Pygmy-Owl—Uncommon permanent resident of mixed woodlands in mountains and along canyon bottoms. Some known sites include

Santa Anita Canyon, the vicinity of McGill Campground on Mount Pinos, and at Figueroa Mountain north of Santa Barbara. A diurnal species, it is often heard calling at these locations during the day, especially in the morning hours. Coastal canyon occurrences are fairly common from Santa Barbara north and are frequently noted on local RBAs.

Elf Owl—Rare Southern California breeding bird in old woodpecker holes in trees along the Colorado River only. Very local, threatened in California due to habitat loss. There are no known predictable localities to find this species in the state.

Burrowing Owl—Formerly a common Southern California breeding bird in suitable habitat; now uncommon and declining in most areas of its former abundance. Perhaps most easily found on dikes along roads near Salton Sea National Wildlife Refuge; the Carrizo Plain is also a good place to find them, and they are local and regular in rural western San Diego County, as well as in the San Jacinto Valley in western Riverside County. Incongruously, there is a population of Burrowing Owls on some of the Channel Islands; they also show up as transients on the islands.

Spotted Owl—Uncommon permanent resident of dense woodlands in steep-sided canyons and shaded ravines, usually near a stream. Some known sites are Santa Anita Canyon, below Red Box Ranger Station in the San Gabriel Mountains, near Observatory Campground on Palomar Mountain, around Lake Fulmor in the San Jacinto Mountains, and in Holcomb Valley in the San Bernardino Mountains.

Lesser Nighthawk—Abundant summer resident of open areas at lower elevations in the deserts; less common along the coast. Easy to find at Furnace Creek Ranch, Death Valley, and in the Imperial Valley on spring and summer evenings.

Common Nighthawk—Uncommon local summer resident at Bluff Lake near Big Bear Lake, Baldwin Lake, and at Onyx Summit. This bird is more easily found in the Owens Valley in summer, just north of this book's coverage. Identification of lone birds is very difficult. The white bar beyond the wrist in Common is closer to the wrist than in Lesser. Common also has pointier wing tips and is whiter on the lower belly, vent area, and undertail coverts than the Lesser. These features can be readily discerned in direct comparison, but is subjective on individual sightings—beware. See Zimmer, 1985, for a full discussion.

Common Poorwill—Fairly common summer resident of open brushlands in the foothills and mountains. Although some hibernate, exact winter status is not known. The easiest way to find this bird is to drive back roads through the foothill chaparral and deserts just after dark and watch for their orange eyeshine on the road. The chaparral segments of Cerro Noroeste road and the lower slopes of Mount Pinos can be productive in late spring and summer, as are the back roads on the lower slopes of the San Bernardinos.

Whip-poor-will—The *arizonae* subspecies is a rare and local breeding bird in the San Gabriel (Big Pines Highway), San Bernardino (Angelus Oaks and Heart Bar Campground), and San Jacinto (near Lake Fulmor) Mountains.

Black Swift—Rare late-spring and fall migrant west of the deserts, and uncommon summer resident near waterfalls. May nest in Santa Anita Canyon, the Big Falls Picnic Area in Mill Creek Canyon in the San Bernardino Mountains, and near the Tahquitz Trail and at Lawler Park in the San Jacinto Mountains. Check the coastal RBAs in May as they are seen regularly coastally some years, although not at all most years.

Vaux's Swift—Fairly common to abundant spring and fall migrant in most areas—roosts of up to 10,000 birds are regular late April–May and September–October in downtown Los Angeles. **Chimney Swift** is rare in Southern California in late spring and summer (they summer regularly in small numbers around downtown Los Angeles), but are more likely at these seasons here than Vaux's.

White-throated Swift—Common permanent resident of steep cliffs in all areas. Ranges widely while feeding. Fairly easy to find in mountain canyons, at high coastal cliffs, and along the freeways in Los Angeles.

Black-chinned Hummingbird—Fairly common summer resident of the woodlands in the foothills and lower mountain canyons, uncommon locally in the deserts. Sometimes abundant about feeders in the canyons, as at Tucker Sanctuary.

Anna's Hummingbird—Abundant permanent resident wherever it can find flowers for feeding, mostly west of the deserts; summer resident of Southern California mountains to approximately 8,000 feet. Easy to find about gardens in all of the coastal cities.

Costa's Hummingbird—During the late fall and midwinter months most of these birds are in Baja California, but a few linger in the coastal areas north to Los Angeles and the lower Colorado Desert, and also in Brawley. This is the common hummingbird of California deserts in spring and summer, occurring wherever there is suitable habitat and forage. Yaqui Well and the Anza-Borrego Desert Museum in Borrego Valley are sure bets at the appropriate season. They can also be found spring through summer on the dry chaparral-clad slopes of the drier interior portions of the coast range throughout Southern California, where they are fairly common to common.

Calliope Hummingbird—Uncommon to rare spring migrant in the coastal lowlands and mountains. Uncommon summer resident of higher mountains, such as at Iris Meadows on Mount Pinos and at Bluff Lake, but may be found around feeders, as at Angelus Oaks in the San Bernardino Mountains.

Rufous Hummingbird—Common migrant through the lowlands in spring, although coastal numbers vary from year to year with weather conditions, and the mountains in late summer.

Allen's Hummingbird—Represented by two subspecies. A common migrant through the lowlands in spring, and less commonly in the mountains and foothills west of the deserts in late summer; breeds along the northern coast. Members of a resident population can always be found on the near Channel Islands, in Averill Park, on Point Fermin, and at Point Dume and Huntington Central Park in coastal Orange County.

Lewis's Woodpecker—Erratic winter visitor to open oak groves and pecan and walnut orchards. Unpredictable and rarely seen. More common farther north; it is an uncommon and local breeding bird in the Blue Oak belt of northern San Luis Obispo County. Your best chance (apart from a winter RBA stakeout) is in the Blue Oak/Valley Oak woodlands near Pozo Road along Highway 58 in interior San Luis Obispo County.

Acorn Woodpecker—Abundant permanent resident of all oak woodlands, both lowland and mountains. This noisy, colorful bird is hard to miss.

Gila Woodpecker—Locally common in Brawley, fairly common in riparian areas along the Colorado River.

Red-naped Sapsucker—Uncommon to rare winter visitor throughout the region; more common in the desert.

Red-breasted Sapsucker—Fairly common breeder in mountains west of the deserts, wintering in the coastal lowlands.

Williamson's Sapsucker—Uncommon permanent resident at upper elevations in the higher mountains. More common farther north in the Sierra Nevada. In summer occurs mostly in stands of Lodgepole or Jeffery Pines as at Bluff Lake and above Jenks Lake (try the Poopout Trail) in the San Bernardinos or in the San Gabriel and San Jacinto mountain highlands. Casual in lowlands in winter. More widespread in the mountains in winter, but still uncommon.

Ladder-backed Woodpecker—Fairly common permanent resident of the deserts west to the Antelope Valley west of Lancaster. Found wherever suitable nesting sites are available, as in city parks, patches of cholla cactus, Joshua Tree woodland, and trees along desert washes.

Nuttall's Woodpecker—Common permanent resident of woodlands in the foothills and lowlands west of the desert. It coincides with the western edge of the Ladder-backed's range in the vicinity of San Gorgonio Pass and Palmdale, and care should be taken in these areas (e.g., it is more common than Ladder-backed at Morongo Valley). This coastal counterpart of the Ladder-backed is easily found in most oak groves or in riparian woodland.

White-headed Woodpecker—Fairly common permanent resident of coniferous mountain forests, mainly mature Jeffrey, Ponderosa, and Coulter Pines. Although fairly common, it can be hard to find. You should find it on Mount Pinos, at Charlton Flats and Chilao Campgrounds in the San Gabriel Mountains, Green Valley and Grout Bay Campgrounds in the San Bernardino Mountains, and Black Mountain, Hurkey Creek, and near the fire station at Idyllwild in the San Jacintos.

Gilded Flicker—Very uncommon to uncommon resident in riparian areas of Colorado River, especially north of Blythe. Also uncommon, possibly declining, in Joshua Tree forests around Cima, San Bernardino County.

Willow Flycatcher—Fairly common late migrant in spring, especially through the eastern deserts. Early fall migrant. Virtually extirpated from Southern California as a breeding species except in areas where there is active control of Brown-headed Cowbirds (e.g., locally along the Colorado River, in Mission Gorge, San Diego County, and the Kern River delta above Lake Isabella, Kern County).

Dusky Flycatcher—Fairly common summer resident of patches of dense brush with scattered trees at higher elevations in the mountains. Some known sites are below the parking lot on top of Mount Pinos, near Dawson Saddle and Blue Ridge in the San Gabriel Mountains, at Lake View Point in the San Bernardino Mountains, and above Hurkey Creek Campground in the San Jacinto Mountains. **Hammond's Flycatcher**, which does not nest in Southern California, but migrates through, is most likely to be seen at Point Loma, in spring among the coastal slope woodlands of Los Angeles County—less commonly, and somewhat irruptive, north of there—or at the desert oases.

Gray Flycatcher—Fairly common summer resident in arid pinyon-juniper-sagebrush woodlands of the desert mountain ranges. Uncommon in Joshua Tree National Park. Rare migrant and casual winter visitor along the coast.

Pacific-slope Flycatcher—Fairly common summer resident, breeding in the cool, shaded canyons of the foothills of the coastal ranges, and riparian areas to the west, migrating south and east through the lowlands in fall. A split of Western Flycatcher, it is progressively a more common breeding bird as one travels northward in Southern California. Call note an upward-slurred *tseep* as compared to the other split, **Cordilleran Flycatcher**, which has a two-note call. Although it *may* be reasonable to assume that Cordilleran Flycatcher occurs in desert oases during migration to and from breeding sites to the north, there are *no records* in Southern California away from their known breeding locales (e.g., Clark Mountain in eastern San Bernardino County).

Black Phoebe—Common permanent resident near fresh water at lower elevations in all areas. Often common in urban areas. Check under bridges where there is water and you may find nesting phoebes.

Say's Phoebe—Common winter visitor to open country in all areas. Uncommon summer resident in the deserts, particularly the Mojave Desert, and dry interior valleys like the Carrizo Plain and Cuyama Valley. Usually feeds near the ground from a low bush, weed, or fence-line. Nests under the eaves of deserted buildings, bridges, or overhanging rocks.

Vermilion Flycatcher—Very local, uncommon breeder along the Colorado River, the Morongo Valley and, less regularly, Mojave Narrows. Rare fall migrant on the coast, occasionally winters west of the deserts—if any are present at this time they will be on local RBAs.

Ash-throated Flycatcher—Common summer resident of foothill and desert brushlands, riparian, and oak woodlands that have at least some trees with nesting holes. Casual in winter. A shy bird, but not particularly hard to find because it is very active.

Brown-crested Flycatcher—Fairly common resident along the Colorado River, local breeder west of there, as at Morongo Valley and the Kern River delta above Lake Isabella.

Tropical Kingbird—Rare fall and winter visitor along the coast, sure to appear on local RBAs if present.

Cassin's Kingbird—Fairly common resident of open areas with scattered trees in most areas, although absent from the southeast portion of the region. Uncommon to locally fairly common (especially to the south) in winter. Western Kingbird, generally a bird of drier country, is a far more common summer resident, but is absent in winter.

Western Kingbird—Common in summer (absent in winter) in open habitats throughout region; abundant around the Salton Sea and along the Colorado River.

Violet-green Swallow—Common summer resident of mountain and foothill forests, using old woodpecker holes for nesting. Ranges widely while feeding and in migration. A few winter locally.

Bank Swallow—Uncommon migrant; more common in interior, especially the Salton Sea.

Steller's Jay—Common permanent resident of oak and coniferous forests, locally down to about 2,000 feet. Noisy and easy to find. Very rare winter visitor to lowlands, although in San Luis Obispo County they are locally resident in lowland oak canyons and in pine forest at sea level in Cambria on the region's extreme north coast.

Island Scrub-Jay—Common endemic resident of Santa Cruz Island off Santa Barbara County. The bird is common in live oak forests on the island; it also inhabits exotic eucalyptus and pine groves. Western Scrub-Jay does not occur on the island. For information on trip arrangements see the Pelagic and Island Birding section of this guide.

Pinyon Jay—Uncommon permanent resident of pinyon and open pine forests on the arid eastern and northern side of the eastern Transverse Ranges, and in desert ranges with extensive Pinyon Pine growth. Goes about in noisy flocks, often walking on the ground like crows. Some known locations are near Baldwin Lake in the San Bernardino Mountains, along Highway 74 between Hurkey Creek Campground and Pinyon Flats in the San Jacinto Mountains, and in the Providence Mountains east of Kelso.

Clark's Nutcracker—Fairly common permanent resident of the higher mountains. In summer found up to the very summits of the mountains, where the trees are stunted and separated by rocky slopes and meadows. Moves downslope slightly in winter, but casual at best in lowlands.

Yellow-billed Magpie—Common permanent resident of open valleys with scattered or streamside trees, from central Santa Barbara County northward. Found easily along Highway 154 in the Santa Ynez Valley, Santa Barbara County; along US-101 north between Highway 154 and Santa Maria; in the western Cuyama Valley and in oak savannah interior valleys in San Luis Obispo County.

Chestnut-backed Chickadee—Common local resident in coastal woodlands (especially willows) as far south as the mouth of the Santa Ynez River in extreme western Santa Barbara County.

Oak Titmouse—Common permanent resident of all oak-riparian and pine-oak woodlands of the coast ranges and nearby oak groves. Usually noisy and conspicuous. This bird, and the species following, is a split of the old Plain Titmouse. Responds well to pishing.

Juniper Titmouse—Fairly common resident of the pinyon/juniper woodlands of the ranges in the eastern Mojave Desert, as at Mid Hills Campground in the Mojave National Preserve. The other half of Plain Titmouse.

Verdin—Common permanent resident of brushy areas of low deserts. Can be found in such areas as Yaqui Well, Palm Canyon, Joshua Tree/creosote bush associations in Antelope Valley, and around Ramer and Finney Lakes.

Bushtit—Common permanent resident of gardens, chaparral, woodlands, and urban areas of the plains and foothills west of the deserts. Occurs somewhat more locally in the deserts, in the mountains of Inyo and eastern San Bernardino Counties. Forages in twittering flocks; easy to find.

Pygmy Nuthatch—Common permanent resident of mature Jeffrey and Ponderosa Pine forests in the mountains, and an uncommon resident in the coastal pine forest at Cambria, San Luis Obispo County. Usually easy to locate by its insistent peeping calls.

Cactus Wren—Common permanent resident in the region's deserts. The endangered coastal population is found in scattered local pockets of Prickly Pear cactus from San Diego to Ventura Counties. It is a noisy bird, usually located by its loud, rolling call.

Rock Wren—Fairly common permanent resident of rocky sites in all areas. More common in the deserts. Fairly easy to find in Joshua Tree National Park and along the rocky foothills near Palm Springs and Borrego Springs.

Canyon Wren—Fairly common permanent resident of steep, rocky canyons with drainages in the foothills throughout; also present on rocky ocean-facing cliffs at Shell Beach and at Morro Rock, where it may be fighting a losing battle with feral cats. Fairly noisy, but even after its beautiful descending song or its sharp whistled note is heard, it can be hard to pick out among the cliffs where it lives.

American Dipper—Uncommon and localized permanent resident in Southern California. Found along clear, fast mountain streams as in Santa Anita Canyon, north fork of San Gabriel River, and along the upper Santa Ana River in the San Bernardino Mountains. May be found in winter along clear streams in the foothills throughout, but uncommon enough to usually appear on local RBAs in this season.

California Gnatcatcher—Uncommon resident where present, but is endangered due to habitat destruction. Found in coastal arid sage scrub on lower slopes and in washes. Told from allopatric Black-tailed by darker underparts and by call (see illustration in the Palos Verdes Peninsula chapter). Found on brushy slopes at Upper Newport Bay, the south side of San Elijo Lagoon, San Dieguito River Park at Lake Hodges, Crystal Cove, and at Otay Lakes east of Chula Vista.

Black-tailed Gnatcatcher—Uncommon permanent resident of brushy areas of the lower deserts. Some known sites include along the Colorado River, in the brushy areas around Ramer Lake and Finney Lake, along Highway 195 and Lincoln Road at the north end of the Salton Sea, and at Yaqui Well. Not known to overlap in California with California Gnatcatcher.

Western Bluebird—Fairly common permanent resident of open woodlands of the foothills and mountains west of the deserts; at lower elevations in winter. Often sits on fence-lines and telephone wires. Not hard to find.

Mountain Bluebird—Erratic winter visitor to open terrain at lower elevations in all areas. Fairly common in some winters. Often seen hovering over grassy fields. A few spots where they are regular in winter include Lake Henshaw, Antelope Valley, San Jacinto Valley, Cuyama Valley, and on the Carrizo Plain. Nests in the San Bernardino Mountains and on Mount Pinos, and in high mountains to the north. Can be found near cabins around Baldwin Lake.

Townsend's Solitaire—Fairly common permanent resident of higher mountain forests. Lower in winter. In summer usually found in areas of mature White Fir or Jeffrey Pine, where it flycatches in fairly open forest at all levels. It nests on the ground among the roots of trees, on cliffs, or at the top of road-cuts just under the over-hanging vegetation. Depends on berries extensively in winter and can be looked for in lower mountains and even desert oases where mistletoe or fruiting junipers are abundant. Rare in the coastal lowlands.

Varied Thrush—Irregular winter visitor in lowlands, foothills, and lower mountains; mostly in moist oak woodlands from Ventura County northward. Somewhat regular, but uncommon, in winter at Kinevan Road in the Santa Ynez Mountains. Rare in deserts, casual at Salton Sea and along the Colorado River.

Wrentit—Common permanent resident of the chaparral in the foothills and low tangled growth close to the coast. Its call has the cadence of a dropped ping-pong ball and is heard more often than the bird is seen; if you stop at any patch of chaparral and squeak long enough, you can usually coax one into view.

Sage Thrasher—Uncommon migrant to arid areas with scattered brush at lower elevations. More common in the deserts, as in Joshua Tree National Park or near Cabazon. Can be found in winter in small numbers near Maricopa, near Red Rock Canyon north of Mojave, on Carrizo Plain near Soda Lake, and around Lake Mathews and the San Jacinto Valley. Sage Thrashers may be worn and duller in mid-summer, causing some confusion with Bendire's Thrasher. True, their bill is always much shorter than Bendire's bill—but it can still be confusing. Note that the ground color of Bendire's is soft brown, while Sage gives a bicolored look: gray-brown above, whitish below. The discrete chevrons on the Sage's breast become streaks on sides and belly, but never do on Bendire's. See Kaufman, 1990, for a full discussion.

Bendire's Thrasher—Rare and localized early-summer resident of the eastern deserts. Can be seen in Joshua Tree National Park around Ryan Campground and the valley to the east. Probably easiest to find in the Joshua Tree forests near Cima. Casual fall migrant to coastal localities where it will be on local RBAs if present.

California Thrasher—Common permanent resident of the chaparral west of the deserts. Occurs in western Anza-Borrego Desert at Vallecito and Yaqui Wells, and in Mojave Desert at Morongo Valley and along the Mojave River. Can usually be coaxed into view by squeaking.

Crissal Thrasher—Fairly common but hard-to-find permanent resident of dense brush in lower deserts. Declining overall because of habitat destruction. Some known locations are around Ramer and Finney Lakes, along Highway 195 at north end of Salton Sea, and in patches of dense brush along the Colorado River. Note that it lacks the light supercillium of the California Thrasher, and has dark cinnamon undertail coverts in contrast to California.

Le Conte's Thrasher—Uncommon, localized, and hard-to-find permanent resident of very arid terrain with scattered vegetation. Easiest to find near Maricopa and Jawbone Canyon (see Carrizo Plain and Eastern Kern County chapters). Other predictable—if difficult—locations include the Anza-Borrego Desert, the Lucerne Valley, and Antelope Valley. As noted in the Antelope Valley chapter, it sometimes helps to pretend that you're looking for a mouse—watch for a pale brownish-gray mockingbird-sized bird running away with its tail cocked vertically. Its tail is darker brown, contrasting with the pale back, undertail coverts tawny, and its eye stands out distinctly in an otherwise plain face.

Red-throated Pipit—Casual fall migrant. Most records are between late September and late October. Found at estuaries, in wet fields, pastures, and at sod farms along the coast (especially near Oxnard and the Tijuana River Valley).

Phainopepla—Permanent resident of mistletoe-infested plants in the deserts, fairly common to common where berries are present throughout the dry interior west of the deserts. Less common in the coastal north. Uncommon west of the deserts in winter. Usually perches on the top of bushes, making it easy to find. Easy to find at Yaqui Well, Ramer Lake, Morongo Valley, or any southern desert oasis where mistletoe exists.

Bell's Vireo—Rare and local summer resident in dense riparian growth along watercourses at lower elevations west of the desert. A fairly noisy bird that is easily located by its song, but harder than heck to see. Declining in the Morongo Valley, a former stronghold, but recovering its population density in Mission Gorge, San Diego County, and the Prado Basin, Riverside County, due to active Brown-headed Cowbird control. The subspecies breeding in Southern California, the "Least" Bell's Vireo, is a threatened race, and playing a tape to these birds is always inappropriate.

Gray Vireo—Uncommon and localized summer resident of dry chaparral and stands of pinyon and juniper. Some known locations include the Providence Mountains near Kelso, along the Rose Mine Road below Lake Baldwin, along the base of Santa Rosa Mountain (San Jacintos), and just north of Interstate 8 east of San Diego (Kitchen Creek Road).

Cassin's Vireo—Fairly common transient and breeding bird. Look in desert oases and coastal migrant traps during migration seasons and, in summer, in dense oak woodlands for breeding pairs. (See Heindel, Field Identification of the Solitary Vireo Complex, in References.)

Plumbeous Vireo—Uncommon breeding bird in certain of the desert mountains (e.g., Clark Mountain), and very locally in the eastern San Bernardino Mountains. Rare but regular vagrant to the coast during fall migration. If any are present on the coast, they appear on local RBAs.

Hutton's Vireo—Fairly common permanent resident of oak woodlands in foothills and lower mountains. Responds well to taped calls, particularly in the spring. Easy to find in appropriate habitat virtually throughout; easily found at Santa Barbara Botanic Garden and Placerita Canyon State Park.

Virginia's Warbler—Uncommon and local. Nests on Clark Mountain northeast of Cima, and in the White and New York Mountains. Rare fall vagrant to the coast.

Lucy's Warbler—Common and local summer resident of dense tangles in the lower deserts (e.g., Mojave River, Morongo Valley, Borrego Valley, Furnace Creek). Most common along the Colorado River. Rare early fall vagrant to the coast.

Black-throated Gray Warbler—Fairly common summer resident on dry wooded slopes of the higher mountains, desert mountains, and northern coast range in the region. It breeds predominantly in associations in which

Pinyon Pine, junipers, scrub oaks, or Canyon Oaks are dominant. Fairly common migrant throughout; rare to uncommon winter visitor on coast.

Townsend's Warbler—Fairly common to common migrant and uncommon winter visitor in conifers and live oaks in the mountains, foothills, and coastal lowlands.

Hermit Warbler—Uncommon migrant through the desert and along the coast in spring and through the mountain forests in fall. A localized, very scarce breeder in the San Gabriel and San Bernardino Mountains in the region, the bulk of the population nests well to the north of Southern California. A few are present in coastal pines in winter.

MacGillivray's Warbler—Uncommon migrant that skulks in dense cover near the ground in all areas. Uncommon summer resident in willow thickets in San Gabriel and San Bernardino Mountains above 6,500 feet, and in similar habitat at much lower elevation locally in Santa Barbara and San Luis Obispo Counties.

Green-tailed Towhee—Fairly common summer resident of high mountain brushlands. Rare at lower elevations in southern part of the region in migration and winter. Can be found easily in such areas as Mount Pinos, the Chilao area and along higher parts of Angeles Crest Highway in the San Gabriel Mountains, the sagebrush flats around Baldwin Lake, and along the trail to the top of Mount San Jacinto.

California Towhee—Abundant permanent resident of gardens and brushlands at lower elevations west of the deserts. You will soon be saying "it's just another California Towhee." Overall much darker than Canyon Towhee, which is unrecorded in California.

Abert's Towhee—Common but localized permanent resident of thickets near water at lower elevations in the deserts. Because of the clearance of brush for farming, good habitat for this bird is declining. Look for it anywhere along the Colorado River, about Finney and Ramer Lakes, at the SSNWR headquarters, and elsewhere around the Salton Sea.

Rufous-crowned Sparrow—Fairly common permanent resident of chaparral in the foothills west of the desert. Prefers areas where the brush is rather open and not very high, often along road cuts. A few sites include below Sweetwater Dam east of Chula Vista, along Old River Road near Bonsall, Mission Gorge near San Diego, Irvine Park, Lake Mathews, Forrestal Canyon on Palos Verde Peninsula, near Ventura County campus of Cal State Northridge east of Oxnard, along Camino Cielo above Santa Barbara, and Hi Mountain Road behind Lake Lopez in San Luis Obispo County.

Brewer's Sparrow—In summer found in sagebrush flats in the mountains, as around Lake Baldwin. Fairly common on the deserts in winter. Rare to uncommon fall migrant to the coast.

Black-chinned Sparrow—Fairly common but local summer resident of drier chaparral and sagebrush in the foothills and low mountains. In April and May you can hear them singing all over the place and still not see them. Pishing usually brings one or more teed up on a shrub.

"Large-billed" Savannah Sparrow—A candidate for a future split, this bird winters locally in small numbers along the Colorado River, in coastal marshes, and—especially—near the Salton Sea. They differ from the many iterations of Savannah Sparrows in their noticeably larger bill and lack of yellow in the supercillium. When present along the coast, they appear on local RBAs.

Nelson's Sharp-tailed Sparrow—Rare in winter at coastal estuaries from Tijuana Slough National Wildlife Refuge to Morro Bay. Will appear on local RBAs if any are present.

Black-throated Sparrow—Fairly common permanent resident of arid patches of brush and cactus at lower elevations in the deserts. Easy to find in the desert around the base of the San Jacinto Mountains, and in the Anza-Borrego Desert, Joshua Tree National Park, the Providence Mountains, and the southern border of the Antelope Valley east of Palmdale. It reaches its westernmost location in dry canyons at the east edge of the Cuyama Valley in San Luis Obispo and Santa Barbara Counties. A rare vagrant coastally during fall migration.

Sage Sparrow—Fairly common but localized permanent resident of arid chaparral and sagebrush flats west of the deserts (*belli*). Another subspecies (*canescens*) is resident in the high deserts and on the Carrizo Plain. A third subspecies (*nevadensis*), is a winter visitor to the deserts. To find these birds? A few sites include the lower part of Mount Pinos Road, around Lake Baldwin (summer), brush around Soda Lake on the Carrizo Plain, the San Jacinto Valley area, Lake Hodges at San Dieguito River Park, and near Otay Lakes east of Chula Vista.

Golden-crowned Sparrow—Common winter visitor in rather dense chaparral and other brushland in the foothills west of the deserts. Also occur as minority members of White-crowned Sparrow flocks at feeders in winter. Easily found in chaparral by pishing.

"Thick-billed" Fox Sparrow—Yet another possible future split, these birds (*stephensi*) are fairly common breeding birds in the high mountains; found in both yellow pine forests and thickets. They differ markedly from "classic" Fox Sparrows, most obviously in having unstreaked slate-gray backs, crowns the same—possibly with some brownish streaking—and obviously swollen bills. Uncommon winter visitor to chaparral lowlands.

Tricolored Blackbird—Uncommon local resident of lowlands, mainly west of the deserts. Nests irregularly in large colonies in tule marshes, as in the Cuyama Valley and San Jacinto Wildlife Area. Also occurs at the Kern River Preserve and the Antelope Valley. Feeds in open fields with other blackbirds. Somewhat nomadic.

Hooded Oriole—Fairly common summer resident of gardens and woodlands at lower elevations. Rarely winters where there are hummingbird feeders and/or blooming eucalyptus. This oriole shows a preference for fan palms as nesting sites. It is easy to find at the Twentynine Palms Oasis, Palm Canyon, Borrego Springs, and along nearly any city street in the coastal lowlands where there are ornamental plantings and palms.

Scott's Oriole—Fairly common summer resident of Joshua Trees, Pinyon Pines, and riparian woodlands in the western deserts and in the Providence Mountains. Some good sites include Butterbredt Spring, Joshua Tree National Park, Anza-Borrego Desert, Pinyon Flats in San Jacinto Mountains, and Joshua Tree woodlands in the south and east Antelope Valley. Also found at the northwest edge of their range in Ballinger and Quatal Canyons in Santa Barbara and Ventura Counties.

Cassin's Finch—Fairly common permanent resident at higher elevations from San Jacinto Mountains northward. Rarely lower in winter. Shows a preference for the cool arid boreal forests near the tops of the mountains, usually above the elevational range of the Purple Finch. In summer it can be found along the trails to the tops of Mount San Jacinto and San Gorgonio, on Mount Pinos, and throughout the high San Gabriel Mountains. In fall and winter easy to find around Big Bear and Pine Cove.

Lesser Goldfinch—Common permanent resident of open woodlands, brushy fields, and riparian thickets of foothills, the coastal lowlands, and lower mountains west of the deserts. Easy to find.

Lawrence's Goldfinch—Uncommon and erratic summer resident, its complex status is derived from the fact that it is nomadic as well as migratory. During migration it may be chanced upon in weedy fields in the lowlands: regular at Kern County oases in spring (listen for tiny bell-like notes), at Morongo Valley, and in interior San Diego County. Frequently encountered in dry interior grasslands and at water sources in interior Los Angeles, Ventura, Santa Barbara, and San Luis Obispo Counties. It can be found breeding in all mid- to lowland zones extending to the coast, although it may be absent in some years from locations where it was abundant the previous year. Also breeds along South Fork Kern River, near Chilao Campground in the San Gabriels, and above 6,000 feet in the Greenhorn Mountains. Usually hard to find along the coast in winter, but may be common some years, especially in the southern part of the region.

BIRDS OF SOUTHERN CALIFORNIA

The following bar-graphs include all birds which regularly occur in Southern California. A few of the species in the bar-graphs, however, are well-known vagrants that, although rare, are fairly regular (e.g., Magnificent Frigatebird, Reddish Egret, Tricolored Heron, Northern Waterthrush, Bobolink). Others that are seldom seen (almost annually somewhere in the region) or are accidental (fewer than 10 total records) are listed separately following the bar-graph section.

The bar-graphs, largely adapted from Garrett and Dunn, 1981, are designed to show the *probability* of seeing the bird rather than depicting its actual abundance. Such an approach to bar-graphs is not an exact science, but it is an attempt to predict an experience under "average" birding conditions—whatever they are. Thus, a large bird such as Red-tailed Hawk may be shown as "hard to miss," while a small, shy bird such as Black-chinned Sparrow may actually occur in significant numbers, but be shown as "may see". Use these graphs as a representation of what to expect during a visit, not as an indication of a species' true status.

HARD TO MISS

SHOULD SEE

MAY SEE

LUCKY TO FIND

COSMIC GOOD LUCK

IRREGULAR

On your first trip to the area, you may think that some species are harder to find than indicated. However, if you are in the *right habitat* and the *right area* at the *proper season*, you should be able to find the **hard to miss** birds on nearly every field trip, the **should see** on 3 out of 4 trips, the **may see** on 1 out of 4 trips, and the **lucky to find** on1 out of 10 trips or even less often. The **cosmic good luck** species are not to be expected, but occur rarely. **Irregular species** are those which are sporadic and erratic in *occurrence* and *abundance*; in short, they are unpredictable from one year to the next.

If you find an unusual bird, take notes and report your find to the regional editor of *Field Notes*: Guy McCaskie, San Diego Museum of Natural History, Balboa Park, PO Box 1390, San Diego, CA 92112. Local birders would appreciate it if you also would take the time to call the local Rare Bird Alert to report the sighting. See a list of RBA numbers under "Resources" in the Introduction.

When interpreting the habitat categories on the left side of the bar graphs, think in terms of the state from west to east, i.e., from left to right across the map. If you see an area where a bar is across only one-half of the category, you can interpret this fact as showing occurrence in one segment of the category, but not—or in differential abundance—in the other. For instance, shorebirds typically are shown in the right side of "coastal" because they are not habitués of open water; Black Phoebe is shown as "lucky to find" in the *western* high mountains, but not to be expected in the *eastern*. The areas where the birds are found can be broken down as follows:

PELAGIC—open ocean well offshore.

COASTAL—inshore ocean, bays, marshes, mudflats, beaches, and sea cliffs. If a species is graphed for one-half of the coastal region, this means that it is either on water only (left side) or on shore and in coastal marshes (right side).

LOWLANDS—grasslands (including the coastal shelf), fields, lowland oak or pine groves, and riparian woodlands.

FOOTHILLS—chaparral, wooded canyons and streamsides, pinyon/juniper in low hills.

MOUNTAINS—high-mountain brushlands and forests.

DESERTS—arid lands east of the major mountains.

SALTON SEA—the Sea and the Imperial Valley.

COLORADO RIVER—the Colorado River and the Colorado River Valley.

✓	Pelagic	Coastal	Lowlands	Foothills	Mountains	Deserts	Salton Sea	Colo. River	January	February	March	April	May	June	July	August	September	October	November	December

☐ Red-throated Loon

☐ Pacific Loon

☐ Common Loon
Ocean and large lakes.

☐ Pied-billed Grebe

☐ Horned Grebe

☐ Eared Grebe
" "

☐ Western Grebe
Ocean and large lakes.

☐ Clark's Grebe
Ocean and large lakes.

☐ Black-footed Albatross

☐ Northern Fulmar

☐ Pink-footed Shearwater

☐ Flesh-footed Shearwater

☐ Buller's Shearwater

☐ Sooty Shearwater

☐ Short-tailed Shearwater

☐ Black-vented Shearwater
Abundance varies annually.

☐ Leach's Storm-Petrel

☐ Ashy Storm-Petrel

☐ Black Storm-Petrel

☐ Least Storm-Petrel
Less frequent north of Pt. Conception.

☐ Red-billed Tropicbird

☐ Blue-footed Booby

☐ Brown Booby

☐ American White Pelican
A number winter regularly at Morro Bay.

✓

	Pelagic	Coastal	Lowlands	Foothills	Mountains	Deserts	Salton Sea	Colo. River		January	February	March	April	May	June	July	August	September	October	November	December

☐ Brown Pelican

☐ Double-crested Cormorant

☐ Brandt's Cormorant

☐ Pelagic Cormorant
More common in northern counties.

☐ Magnificent Frigatebird

☐ American Bittern

☐ Least Bittern

☐ Great Blue Heron

☐ Great Egret

☐ Snowy Egret

☐ Little Blue Heron
Breeds locally in San Diego area.

☐ Tricolored Heron

☐ Reddish Egret

☐ Cattle Egret

☐ Green Heron

☐ Black-cr. Night-Heron

☐ White-faced Ibis

☐ Wood Stork
Accidental on coast.

☐ Fulvous Whistling-Duck
Accidental on coast.

☐ Tundra Swan
Large lakes.

☐ Greater White-fr. Goose
Erratic.

☐ Snow Goose

☐ Ross's Goose
On coast golf courses, city parks.

☐ Brant

✓ | Pelagic | Coastal | Lowlands | Foothills | Mountains | Deserts | Salton Sea | Colo. River | January | February | March | April | May | June | July | August | September | October | November | December

☐ Canada Goose

☐ Wood Duck

☐ Green-winged Teal

☐ Mallard

☐ Northern Pintail

☐ Blue-winged Teal

☐ Cinnamon Teal

☐ Northern Shoveler

☐ Gadwall

☐ Eurasian Wigeon

☐ American Wigeon

☐ Canvasback

☐ Redhead
Fairly common nester at Salton Sea.

☐ Ring-necked Duck

☐ Greater Scaup

☐ Lesser Scaup

☐ Oldsquaw
Regular in northern counties coastally.

☐ Black Scoter

☐ Surf Scoter

☐ White-winged Scoter

☐ Common Goldeneye

☐ Barrow's Goldeneye

☐ Bufflehead

☐ Hooded Merganser

☐ Common Merganser

☐ Red-breasted Merganser

☐ Ruddy Duck

✓	Pelagic	Coastal	Lowlands	Foothills	Mountains	Deserts	Salton Sea	Colo. River		January	February	March	April	May	June	July	August	September	October	November	December

☐ Turkey Vulture

☐ California Condor
Santa Barbara Co., Western Kern Co.

☐ Osprey
Occasional migrant overhead in desert.

☐ White-tailed Kite

☐ Bald Eagle
Large lakes.

☐ Northern Harrier

☐ Sharp-shinned Hawk
" "

☐ Cooper's Hawk

☐ Northern Goshawk

☐ Red-shouldered Hawk

☐ Broad-winged Hawk

☐ Swainson's Hawk

☐ Zone-tailed Hawk

☐ Red-tailed Hawk

☐ Ferruginous Hawk

☐ Rough-legged Hawk

☐ Golden Eagle

☐ American Kestrel

☐ Merlin

☐ Peregrine Falcon

☐ Prairie Falcon

☐ Chukar

☐ Ring-necked Pheasant
Local.

☐ Wild Turkey

☐ Gambel's Quail

✓	Pelagic	Coastal	Lowlands	Foothills	Mountains	Deserts	Salton Sea	Colo. River	January	February	March	April	May	June	July	August	September	October	November	December
☐ California Quail																				
☐ Mountain Quail																				
☐ Black Rail																				
☐ Clapper Rail																				
☐ Virginia Rail																				
☐ Sora Local in foothills, deserts.																				
☐ Common Moorhen																				
☐ American Coot																				
☐ Sandhill Crane																				
☐ Black-bellied Plover																				
☐ Pacific Golden-Plover																				
☐ American Golden-Plover																				
☐ Snowy Plover																				
☐ Semipalmated Plover																				
☐ Killdeer																				
☐ Mountain Plover Very local.																				
☐ Black Oystercatcher Rocky coasts and jetties.																				
☐ Black-necked Stilt																				
☐ American Avocet																				
☐ Greater Yellowlegs																				
☐ Lesser Yellowlegs																				
☐ Solitary Sandpiper																				
☐ Willet																				
☐ Wandering Tattler																				
☐ Spotted Sandpiper																				
☐ Whimbrel																				

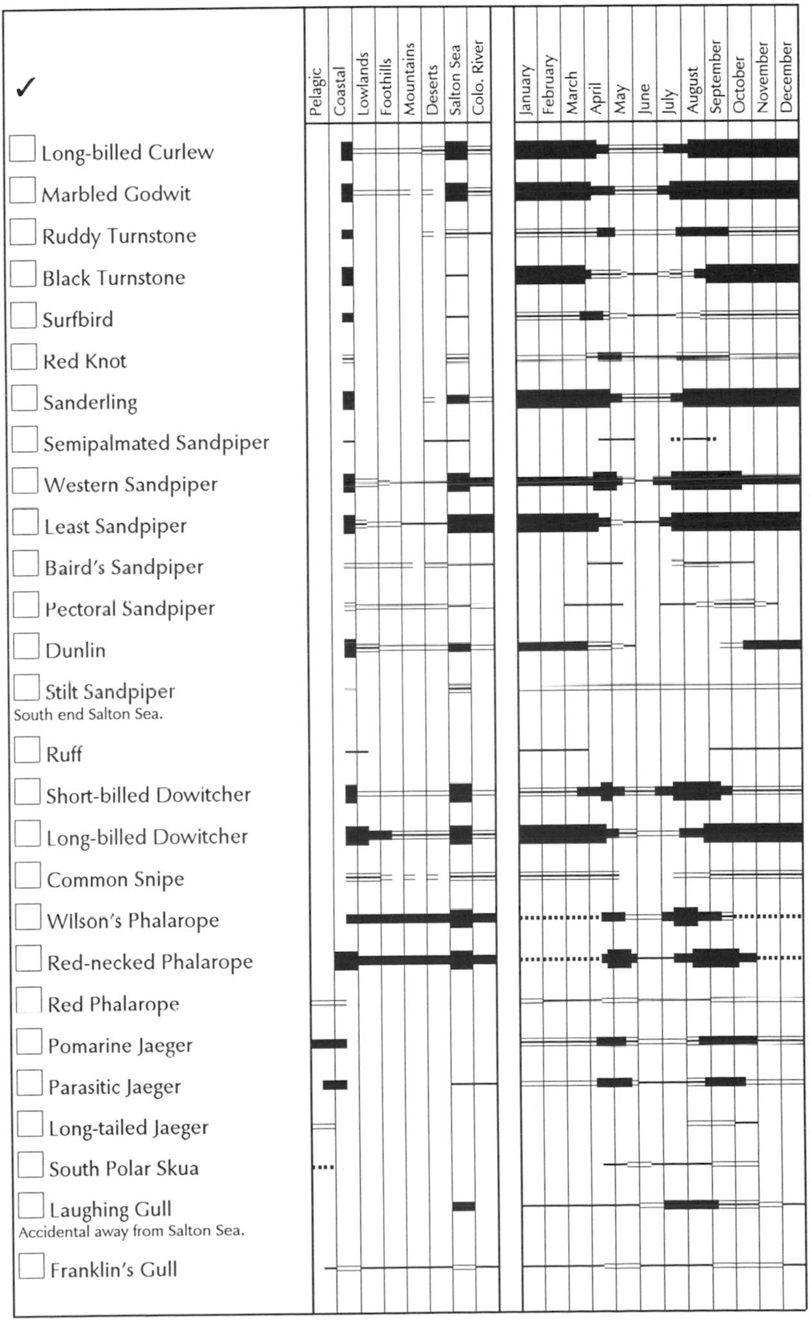

✓	Pelagic	Coastal	Lowlands	Foothills	Mountains	Deserts	Salton Sea	Colo. River		January	February	March	April	May	June	July	August	September	October	November	December

Long-billed Curlew

Marbled Godwit

Ruddy Turnstone

Black Turnstone

Surfbird

Red Knot

Sanderling

Semipalmated Sandpiper

Western Sandpiper

Least Sandpiper

Baird's Sandpiper

Pectoral Sandpiper

Dunlin

Stilt Sandpiper
South end Salton Sea.

Ruff

Short-billed Dowitcher

Long-billed Dowitcher

Common Snipe

Wilson's Phalarope

Red-necked Phalarope

Red Phalarope

Pomarine Jaeger

Parasitic Jaeger

Long-tailed Jaeger

South Polar Skua

Laughing Gull
Accidental away from Salton Sea.

Franklin's Gull

Columns: Pelagic, Coastal, Lowlands, Foothills, Mountains, Deserts, Salton Sea, Colo. River | January, February, March, April, May, June, July, August, September, October, November, December

☑

☐ Bonaparte's Gull

☐ Heermann's Gull
Non-breeding.

☐ Mew Gull

☐ Ring-billed Gull
Non-breeding.

☐ California Gull
Non-breeding.

☐ Herring Gull

☐ Thayer's Gull

☐ Yellow-footed Gull
Non-breeding; a few coastal records
in San Diego County.

☐ Western Gull

☐ Glaucous-winged Gull

☐ Glaucous Gull

☐ Black-legged Kittiwake
Erratic; irregular numbers.

☐ Sabine's Gull

☐ Gull-billed Tern
Salton Sea and San Diego Bay.

☐ Caspian Tern
Nests South San Diego Bay, Bolsa Chica.

☐ Royal Tern
Nests South San Diego Bay, Bolsa
Chica; less common north in summer.

☐ Elegant Tern
Nests South San Diego Bay, Bolsa Chica.

☐ Common Tern

☐ Arctic Tern

☐ Forster's Tern
Nests South San Diego Bay, Bolsa
Chica, and Salton Sea.

☐ Least Tern

✓	Pelagic	Coastal	Lowlands	Foothills	Mountains	Deserts	Salton Sea	Colo. River		January	February	March	April	May	June	July	August	September	October	November	December
☐ Black Tern	▬																				
" " Non-breeding.							▬							▬▬▬▬▬▬▬▬▬						
☐ Black Skimmer	▬						▬			▬▬▬▬▬▬▬▬▬▬▬▬▬▬										
☐ Common Murre	▬																				
☐ Pigeon Guillemot Channel Islands, coast north of Point Conception.	▬												▬▬▬▬▬▬							
☐ Marbled Murrelet	▬																				
☐ Xantus's Murrelet Channel Islands.	▬												▬▬▬▬▬							
☐ Craveri's Murrelet	▬															····▬					
☐ Ancient Murrelet	▬																				
☐ Cassin's Auklet Nests on Channel Islands.	▬																				
☐ Rhinoceros Auklet	▬																				
☐ Tufted Puffin	▬																				
☐ Rock Dove		▬▬▬▬▬▬▬▬▬								▬▬▬▬▬▬▬▬▬▬▬▬▬▬▬▬▬▬▬▬										
☐ Band-tailed Pigeon			▬																		
☐ Spotted Dove		▬▬▬								▬▬▬▬▬▬▬▬▬▬▬▬▬▬▬▬▬▬▬▬										
☐ White-winged Dove						▬				▬▬▬▬▬▬▬										
☐ Mourning Dove		▬▬▬▬▬▬▬▬▬								▬▬▬▬▬▬▬▬▬▬▬▬▬▬▬▬▬▬▬▬										
☐ Inca Dove Very local.																					
☐ Common Ground-Dove Rare north of Ventura.						▬				▬▬▬▬▬▬▬▬▬▬▬▬▬▬▬▬▬▬▬▬										
☐ Yellow-billed Cuckoo Very local breeder; see Specialties section.																▬▬▬					
☐ Greater Roadrunner		▬▬▬▬▬				▬▬				▬▬▬▬▬▬▬▬▬▬▬▬▬▬▬▬▬▬▬▬										
☐ Common Barn Owl																					
☐ Flammulated Owl Very local.														▬▬							
☐ Western Screech-Owl																					

✓	Pelagic	Coastal	Lowlands	Foothills	Mountains	Deserts	Salton Sea	Colo. River		January	February	March	April	May	June	July	August	September	October	November	December

☐ Great Horned Owl

☐ Northern Pygmy-Owl

☐ Elf Owl

☐ Burrowing Owl
Occasional on dikes in Salicornia marshes.

☐ Spotted Owl

☐ Long-eared Owl
Very local.

☐ Short-eared Owl

☐ Northern Saw-whet Owl
Very local.

☐ Lesser Nighthawk

☐ Common Nighthawk
Eastern San Bernardino Mountains.

☐ Common Poorwill

☐ Whip-poor-will

☐ Black Swift
Very local.

☐ Chimney Swift

☐ Vaux's Swift

☐ White-throated Swift

☐ Black-chinned Hummingbird

☐ Anna's Hummingbird

☐ Costa's Hummingbird
   " "

☐ Calliope Hummingbird
   " "

☐ Rufous Hummingbird

☐ Allen's Hummingbird
   " "

☐ Allen's Hummingbird
    "insular" subspecies
Palos Verde Peninsula, Channel Islands.

✓

	Pelagic	Coastal	Lowlands	Foothills	Mountains	Deserts	Salton Sea	Colo. River		January	February	March	April	May	June	July	August	September	October	November	December

☐ Belted Kingfisher

☐ Lewis's Woodpecker
Small resident population east
of San Luis Obispo.

☐ Acorn Woodpecker
Limited to oak groves, save migrants.

☐ Gila Woodpecker

☐ Red-naped Sapsucker

☐ Red-breasted Sapsucker
Lowlands in winter.

☐ Williamson's Sapsucker
Foothills and deserts in winter only.

☐ Ladder-backed Woodpecker

☐ Nuttall's Woodpecker

☐ Downy Woodpecker

☐ Hairy Woodpecker

☐ White-headed Woodpecker
Rarely irrupts into lowlands in winter.

☐ Northern Flicker
" "

☐ Gilded Flicker

☐ Olive-sided Flycatcher

☐ Western Wood-Pewee

☐ Willow Flycatcher

☐ Hammond's Flycatcher

☐ Dusky Flycatcher

☐ Gray Flycatcher
Rarely winters.

☐ Cordilleran Flycatcher
Local (and casual?) in eastern
desert mountains.

☐ Pacific-slope Flycatcher

☐ Black Phoebe

✓	Pelagic	Coastal	Lowlands	Foothills	Mountains	Deserts	Salton Sea	Colo. River		January	February	March	April	May	June	July	August	September	October	November	December

☐ Say's Phoebe
   "   "

☐ Vermilion Flycatcher
Regular at Morongo Valley.

☐ Ash-throated Flycatcher

☐ Brown-crested Flycatcher
Regular at Morongo Valley.

☐ Tropical Kingbird

☐ Cassin's Kingbird

☐ Western Kingbird

☐ Horned Lark
   "   "

☐ Purple Martin
Coastal lowlands occasionally
  during migration.

☐ Tree Swallow
   "   "

☐ Violet-green Swallow
Below Parker Dam on Colorado River.
   "   "

☐ N. Rough-winged Swallow

☐ Bank Swallow

☐ Cliff Swallow

☐ Barn Swallow
   "   "

☐ Steller's Jay
Lowlands in winter.

☐ Western Scrub-Jay

☐ Pinyon Jay
Lowlands in winter.

☐ Clark's Nutcracker
Lowlands in winter rarely.

☐ Yellow-billed Magpie
Interior valleys in Santa Barbara and
San Luis Obispo Counties.

✓	Pelagic	Coastal	Lowlands	Foothills	Mountains	Deserts	Salton Sea	Colo. River	January	February	March	April	May	June	July	August	September	October	November	December

☐ American Crow

☐ Common Raven
Obvious, but local, coastally.

☐ Mountain Chickadee
Lowlands in winter occasionally.

☐ Chestnut-bkd Chickadee

☐ Oak Titmouse

☐ Juniper Titmouse
In junipers in desert mountians,
eastern San Bernardino Co.

☐ Verdin

☐ Bushtit

☐ Red-breasted Nuthatch
Lowlands in winter.

☐ White-breasted Nuthatch
Lowlands in winter.

☐ Pygmy Nuthatch
Lowlands in winter.

☐ Brown Creeper
Lowlands in winter.

☐ Cactus Wren
Very local (Prickly Pear thickets) on coast
from Ventura County south.

☐ Rock Wren

☐ Canyon Wren
Below Parker Dam on Colorado River.

☐ Bewick's Wren

☐ House Wren
    "   "

☐ Winter Wren

☐ Marsh Wren

☐ American Dipper

✓	Pelagic	Coastal	Lowlands	Foothills	Mountains	Deserts	Salton Sea	Colo. River	January	February	March	April	May	June	July	August	September	October	November	December

☐ Golden-crowned Kinglet
Very local.
   " "

☐ Ruby-crowned Kinglet
   " "

☐ Blue-gray Gnatcatcher
   " "

☐ California Gnatcatcher

☐ Black-tailed Gnatcatcher

☐ Western Bluebird
Lowlands in winter.

☐ Mountain Bluebird
Winters regularly in grasslands
  of interior valleys.
   " "

☐ Townsend's Solitaire
Lowlands in winter.

☐ Swainson's Thrush

☐ Hermit Thrush
   " "
Very local in mountains.

☐ American Robin

☐ Varied Thrush
Irruptive, irregular in winter in lowlands
  and foothills.

☐ Wrentit

☐ Northern Mockingbird

☐ Sage Thrasher

☐ Bendire's Thrasher

☐ California Thrasher

☐ Crissal Thrasher

☐ Le Conte's Thrasher
Very local; dry washes.

☐ American Pipit

✓

☐ Cedar Waxwing

☐ Phainopepla
" "

☐ Loggerhead Shrike

☐ European Starling

☐ Bell's Vireo
Local

☐ Gray Vireo
Very local.

☐ Plumbeous Vireo
Very local, rare.
" "
Very local, rare.

☐ Cassin's Vireo

☐ Hutton's Vireo

☐ Warbling Vireo

☐ Tennessee Warbler

☐ Orange-crowned Warbler
" "

☐ Nashville Warbler

☐ Virginia's Warbler
" "
Nests on Clark Mtn, New York Mtns,
and NE San Bernardino Mtns.

☐ Lucy's Warbler
" "

☐ Yellow Warbler

☐ Yellow-rumped Warbler
" "

☐ Black-throated
    Gray Warbler

☐ Townsend's Warbler

☐ Hermit Warbler

Columns: Pelagic, Coastal, Lowlands, Foothills, Mountains, Deserts, Salton Sea, Colo. River | January, February, March, April, May, June, July, August, September, October, November, December

✓ — Pelagic, Coastal, Lowlands, Foothills, Mountains, Deserts, Salton Sea, Colo. River — January, February, March, April, May, June, July, August, September, October, November, December

Palm Warbler

Blackpoll Warbler

Black-and-white Warbler

American Redstart

Northern Waterthrush

MacGillivray's Warbler

Common Yellowthroat

Wilson's Warbler
" "

Yellow-breasted Chat

Hepatic Tanager
Has nested in San Bernardino Mountains.

Summer Tanager

Western Tanager
" "

Northern Cardinal
Small Los Angeles Area population
introduced; Colorado River
population quite rare.

Rose-breasted Grosbeak

Black-headed Grosbeak

Blue Grosbeak

Lazuli Bunting

Indigo Bunting
Very local.

Dickcissel

Green-tailed Towhee
" "

Spotted Towhee

California Towhee

Abert's Towhee

✓	Pelagic	Coastal	Lowlands	Foothills	Mountains	Deserts	Salton Sea	Colo. River		January	February	March	April	May	June	July	August	September	October	November	December

☐ Rufous-crowned Sparrow

☐ Chipping Sparrow
    " "

☐ Clay-colored Sparrow

☐ Brewer's Sparrow
    " "

☐ Black-chinned Sparrow

☐ Vesper Sparrow
Breeds at Baldwin Lake
in San Bernardino Mtns.

☐ Lark Sparrow

☐ Black-throated Sparrow

☐ Sage Sparrow
Local.
    " "

    " " (Bell's)
Very local

☐ Lark Bunting

☐ Savannah Sparrow
    " " (Belding's)
    " " (Large-billed)

☐ Grasshopper Sparrow

☐ Fox Sparrow
    " " (Thick-billed)

☐ Song Sparrow

☐ Lincoln's Sparrow
    " "
Very local.

☐ Swamp Sparrow

☐ White-throated Sparrow

☐ Golden-crowned Sparrow

☐ White-crowned Sparrow

☐ Harris's Sparrow

✓	Pelagic	Coastal	Lowlands	Foothills	Mountains	Deserts	Salton Sea	Colo. River		January	February	March	April	May	June	July	August	September	October	November	December
☐ Dark-eyed Junco "Oregon"																					
" "																					
"Gray-headed" Junco																					
"Slate-colored" Junco																					
☐ McCown's Longspur																					
☐ Lapland Longspur																					
☐ Chestnut-collared Longspur																					
☐ Bobolink																					
☐ Red-winged Blackbird																					
☐ Tricolored Blackbird Very local.																					
☐ Western Meadowlark																					
☐ Yellow-headed Blackbird																					
" "																					
☐ Rusty Blackbird																					
☐ Brewer's Blackbird																					
☐ Great-tailed Grackle Expanding range.																					
☐ Bronzed Cowbird																					
☐ Brown-headed Cowbird																					
☐ Orchard Oriole																					
☐ Hooded Oriole																					
☐ Baltimore Oriole																					
☐ Bullock's Oriole																					
☐ Scott's Oriole																					
☐ Purple Finch																					
" "																					
☐ Cassin's Finch Lowlands in winter.																					
☐ House Finch																					

	Pelagic	Coastal	Lowlands	Foothills	Mountains	Deserts	Salton Sea	Colo. River		January	February	March	April	May	June	July	August	September	October	November	December
☐ Red Crossbill																					
Lowlands in winter.																					
☐ Pine Siskin																					
" "																					
☐ Lesser Goldfinch																					
☐ Lawrence's Goldfinch																					
" "																					
☐ American Goldfinch																					
" "																					
☐ Evening Grosbeak																					
☐ House Sparrow																					

BIRDS SELDOM SEEN BUT POSSIBLE

None of the following birds is to be expected on a given day at any season, although they have occurred enough times in Southern California to be expected again. They range in rarity from such birds as Eastern Kingbird, an annually occurring vagrant, to Curve-billed Thrasher with only a handful of winter records. For a clear appreciation of these species' status, see Garrett and Dunn, 1981. Those species on the California Bird Records Committee Review List are noted by an asterisk.

Red-necked Grebe	Northern Shrike
Laysan Albatross	*White-eyed Vireo
Cook's Petrel	Solitary Vireo
Wilson's Storm-Petrel	*Yellow-throated Vireo
Fork-tailed Storm-Petrel	*Philadelphia Vireo
*Yellow-crowned Night-Heron	Red-eyed Vireo
*Roseate Spoonbill	*Yellow-green Vireo
Tufted Duck	*Golden-winged Warbler
Harlequin Duck	Northern Parula
Harris's Hawk	Chestnut-sided Warbler
Sharp-tailed Sandpiper	Magnolia Warbler
Rock Sandpiper	Cape May Warbler
Buff-breasted Sandpiper	Black-throated Blue Warbler
*Little Gull	Black-throated Green Warbler
Horned Puffin	Blackburnian Warbler
*Ruddy Ground-Dove	*Yellow-throated Warbler
*Broad-billed Hummingbird	*Grace's Warbler
Broad-tailed Hummingbird	*Pine Warbler
*Greater Pewee	Prairie Warbler
Least Flycatcher	Bay-breasted Warbler
Eastern Phoebe	Prothonotary Warbler
*Dusky-capped Flycatcher	*Worm-eating Warbler
Eastern Kingbird	Ovenbird
*Scissor-tailed Flycatcher	*Kentucky Warbler
*Gray Catbird	Hooded Warbler
Brown Thrasher	Canada Warbler
*Curve-billed Thrasher	*Scarlet Tanager
*Sprague's Pipit	*Painted Bunting
Red-throated Pipit	American Tree Sparrow
Bohemian Waxwing	*Common Grackle

ACCIDENTALS

The species in the following list are the rarest of Southern California's rarities records. All species but those with a double asterisk are on the California Bird Records Committee Review List.

Arctic Loon
Yellow-billed Loon
Least Grebe
Short-tailed Albatross
Mottled Petrel
**Murphy's Petrel
Wedge-tailed Shearwater
Manx Shearwater
Band-rumped Storm-Petrel
Wedge-rumped Storm-Petrel
White-tailed Tropicbird
Red-tailed Tropicbird
Masked Booby
Red-footed Booby
Neotropic Cormorant
Anhinga
White Ibis
Black-bellied Whistling-Duck
Trumpeter Swan
Emperor Goose
Baikal Teal
Garganey
Common Pochard
King Eider
Mississippi Kite
Common Black-Hawk
Yellow Rail
Purple Gallinule
Mongolian Plover
Wilson's Plover
Piping Plover
American Oystercatcher
Spotted Redshank
Gray-tailed Tattler
Upland Sandpiper
Little Curlew
Hudsonian Godwit
Bar-tailed Godwit
Red-necked Stint
Little Stint
White-rumped Sandpiper
Curlew Sandpiper
Belcher's Gull
Black-headed Gull
Black-tailed Gull
Lesser Black-backed Gull
Red-legged Kittiwake
Ivory Gull

Sandwich Tern
Sooty Tern
Thick-billed Murre
Kittlitz's Murrelet
Parakeet Auklet
Black-billed Cuckoo
Groove-billed Ani
Xantus's Hummingbird
Violet-crowned Hummingbird
Red-headed Woodpecker
Yellow-bellied Flycatcher
Alder Flycatcher
Great Crested Flycatcher
Sulphur-bellied Flycatcher
Couch's Kingbird
Thick-billed Kingbird
Cave Swallow
Blue Jay
**Black-billed Magpie
Sedge Wren
Dusky Warbler
Arctic Warbler
Northern Wheatear
Veery
Gray-cheeked Thrush
Wood Thrush
Rufous-backed Robin
Yellow Wagtail
White Wagtail
Black-backed Wagtail
Blue-winged Warbler
Cerulean Warbler
Louisiana Waterthrush
Connecticut Warbler
Mourning Warbler
Red-faced Warbler
Pyrrhuloxia
Little Bunting
Varied Bunting
Cassin's Sparrow
Field Sparrow
Baird's Sparrow
Le Conte's Sparrow
Smith's Longspur
Snow Bunting
Streak-backed Oriole
**Gray-crowned Rosy-Finch

SOUTHERN CALIFORNIA BUTTERFLIES

San Luis Obispo County eastward, including mountains around Kern River.

Swallowtails:
Anise
Baird's
Black
Giant
Indra
Pale
Pipevine
Two-Tailed
Western Tiger

Whites:
Becker's
Cabbage
Checkered
Mustard
Pine
Spring

Marbles:
Gray
Large
Pearly

Orangetips:
Desert
Pima
Sara

Sulfurs:
Clouded
Cloudless
Dainty
Large Orange
Lyside
Orange
Orange-barred
Queen Alexandra's

Orange:
Sleepy

Yellows:
Boisduval's
Little
Mexican
Mimosa

Dogface:
California
Southern

Coppers:
Blue
Edith's
Gorgon
Great
Hermes

Lustrous
Purplish
Ruddy
Tailed

Hairstreaks:
Behr's
Bramble
California
Golden
Gold-Hunter's
Gray
Great Purple
Hedgerow
Juniper
Mt. Mahogany
Sheridan's
Silver-banded
Sylvan
Thicket

Ministreak:
Leda

Scrub-hairstreaks:
Avalon
Mallow

Elfin:
Brown
Desert
Moss
Western Pine

Blues:
Acmon
Arctic
Arrowhead
Boisduval's
Ceraunus
Dotted
Eastern Tailed
Greenish
Lupine
Marine
Melissa
Reakirt's
Rita
San Emigdio
Silvery
Small
Sonoran
Square-spotted
Veined
Western Pygmy
Western Tailed
Spring Azure

Metalmarks:
Fatal
Mormon
Palmer's
Wright's

Fritillaries:
Callippe
Coronis
Great Basin
Gulf
Hydaspe
Mormon
Pacific
Unsilvered
Variegated

Checkerspots:
Arachne
Edith's
Gabb's
Leanira
Northern
Sagebrush
Tiny
Variable

Crescents:
Field
Mylitta
Pearl
Phaon

Patches:
Bordered
California

Buckeyes:
Common
Tropical

Ladies:
American
Painted
West Coast
Red Admiral

Commas:
Hoary
Oreas
Satyr

Tortoiseshells:
California
Milbert's

Milkweed Butterflies:
Monarch
Queen

308

Miscellaneous Brushfoots:
Mourning Cloak
Lorquin's Admiral
California Sister
Viceroy
American Snout

Satyrs:
Common Ringlet
Great Basin Wood-Nymph

Checkered-Skippers:
Common
Small
Two-banded

Cloudywings:
Mexican
Northern

Duskywings:
Afranius
Funereal
Mournful
Pacuvius

Persius
Propertius
Sleepy

Sootywings:
Common
Mojave
Saltbush

White-Skippers:
Erichson's
Northern

Miscellaneous Spreadwing Skippers:
Hammock
Longtailed
Arizona Powdered-Skipper
Golden-headed Scallopwing
Silver-Spotted Skipper

Grass Skippers:
Alkali
Brazilian
Carus
Columbian

Common Branded
Dun
Eufala
Fiery
Juba
Julia's
Lindsey's
Pahaska
Rural
Sachem
Sandhill
Sierra
Sonoran
Umber
Wandering
Woodland
Yuma
Orange Skipperling

Giant-Skippers:
Arizona
California
Mojave
Yucca

SOUTHERN CALIFORNIA MAMMALS

For more information consult Ingles' *Mammals of the Pacific States.*

Opossum

Ornate Shrew
Gray or Desert Shrew
California Mole
California Leaf-nosed Bat
Pallid Bat
Big Brown Bat
Silver-haired Bat
California Myotis
Small-footed Myotis
Long-eared Myotis
Little Brown Bat
Fringed Myotis
Long-leggged Myotis
Yuma Myotis
Western Pipistrelle
Townsend's Big-eared Bat
Mexican Free-tailed Bat
Spotted Bat
Red Bat
Hoary Bat
Western Mastiff Bat
Black Bear
Raccoon
Ring-tailed Cat
Long-tailed Weasel
Sea Otter
Badger
Spotted Skunk
Striped Skunk
Coyote
Kit Fox
Gray Fox
Mountain Lion
Bobcat
Steller's Sea Lion
California Sea Lion
Northern Fur Seal
Guadalupe Fur Seal
Harbor Seal
Elephant Seal
California Ground Squirrel
Rock Squirrel
Mojave Ground Squirrel
Round-tailed Ground Squirrel
Golden-mantled Ground Squirrel
White-tailed Antelope Squirrel
Yuma Antelope Squirrel

San Joaquin Antelope Squirrel
Merriam's Chipmunk
Panamint Chipmunk
Lodgepole Chipmunk
Western Gray Squirrel
Eastern Fox Squirrel
Northern Flying Squirrel
Valley Pocket Gopher
Pocket Mouse (9 species)
Kangaroo Rat (6 species)
Beaver
Western Harvest Mouse
Southern Grasshopper Mouse
White-footed or Deer Mouse (6 species)
Woodrat or Packrat (3 species)
California Vole or Meadow Mouse
Long-tailed Vole
Muskrat
Porcupine
Black-tailed Jackrabbit
Desert Cottontail
Brush Rabbit
Mule Deer
Bighorn Sheep
Pacific Bottle-nosed Dolphin
Common Dolphin
Pacific White-sided Dolphin
Long-beaked Dolphin
Right Whale Dolphin
Pacific Pilot Whale
Baird's Beaked Whale
Pacific Beaked Whale
Goose-beaked Whale
Sperm Whale
Pygmy Sperm Whale
Pacific Killer Whale
False Killer Whale
Grampus or Risso's Dolphin
Gray Whale
Fin-backed Whale
Humpback Whale
Rorqual or Sei Whale
Piked or Minke Whale
Blue Whale
Pacific Right Whale

SOUTHERN CALIFORNIA REPTILES AND AMPHIBIANS

For more information, see Stebbins' *A Field Guide to Western Reptiles and Amphibians.*

California Newt
Ensatina
Arboreal Salamander
California Slender Salamander
Pacific Slender Salamander
Western Spadefoot
Colorado River Toad
Woodhouse's Toad
Great Plains Toad
Desert or Red-spotted Toad
Western Toad
Southwestern Toad
Pacific Tree Frog
Canyon Tree Frog
Red-legged Frog
Yellow-legged Frog
Leopard Frog
Bullfrog
Western Pond Turtle
Sonoran Mud Turtle
Spiny Soft-shelled Turtle
Desert Tortoise
Western Banded Gecko
Leaf-toed Gecko
Desert Iguana
Chuckwalla
Zebra-tailed Lizard
Fringe-toed or Sand Lizard
Collared Lizard
Leopard Lizard
Desert Spiny Lizard
Granite Spiny Lizard
Banded Rock Lizard
Side-blotched Lizard
Western Fence Lizard
Sage-brush Lizard
Long-tailed Brush Lizard
Tree Lizard
Small-scaled Lizard
Coast Horned Lizard
Desert Horned Lizard

Flat-tailed Horned Lizard
Desert or Yucca Night Lizard
Granite Night Lizard
Island Night Lizard
Western Skink
Gilbert's Skink
Orange-throated Whiptail
Western Whiptail
Southern Alligator Lizard
California Legless Lizard
Western Blind or Worm Snake
Rosy Boa
Rubber Boa
Western Ring-necked Snake
Spotted Leaf-nosed Snake
Yellow-bellied Racer
Coachwhip
Striped Racer
Western Patch-nosed Snake
Glossy Snake
Gopher Snake
Common Kingsnake
California Mountain Kingsmale
Long-nosed Snake
Western Garter Snake
Common Garter Snake
Checkered Garter Snake
Western Ground Snake
Western Shovel-nosed Snake
Western Black-headed Snake
California Lyre Snake
Arizona Lyre Snake
Night Snake
Western Diamond-backed Rattlesnake
Red Diamond-backed Rattlesnake
Speckled Rattlesnake
Sidewinder
Western Rattlesnake
Mojave Rattlesnake

REFERENCES

Austin, Mary. 1903. *Land of Little Rain.* Houghton Mifflin Co., Boston. Evocative, eloquent, one of the finest pieces of literature produced in California, about California. Austin's description of life in southern and eastern California includes encounters with California Condors and other wild things. A joy to read and re-read. Reprinted in paperback by various publishers, it is available in National Park visitors center bookstores in California, as well as through many book dealers.

Bailey, Harry P. 1966. *The Weather of Southern California.* University of California Press, Berkeley.

Birch, Andrew, and Cin-Ty Lee. 1997. Arctic and Pacific Loons: Field Identification. *Birding* 29(2):107-115. American Birding Association. Compendium of the known details concerning identification of this ultra-rare species to our area.

Childs, Henry E. Jr. 1993. *Where Birders Go in Southern California.* Los Angeles Audubon Society, Los Angeles.

Clarke, Herbert. 1989. *An Introduction to Southern California Birds.* Mountain Press Publishing Co., Missoula.

Cornett, James W. 1987. *Wildlife of the North American Deserts.* Nature Trails Press, Palm Springs.

Dameron, Wanda. 1997. *Searching for Butterflies in Southern California.* Flutterby Press, Los Angeles. A contemporary guide, available from Los Angeles Audubon Society Bookstore.

Dunn, Jon L., and Kimball L. Garrett. 1997. *A Field Guide to the Warblers of North America.* Houghton Mifflin Co., Boston.

Emmel, Thomas C., and John F. Emmel. 1973. *The Butterflies of Southern California.* Natural History Museum of Los Angeles County, Los Angeles.

Gallagher, Sylvia Ranney. 1996. *Atlas of Breeding Birds in Orange County, California.* Sea and Sage Press, Santa Ana.

Garrett, Kimball, and Jon Dunn. 1981. *Birds of Southern California: Status and Distribution.* Los Angeles Audubon Society. Since its publication, the standard reference on status and distribution of Southern California birds.

Garth, John S., and J. W. Tilden. 1986. *California Butterflies.* University of California Press, Berkeley.

Grinnell, Joseph, and Alden H. Miller. 1944. *The Distribution of the Birds of California.* 1944. Cooper Ornithological Club, Berkeley. Pacific Avifauna #27. Classic reference on status and distribution of California birds, indispensable. Available in a 1986 reprint, with a new introduction only, from Artemisia Press, Lee Vining, CA.

Hamilton, Robert A., and Douglas R. Willick. 1996. *The Birds of Orange County California: Status and Distribution.* Sea and Sage Audubon Society, Irvine. As the title states, plus helpful information on the county's geography and habitats.

Harrison, Peter. 1983. *Seabirds: An Identification Guide.* Houghton Mifflin Co., Boston.

Heindel, Matt T. Field Identification of the Solitary Vireo Complex. 1996. *Birding* 28(6):458-471. American Birding Association. Outstanding discussion of our understanding of the field identification for the three species in the "Solitary" complex.

Hoffman, Ralph. 1927. *Birds of the Pacific States.* Riverside Press, Cambridge, Massachusetts. A classic, although with a scope extending beyond California. Possibly the best-written field guide extant. Now, sadly, out of print.

Ingles, Lloyd G. 1965. *Mammals of the Pacific States.* Stanford University Press, Palo Alto.

Jaeger, Edmund C. 1965. *The California Deserts.* Fourth edition. Stanford University Press, Palo Alto. A classic discussion of California deserts.

Kaufman, Kenn. 1990. *A Field Guide to Advanced Birding.* Houghton Mifflin Co., Boston. Thorough treatment of field identification of many more difficult to identify species.

Lee, Cin-Ty. 1995. Birdwatching in Riverside, California. *Quarterly* 42(4). San Bernardino County Museum Association, Redlands.

Lehman, Paul E. 1980. The Identification of Thayer's Gull in the Field. *Birding* 12(6):198-210. American Birding Association. The classic article defining field identification of this cryptic species.

_____ 1994. *The Birds of Santa Barbara County, California.* UCSB Vertebrate Museum, Santa Barbara. Thorough recounting of the status and distribution of birds in this fascinating county; includes much valuable information on topography and climate with their relation to the bird life of the area.

Massey, Barbara W. 1998. *Guide to the Birds of the Anza-Borrego Desert.* Anza-Borrego Desert Natural History Association, Borrego Springs.

Matelson, Helen. 1996. *The Birds Come Flocking, A Field Guide to Santa Barbara County for Birders and Other Travelers* (revised). Published by the author.

Miller, Alden H., and Robert C. Stebbins. 1964. *Lives of Desert Animals in Joshua Tree National Monument.* University of California Press, Berkeley.

Niehaus, Theodore F., and Charles L. Ripper. 1976. *A Field Guide to Pacific States Wildflowers.* Houghton Mifflin Co., Boston. *The Peterson Field Guide.*

Norris, Robert M., and Robert W. Webb. 1976. *Geology of California.* John Wiley and Sons, New York. A good introduction to California's complex geology, a college text.

Pavlik, Bruce M., Pamela C. Muick, Sharon G. Johnson, and Marjorie Popper. 1991. *Oaks of California.* Cachuma Press, Los Osos, California. Illustrated with stunning photographs throughout. A scholarly layman's treatment of California's 18 species of oaks and, of necessity, their environment. Highly recommended.

Roberson, Don. 1980. *Rare Birds of the West Coast.* Woodcock Publications, Pacific Grove. A section on eastern warblers in California includes average number of occurrences annually per species, as well as other useful information.

Rosenberg, K.V., R.D. Ohmart, W.C. Hunter, and B.W. Anderson. 1991. *Birds of the Lower Colorado River Valley.* University of Arizona Press, Tucson. The definitive work on the birds of this region.

Schoenherr, Allan A. 1992. *A Natural History of California.* University of California Press, Berkeley. "A book of astonishments...The most comprehensive look at California's natural diversity yet attempted," *Pacific Discovery.*

Sharp, Robert P. 1994. *A Field Guide to Southern California,* Third edition. Kendall/Hunt Publishing Co., Dubuque, Iowa. A fascinating treatment of Southern California's geology as seen from the roadside. It really belongs in every car traversing Southern California.

Small, Arnold. 1994. *California Birds: Their Status and Distribution.* Ibis Publishing, Vista. Updated, revised, and expanded from the 1974 edition. Includes information on every species on the California list and 54 pages of outstanding color photographs of California birds.

Stallcup, Rich. 1990. *Ocean Birds of the Nearshore Pacific.* Point Reyes Bird Observatory, Stinson Beach. A presentation of much useful material for a Southern California pelagic trip—more than just identification.

Stebbins, Robert C. 1966. *A Field Guide to Western Reptiles and Amphibians.* Houghton Mifflin Co., Boston. The Peterson Field Guide to herps of the West.

Stienstra, Tom. 1993. *California Camping: the Complete Guide to More than 50,000 Camping Sites.* Foghorn Press, San Francisco.

Unitt, Philip. 1984. *Birds of San Diego County.* San Diego Society of Natural History. Meticulously done, a marvelous reference on the status and distribution of birds in San Diego County—and much more.

Wheeler, Brian K., and William S. Clark. 1995. *A Photographic Guide to North American Raptors.* Academic Press, San Diego.

Zimmer, Kevin J. 1985. *The Western Bird Watcher: An Introduction to Birding in the American West.* Prentice-Hall, Inc., Englewood, NJ. Now out of print, though a revised edition is due in 1998. Valuable information—well presented—on birding the West, including a thorough treatment of identification points of difficult-to-identify species that are relevant in Southern California.

AMERICAN BIRDING ASSOCIATION

ABA is the organization of North American birders, and its mission is to bring all the excitement, challenge, and wonder of birds and birding to you. As an ABA member you will get the information you need to increase your birding skills so that you can make the most of your time in the field.

ABA supports the interests of birders of all ages and experiences, and promotes birding publications, projects, and partnerships. It focuses on bird identification and birdfinding skills and the development and dissemination of information on bird conservation. ABA also champions ethical birding practices.

Each year members receive six issues of ABA's award-winning magazine *Birding* and twelve issues of *Winging It*, a monthly newsletter. ABA conducts regular conferences and biennial conventions in the continent's best birding locations, publishes a yearly *Membership Directory and Yellow Pages*, compiles an annual *Directory of Volunteer Opportunities for Birders*, and offers discount prices for many bird books, optical gear, and other birding equipment through ABA Sales. The organization's *ABA/Lane Birdfinding Guide Series* sets the standard for accuracy and excellence in its field.

ABA is engaged in bird conservation through such institutions and activities as Partners in Flight and the American Bird Conservancy's Policy Council. ABA also actively promotes the economic and environmental values of birding.

ABA encourages birding among young people by sponsoring birding camp scholarships and "ABA/Leica Young Birder of the Year" competition, and by publishing *A Bird's-Eye View*, a bimonthly newsletter by and for its younger members.

In cooperation with the National Audubon Society, ABA also publishes *Field Notes*, a quarterly which reviews all imprortant bird sightings and significant population trends for the US, Canada, and the West Indies.

In short, ABA works to ensure that birds and birding have the healthy future that they deserve. In the words of the late Roger Tory Peterson, the American Birding Association is "the best value in the birding community." The American Birding Association gives active birders what they want. Consider joining today. You will find a membership form on the other side of this page.

American Birding Association Membership Services
PO Box 6599
Colorado Springs, CO 80934
telephone 800/850-2473 or 719/578-1614 - fax 719/578-1480
e-mail: member@aba.org
web site: http://www.americanbirding.org

315

AMERICAN BIRDING ASSOCIATION
Membership Application

All memberships include six issues of *Birding* magazine, monthly issues of *Winging It,* ABA's newsletter, and full rights of participation in all ABA activities.

Membership Classes and Dues:

❑ Individual - US	$36.00 / yr	❑ Student - Canada**	$27.00 / yr
❑ Individual - Canada *	$45.00 / yr	❑ Family - US	$43.00 / yr
❑ Individual - Int'l	$45.00 / yr	❑ Family - Canada*	$52.00 / yr
❑ Student - US**	$18.00 / yr	❑ Family - Int'l	$52.00 / yr
		❑ Hooded Merganser	$136.00 / yr

* Canadian dues include GST, which is paid to the Canadian government
All membership dues include $27 for **Birding** *magazine and $9 for* **Winging It** *newsletter.*
** **Students** - Write your date of birth, name and location of school, and expected date of graduation on the bottom of this form. This information is **required** to receive Student rates.

Application Type

❑ New Membership ❑ Renewal ❑ Gift

Please call 800/850-2473 or 719/578-1614 for information about how you may subscribe to Field Notes.

Member Information

Name _____

Address _____

_____

Phone _____

Payment Information

❑ Check or Money Order enclosed (US funds only)

❑ Charge to VISA / MasterCard (circle one)

Account Number _____

Exp Date _____

Signature _____

Send this completed form with payment to: **ABA Membership**
PO Box 6599
Colorado Springs, CO 80934

SoCal 8/98

316

OTHER ABA BIRDFINDING GUIDES

A Birder's Guide to the Bahama Islands
Anthony W. White
June 1998 — $26.95

A Birder's Guide to Idaho
Dan Svingen and Kas Dumroese
October 1997 — $18.95

A Birder's Guide to Virginia
David Johnston
May 1997 — $18.95

A Birder's Guide to Colorado
Harold R. Holt
February 1997 – $21.95

A Birder's Guide to Florida
Bill Pranty
May 1996 – $21.95

A Birder's Guide to New Hampshire
Alan Delorey
January 1996 – $18.95

Birdfinder: A Birder's Guide to Planning North American Trips
Jerry A. Cooper
November 1995 – $21.95

A Birder's Guide to Southeastern Arizona
Rick Taylor
August 1995 – $19.95

A Birder's Guide to Arkansas
Mel White
May 1995 – $18.95

A Birder's Guide to Eastern Massachusetts
Bird Observer
August 1994 – $18.95

A Birder's Guide to Churchill
Bonnie Chartier
January 1994 – $17.95

A Birder's Guide to the Texas Coast
Harold R. Holt
May 1993 – $18.95

A Birder's Guide to Wyoming
Oliver K. Scott
February 1993 – $18.95

A Birder's Guide to the Rio Grande Valley of Texas
Harold R. Holt
January 1992 – $18.95

American Birding Association Sales
PO Box 6599, Colorado Springs, Colorado 80934
Phone: 800/634-7736 or 719/578-0607 Fax: 800/590-2473 or 719/578-9705

AMERICAN BIRDING ASSOCIATION

PRINCIPLES OF BIRDING ETHICS

Everyone who enjoys birds and birding must always respect wildlife, its environment, and the rights of others. In any conflict of interest between birds and birders, the welfare of the birds and their environment comes first.

CODE OF BIRDING ETHICS

1. Promote the welfare of birds and their environment.

1(a) Support the protection of important bird habitat.

1(b) To avoid stressing birds or exposing them to danger, exercise restraint and caution during observation, photography, sound recording, or filming.

Limit the use of recordings and other methods of attracting birds, and never use such methods in heavily birded areas or for attracting any species that is Threatened, Endangered, or of Special Concern, or is rare in your local area.

Keep well back from nests and nesting colonies, roosts, display areas, and important feeding sites. In such sensitive areas, if there is a need for extended observation, photography, filming, or recording, try to use a blind or hide, and take advantage of natural cover.

Use artificial light sparingly for filming or photography, especially for close-ups.

1(c) Before advertising the presence of a rare bird, evaluate the potential for disturbance to the bird, its surroundings, and other people in the area, and proceed only if access can be controlled, disturbance can be minimized, and permission has been obtained from private land-owners. The sites of rare nesting birds should be divulged only to the proper conservation authorities.

1(d) Stay on roads, trails, and paths where they exist; otherwise keep habitat disturbance to a minimum.

2. Respect the law and the rights of others.

2(a) Do not enter private property without the owner's explicit permission.

2(b) Follow all laws, rules, and regulations governing use of roads and public areas, both at home and abroad.

2(c) Practice common courtesy in contacts with other people. Your exemplary behavior will generate goodwill with birders and non-birders alike.

3. Ensure that feeders, nest structures, and other artificial bird environments are safe.

3(a) Keep dispensers, water, and food clean and free of decay or disease. It is important to feed birds continually during harsh weather.

3(b) Maintain and clean nest structures regularly.

3(c) If you are attracting birds to an area, ensure the birds are not exposed to predation from cats and other domestic animals, or dangers posed by artificial hazards.

4. Group birding, whether organized or impromptu, requires special care.

Each individual in the group, in addition to the obligations spelled out in Items #1 and #2, has responsibilities as a Group Member.

4(a) Respect the interests, rights, and skills of fellow birders, as well as those of people participating in other legitimate outdoor activities. Freely share your knowledge and experience, except where code 1(c) applies. Be especially helpful to beginning birders.

4(b) If you witness unethical birding behavior, assess the situation and intervene if you think it prudent. When interceding, inform the person(s) of the inappropriate action and attempt, within reason, to have it stopped. If the behavior continues, document it and notify appropriate individuals or organizations.

Group Leader Responsibilities [amateur and professional trips and tours].

4(c) Be an exemplary ethical role model for the group. Teach through word and example.

4(d) Keep groups to a size that limits impact on the environment and does not interfere with others using the same area.

4(e) Ensure everyone in the group knows of and practices this code.

4(f) Learn and inform the group of any special circumstances applicable to the areas being visited (e.g., no tape recorders allowed).

4(g) Acknowledge that professional tour companies bear a special responsibility to place the welfare of birds and the benefits of public knowledge ahead of the company's commercial interests. Ideally, leaders should keep track of tour sightings, document unusual occurrences, and submit records to appropriate organizations.

PLEASE FOLLOW THIS CODE— DISTRIBUTE IT AND TEACH IT TO OTHERS.

Additional copies of the Code of Birding Ethics can be obtained from: ABA, PO Box 6599, Colorado Springs, CO 80934-6599, (800) 850-2473 or (719) 578-1614; fax: (800) 247-3329 or (719) 578-1480; e-mail: member@aba.org

This ABA Code of Birding Ethics may be reprinted, reproduced, and distributed without restriction. Please acknowledge the role of ABA in developing and promoting this code.

7/1/96

NOMENCLATURE

Bird names follow the American Ornithologists' Union **Check-list of North American Birds**, 7th Edition (June 1998). Taxonomic sequence follows the American Birding Association's **ABA Checklist of Birds of the Continental United States and Canada**, 5th Edition (1996). Below are some bird names which differ from those used in the older field guides and in previous editions of this book. Further "field-identifiable forms" are listed in the bar-graphs and Specialties section. Learning to identify these forms will prepare you for future taxonomic splits.

Names Used in this Book . . . . *Former Name or Derivation*

Tricolored Heron	*formerly* Louisiana Heron
Green Heron	*formerly* Green-backed Heron
Tundra Swan	*formerly* Whistling Swan
White-tailed Kite	*formerly* Black-shouldered Kite
Pacific Golden-Plover	*split from* Lesser Golden-Plover
American Golden-Plover	*split from* Lesser Golden-Plover
Red-necked Stint	*formerly* Rufous-necked Stint
Black-headed Gull	*formerly* Common Black-headed Gull
Belcher's Gull	*split from* Band-tailed Gull
White-winged Parakeet	*split from* Canary-winged Parakeet
Yellow-chevroned Parakeet	*split from* Canary-winged Parakeet
Red-naped Sapsucker	*split from* Yellow-bellied Sapsucker
Red-breasted Sapsucker	*split from* Yellow-bellied Sapsucker
Gilded Flicker	*split from* Northern Flicker
Pacific-slope Flycatcher	*split from* Western Flycatcher
Cordilleran Flycatcher	*split from* Western Flycatcher
Island Scrub-Jay	*split from* Scrub Jay
Western Scrub-Jay	*split from* Scrub Jay
Oak Titmouse	*split from* Plain Titmouse
Juniper Titmouse	*split from* Plain Titmouse
California Gnatcatcher	*split from* Black-tailed Gnatcatcher
American Pipit	*formerly* Water Pipit
Plumbeous Vireo	*split from* Solitary Vireo
Cassin's Vireo	*split from* Solitary Vireo
California Towhee	*split from* Brown Towhee
Spotted Towhee	*split from* Rufous-sided Towhee
Nelson's Sharp-tailed Sparrow	*split from* Sharp-tailed Sparrow
Dark-eyed Junco	*lumped from* Oregon, White-winged, Slate-colored, and Gray-headed Juncos
Baltimore Oriole	*resplit from* Northern Oriole
Bullock's Oriole	*split from* Northern Oriole
Gray-crowned Rosy-Finch	*resplit from* Rosy Finch

INDEX